UNMANNED AIRCRAFT
—— IN THE ——
NATIONAL AIRSPACE

Critical Issues, Technology, and the Law

Donna A. Dulo, Editor

ABA SECTION OF
SCIENCE & TECHNOLOGY LAW

Cover design by Andrew Alcala/ABA Publishing.

Printed in the United States of America.

19 18 17 16 15 5 4 3 2 1

Library of Congress Cataloging-in-Publication Data

Unmanned aircraft in the national airspace : critical issues, technology, and the law / Donna A. Dulo, Editor.
    pages cm
  Includes index.
   ISBN 978-1-62722-998-2 (softcover : alk. paper) -- ISBN 978-1-62722-999-9 (e-book) 1. Drone aircraft--United States. 2. Drone aircraft--Government policy--United States. 3. Air traffic rules--United States. 4. Aeronautics--United States--Safety measures. 5. National Airspace System (U.S.) 6. Aeronautics, Commercial--United States. I. Dulo, Donna A., editor.
  KF2406.U56 2015
  343.7309'75--dc23   2015015640

Discounts are available for books ordered in bulk. Special consideration is given to state bars, CLE programs, and other bar-related organizations. Inquire at Book Publishing, ABA Publishing, American Bar Association, 321 N. Clark Street, Chicago, Illinois 60654-7598.

www.ShopABA.org

This book is dedicated to my late mother,

Joan Mary Barbieri.

Contents

About the Editor and Lead Author

Donna A. Dulo is a mathematician, computer scientist, software/systems engineer, and legal scholar. She has been with the Department of Defense in military and civilian capacities for over twenty-seven years. She is also a systems and software engineer for Icarus Interstellar, where she focuses on the safety, reliability, and resilience of spacecraft for long-term missions, and is the founder of the Icarus Interstellar Center for Space Law. She is the Director of Advanced Computational Technologies and is a computer science professor at Sofia University in Palo Alto, California, where she founded and developed the university's Unmanned Aircraft Computing Master's Degree and Professional Certificate programs. She is also a faculty member at Embry-Riddle Aeronautical University where she develops and teaches graduate and undergraduate cyberlaw, cybersecurity, and information assurance courses. Donna is the president and founder of Unmanned Aircraft Safety and Security Society, Inc., and speaks and consults all over the world in the areas of unmanned aircraft technology, safety, and security; aviation/aerospace cybersecurity and software safety; and systems information assurance/cybersecurity and safety.

Donna received her Doctor of Jurisprudence from the Monterey College of Law and is a PhD candidate in Software Engineering at the US Naval Postgraduate School. She has an MS in Systems Engineering from Johns Hopkins University, an MS in Computer Science from the US Naval Postgraduate School, an MA in National Security & Strategic Studies from the US Naval War College, an MAS in Aeronautics and Aerospace Safety from Embry-Riddle Aeronautical University, an MBA in Engineering Management from City University, and an MS in Computer Information Systems from the University of Phoenix. She did her undergraduate work in Economics at the US Coast Guard Academy. She has graduate diplomas from both the US Navy College of Naval Command and Staff and the US Marine Corps Command and Staff College. She has a certificate in Computer Security from Stanford University and three Software Engineering certificates from the US Air Force Institute of Technology. She is also a graduate of the Defense Language Institute's Arabic Program.

Donna is a leading scholar, legal writer, and researcher in the area of unmanned aircraft law. She has published extensively in the areas of unmanned aircraft law, unmanned aircraft cybersecurity and safety, unmanned aircraft technology, spacecraft safety systems, computer science, and software/systems engineering and has published a book on computer programming. She has been featured in the national media including the Associated Press, NPR, *Slate*, and *Discovery News*. She was named as one of the 2015 Women of Influence in Silicon Valley by the *Silicon Valley Business Journal*. She lives in Monterey, California.

About the Contributing Authors

Stephen S. Wu is Of Counsel with Silicon Valley Law Group in San Jose, California. He advises clients on liability matters arising from the manufacture and use of drones and other robots. He also advises clients and resolves disputes in information assurance matters in areas including privacy, information security, data breach response, computer fraud, records and information management, and secure e-commerce. Mr. Wu acts as outside general counsel to Silicon Valley startups and technology companies, drafting and negotiating software licensing, hardware sales, information technology services, cloud computing, and marketing agreements, as well as other technology transactions. Finally, he advises clients concerning cutting-edge information technologies, such as artificial intelligence, mobile computing, cloud computing, augmented and virtual reality, Big Data, human–computer interfaces, and the Internet of Things.

Mr. Wu has written or cowritten six books on information assurance topics, a law review article on robotics product liability, and two conference papers on robotics product liability for the We Robot Conference. He served as the 2010–2011 chair of the American Bar Association Section of Science & Technology Law and is one of the founding members of the section's Artificial Intelligence and Robotics Committee. He currently serves as chair of the High Technology Law Section of the Santa Clara County Bar Association and leader of the section's Artificial Intelligence and Robotics Interest Group. In addition, he has taught as a lecturer in information technology law at Santa Clara University School of Law. Mr. Wu holds a JD from Harvard Law School and received a BA from the University of Pittsburgh.

Cameron R. Cloar is a former pilot for a national airline; he represents some of the world's largest aircraft manufacturers and aviation service providers in federal and state court litigation. He also advises corporate entities on complex aviation-related regulatory matters. Cloar devotes much of his practice to representing aviation companies faced with large disputes around the United States. His experience as an airline pilot with over 5,000 accumulated flight hours makes him a valuable asset to the aviation team, and he is often called upon to provide piloting and regulatory advice in connection with aviation litigation matters. Most recently, Cloar was part of a three-attorney team representing a European aviation services company sued for claims of breach of contract, fraud, and several other business torts. Their early aggressive defense strategy resulted in full vindication for the company and all claims against it were dismissed.

Jonathan B. Rupprecht is a commercial pilot with single-engine, multi-engine, and instrument ratings. He is also an airplane flight instructor and instrument flight instructor. Jonathan obtained a Bachelor of Science, magna cum laude, in Professional Aeronautics from Embry-Riddle Aeronautical University and a Juris Doctor from Florida International University School of Law. He has conducted extensive research of the integration of unmanned aircraft into the Japanese airspace compared to the integration in the United States' airspace. In his youth, he became an Eagle Scout and obtained an FCC technician radio license with Morse code privileges. Prior to forming Rupprecht Law, PA, Jonathan practiced at a criminal defense law firm, but he has taken those skills and set out to focus on his true passion, aviation. Jonathan is a member of the Florida Bar and the U.S. Southern District of Florida. Jonathan lives in southern Florida with his wife, Ashley, and their daughter Anna.

David K. Beyer has been a licensed insurance broker since 1990; he has spent the last nineteen years developing new insurance products for emerging technology risks. He specializes in technology, information security, and privacy liability for main street and e-commerce companies. In the mid 1990s, he helped identify, develop, and bring to market some of the world's first cyberinsurance products, including Security Breach Liability and Privacy Liability products. Today, he is the cofounder of Digital Risk Resources, an insurance product development and distribution company that enables insurance companies to offer cyberinsurance to protect their small to mid-sized business policyholders.

Gale A. Townsley is a member of the ABA Science & Technology Section's Information Security Committee and the Robotics & Artificial Intelligence committee. She is Senior Counsel in the law firm of Severson & Werson's Insurance Law group in San Francisco where she is leading the expansion of the group's coverage and monitoring services to clients developing technology, privacy, and cybersecurity products and programs. With nearly twenty-five years of insurance coverage experience, Ms. Townsley advises insurers regarding coverage, product development, and policy drafting. She also serves as monitoring counsel for London, European, and U.S. underwriters: negotiating pre-litigation settlements, handling claims, supervising outside coverage and litigation counsel, and counseling insureds on loss prevention, risk management, professional responsibility, and ethics.

Hillary B. Farber is an associate professor of law at the University of Massachusetts. She teaches criminal law, criminal procedure, and evidence. Her research focuses on criminal law and criminal procedure issues, with a particular focus on juveniles and issues of privacy. She has published articles on topics such as juvenile interrogations, a parent-child testimonial privilege, and the privacy and regulatory issues implicated by the use of unmanned aircraft systems. Professor Farber serves on the Advisory Board of the Boston Chapter of the American Constitution Society, the Board of Directors for Suffolk Lawyers for Justice, and the Massachusetts Chapter of the National Lawyers' Guild. She is a founding member of the New England Innocence Project. Professor Farber earned a BA in political science with high honors from the University of Michigan and received her JD from Northeastern University School of Law.

Timothy M. Ravich is a past chair of the Florida Bar Aviation Law Committee and a Member of the ABA Air and Space Law Forum. His aviation law and consulting practice is based in Florida where he served as the president of the Dade County Bar Association and where he is recognized as one of only thirty-seven Board Certified Specialists in Aviation Law. He has received the highest possible rating from Martindale-Hubbell® and has been recognized as a "Leading Lawyer" and Florida "Super Lawyer" by the South Florida Legal Guide.

In addition to his practice, Mr. Ravich is an assistant professor with the University of Central Florida and has taught aviation and space law as an adjunct professor at the University of Miami School of Law and Florida International University's College of Law. He earned his MBA in Aviation Policy and Planning from Embry-Riddle Aeronautical University. Mr. Ravich has appeared in local, national, and international news programs and podcasts featuring aviation and aerospace issues, including National Public Radio, NBC Universal, and China Central Television. He is the author of the *LexisNexis Expert Aviation Series* and has contributed to Thomson Reuters/ Aspatore Special Reports. He has also written extensively about aviation issues in peer-reviewed journals such as the American Bar Association Section of Litigation— Mass Torts, Southern Methodist University's *Journal of Air Law and Commerce*, the *North Dakota Law Review*, the *Florida Bar Journal*, the *University of Miami Law Review*, and the *Journal of the Transportation Research Forum*.

Christine L. Keyzers holds a BS in Business and a Juris Doctorate and has been a corporate executive and business owner for more than twenty-five years. Having worked in the shopping center, commercial, and multi-family real estate industry, she has been instrumental in establishing policies and procedures for regulating appropriate time, place, and manner restrictions on publicly expressive activity for private property owners in consideration of their property and privacy rights as owners whose property is open to the public for commercial purposes versus the constitutional speech and petitioning rights entitled to entrants and tenants under both the federal and respective state constitutions. Her development of commercial property owner guidelines and regulations focused on the impingement of private property rights relative to areas such as political petitioning and activities and labor union picketing, as well as gang affiliate and media access.

Christine has leveraged her management experience and proficiency developing and implementing effective public access regulations into that of author. Christine has written on the constitutionality of drone use in law enforcement, and she has contributed to and edited multiple articles regarding system safety and security concerns of unmanned aviation, as well as privacy and free speech constitutional implications. Christine also serves on the board of directors of the Unmanned Aircraft Safety and Security Society, Inc.

Preface

The national airspace, as well as the entire world of aviation, is undergoing a major transformation with the advent and rapid advancement of unmanned aircraft being used for myriad commercial, academic, government, and recreational endeavors. The rising popularity of unmanned aircraft is revolutionizing the field of aviation at a record rate, with new and innovative aircraft and payload technologies emerging every day. Yet the laws governing unmanned aircraft are advancing at a much slower pace, as law typically does with respect to technology and technological operations.

Laws and legal areas affecting unmanned aircraft are vast, including but extending significantly beyond the areas of privacy and airspace integration, which are prominent legal topics in the news today. Issues of law surrounding the safety and security of unmanned aircraft, for example, couple together to form a complex set of compound legal challenges. The emergence of unmanned aircraft insurance, risk management, and product liability further this legal complexity. Constitutional issues are also emerging, especially in the areas of the First, Second, Fourth, and Fifth Amendments, giving rise to an expanding arena of potential unmanned aircraft-related constitutional challenges by both citizens and entities such as the media.

This book provides insight into the emerging areas of unmanned aircraft law with a technological perspective. With the understanding that the law and the technology it regulates form a complex and intertwined bond, this book covers both the laws of unmanned aircraft and the respective technological foundations required to understand and work with the law in an informed manner. Unmanned aircraft law is a subset of aviation law, with its own unique perspective. As such, aviation law foundations are critical to the unmanned aviation legal scholar/practitioner and are covered appropriately throughout the book. Also covered are the legal foundations of insurance and risk, product liability, system security, information assurance, and safety. Additionally, this book has a section on constitutional law, covering emerging areas that may impact civil rights and civil liberties, as well as issues concerning the media, such as freedom of the press and freedom to cover stories involving collaboration with law enforcement.

Overall, this book strives to open a dialog surrounding the emerging area of unmanned aircraft and aviation law. It provides a balanced view of the various legal issues and perspectives surrounding the regulation and use of civilian unmanned aircraft in the national airspace. It also provides suggestions, recommendations, and proposed legal frameworks to help develop and enhance the understanding of specific unmanned aircraft legal areas.

Finally, this book is written to accommodate all readers, from the general public to those in the legal profession, as well as those operating or utilizing unmanned aircraft for commercial, academic, government, or recreation purposes. Topics are developed systematically to ensure that all readers can learn and benefit from the material. Legal issues and technological issues are intertwined to ensure holistic understanding and practical application of the legal topics. In essence, this book brings together the legal, technological, and operational perspectives of unmanned aircraft law into one comprehensive resource.

Acknowledgments

This book would not be possible without the extensive assistance, dedication, and support of many people. I first and foremost would like to thank Sarah Forbes Orwig, Executive Editor, Book Development and Publication for the ABA for her support, guidance, and dedication in helping this book become a reality. I would also like to thank Benjamin Wilson, chair of the book publishing board of the ABA Section of Science and Technology Law, and Krista Carver, member of the board, for all of their help, guidance, and support. I would like to sincerely thank the contributing authors for their expertise and writing talents; without their hard work this book would not have become a reality.

I would like to thank Dr. Oleg Yakimenko, Bob Bluth, Ray Jackson, and the folks at the Center for Interdisciplinary Remotely-Piloted Aircraft Studies (CIRPAS) at the Naval Postgraduate School for their dedicated assistance and for providing access to their aerial systems and operations. Many thanks as well to SSG Carlos Altamirano and the soldiers of Det. 1 D Company, 578th BEB (TUAS) at Camp Roberts, California, for their technical assistance and for providing access to their systems.

I would like to thank Dr. Luqi and Dr. Bret Michael at the Naval Postgraduate School for their inspiration, which helped me to find my way into the areas of aviation software safety and unmanned systems. I would also like to thank Professors Richard Riehle, Mikhail Auguston, Neil Rowe, Gurminder Singh, Ray Madachy, and Man-Tak Shing at the Naval Postgraduate School as well as the professors of the US Naval War College, Monterey Campus, for all of their assistance and dedication over the years.

Sincere thanks and appreciation go out to Sharon M. Wesley, MD, for all of her support, encouragement, and guidance over the years, especially during the preparation of this book, which helped me keep both feet firmly and healthfully on the ground.

A special thank you goes out to Anjali Mahaldar, who expertly proofread every word and page of this manuscript. Her expertise and strong command of the English language contributed significantly to the quality of the book and is sincerely appreciated. Thanks as well to Eileen Advincula who did the initial proofreading on chapter 3 and to Christine Keyzers who helped edit and proofread chapter 10.

I have been blessed to have the support of so many friends and family over the years. First and foremost, I would like to thank my dear friend Gonzalo J. Roig for all of his support and unconditional friendship for many, many years. Special thanks go out to my adopted Serbian family, Steve, Nada, and Mirko Vicijan, for all of their love, support, and guidance. Thanks as well to my sister Luann Stewart, my brothers, Bobby Dulo and Johnny Dulo, and my nephew, Jimmy Minugh, for their love and support. I would also like to thank my friends Tami Huntley, Ada Hynes, Bonnie Buckwade, Carol Ross, Chris Keyzers, Paul DeBone, Sameera Sharif, Maria Moffa, Heidi Storm, Jamie Young, Monica Farah-Stapleton, Maribel Simpauco, Sara Javid, and Barbara Hecker for standing by me and my work, even when it made me disappear for weeks at a time.

Finally, I would like to thank my late mother, for all of the incredible things she did for me throughout my life and for her inspiration, continual guidance, and unwavering love and support. She taught me the value of education and relentless hard work, and she always wanted for me to enter the field of law, despite my strong arguments to be an aviator and an engineer. Hopefully she can see that we have finally come to a happy compromise.

—Donna A. Dulo

1

Introduction to Unmanned Aircraft Technology and Law

1

Introduction to Unmanned Aircraft Law

Donna A. Dulo

"Recent years have proved such a splendid success for aeronautics that it really seems justifiable for law to begin to take its share in the aerial labour."

—Johanna Francina Lycklama á Nijeholt[1]

The national airspace of the United States is undergoing a major revolution, one it has not seen in many decades. For the first time in history, unmanned aircraft are penetrating the nation's airspace in significant numbers, flying in the same airspace that has been traditionally reserved for manned aircraft. While unmanned aircraft have been in existence since the founding days of aviation, their use had not been perfected for widespread commercial, academic, government, and recreational applications like it is today. Yet, this is only the beginning. With the advent of inexpensive, easy-to-operate unmanned aircraft, the field of aviation is opening up to everyone who has a desire to control an aircraft in the skies.

Unmanned aircraft technology is advancing rapidly and precipitously, with advanced sensing, imaging, and operational payloads becoming accessible to virtually any potential operator with an interest in aerial applications. The sky is truly the limit with the

---

1. Johanna Francina Lycklama á Nijeholt, Air Sovereignty (The Hague: Martinus Nijhoff) (1910). Dr. Nijeholt's treatise was one of the seminal and prominent legal treatises on the topic of aviation and air law, and her work is considered by many to be one of the first major legal treatises in history to be written by a woman. Her work and pioneering spirit in the field of aviation law was one of the inspirations for this book.

myriad uses of these innovative and relatively inexpensive aircraft. In fact, their use is becoming so pervasive that the lines are becoming increasingly blurred between the application of these aerial vehicles as toys, models, and professional aerial instruments. What can be thought of as a model or hobby aircraft taking pictures for the personal photo album of its operator, for example, can suddenly be classified as a commercial aerial application if one of the photographs is sold for a profit. The legal complexities of unmanned aircraft law are thus increasing as their use becomes more widespread and diverse.

Figure 1.1

An Airborne Sentry Unmanned Aircraft (Photo courtesy of Donna Dulo)

The area of unmanned aircraft law is highly dynamic. The Federal Aviation Administration (FAA), NASA, and the Federal Communications Commission (FCC), as well as various authorized working groups across the country, are currently developing and honing the details of unmanned aircraft regulations that will supplement the current FAA and FCC regulations. While FAA regulations govern the operation of aircraft through the Federal Aviation Regulations, the FCC regulations govern the use of communication systems including satellite communication systems, and they are currently being tailored to accommodate unmanned aircraft command, control, and communications traffic. The Federal Aviation Regulations, as well as current FCC regulations in general, were not intended for unmanned aircraft and in many ways will not apply to their operations. Therefore, a new body of regulations is evolving to encompass the growing spectrum of unmanned aircraft operations and communications. Unmanned aviation laws overall are being developed and designed to regulate the national airspace, to regulate the manufacturing and design of unmanned aircraft, and to facilitate the complex communication schemes of airborne systems.

Figure 1.2

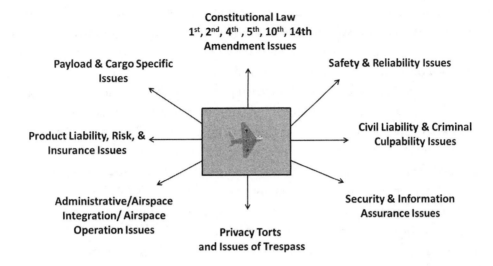

The Diverse Legal Issues Surrounding Unmanned Aircraft Use in the National Airspace (Photo courtesy of Donna Dulo)

Unmanned aircraft integration into the national airspace opens up a variety of legal issues that must be addressed. Myriad legal issues range from aircraft certification and airspace integration issues, to insurance issues, safety and reliability regulations, privacy and trespass issues, and security issues, such as information security and physical security. Constitutional issues also arise with the use of unmanned aircraft, such as Second Amendment issues of weapons as an extension of gun rights, Fourth Amendment issues of unreasonable search and seizure, Fifth and Fourteenth Amendment issues of Due Process, Tenth Amendment issues of states' rights to regulate unmanned aircraft activities, as well as First Amendment free speech issues regarding unmanned aircraft use for both the media and the public.

Extending from these legal issues are the complex issues of liability; who will be ultimately responsible in the event of an accident or incident is a central question. This question advances the issues of criminal culpability and civil liability as well as product liability issues, creating a wide-ranging set of legal challenges to owners, operators, manufacturers, and distributors of unmanned aircraft. Stemming directly from and intertwining with these liability issues are the laws of insurance and the regulation of the unmanned aviation insurance industry. Since the ingestion of a small, unmanned aircraft into the engine of a passenger airliner can result in a complete hull and passenger loss, the legal and financial stakes are high for insurance holders and the aviation insurance industry in general. The resolution of liability issues is therefore paramount to create a more predictable, holistic, aerial-operations legal domain.

A significant problem, in addition to the fact that many of the laws of unmanned aviation are not yet enacted, is due to the immature nature of the industry. This immaturity ultimately results in a dearth of relevant judicial precedents, as very few unmanned aircraft cases have been tried in the courts. Thus, even though an unmanned aircraft law or regulation may be written and in effect, how that law is interpreted by the courts is another critical facet of the legal process. To date, few unmanned aircraft laws and regulations have been interpreted, resulting in a lack of judicial precedent. This aspect of the law can take years, if not decades, to yield relevant, applicable case law. However, the industry is beginning to evolve, as we are beginning to see unmanned aviation–related cases in the courts, and in some cases judicial decisions have already been published. Additionally, relevant judicial decisions in manned aviation or other applicable scenarios can be applied to unmanned aviation situations providing applicable and relevant legal guidance.

This book aims to address many of the emerging legal issues that are facing the aviation industry. It strives to provide an overview of the law and the corresponding technical issues that drive and shape the law as unmanned aircraft become major participants in the national airspace.

Section 1 provides a brief introduction to the history of unmanned aircraft that stems from the early days of aviation. It describes the various uses of unmanned aircraft from the turn of the twentieth century to their current commercial and recreational uses. It also provides an introduction to the airframe technologies and classifications of unmanned aircraft to ensure that the reader thoroughly understands the aerial concepts being regulated and flown in the skies.

Section 2 describes the process of federal rulemaking, spotlighting the FAA and its rulemaking process for both manned and unmanned aviation. It tracks the current rules of unmanned aircraft from the early laws of aviation and presents the future direction of current laws. It also discusses the issue of autonomous aerial operations and the various legal issues of autonomous systems control. Finally, issues of an autonomous operation legal framework are presented, providing insight and guidance toward the integration of fully automated unmanned aircraft into the national airspace.

Section 3 highlights the emerging information assurance and security issues surrounding the use of unmanned aircraft as wireless entities in the skies. It presents the history of national information assurance and computer security regulations as well as the current regulatory mandates, and frames them for the use of unmanned aircraft, exposing many security and information assurance issues that operators will face as aerial operations become more pervasive in the national skies. It also provides concrete information assurance and security concepts to ensure that the reader thoroughly understands security principles and how they apply to unmanned aircraft operations and law.

Section 4 develops the constitutional issues surrounding the use of unmanned aircraft. The issues of the media and the First and Fourth Amendments are presented as well as issues of the Fourth Amendment and the general public. The section rounds out with a discussion of the use of weapons on unmanned aircraft and the Second Amendment implications of arming an aerial instrument.

Finally, Section 5 discusses the concepts of product liability, safety, and risk, including their impact on the field of unmanned aviation insurance. It presents a detailed description of the area of product liability law and the various legal issues that surround the manufacturing of complex systems. It also develops the concept of unmanned aviation insurance and how the insurance field works to identify risk triggers and to mitigate and address issues of risk. The section finishes with an original detailed study of unmanned aircraft accidents and how product liability and insurance may be impacted by the results of the study.

CHAPTER

2

A Brief History of Unmanned Aircraft

Jonathan B. Rupprecht and Donna A. Dulo

"Flying has torn apart the relationship of space and time. It uses our old clock but with new yardsticks."

—Charles A. Lindbergh

Unmanned aircraft are a major component of the aviation domain with their origins stemming back to pre-manned aircraft days. Unmanned aircraft were not only developed before manned aircraft but served as a vital predecessor to them. Unmanned aircraft were the foundational scientific, engineering, and aeronautics test beds and prototypes that propelled aviation into the future so that manned aviation would be possible. It was through unmanned aviation research and development that the Wright Brothers had the seminal aeronautical engineering insights to develop the first controlled, powered manned aircraft.

In theory, every aircraft in the sky today can be flown as an unmanned aircraft, with the proper remote control mechanisms and communications. The largest aircraft and airliners in the skies can be commanded from the ground, at remote control stations, through line-of-sight or satellite-based communication relays. In fact, the future is bright for the return of aviation to its unmanned flying roots, with technologies being developed not only to advance and integrate common unmanned aircraft types into the national airspace but also to automate aircraft that are traditionally flown with pilots in the cockpit such as air freighters and passenger airliners. In essence, the distant future may reveal that unmanned aircraft will have come full circle in the realm of aviation dominance.

The use of unmanned aircraft paradigm to perform the "dirty, dangerous, and dull" tasks of aviation may soon evolve to add another *d*: dollar-wise. Eliminating the pilot helps streamline the aircraft, with cockpit space aligned with more functional payload space, allowing for smaller aircraft to be developed that save money in propulsion system costs as well as fuel costs. The lack of an onboard operator also allows a centralization of control functions, with pilot-operators working from centralized locations and in some cases with the ability to operate more than one aircraft, augmenting the autonomous controls of the aircraft in the skies rather than being a central mechanism in direct control. This logistical advantage allows more aircraft from an organization to be in the sky at one time, supporting accelerated delivery or mission timelines and improving the airborne operations of the organization.

Figure 2.1

A Sentry Unmanned Aircraft in the Hangar (Photo courtesy of Donna Dulo)

To advance into the future, lessons of the past must be observed. Developers of unmanned aviation law and technology need insights on the emergence of unmanned aircraft and how these aircraft not only accelerated the development of more sophisticated and safer aircraft but also advanced the field of aviation and impacted the sociological aspects of aviation upon the general population. For example, many individuals today feel that unmanned aircraft are offshoots of the military and ultimately have a militaristic purpose in civilian airspace. Many individuals also believe that unmanned aircraft are inherently dangerous, are devices for the invasion of privacy, and have no logical purpose in the national airspace. The issues of who owns the skies and aerial property rights may also emerge as they did in the early days of manned aviation, begging the question of the scope of private, commercial, and government operations of low-flying unmanned aircraft on individual property rights.

In order to develop an understanding of the law and technology of unmanned aircraft, an understanding of their origins is important. Historical study of unmanned aviation yields critical lessons that have been learned in the past, in addition to yielding sound technological and sociological trends developed since the first manned aircraft entered the skies. Historical studies also shed light on potential future technologies and uses of unmanned aircraft, developed from useful and successful trends of the past.

This chapter provides a brief overview of the history of unmanned aircraft and their uses throughout aviation history as well as their importance in the advancement of aviation and the advancement of aeronautical science and engineering. It also provides insight on the various uses of unmanned aircraft and how these applications aided in the development of specific types of unmanned aircraft as well as in the development of novel uses for them. Through both unmanned operations and technology, new laws have ultimately emerged in the aviation domain and will continue to emerge as technologies and operations advance. Through an understanding of the technical and utility aspects of unmanned aircraft as revealed through unmanned aviation history, future legal issues can be predicted and researched to ensure safer and more proactively regulated skies.

THE EARLY HISTORICAL UTILIZATION OF UNMANNED AIRCRAFT

Every engineering endeavor has an ultimate goal and purpose. This is especially true in aviation. Aircraft were developed not only for the joy of flying but also for sound scientific, military, and commercial business purposes. Unmanned aircraft throughout history were no exception and were developed for a number of concrete and viable reasons: (A) as weapons; (B) to provide realistic target practice for military training; (C) as military decoys; (D) for aerodynamic research and development; (E) for data, remote sensing, and image gathering; and (F) for recreation. These ideas will be briefly discussed with interesting associated historical facts to demonstrate the holistic value of unmanned aircraft and to shed light on the future implications of each of these uses in the national airspace.

Unmanned Aircraft as a Weapon

When engineers started learning about the different types of aircraft, it was not long after that they adapted aircraft for strategic advantage in warfare. Strategic advantage in war stems historically from two areas: logistics and weapons technologies. The advent of aviation improved both areas exponentially over time, as with aviation today, both manned and unmanned, playing a major role in combat operations and logistics. The first uses of unmanned aircraft in human history, in fact, were for the advancement of strategic surprise as well as tactical and strategic advantage.

Unmanned Rockets

Early in the third century, a Chinese general named Zhuge Liang used paper balloons fitted with oil-burning lamps to lift the balloons up in the air and to fly over the enemy at night to frighten them.[1] The Chinese also developed the seminal concept of rockets, which were eventually turned into weapons. The Ming Dynasty (1362–1644), for example, enhanced military dominance through the use of gunpowder-based rockets. A military inventor during the dynasty, General Qi Jiguang developed several strategic types of rockets that could be launched by ground troops or by naval forces against enemy combat units.

Ultimately, the general's arsenal proved both deadly to China's enemies and groundbreaking in the area of military weapons technology, inspiring many nations of the world to develop rockets for both defensive and offensive warfare. Rockets soon became a mainstay of military strategy and tactics for ground and naval warfare; they are recorded prominently in history, such as the ones the British used to attack Fort McHenry during the War of 1812, inspiring Francis Scott Key to write "And the rockets' red glare, the bombs bursting in air[.]"

Unmanned Balloons

Unmanned balloons are another type of aerial vehicle that emerged from Chinese roots to aid in military strategic advantage. The earliest uses of balloons by the Chinese were aerial lanterns called Kongming lanterns that were used to signal allied forces. The Mongols adapted the technology of Kongming lanterns in the Battle of Legnica in 1241 against the Kingdom of Poland, marking the first time in Western history that balloons were used in warfare.[2] On August 22, 1849, the Austrians used

---

1. *See* Charles Jarnot, *History*, *in* INTRODUCTION TO UNMANNED AIRCRAFT SYSTEMS 1 (Richard K. Barnhart et al. eds., 2012).

2. JOSEPH NEEDHAM, SCIENCE AND CIVILISATION IN CHINA: VOLUME 4, PHYSICS AND PHYSICAL TECHNOLOGY, PART 2, MECHANICAL ENGINEERING (rpr. Taipei: Caves Books Ltd).

unmanned balloons to drop bombs on Venice by transmitting electricity over a copper wire attached to the balloon.[3]

Uses of unmanned balloons in warfare continued throughout history, including uses by the Japanese in World War II. The Japanese saw the potential of long-range unmanned aerial weapon systems and developed an arsenal of balloon bombs that would monopolize on the aerial jet stream, sending its balloon bombs all over the world, but particularly to the continent of North America. These balloon bombs, although primitive and highly ineffective, became the first intercontinental weapon systems in history. The first balloon bombs were launched by the Japanese on November 3, 1944, and Japanese records indicate that approximately 9,000 were launched. Records from Canada and the United States indicate that evidence and remnants of 284 balloon bombs were found that had reached North America, many as far east as Michigan.[4]

Unmanned balloons continue to be used in special circumstances in warfare today, although many are controlled electronically as lighter-than-air unmanned aircraft. They have both strategic purposes as well as humanitarian purposes in war zones, offering a cheap alternative to other types of military aerial vehicles. Overall, unmanned rockets and balloons have been used for strategic warfare throughout history, revolutionizing the areas of military surveillance and reconnaissance, as well as aerial weapons delivery. They have played a vital role in the genesis of military aviation history from the first days of unmanned aviation to the present. However, a greater and more ominous player was about to enter the skies: the powered and controllable unmanned airplane.

Unmanned Airplanes

During the late 1800s, a young inventor named Nikola Tesla had an idea of creating a remote-controlled airplane that "could change its direction in flight, explode at will, and . . . never make a miss."[5] Tesla later started developing remote-controlled torpedoes for the United States Navy, which he called "Telautomatons," testing them out between 1914 to 1916, but the Navy did not pursue the idea any further.[6] Tesla ultimately never developed an unmanned airplane, but he did develop the idea of remotely controlling weapon systems, such as torpedoes and aircraft, setting the stage for further aerial systems research and development.

---

3. *See Remote Piloted Aerial Vehicles: An Anthology*, http://www.ctie.monash.edu/hargrave/rpav_home.html#Beginnings.

4. J. Rizzo, *Japan's Secret WWII Weapon: Balloon Bombs*, NATIONAL GEOGRAPHIC ONLINE (2013), http://news.nationalgeographic.com/news/2013/05/130527-map-video-balloon-bomb-wwii-japanese-air-current-jet-stream/.

5. LAURENCE R. NEWCOME, UNMANNED AVIATION: A BRIEF HISTORY OF UNMANNED AERIAL VEHICLES 13 (American Inst. of Aeronautics and Astronautics 1st ed. 2004).

6. *See id.* at 14.

Elmer Sperry started developing a gyrostabilizer for airplanes in 1909.[7] Two weeks before World War I broke out, on June 18, 1914, Sperry's son successfully demonstrated his father's gyrostabilizer to a crowd at a competition, winning a 15,000-franc prize.[8] After this, Peter Cooper Hewitt approached Sperry and offered him $3,000 to codevelop a pilotless flying bomb using the gyrostabilizer technology.[9] Sperry worked with Glenn Curtiss, an airframe designer, to design an aerial torpedo, and on March 6, 1918, the aircraft was successfully launched; it flew, and it dived on its target as intended.[10] Sperry's aerial torpedo more closely resembled a modern-day cruise missile with its internal gyrostabilizer "autopilot." While this was not how modern unmanned aircraft are used, it laid the foundation of modern unmanned aircraft architectures and autonomous control systems.

The inaccuracy of unmanned airplanes posed a significant problem of control and precision, vital components of military weapon systems; there needed to be some sort of way to better guide and control the aircraft once launched. In October 1915, Siemens-Chucker Were began developing unmanned aircraft gliders that would hold a bomb, be launched from a Zeppelin, and be controlled via a thin trailing copper wire.[11] Years later, the United States military, during World War II, started experiments with converting PB4Y Privateer bombers (the Navy version of the B-24 Liberators) to be aerial torpedoes.[12] The idea was to convert the PB4Ys into huge "flying bombs" with ten tons of explosives which would be flown by a pilot inside; the pilot would then parachute out over England, and the "flying bomb" would be remotely piloted from another bomber to fly into a target.[13] John F. Kennedy's older brother was a pilot of one of these converted PB4Ys, but he died in an unexpected mid-air explosion while on the way to attack a Nazi super-cannon.[14] There was only one more development needed in military unmanned aircraft technology: the aircraft being a vehicle for delivery of a weapon and not a weapon itself.

In 1962, the QH-50 DASH (Unmanned aircraft Anti-Submarine Helicopter) was introduced to the U.S. Navy to allow the Navy to attack Russian submarines beyond Russian and normal U.S. torpedo ranges.[15] The idea was that the unmanned helicop-

7. *See id.* at 16.
8. *See id.*
9. *See id.*
10. *See* JARNOT, *supra* note 1, at 4.
11. *See* NEWCOME, *supra* note 5 at 50.
12. *See* JARNOT, *supra* note 1, at 8.
13. *See id.*
14. *See id.; see also* Anthony Leviero, *Kennedy Jr. Died In Air Explosion*, N.Y. TIMES, (Oct. 25, 1945), *available at* http://select.nytimes.com/gst/abstract.html?res=FB0B11FB3D5E1B7B93C7AB178BD95F418485F9 (requires subscription or individual payment for article); John David Blom, *Unmanned Aerial Systems: A Historical Perspective* 48, COMBAT STUDIES INST. 1st ed. (2010), *available at* http://usacac.army.mil/cac2/cgsc/carl/download/csipubs/OP37.pdf.
15. *See* John David Blom, *Unmanned Aerial Systems: A Historical Perspective* 48, COMBAT STUDIES INST. 1st ed. (2010), *available at* http://usacac.army.mil/cac2/cgsc/carl/download/csipubs/OP37.pdf, page 38. *See also*

ter would be launched from the back of a destroyer, be flown to the area where the submarine was detected, drop nuclear depth charges or launching homing torpedoes at the target, and then be returned back to the ship.[16] This opened the modern era of how many unmanned aircraft are being used today in the military as aerial weapons delivery systems.

Israel was one of the first countries to strategically incorporate unmanned airplanes into their battle plans during the Yom Kippur War in 1973, where it was able to reduce its pilot and airplane losses and captures by using Chukar unmanned aerial decoys to both deceive and saturate Egyptian surface-to-air missile batteries along the Suez Canal. It soon thereafter developed small, versatile, and low-signature unmanned airplanes to collect real-time video, pictures, and intelligence that could be operated by ordinary soldiers on the battlefield.[17]

Israel continued to lead the world in unmanned military airplanes with the development, in 1973, of the Tadrian Electronic Industries Mastiff unmanned aircraft, which had modern data-link capabilities, making it one of the first modern unmanned surveillance aircraft, and its competitor, the Israel Aircraft Industries (IAI) Scout, which was developed soon after. Both types of unmanned aircraft were used in June 1982, when Israel commenced the "Peace for Galilee" offensive against the Syrian military forces in Lebanon.

The offensive resulted in major damage to Syrian radar systems and subsequently their air defense systems, which were totally eliminated with a wave of following manned aircraft. In this strategic use of both manned and unmanned aircraft in battle, Israel suffered zero losses of manned aircraft.[18] The use of the Scout, in particular, by Israel, with a top speed of 95 knots, an endurance of 7 hours, and a range of 54 miles, made the unmanned aircraft a tactical asset as opposed to an aerial instrument of strategic reconnaissance, opening up the use of unmanned airplanes as a tactical military weapon delivery system. This set the stage for the modern use of the unmanned aircraft in tandem with manned aircraft for strategic, operational, and tactical battlespace dominance.

Unmanned Aircraft Providing Realistic Target Practice for Military Training

In 1921, United States General Billy Mitchell demonstrated to the world that a battleship could be destroyed by aircraft.[19] During the interwar period of peace, 1919–1939, militaries started to develop unmanned aircraft to test anti-aircraft weaponry because

---

http://www.aero.psu.edu/facilities/images/36_DASH_QH-50.pdf.

16. *See id.*
17. K. MUNSON, WORLD UNMANNED AIRCRAFT (United Kingdom: Jane's Publishing Company Limited 1988).
18. *See id.*
19. *See* JARNOT, *supra* note 1, at 5.

they began to see the aircraft's ability to change the results of a battle.[20] The "old school" military response to aircraft attacks was to add more guns to the ships to help eliminate the enemy aircraft before they could hit their targets. Realistic unmanned target aircraft were therefore needed for real-time target training of the gunners on these ships.

The British Navy held the belief that many guns would provide adequate protection, but they were proven wrong when a target unmanned aircraft flew forty successful missions over Royal Navy warships equipped with modern anti-aircraft guns.[21] In March 1939, less than three years before the Japanese attack on Pearl Harbor, the USS *Utah*, one of the ships that sank at Pearl Harbor, received an ominous premonition when, during a live-fire exercise on many target unmanned aircraft, the crew managed to shoot down only two of them.[22] The unmanned aircraft thus provided realistic training but also pointed out the vulnerabilities of naval ships to fast-moving aircraft.

In the 1930s, Reginald Denny, an actor, started a business of making radio-controlled planes in Hollywood, California, a business which later became very successful through the award of a military contract to produce target radio-controlled aircraft in 1941.[23] He created a radio-controlled small aircraft design for target practice that turned out to work so well, 15,374 of the aircraft were purchased by the military to train American anti-aircraft gunners during World War II.[24] This was the first mass-produced remote-controlled aircraft.

It is interesting to know that as the war started coming to a close, Denny contacted a fellow Screen Actors Guild member named Ronald Reagan, a captain in the U.S. Army Air Force 1st Motion Picture Company, about documenting his Hollywood company's contribution to the war effort.[25] Reagan sent a private to take photos for *Yank* magazine on June 26, 1945; while taking photos, the private discovered an attractive young lady named Norma Jean Dougherty working on the target unmanned aircraft assembly line. Miss Dougherty later left the company, did a brief bit of modeling, and started acting under the name Marilyn Monroe.[26]

Unmanned Aircraft as Military Decoys

As aviation technology increased, rockets soon were equipped with guidance systems, turning them into guided missiles. Air warfare rapidly changed because pilots began

---

20. *See id.*
21. *See id.*
22. *See* John F. Keane & Stephen S. Carr, *A Brief History of Early Unmanned Aircraft*, 32 Johns Hopkins APL Technical Digest 563 (2013), *available at* http://www.jhuapl.edu/techdigest/TD/td3203/32_03-Keane.pdf.
23. *See id.* at 563–64.
24. *See* Newcome, *supra* note 5, at 58.
25. *See id.*
26. *See id.*

facing deadly surface-to-air missiles (SAMs) on a regular basis. SAMs were expensive, but unmanned aircraft decoy targets were not. During the Vietnam War, the U.S. Air Force used the unmanned McDonnell ADM-20 Quail, which mimicked the radar signature of a B-52 bomber, to protect its real B-52s from SAMs.[27]

Later, during the Yom Kippur War of October 1973 as discussed previously, "the Israeli Air Force employed pilotless aircraft as a first wave of an aerial attack against Arab forces. The UAVs fooled radar operators and defense systems. The ruse caused Arab defenses to expend their surface-to-air missiles (SAMs) . . . giving the second wave of manned aircraft a chance[.]"[28] Unmanned aircraft were therefore successfully utilized, and they continue to be used as decoys to protect pilots' lives on very dangerous missions.

Unmanned Aircraft for Aerodynamic Research and Development

Unmanned aircraft were developed in tandem with early manned aircraft because aviation pioneers first tested out their designs with an unmanned version before they risked their own lives.[29] As Laurence Newcome puts it,

> The lessons learned in aerodynamic stability by conducting early unmanned flight, unpowered and powered, were applied directly to the betterment of manned flight attempts. From Cayley's 1804 model glider to Du Temple's clockwork-powered 1857 model and Langley's 1896 steam-powered model, unmanned flight forerunners often succeeded where their follow on manned flight attempts did not.[30]

Unmanned aircraft, in aeronautical research, provided less overhead and generally lighter aircraft on which to test an aerial platform. Even if the design is a manned aircraft, the unmanned prototype version is generally easier to manage and configure than a manned counterpart. Early aviation pioneers like Orville Wright and Glen Curtiss used both manned and unmanned aircraft in the development of their aircraft models. However, the purposes were distinct: Unmanned aircraft were used in limited production as experimental and test aircraft; manned aircraft, once the unmanned prototypes were perfected, were then used almost exclusively in aerodynamic research and development.[31]

---

27. *See* JARNOT, *supra* note 1, at 10.
28. *See* BLOM, *supra* note 15, at 6.
29. *See* NEWCOME, *supra* note 5, at 49.
30. *Id.*
31. *See* NEWCOME, *supra* note 5, at 15.

Unmanned Aircraft Gathering Data

When balloons were invented, the military discovered that they would make excellent platforms to observe the enemy. The problem was that data could be easily gathered by an observer in the balloon, but transmitting the information accurately and quickly was difficult. Balloons themselves also had disadvantages; they could not fly in high winds or bad weather, and they were big aerial targets. On June 16, 1861, Thaddeus Lowe experimented with using a telegraph wire to transmit signals from a balloon for the purpose of being used in military reconnaissance.[32] This provided primitive real-time and somewhat accurate updates of what was being observed, but something better was still needed.

When airplanes arrived on the scene, it was not long before various innovative militaries started using them for reconnaissance. However, even though the airplanes could get better pictures compared to the balloons, the aerial photographs and information were not received fast enough to provide sound military intelligence. In 1955, Reginald Denny's company, Radioplane, modified its OQ-19 Shelduck unmanned aircraft to be a reconnaissance aircraft called the RP-71 by adding film cameras, thereby creating the first remotely controlled unmanned reconnaissance aircraft.[33] The RP-71 was flown by a pilot via a stick box that also operated a TV camera for about 30 minutes at 185–224 miles per hour.[34] The controller would fly the mission, turn around, and then kill the engine, deploying a parachute to safely land the aircraft once over friendly territory.[35]

Italy developed one of the early data collection unmanned aircraft in 1966, known as the Meteor P.1/R. This system, which had a television camera system, was only line-of-sight but led to the development of the Meteor P.2 soon after, which was able to collect data on beyond line-of-sight reconnaissance missions.[36] The Meteor series of aircraft set a precedent for advanced optics and data recording systems in unmanned aircraft, advancing the cause of aerial data collection in unmanned aircraft worldwide. Advanced visual systems thus became a mainstay for unmanned aviation throughout the 1970s and beyond.

Unmanned Aircraft for Recreation

Some people just enjoy flight. Whether individuals were building balloons, kites, or airplanes, the joy of flight encompassed all types of aircraft. The Academy of

---

32. *See Balloon Reconnaissance and Aerial Telegraph*, THE SCIENTIFIC AMERICAN, June 29, 1861, at 409, *available at* https://ia600805.us.archive.org/1/items/scientific-american-1861-06-29/scientific-american-v04-n26-1861-06-29.pdf.
33. *See* NEWCOME, *supra* note 5, at 59.
34. *See* BLOM, *supra* note 15, at 50.
35. *See id.*
36. *See* NEWCOME, *supra* note 5, at 54.

Model Aeronautics (AMA) was formed in 1936 with the idea that "there should be expert guidance of, for, and by model builders. Modelers wanted a single voice to develop national rules for aero-modeling contests as well as one voice to speak to the government."[37]

Many of the present-day owners, operators, and manufacturers of unmanned aircraft started in model aircraft through flying at AMA clubs. To the present day, unmanned aircraft are flown for the sheer joy of flight, making the flying of unmanned aerial vehicles an emerging national pastime, especially with the increased development and sales of toy "unmanned aircraft" which can be bought for less than fifty dollars and flown less than ten minutes out of the box by anyone wanting to enjoy the aerial pastime.

UNMANNED AIRCRAFT TAXONOMY

A review of the history of unmanned aircraft will reveal that the lines between guided bombs, missiles, and unmanned aircraft are not clear. A chart (see Figure 2.2) has been compiled to demonstrate how unmanned aircraft may be categorized in conjunction with their aerial counterparts.

As can be seen in the chart, manned and unmanned aircraft can serve the same purposes and, in fact, can be used simultaneously on missions to augment one another. As stated previously, an unmanned aircraft can perform basically the same functions as a manned aircraft, but without the danger to the pilot. However, this may not equate to a dangerless mission, as unmanned aircraft pose new risks in the skies due to potential issues with communications and controls, leading to the risk of aerial and ground collisions, as will be discussed throughout this book.

Overall, the key is to recognize the value of unmanned aircraft and their role in the skies as counterparts to manned aircraft. Through proper integration, both manned and unmanned aircraft can serve strategic, operational, and tactical functions, providing added value and flexibility to operators that need comprehensive aerial services.

---

37. *The AMA History Project Presents: History of the* ACADEMY OF MODEL AERONAUTICS, NATIONAL MODEL AVIATION MUSEUM *&* MODEL AVIATION *magazine*, 1 Apr. 2012, https://www.modelaircraft.org/files/AMANMAMMAhistory.pdf.

Figure 2.2

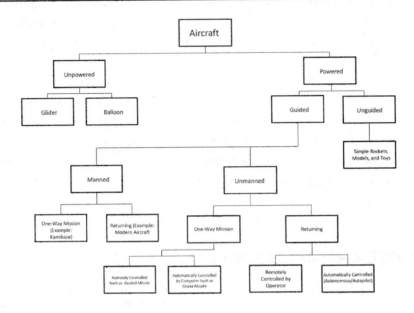

Unmanned Aircraft Taxonomy[1]

---

1. This chart was adapted from Norman Sakamoto's UAV Family Tree PowerPoint slide, which is available at http://www.nps.edu/Academics/Institutes/Meyer/docs/August%2026%202004%20History%20of%20UAVs.pdf.

CONCLUSION

Unmanned aircraft are not new. They have been with us in the past and will continue to be with us in increasing roles and functionality far into the future. The technology used in unmanned aircraft in the past did not allow for them to intersect with everyday life, but this is rapidly changing with the precipitous rise in unmanned aircraft development and utilization at all levels. As technology progresses, unmanned aircraft will further assimilate into our everyday lives and become as ubiquitous as cell phones, televisions, or laptops. Unmanned aircraft have been around since the beginning of aviation, and they are here to stay.

CHAPTER

3

Aeronautical Foundations of the Unmanned Aircraft

Donna A. Dulo

"Aeronautics was neither an industry nor a science. It was a miracle."
—Igor I. Sikorsky, 1889–1972, Father of the Helicopter

The unmanned aircraft or unmanned aerial system (UAS)[1] encompasses a wide range of technologies and aeronautical platforms ranging from the highly sophisticated to the most basic aircraft models. The functions, cost, and ability of operators to acquire a UAS vary based on the level of sophistication for each system. Additionally, many technological features and aerodynamic functions are ubiquitous across all systems. The key point is that aeronautical technology drives the development and operation of unmanned aircraft, which subsequently drives the development of the laws that will regulate aeronautical technology in the skies. The goal of this chapter is not to provide a treatise on unmanned aircraft technology but rather to provide a technological foundation with which to assist in the understanding of the broader legal concepts of unmanned aircraft.

---

1. Various terms apply to the unmanned aircraft: Unmanned Aerial Vehicle (UAV), Unmanned Aircraft (UA), Unmanned Aerial System (UAS), which refers either to the system of systems in the aircraft or the aircraft-ground station system, Remotely Piloted Aircraft System (RPAS), Aerial Robot (AR), etc. The term "drone" is an unofficial, slang term, used throughout aviation history. This term will not be used in this book except when citing an external reference that uses the term. The terms "Unmanned Aircraft," "Unmanned Aerial System," and "Unmanned Aerial Vehicle" are used throughout the book.

The potential use of unmanned aircraft technology has grown exponentially over the past few years in the civilian sector. Compared to the traditional manned aircraft, unmanned aerial applications are limited only to the imaginations of their operators. Incorporating lighter composites, advanced embedded electronics, and efficient computational algorithms, the unmanned aircraft is becoming the platform of choice for increased aerial mobility and functionality for a wide range of operators ranging from police departments monitoring crime to science departments mapping archaeological sites.

The key to UAS popularity is the potential for expanded operations in three-dimensional space. Current UAS technology allows operators to negotiate three-dimensional space in a more rapid and customized manner which transcends military use of the UAS for operations that are too "dull, dirty, or dangerous" for manned aircraft. Rather, it facilitates new and innovative uses of unmanned aircraft due to their compact and relatively inexpensive nature as compared to their manned counterparts. This newly found aeronautical ability of operators enhances real-time situational awareness, allowing information to be gathered and disseminated in an effective and more efficient manner.

Figure 3.1

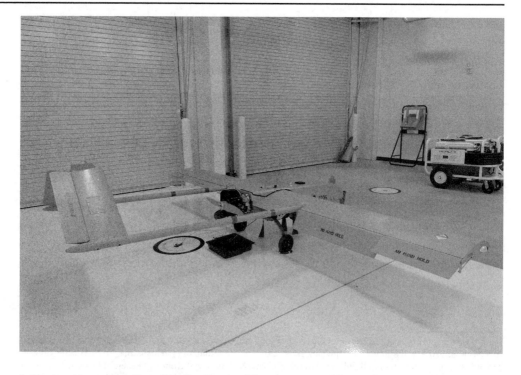

A Shadow Unmanned Aircraft in the Hangar (Photo courtesy of Donna Dulo)

The increased aerial information intake allows for significant reductions in decision cycles that result in faster situational resolutions and reduced information and photographic product turnarounds. In essence, UAS technology has the potential to transform the manner in which organizations and operators do business through enhanced information gathering and photography from a three-dimensional aerial vantage point.

The FAA Modernization and Reform Act of 2012 Subtitle B,[2] currently mandates that a plan to integrate UAS technology into U.S. national airspace be developed by the Secretary of Transportation in consultation with the aviation industry and applicable federal agencies. The types of UAS technology are not specified, but rather, the legislation states that agencies and organizations will be allowed access to the national airspace as "standards are completed and technology issues are resolved." This plan leaves the technological door open for a wide range of UAS platforms, payloads, and airframe uses in the national airspace. This plan also allows for a wide range of flexibility for the FAA to implement the mandates. As such, the future is bright for the aerial integration of a plethora of UAS technologies, airframes, and classifications.

MANNED VS. UNMANNED TECHNOLOGIES

The most basic principle to understand is that an unmanned aerial system is an aircraft, and it obeys the same aerodynamic principles and laws of physics as a manned aircraft. In fact, technologically speaking, all aircraft, ranging from large aircraft such as airliners to high speed jets, can be remotely operated. However, unmanned aircraft are distinguished based on their technological design which does not center on a cockpit but rather on a design based on potential mission functionality. In fact, all unmanned aircraft are designed around a specific functionality or set of functionalities, principally their payload or payload systems.

Without the specificity of their payload, or without a payload altogether, unmanned aircraft may be classified as recreational model aircraft or experimental systems. Thus, unmanned aircraft tend to be crafted and designed for specific missions or functions from concept through implementation, while their basic aeronautical and physical

---

2. The Federal Aviation Administration proposed a framework of regulations in February 2015 that would allow routine use of certain small unmanned aircraft systems (UAS) in today's aviation system, while maintaining flexibility to accommodate future technological innovations. The proposal presents various safety rules for small UAS (under 55 pounds) conducting nonrecreational, commercial-type operations. The rule would limit flights to daylight and visual-line-of-sight operations and addresses height restrictions, operator certification, optional use of a visual observer, aircraft registration and marking, and operational limits. *See* http://www.faa .gov/regulations_policies/rulemaking/media/021515_sUAS_Summary.pdf.

foundations mirror those of their manned counterparts. The following definitions demonstrate this principle.

The Federal Aviation Administration (FAA) defines an aircraft in the Federal Aviation Regulations § 1.1 (2015)[3] as: "A device that is used or intended to be used for flight in the air."

This definition, which ultimately derives its authority from 49 U.S.C. §§ 106(g), 40113, and 44701, applies to both manned and unmanned aircraft. The definition of an airplane, which emerges from the same authority, states that an airplane is: "An engine-driven fixed-wing aircraft heavier than air, that is supported in flight by the dynamic reaction of the air against its wings."

The definition rightly applies to both manned and unmanned systems. Exploring this concept a step further under the same authority, the definition of a rotorcraft[4] is: "A heavier-than-air aircraft that depends principally for its support in flight on the lift generated by one or more rotors."

Since an unmanned aircraft can be composed of either fixed-wing (airplane) or rotorcraft form, all of the above definitions apply perfectly to an unmanned aircraft since the unmanned aircraft obeys the same three-dimensional aerodynamic principles as its manned counterpart and requires the same basic technological components to operate in the air. So where is the definitional variance? The definition of unmanned aircraft can be found in the FAA Modernization and Reform Act of 2012, Subtitle B § 331: "An aircraft that is operated without the possibility of direct human intervention from, within, or on the aircraft."

Thus, it is clear that the sole distinguishing factor of manned and unmanned aircraft from a legal definitional standpoint is the absence of a human pilot onboard the physical aircraft. This is a major legal point as well as a technological reality. Without the human inside the aircraft, its legal role in the national airspace is vastly different than its manned counterpart, although they both are aerodynamically and technologically similar.

Yet, despite the fact that they are by definition "unmanned," unmanned aircraft have an operational human component which in many cases encompasses more personnel than their manned counterparts. While a human may not be in the cockpit, they are

---

3. CODE OF FEDERAL REGULATIONS TITLE 14: Aeronautics and Space, Chapter 1 Subchapter A Part 1 §1.1 (2015).

4. The term "rotorcraft" encompasses a wide variety of rotary wing aircraft that generate lift from rotor blades that are mounted on a single or multiple masts. This term includes helicopters, gyrodynes, autogyros, as well as other forms of masted rotor-based aircraft.

pervasive in the mission from launch to recovery. Humans in the loop during UAS operations include the following:

- **Remote Pilots:** human operators that control or partially control the aircraft from a distance
- **Payload Specialists:** personnel that control and operate the payloads of the aircraft to ensure optimal performance
- **Safety Personnel:** personnel that monitor operations to ensure safety in all areas of UAS operations including spotting and collision avoidance
- **Launch and Recovery Personnel:** personnel that provide support for safe launch and recovery operations
- **Operations Supervisors:** personnel that provide overall supervision to the UAS flight evolution
- **Navigation and Communication Specialists:** personnel that direct and control communications and navigation operations

As clearly demonstrated, UAS operations are far from "unmanned." This term is quite the misnomer, however there are significant operational differences in aircraft flight and control between manned and unmanned aircraft. Unlike onboard pilots, remote operators cannot "feel" the aircraft, which causes a variance in flight operations, aircraft control, and procedures. Additionally, with many smaller unmanned aircraft, the vantage point of the operator is vastly different than that of the onboard aircraft pilot. For example, an onboard pilot's vision differs from the on-ground operator's line of sight. Vision through onboard cameras in an unmanned aircraft is quite different as well from the window-based view of an onboard pilot, making unmanned aircraft operations feel more like a video game than a real-time flight operation. These overall differences effectuate major operational and procedural variances in the two types of aerial platforms, manned and unmanned, necessitating myriad technological and training solutions.

Figure 3.2

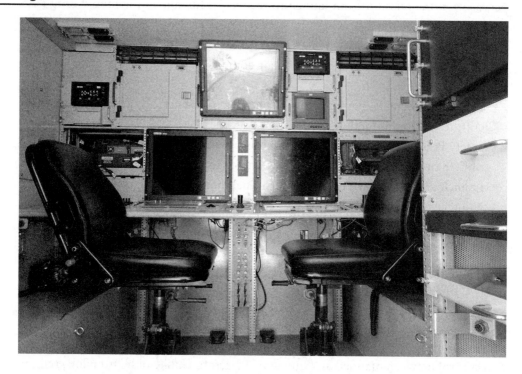

A Control Center for a Shadow Unmanned Aircraft (Photo courtesy of Donna Dulo)

Therefore, the true difference between manned and unmanned aircraft is more complex than their definitional standpoints. This complexity translates to safety and operational issues that must be resolved through the use of technology as well as modified operational procedures. It also translates to more variances that are necessary in aviation laws and regulations to ensure the safe operation of unmanned aircraft in the skies. Through the understanding of the basic classifications and technologies, these differences will become clearer, making it quite evident that the laws and regulations of manned aviation were not developed with unmanned operations in mind.

TYPES OF UNMANNED AERIAL SYSTEMS

There are several ways to classify an unmanned aircraft. Methods of classification vary between the military services, between the military and civilian sectors, and between different countries. This chapter will follow the more standard civilian terminologies and categorizations of the United States. In general, it is useful to classify an unmanned aircraft according to three specific criteria:

1. FAA Operational Categories
2. General Airframe Technologies
3. Functional Size Categories

Each unmanned aircraft will have a specification within each of the three criteria, allowing for a specific type of identification for the aircraft. This facilitates a general understanding of the performance, range, and maneuverability of the aircraft at an initial glance. Classification is also helpful when dealing with legal cases involving unmanned aircraft, as initial generalizations can be formed about the aircraft at issue to aid in the understanding of the facts of the case. The following sections expand upon each of the three classifications in greater detail.

FAA Operational Categories

The three types of civilian operational categories of the UAS as defined by the FAA are as follows:

- Experimental Unmanned Aircraft
- Model Unmanned Aircraft
- Public Unmanned Aircraft

These are the general categories of UAS that currently exist in the rapidly evolving realm of regulatory definitions. While each is considered unmanned aircraft, they have unique characteristics that warrant their own special category.

Experimental Aircraft

Experimental aircraft are unmanned aircraft that serve various scientific and engineering purposes such as airframe testing, payload testing, research and development, pilot and aircrew training, academic and educational training, and systems demonstration aside from air shows and air racing events. Their technologies range from fixed wing and rotorcraft, to a combination of the two with a plethora of propulsion and payload technologies. The FAA issues special experimental category airworthiness certificates under the Federal Aviation Regulations § 21.191 for operations of experimental aircraft. These aircraft must be operated with full FAA approval. In many cases these aircraft encompass the cutting-edge elements of aeronautical design, advanced technology, and enhanced development methodologies.

Model Unmanned Aircraft

Model aircraft are recreational unmanned aircraft, with technologies ranging from fixed wing to rotorcraft to lighter-than-air models, that are regulated by Advisory Circular AC 91-57 and more currently by the FAA Modernization and Reform Act of 2012 § 336, Special Rule for Model Aircraft. Section 336 defines a model unmanned aircraft as:

1. capable of sustained flight in the atmosphere
2. flown within visual sight of the person operating the aircraft
3. flown for hobby or recreational purposes

The guidelines for model aircraft in § 336 state that model aircraft are flown strictly for hobby or recreational use, are not more than 55 pounds unless otherwise certified, are operated in a manner that does not interfere with and gives way to manned aircraft, and when flown within 5 miles of an airport the airport operator and air traffic control tower are notified and mutual arrangements are made.

Model aircraft are flown within a community-based set of safety regulations that are founded upon the works of national community-based model aircraft organizations. These organizations design, develop, and implement their own safety programs for use in the model aircraft community.

Public Aircraft

Public unmanned aircraft are discussed in § 334, Public Unmanned Aircraft Systems. Section 334 provides the provisions for the establishment of unmanned aircraft in the national airspace. While the ultimate size and limits of the aeronautical technologies of public unmanned aircraft are not defined in § 334, the section does permit government public safety agencies to operate small unmanned systems while the issues of the national airspace are being worked out legislatively. Section 334 allows for an agency to operate an unmanned aircraft weighing 4.4 pounds or less if operated:

1. within sight of the operator;
2. less than 400 feet above the ground;
3. during daylight hours;
4. within class G airspace; and
5. outside of 5 statute miles from any airport, heliport, seaplane base, spaceport, or other location with aviation activities.

The above operational categories are general classifications of UAS. These categories can encompass a wide variety of aeronautical designs and capabilities. These designs and capabilities ultimately revolve around the choice of airframe as well as size of aircraft being used for a particular mission or operation. The following sections define the airframes and sizes of unmanned aircraft including the aeronautical technologies that encompass them.

UAS Airframe Technologies

When observing an unmanned aerial system, the airframe is the key determinant to the degree of maneuverability that the aircraft will have in three-dimensional airspace. The speed, range, and maneuverability requirements of a UAS will be key factors in determining the choice of the airframe technology used to achieve the required mobility for fulfilling the mission of the organization or operator. The size and weight of the payload, too, will determine the choice of a UAS airframe technology, as well as time in air or "persistence" requirements. There are four basic types of UAS airframe technologies, as well as hybrid models, that operators and organizations will be choosing from to achieve their maneuverability, speed, range, and payload operational requirements:

1. Fixed-Wing UAS
2. Rotorcraft UAS
3. Tilt Rotor UAS
4. Lighter-than-Air UAS

The choice of the airframe will also depend on a careful analysis of long-term mission requirements, cost, launch capabilities, remote pilot and operational capabilities, as well as ground station availability and location.

Fixed-Wing UAS

The first airframe category to be discussed is the fixed-wing UAS. This aircraft technology uses forward motion to generate lift and move the UAS through the air. The fixed-wing unmanned aircraft has the same basic aerodynamic structures as the fixed-wing manned aircraft:

- **Fuselage:** the body of the aircraft upon which the main usable volume is found
- **Empennage:** the tail assembly consisting of various horizontal and vertical stabilizers, the elevator, and the rudder
- **Wings:** the main source of aerodynamic lift within the flight envelope
- **Engines:** the system of propulsion

The fixed-wing configuration will depend upon the design of the particular UAS model. The empennage will vary considerably from model to model, and will vary in comparison to manned aircraft based on aerodynamic requirements. The empennage is the most deviant in appearance due to the smaller size and aerodynamic differences of UAS as compared to manned aircraft. However, in general, the fixed-wing unmanned aircraft closely resembles its manned counterpart.

Rapid point-to-point transversal and large-area coverage are the key benefits to this type of UAS. Vast amounts of airspace at many altitudes can be covered in short amounts of time, making this type of UAS ideal for large-area surveillance, photography, and information gathering. The extended ranges of fixed-wing UAS platforms make rapid, long-distance missions possible. This leads to the potential expansion of the range of capabilities for agencies and user organizations as compared with their current ground-based technology.

Figure 3.3

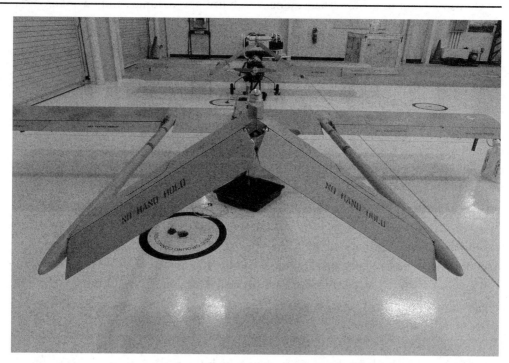

A Shadow UAS Highlighting the Aircraft's Empennage (Photo courtesy of Donna Dulo)

Fixed-wing unmanned aircraft can also cover higher altitudes than their rotorcraft counterparts, facilitating wider airspace coverage areas in smaller time frames. This higher altitude coverage makes them ideal for experiments and research. Additionally, fixed-wing fuselages can typically remain airborne longer than rotorcraft, due to larger fuel carrying capabilities, extending mission time and coverage.

The fixed-wing UAS must have a launch mechanism. It launches in what is termed a horizontal takeoff and landing (HTOL) methodology. This necessitates either a runway, a mechanical launcher, or, with smaller unmanned aircraft, a human to basically throw the aircraft into the air allowing it to gain lift and propel forward thereafter on its own. This HTOL requirement can be a disadvantage as airports must be located and utilized in many cases. In other cases, sometimes heavy and bulky launch mechanisms must be hauled into the area of operations, which can pose safety hazards. Even human-based launches can be safety hazards. Human-based launches have the potential for failed launches, inaccurate takeoffs, or other anomalies.

Figure 3.4

A Sentry UAS with Its Control Station (Photo courtesy of Donna Dulo)

In short, fixed-wing UAS have advantages and disadvantages that must be weighed in light of the mission, airspace conditions, needs of the user organization, availability of takeoff capabilities, and many other factors. These factors also play a major part in the safety and reliability of the aircraft in the overall strategic, operational, and tactical missions of the user organization.

Rotorcraft UAS

The second UAS airframe alternative is the rotary wing airframe, also known as a rotorcraft. This is a UAS that generates lift through rotating rotor blades that revolve around a mast. A UAS can be in the standard single rotor "helicopter" frame or the popular quad rotor airframe, where four masts and blade systems propel the aircraft. It can also have configurations of two or three rotors per mast depending on the design. Recent unmanned rotorcraft designs have even sported eight or more masts with single or multiple rotor blades on each mast.

However, the most popular UAS are the single blade rotorcraft, also known as a standard rotorcraft, the quad rotor, and the single mast dual rotor model. The main components of a standard rotorcraft are as follows:

- **Airframe:** the primary structure where components are attached
- **Main Rotor System:** the primary rotor producing lift
- **Tail Rotor System:** a smaller rotor on the tail which counters the torque of the main rotor to maintain directional control of the aircraft
- **Landing Gear:** the gear that provides antiskid and antishock capabilities for landing

The rotorcraft UAS can appear quite different depending on the number of rotors and masts it carries. The single rotor rotorcraft looks like a traditional helicopter. A single mast dual rotor (coaxial rotor) UAS has blades that rotate in opposite directions which cancels the torque from each blade, thus in many cases a tail rotor assembly is not needed. Single mast dual rotor types of rotorcraft are often symmetric in design and are more stable in the atmosphere than many other rotorcraft designs, making this an ideal airframe for overhead station-keeping operations such as surveillance, video documentation, and real-time area monitoring.

The quad rotor is the final design of rotorcraft that will be discussed. It is quite different from the standard manned helicopter that most people are familiar with. In fact, a quad rotor that is airborne can appear quite odd in the sky to the untrained observer. The quad rotor is a relatively new design in the rotorcraft world, but it is becoming increasingly popular in the model UAS aircraft and small UAS operations arenas.

The key feature of the quad rotor UAS is its ease of use in small configurations despite the intricate aerodynamic challenges of its design. From a micro design the size of a hand to designs that are several feet across, the aerodynamic stability, ease of maneuverability, and station-keeping capability make this an ideal model for operators that need an out-of-the-box solution with minimal training and high operational functionality. This is therefore a popular model for police and fire agencies, news organizations, researchers, photographers, as well as hobbyists searching for a low-cost, easy-to-learn-and-operate unmanned aerial system. Newer multimasted unmanned aircraft with eight or more masts add additional stability and functionality to the quad rotor basic design.

One of the main benefits of the rotorcraft airframe is its vertical takeoff and landing (VTOL) capability. This capability allows it to launch from virtually anywhere and land virtually anywhere, the only requirement being a hard, relatively flat surface. This enables rapid transportation to and from the scene of operation in a support land vehicle, with the requirement of an airport being virtually non-existent. VTOL also facilitates launch and recovery in tight areas providing safety and security as well as maneuverability.

The rotorcraft airframe has the ability to maintain station, also called "station-keep," a critical feature for many operators who are looking for precision video, surveillance, or some type of environmental sensing or monitoring. While having significantly less range and altitude capabilities than a fixed-wing UAS, the enhanced in-space tight maneuverability, vertical flight, vertical takeoff and landing (VTOL), and station-keeping ability of the rotary wing UAS make it especially useful for a wide range of unmanned aerial applications.

Tilt Rotor UAS

For operators requiring the best of both the fixed-wing and rotorcraft worlds, the tilt rotor may be the UAS technology of choice. This UAS is an airframe that uses a pair of powered rotors mounted on rotating shafts, which are located at the end of a fixed aircraft wing. The wing of this aircraft is fixed, but the rotors and pylons on which they are mounted tilt in the order of a 90-degree or better range, allowing for various combinations of horizontal or vertical flight. This allows the UAS to generate lifting in either the fixed-wing mode, for rapid, long-range travel, or in the rotary-wing mode, for vertical flight, VTOL, and station-keeping hovering operation. The flexibility of this UAS technology makes it a popular candidate for operators and organizations with a wide variety of missions.

The tilt rotor UAS is not as popular as the other UAS airframes, and it tends to be found in niche operational areas such as nautical search and rescue. The mechanical complexity of this design makes it more difficult to design and thus more expensive to produce. However, as unmanned aerial systems become more pervasive, this airframe will surely take its place in unmanned operations due to its versatility and interoperability in both the horizontal flight mode and vertical hover mode.

Lighter-than-Air UAS

The final UAS airframe technology is the lighter-than-air UAS, also referred to in old-fashioned terms as a "blimp." It is also called an "unmanned airship." It uses buoyancy to float through the use of one or more large gas bags or canopies. This is an ideal technology for persistent, long-term, vertical mobility for such applications as stationary surveillance.

The lighter-than-air UAS has many advantages. It is relatively inexpensive to acquire, operate, and maintain compared with most other UAS airframes. It is extremely easy to operate with flexible takeoff and landing operations in the vertical mode. It can stay aloft for significantly longer than other types of UAS, making it ideal for operations requiring airborne "persistence," which is extended station-keep to monitor or conduct surveillance on a targeted area. The stable performance of the UAS permits days, weeks, or even more of persistent aerial operations. Scalability is also a beneficial factor; with increasing payloads, operators can easily scale up to more robust airframes at a significantly less cost than through the acquisition of fixed-wing or rotorcraft models.

One of the downsides of this type of airframe is its volatility in inclement weather, especially weather with high wind conditions. Thus, the use of this type of UAS must be matched with the local area and potential weather conditions to ensure safe and productive unmanned operations. However, more robust lighter-than-air UAS airframe designs are currently being researched, as this model of UAS is likely to be popular with its plethora of potential aerial applications.

Of particular note is the tethered/moored balloon, or a free balloon, which in some circles are called an unmanned aircraft. The differences between these aerial entities must be understood for both legal and operational purposes. A moored balloon has a specific set of regulations, § 101.11 of 14 C.F.R.[5] This subpart applies to the operation of moored balloons and kites. However, a person operating a moored balloon or a kite within a restricted area must comply only with 14 C.F.R. § 101.19 and with additional limitations imposed by the using or controlling agency, as appropriate. Specifically, the operation of a moored balloon has the following operational limitations[6]:

§ 101.13 Operating limitations.

(a) Except as provided in paragraph (b) of this section, no person may operate a moored balloon or kite—

(1) Less than 500 feet from the base of any cloud;

(2) More than 500 feet above the surface of the earth;

---

5. 14 C.F.R. Chapter 1 Subchapter F § 101 (Jan. 1, 2012).
6. *Id.*

(3) From an area where the ground visibility is less than three miles; or

(4) Within five miles of the boundary of any airport.

(b) Paragraph (a) of this section does not apply to the operation of a balloon or kite below the top of any structure and within 250 feet of it, if that shielded operation does not obscure any lighting on the structure.

An unmanned free balloon also has a special set of regulations, § 101.31. This subpart applies specifically to the operation of unmanned free balloons. However, a person operating an unmanned free balloon within a restricted area must comply only with § 101.33 (d) and (e) and with any additional limitations that are imposed by the using or controlling agency, as appropriate. The operation of an unmanned free balloon must follow the following regulations[7]:

§ 101.33 Operating limitations.

No person may operate an unmanned free balloon—

(a) Unless otherwise authorized by ATC, below 2,000 feet above the surface within the lateral boundaries of the surface areas of Class B, Class C, Class D, or Class E airspace designated for an airport;

(b) At any altitude where there are clouds or obscuring phenomena of more than five-tenths coverage;

(c) At any altitude below 60,000 feet standard pressure altitude where the horizontal visibility is less than five miles;

(d) During the first 1,000 feet of ascent, over a congested area of a city, town, or settlement or an open-air assembly of persons not associated with the operation; or

(e) In such a manner that impact of the balloon, or part thereof including its payload, with the surface creates a hazard to persons or property not associated with the operation.

This clearly indicates that lighter-than-air unmanned aircraft must have three-dimensional control and propulsion mechanisms for steering and transversal in all three axes. A simple free balloon or gas bag with a tether/moor or a kite do not fit the definition for an unmanned aircraft; therefore, regulations on the use of balloons should be followed for situations involving free or tethered balloons. They should not be called unmanned aircraft as defined by federal regulations.

---

7. *Id.*

Manned–Unmanned Hybrids

As discussed earlier in this chapter, almost any type of aircraft can be flown remotely. In the past, jetliners, fighter jets, and all types of helicopters have been flown remotely, but mainly for test or experimental purposes. However, there is a new design trend in the aviation community: manned–unmanned hybrids. These are not manned aircraft rigged for remote flight for experimental purposes but aircraft designed specifically for operation in both situations. For operations requiring the feel of the aircraft and rapid onboard human decision-making and actions, these aircraft are designed to accommodate one or more physically onboard pilots. They will fly in accordance with manned aircraft flight rules when a pilot is onboard.

Hybrids have the potential to encompass all four types of airframe designs. However, at the present time research and development are centered on the fixed-wing hybrid and the single rotor rotorcraft design, both of which appear from the ground as regular manned aircraft. In fact, only close inspection of the aircraft would reveal if the aircraft is in fact unmanned during an operation.

For "D³" operations, also known as "dull, dirty, or dangerous" operations, the aircraft will have the capability of fully autonomous or remotely piloted control. It will fly in accordance with unmanned flight rules. Hybrid types will be able to switch between modes with little configuration changes, making them the ideal aircraft for many operators and organizations that have challenging missions that require flexibility in operations due to safety, security, or other special circumstances. Hybrids are currently in research and development at many major aircraft manufacturers and will likely become a strong participant in the civilian unmanned aircraft population in the future.

UAS Size Categorizations

A final categorization of unmanned aircraft is its functional size. This category is particularly important in the legal arena, as future airspace regulations are likely to revolve around UAS size as well as operational capabilities. The functional size of a UAS determines its robustness not only in terms of aeronautical capabilities and payload abilities but also in terms of its visibility in the air and its maneuverability. Both of these factors contribute to the safe operation of the aircraft in the national airspace.

Functional size categorizations, like other categorizations of unmanned aircraft, vary widely between military services, civilian agencies, and countries. The categories listed in this chapter are meant to provide clear guidance in the realm of civilian use in the United States both at the present time and in the future. It should be noted that there are myriad terms for many of the categories, and as such, several of the alternative terms are mentioned for reference purposes. In many cases, the terms can be used interchangeably, although in this book the primary terms will be used throughout.

The functional size categories in the civilian world are arbitrary, except for the small category, which is specifically defined in the FAA Modernization and Reform Act of 2012. The categories are as follows:

- Large UAS
- Medium UAS
- Small UAS
- Micro/Mini UAS
- Nano UAS

These categories cover all airframe types, although the manned–unmanned hybrids would more likely be categorized with their manned counterparts. Additionally, lighter-than-air unmanned aircraft tend to be larger by nature and, as such, are usually categorized by their specific volume size.

Large UAS
The large UAS category covers unmanned aircraft that rival the size of small manned aircraft. These unmanned aircraft tend to be strategic in nature as opposed to tactical, and they are extremely expensive to acquire, operate, and maintain. Large UAS have high-altitude capabilities and extended ranges and possess the longest endurance. They are able to carry extensive payloads. Current operators of these aircraft in the national airspace are limited to mainly federal agencies such as the Department of Homeland Security. Large UAS are primarily fixed-wing or single main rotor airframes and have extended aerial endurance. Extensive remote pilot and support personnel training is required to operate this type of unmanned aircraft.

Medium UAS
The medium UAS category is of a more tactical nature than the large UAS. It is smaller than a large UAS but larger than the FAA-defined size of a small UAS, thus weighing 55 pounds or more up to the size of a large UAS. They have extended ranges and can operate for extended periods in many fixed-wing models. Medium UAS airframes include fixed-wing, tilt rotor, and single or dual mast rotorcraft. They have payload capabilities far greater than the small UAS and can carry multiple payload systems that can operate independently of each other. Medium UAS are quite expensive and, like the large UAS, require extensive remote pilot training and support personnel training and experience.

Small UAS

The small UAS is the primary UAS targeted by the FAA for initial integration into the national airspace. The FAA Modernization and Reform Act of 2012 § 331 defines a small unmanned aircraft as "an unmanned aircraft weighing less than 55 pounds." While this is a narrow definition, it sets a concrete and specific definitional standard for small UAS airframe reference. This unmanned aircraft is currently the most pervasive in the civilian world and its use and presence in the skies will increase exponentially as the FAA works out the rules and regulations for its use.

The small UAS is significantly different from its large and medium size counterparts: Its size allows it to be more maneuverable, more flexible, and easier to fly. Its cost is significantly less than its larger cousins, making many models affordable to a wide variety of civilian organizations and even private citizens. The small UAS can operate in areas previously unflyable by manned aircraft or even the larger unmanned aircraft. Through vertical takeoff and landing (VTOL), for example, the small UAS can transverse the outlines of buildings, follow moving land vehicles, and fit in tight spaces limited only by its diameter and skill of its operator.

The operation of small UAS is significantly cheaper than that of its larger counterparts. In addition, pilots (operators) can be trained more quickly. Payloads tend to be found on external racks compared to being internal semifixed components on the larger UAS and therefore can be interchangeable and quickly modified if necessary to fit the specific operational mission. The small nature of the airframe makes maintenance easier and less expensive, thus reducing the total cost of ownership.

The smaller size does increase the risk of the aircraft. With small size comes lower visibility, and the use of these smaller vehicles in the national airspace will pose many hazards requiring precise sense and avoid systems. The reduced training requirements of small UAS pilot operators also presents another set of inherent risks.

Overall, the small UAS is destined to be the workhorse of the unmanned civilian fleet in the very near future. With primarily tactical and research operations, its flexibility and maneuverability will have many applications in the civilian context. With scalability, portability, and cost advantages, this category is destined to dominate the civilian skies with a virtually unlimited number of applications.

Micro/Mini UAS

The micro/mini UAS is an unmanned aircraft similar in size to a model aircraft. However, it has a distinct operational function with a payload configured for a specific mission. This category tends to be hand-held in size as well as hand-launched. Payloads are usually singular in nature, and the entire aircraft may have only a single, functional payload capability. Research within this category includes security functions such as building security, short-range scientific surveying, such as tree-based wildlife observations, and short-range photography.

Micro UAS are, in most cases, limited to model aircraft, although specific commercial applications are being researched and developed. The use and utility of this size classification is endless due to its size, low cost, portability, and expendable nature.

Nano UAS

This category is mostly experimental and academic, although it has defined applications in the military and clandestine services. They are the size of large insects and can be used alone for very short range surveillance or in large groups for scientific research. This type of UAS is not large enough to be classified for the national airspace, but its mention is important to give a broad overview of the wide potential of this unmanned aircraft and also to demonstrate a potential for privacy issues due to its stealth nature.

Nano UAS are very popular experimental aircraft at universities, and extensive research is being done with these types of UAS in terms of flight capabilities, video and still photography capabilities, as well as altitude and range capabilities. In the future, the use of Nano UAS is expected to expand into a wide range of uses including utility functions, surveillance and security functions, scientific functions, and many other uses.

CONCLUSION

The classification and categorization of the UAS are vital in understanding the operational capabilities of the aircraft. They are also important for understanding the technological capability, maneuverability, range, and endurance specifications of the various unmanned aircraft models and airframes. By understanding the operational and size categories, as well as the airframe technologies of the UAS, a defined picture of system capabilities can be drawn in order to understand specific applications of a particular unmanned aircraft.

Understanding the technical capabilities of a UAS also aids the legal practitioner in understanding the legal ramifications of the use and implementation of the specific UAS technology. Each airframe as well as airframe size classification poses specific legal challenges and issues. By understanding these technological specifications, a clearer picture of emerging legal issues can be gained. Also, through this understanding, privacy, security, and safety laws and regulations can be developed to ensure proper UAS operation and integration in the national airspace.

2

FAA Rulemaking and Unmanned Aircraft Law

CHAPTER

4

The Federal Aviation Administration Rulemaking Process

Jonathan B. Rupprecht

Many individuals who must follow federal regulations do not understand how regulations are created. This is because many individuals understand the idea of the three branches of government as laid out in our Constitution, but as Justice Jackson noted, "The rise of administrative bodies probably has been the most significant legal trend of the last century. . . . They have become a veritable fourth branch of the Government, which has deranged our three-branch legal theories much as the concept of a fourth dimension unsettles our three-dimensional thinking."[1]

Congress creates federal agencies to regulate certain areas and gives them power to create regulations necessary to carry out their missions. The rulemaking process is the way federal agencies go about creating rules or regulations[2] with binding legal effect upon the public. These regulations can either prescribe a certain type of conduct[3] or prohibit a certain type of conduct.[4]

---

1. Fed. Trade Comm'n v. Ruberoid Co., 343 U.S. 470, 487 (1952) (Jackson, J., dissenting).
2. *See* Maeve P. Carey, Cong. Research Serv., RL 32240, The Federal Rulemaking Process: An Overview 1 (2013) (The terms *rule* or *regulation* are often used interchangeably in discussions of the federal regulatory process).
3. *See* 14 C.F.R. § 91.126(b) (Proscribing how a pilot is to enter the traffic pattern).
4. *See* 14 C.F.R. § 91.17(a) (Prohibiting a pilot from flying an airplane within 8 hours of drinking alcohol).

There are different types of agency rulemaking: (1) formal rulemaking, (2) informal rulemaking, (3) direct final rulemaking, (4) hybrid rulemaking, and (5) negotiated rulemaking. Rules are classified as (1) substantive,[5] (2) interpretive or general statements of policy,[6] or (3) management or procedural.[7] The test to determine if something is a substantive rule is if the agency "intends to create a new law, rights or duties[.]"[8] This discusses the informal rulemaking of substantive rules because substantive rules are what the FAA regularly uses and is currently using to create the new laws, rights, and duties of unmanned aircraft regulations.

Generally,[9] the informal rulemaking process for substantive rules is (1) a notice of a proposed rule is published, (2) comments are received on the rule, and (3) the agency publishes the final rule, taking into account the comments received from the first notice. The purpose of this process is to allow the public to voice its opinions on the wisest way to solve a problem and to treat fairly the individuals who will be burdened by the regulation by giving them the ability to participate.[10] This notice and comment process gives the affected party the time to prepare to comply with the new regulation.

"Congress and various Presidents have developed during the past 60 to 70 years" many requirements and procedures for federal agencies.[11] The decades of requirements pile up similar to the layers of old civilizations that archaeologists dig through in Athens and Rome. The overall effect of the layers of requirement is a massive amount of hoops the FAA has to jump through which would rival most of the world's circuses combined. The purpose of this chapter is to make the reader aware of the complexities of this area, to provide resources for further study, and to equip the reader to discuss this area intelligently.

There are some common misconceptions of the rulemaking process. The rulemaking process is not a back-in-time looking ruling by a judge on a case. The rulemaking process is forward looking[12] because the federal agency detects an unsafe situation. Also, the rule is not created by a judge or directly by Congress,[13] but made by a federal agency. The rulemaking process deals with things outside the agency and not with inter-

---

5. These are also called legislative rules because they are issued under a statutory authority. They implement a statute and have the full force of law behind them.

6. 5 U.S.C. § 553(b)(3)(A) (The APA applies except "to interpretative rules, general statements of policy, or rules of agency organization, procedure, or practice").

7. Pickus v. United States Board of Parole, 507 F.2d 1107, 1113 (D.C. Cir. 1974) ("This category . . . should not be deemed to include any action which goes beyond formality and substantially affects the rights of those over whom the agency exercise authority").

8. General Motors Corp. v. Ruckelshaus, 742 F.2d 1561, 1565 (D.C. Cir. 1984) (en banc).

9. There are some exceptions that will be discussed later.

10. *See* United States v. Utesch, 596 F.3d 302, 308–09 (6th Cir. 2010).

11. CAREY, *supra* note 2, at 3.

12. *See* 5 U.S.C. § 551(4) ("future effect designed to implement, interpret, or prescribe law").

13. Congress may pass legislation telling an agency to pass regulations.

nal agency rules, organization, procedure, practice,[14] management or personnel, public property, loans, grants, benefits, contracts,[15] military, or foreign affairs functions.[16]

THE FAA IS AUTHORIZED TO CREATE REGULATIONS

The FAA has been given by Congress the power to create regulations[17] such as regulations for "the use of the airspace necessary to ensure the safety of aircraft and the efficient use of airspace."[18] The FAA was required to create regulations for "(A) navigating, protecting, and identifying aircraft; (B) protecting individuals and property on the ground; (C) using the navigable airspace efficiently; and (D) preventing collision between aircraft, between aircraft and land or water vehicles, and between aircraft and airborne objects."[19] Another section further authorizes the FAA to create regulations inspecting, servicing, and overhauling aircraft, aircraft engines, propellers, appliances,[20] reserve supply of aircraft fuel and oil,[21] maximum number of hours for pilots to fly in a day,[22] and whatever the FAA "finds necessary for safety in air commerce and national security."[23]

Congress passed the FAA Modernization and Reform Act of 2012 (FMRA)[24] which requires the FAA to publish "a final rule on small unmanned aircraft systems that will allow for civil operation of such systems in the national airspace system,[25] . . . a notice of proposed rulemaking to implement the recommendations of the" FAA's unmanned aircraft integration comprehensive plan, and "the final rule to be published not later than 16 months after the date of publication of the notice[.]"[26] The FAA has congressionally delegated authority to create regulations on unmanned aircraft.

---

14. *See* 5 U.S.C. § 553(b)(3)(A).
15. *See* 5 U.S.C. § 553(a)(2).
16. *See* 5 U.S.C. § 553(a)(1).
17. *See* 49 U.S.C. §§ 40103, 40113(a), 106(f)(3).
18. 49 U.S.C. § 40103(b)(1).
19. 49 U.S.C. § 40103(b)(2).
20. *See* 49 U.S.C. § 44701(a)(2)(a).
21. *See* 49 U.S.C. § 44701(a)(3).
22. *See* 49 U.S.C. § 44701(a)(4).
23. 49 U.S.C. § 44701(a)(5).
24. FAA Modernization and Reform Act of 2012, Pub. L. No. 112-95, 126 Stat. 11 (2012) [hereinafter FMRA], *available at* http://www.gpo.gov/fdsys/pkg/PLAW-112publ95/pdf/PLAW-112publ95.pdf.
25. *Id.* § 332(b)(1), 126 Stat. at 74.
26. *Id.* § 332(b)(2), 126 Stat. at 74.

WHAT IS SUBJECT TO THE RULEMAKING PROCESS?

In the context of the FAA, the rulemaking process "applies to the issuance, amendment, and repeal of any regulation[,]"[27] petitions for exemptions from regulations,[28] issuances of airworthiness directives (ADs),[29] special conditions,[30] and airspace designations or modifications.[31] The rulemaking process does not apply "to interpretative rules, general statements of policy, or rules of agency organization, procedure, or practice"[32] or where the agency finds the rulemaking process is "impracticable, unnecessary, or contrary to the public interest."[33]

Located inside the Code of Federal Regulations is Title 14, which is called the Federal Aviation Regulations (FARs).[34] This title has the regulations that govern the certification of civil aircraft,[35] civil pilot licensing,[36] airspace,[37] commercial operations,[38] general pilot operating rules,[39] pilot schools and certificated agencies,[40] airports,[41] and navigational facilities.[42] The FARs have been at times confused with the Federal Acquisition Regulations,[43] which have also been called FARs. To prevent this, the FAA uses 14 C.F.R. Part XXXX when referring to a regulation and not the abbreviation FAR.[44] Future additions or changes to these regulations require the FAA to put the regulations through the rulemaking process. There is also something called Special Federal Aviation Regulations (SFARs), which are regulations but apply only to specific or unique situations[45] and are also subject to the rulemaking process.

Petitions for exemptions are requests for relief from regulations, and exemptions are subject to the rulemaking procedures.[46] The FAA has what is called regulatory

---

27. 14 C.F.R. §§ 11.1, 11.21(a).
28. *See* 14 C.F.R. § 11.15.
29. *See* 14 C.F.R. § 11.21(b).
30. *See* 14 C.F.R. §§ 21.16, 11.19.
31. *See* 14 C.F.R. § 11.21(c).
32. 5 U.S.C. § 553(b)(3)(A).
33. 5 U.S.C. § 553(b)(3)(B).
34. 14 C.F.R. pts. 1–199.
35. 14 C.F.R. pts. 21–49.
36. 14 C.F.R. pts. 61–67.
37. 14 C.F.R. pts. 71–77.
38. 14 C.F.R. pts. 119–135.
39. 14 C.F.R. pts. 91–105.
40. 14 C.F.R. pts. 141–147.
41. 14 C.F.R. pts. 150–161.
42. 14 C.F.R. pts. 170–171.
43. 48 C.F.R. pts. 1–53.
44. *See* Aviation Maintenance Technician Handbook General, Fed. Aviation Admin. 12-3 (2008), *available at* http://www.faa.gov/regulations_policies/handbooks_manuals/aircraft/amt_handbook/media/faa-8083-30_ch12.pdf.
45. *See* 14 C.F.R. § 91.1605 ("Special Federal Aviation Regulation No. 77—Prohibition Against Certain Flights Within the Territory and Airspace of Iraq").
46. *See* 14 C.F.R. § 11.15.

flexibility,[47] which allows deviations,[48] waivers,[49] and authorizations[50] from regulations. If a request cannot fall into one of those three options, then an individual must petition the FAA for an exemption from the regulations under the FAA's exemption authority.[51] A good example of this is where three FAA employees petitioned for an exemption for unmanned aircraft from section 91.151, which requires a certain amount of time in fuel for an airplane flight in good weather.[52] The petitioners correctly reasoned, "Since there is no apparent regulatory flexibility built into this language through authorization by the [FAA], a request for a deviation is not an available remedy. As this rule is not listed in 14 CFR § 91.905, List of rules subject to waivers, a request for a waiver is not applicable. Therefore, an exemption is the only regulatory flexibility available."[53]

A special condition happens when the airworthiness regulations in place do not contain satisfactory or suitable safety standards for an aircraft or related part because of a new or unique design feature of the aircraft or aircraft part. The FAA "prescribes special conditions and amendments thereto for the product. The special conditions . . . contain such safety standards for the aircraft, aircraft engine or propeller as the FAA finds necessary to establish a level of safety equivalent to that established in the regulations."[54] A good example of special conditions is back in the late 1980s when the European Airbus A320 was trying to obtain a type certificate here in the United States and the existing FARs did not contain adequate or appropriate safety standards regarding electronic fly-by-wire flight controls, but the FAA created special conditions[55] for the certification of the aircraft.[56] The FAA believes special conditions are not subject to the APA's notice and comment rules because special conditions are rules of "particular applicability" to a particular aircraft design; however, the "FAA does follow notice and comment procedures anyway, because [the FAA] may receive useful information."[57]

Airworthiness directives are actually considered part of the regulations, but they are not annually codified in the FARs. They are, however, published in the Federal

47. For a great explanation of all of these, *see* ANTHONY J. ADAMSKY & TIMOTHY J. DOYLE, INTRODUCTION TO THE AVIATION REGULATORY PROCESS 111–12 (5th ed. 2005).

48. *See generally* 14 C.F.R. 91.319.

49. *See* 14 C.F.R. § 91.903.

50. *See generally* 14 C.F.R. § 91.817.

51. *See* 49 U.S.C. § 40109.

52. *See* Petition for Exemption; Summary of Petition Received, 79 Fed. Reg. 2,244, 2,245 (proposed Jan. 13, 2014).

53. Mike Wilson, Skip Wiegand, and Brad Howard, *Exemption/Rulemaking*, REGULATIONS.GOV (Apr. 18, 2013), http://www.regulations.gov/#!documentDetail;D=FAA-2013-0376-0001.

54. 14 C.F.R. §§ 21.16, 11.19.

55. *See* Notice of Proposed Special Conditions No. SC-87-5-NM for the Airbus Industrie Model A320 series airplanes, 52 Fed. Reg. 38,772 (proposed Oct. 19, 1987).

56. *See* A320 Special Conditions for Certification, FED. AVIATION. ADMIN., http://lessonslearned.faa.gov/ll_main.cfm?TabID=1&LLID=71&LLTypeID=5.

57. General Rulemaking Procedures, 65 Fed. Reg. 50,850, 50,855 (Aug. 21, 2000) (to be codified at 14 C.F.R. part 11).

Register as amendments to section 39.13.[58] Interestingly, section 91.403 is annually codified and requires owners or operators of aircraft to comply with the applicable ADs in section 39.13.[59] The public needs to be made aware of these ADs because "[A]irworthiness directives are legally enforceable rules that apply to the following products: aircraft, aircraft engines, propellers, and appliances."[60] The "FAA issues an airworthiness directive addressing a product when [the FAA] find[s] that: (a) An unsafe condition exists in the product; and (b) The condition is likely to exist or develop in other products of the same type design."[61] A good example is where the FAA receives multiple reports of a low oil pressure warning on the same types of Sikorsky helicopter and issues an AD that requires an inspection of certain parts on the helicopter to prevent the low oil pressure warning problem.[62] The FAA can unilaterally issue an AD, or an airplane manufacturer can request the FAA to issue one.[63]

Airspace designations are "[a]ctions establishing, amending or revoking terminal and enroute airspace area designations and reporting points, in the United States and its territories,"[64] incorporated by reference into the FARs.[65] This happens by the FAA annually amending section 71.1[66] to include by reference an updated FAA order containing all of the airspace designations and reporting points.[67] The reason the order is by reference and not actually included in the FARs is because the order is large and there are a large number of changes in the airspace.[68] The FAA is allowed to incorporate this order by reference in part 71 because it has been approved by the director of the Federal Register.[69]

---

58. *See* 14 C.F.R § 39.13.

59. *See* 14 C.F.R. § 91.403.

60. 14 C.F.R. § 39.3.

61. 14 C.F.R. § 39.5.

62. *See* Airworthiness Directives; Sikorsky Aircraft Corporation (Sikorsky) Helicopters, 79 Fed. Reg. 31,231 (proposed June 2, 2014) [hereinafter "Sikorsky AD"] ("This proposed [rule] is prompted by several reports of MGB low oil pressure warnings. . . . The proposed actions are intended to prevent failure of the [main gear box] from loss of oil, which could result in subsequent loss of control of the helicopter").

63. *See* Airworthiness Directives; The Boeing Company Airplanes, 78 Fed. Reg. 61,173, 61,174 (Oct. 3, 2013) ("Boeing and American Airlines (AAL) requested that the most recent MPD document be incorporated into the NPRM (77 FR 58791, September 24, 2012)").

64. Fed. Aviation Admin., Order JO 7400.9X, Airspace Designations and Reporting Points 1 (2013), *available at* http://www.faa.gov/documentLibrary/media/Order/JO_7400.9X.pdf.

65. *See* 14 C.F.R. § 71.1.

66. *See* Airspace Designations; Incorporation by Reference, 78 Fed. Reg. 52,847 (Aug. 27, 2013) (to be codified at 14 C.F.R. § 71.1).

67. *See* Fed. Aviation Admin., Order JO 7400.9X, Airspace Designations and Reporting Points 1 (2013), *available at* http://www.faa.gov/documentLibrary/media/Order/JO_7400.9X.pdf.

68. *See id.*

69. *See id.* at 2; *see also* 5 U.S.C. §§ 552(a), 553; 1 C.F.R. §§ 51.1, 51.3.

WHAT ARE THE LAWS GOVERNING THE RULEMAKING PROCESS?

There are many laws applying to the FAA's rulemaking. This is not a complete list of all the laws affecting the rulemaking process. Only the acts that will actually affect the unmanned aircraft rule will be discussed below. Some of the more prominent ones will be discussed in detail and others only briefly mentioned.

Legislation Affecting the Rulemaking Process

Congress has made many different acts over the years. For a great resource on the acts, executive orders, and other legal material that affects the rulemaking process, see the Department of Transportation's Rulemaking Requirements document.[70] Statutes can be categorized as either (1) applying to all agencies or (2) applying only to a specific agency or program.

The Federal Register Act of 1935

The history behind the Federal Register Act[71] needs to be discussed so one can fully understand what led to the passing of it. A TWA airliner crashed on May 6, 1935, killing the beloved and well-respected Senator Bronson Cutting.[72] The Department of Commerce's investigators blamed TWA and the pilot for the cause of the accident, but the president of TWA, Jack Frye, "contended that the Bureau of Air Commerce's regulations which addressed scheduled air transport operation had been improperly promulgated and were therefore not in force at the time the accident occurred."[73] The regulations issued by the Bureau of Air Commerce were so disorganized; the bureau had difficulty in figuring out which of its own regulations were in force.[74] The bureau searched for the current regulations containing the secretary's signature on them and failed to find an original signed copy of an October 1934 regulation amendment regulating TWA's scheduled airline operations.[75] The bureau could not find signatures of the previous secretary on many of the regulations, which led the new secretary to "stop gap" initialing of copies of the regulations to get all the regulations in force.[76]

This regulatory mess was a miniature version of the overall executive branch with its explosion of disorganized regulations and executive orders.[77] The exponentially

---

70. Dep't of Trans., Rulemaking Requirements (2012), *available at* https://dotgov.prod.acquia-sites .com/sites/dot.gov/files/docs/RULE%20REQUIREMENTS%202012.docx.

71. 44 U.S.C. §§ 1501–1511.

72. *See* Anthony J. Adamski & Timothy J. Doyle, Introduction to the Aviation Regulatory Process 5 (5th ed. 2005).

73. *Id.* at 5.

74. *See id.*

75. *See id.*

76. *See id.* at 5–6.

77. *See id.* at 6.

growing regulatory mess created the need for a way that everyone could receive notices of the regulations being passed, which led to the Federal Register Act being passed.

The modern day form of the Federal Register Act (FRA)[78] requires a codification of all the newly created regulations to be put in the Code of Federal Regulations (CFR).[79] The Code of Federal Regulations closely mirrors the United States Codes (USC).[80] Title 49 of the USC deals with transportation; however, the Federal Aviation Regulations are in Title 14 of the CFR and not Title 49 of the CFR as one would expect.

The Federal Register is a legal newspaper, published every business day, that makes available to the public notices from federal agencies on proposed regulations. The Federal Register also publishes other materials including presidential proclamations and executive orders, federal agency documents having general applicability and legal effect, documents required to be published by acts of Congress, and other federal agency documents of public interest.[81] The Federal Register is the primary way the public can be informed about the regulations that have recently been passed.

For purposes of the scope of this book, the FAA publishes in the Federal Register airworthiness directives, exemptions, petitions for rulemaking, airspace changes, and aviation rulemaking advisory committee meetings.[82] In addition to these things which are required to be published, the FAA also publishes advisory circulars,[83] special conditions,[84] policy notices,[85] and interpretations of FAA policy or rules.[86]

Administrative Procedures Act

The Administrative Procedures Act (APA)[87] controls the way federal agencies go about "formulating, amending, or repealing a rule."[88] A "'rule' means the whole or a part of an agency statement of general or particular applicability and future effect designed to implement, interpret, or prescribe law or policy or describing the organi-

---

78. This act has been amended multiple times since 1935.

79. *See* 44 U.S.C. § 1505(a).

80. The C.F.R. and U.S.C. share similar subject and title number in titles 1, 3, 5, 7, 8, 12, 15, 19, 21, 22, 23, 25, 26, 27, 28, 29, 30, 31, 33, 38, 39, 41, 42, 43, 46, 47, and 49.

81. *See* 44 U.S.C. § 1505; *see also* 1 C.F.R. 1.1.

82. *See* RTCA Special Committee 228—Minimum Operational Performance Standards for Unmanned Aircraft Systems, 79 Fed. Reg. 19,705 (Apr. 9, 2014).

83. Advisory Circular: Public Aircraft Operations, 77 Fed. Reg. 7,656 (Feb. 13, 2012).

84. *See* General Rulemaking Procedures *supra*, note 57, at 50,855.

85. *See* Notice of Unmanned Aircraft Operations in the National Airspace System Policy, 72 Fed. Reg. 6,689 (proposed Feb. 13, 2007), *available at* https://www.faa.gov/about/office_org/headquarters_offices/ato/service_units/systemops/aaim/organizations/uas/coa/faq/media/frnotice_uas.pdf and http://www.faa.gov/about/initiatives/uas/media/model_aircraft_spec_rule.pdf.

86. *See* Interpretation of the Special Rule for Model Aircraft, 79 Fed. Reg. 36,171 (June 23, 2014).

87. 5 U.S.C. §§ 551–559. The Freedom of Information Act is 5 U.S.C. § 552 which gives individuals the ability to get information from federal agencies. Individuals have been successful to obtain cease and desist letters targeting unmanned aircraft operators. *See* Jason Koebler, *FAA Commercial Unmanned aircraft Cease-and-Desist orders*, SCRIBD.COM (Feb. 6, 2014), http://www.scribd.com/doc/205201647/FAA-Commercial-Unmanned-aircraft-Cease-and-Desist-orders.

88. 5 U.S.C. § 551(5).

zation, procedure, or practice requirements of an agency[.]"[89] A rule can be classified as either (1) a substantive rule,[90] (2) an interpretive rule,[91] (3) a general statements of policy, or (4) a procedural rule.[92] Only substantive rules are subject to the notice and comment procedures under the APA, unless the agency finds the notice and comment procedures "impracticable, unnecessary, or contrary to the public interest."[93]

Federal Advisory Committee Act of 1972

The Federal Advisory Committee Act (FACA)[94] applies to the advisory committees the FAA uses. Advisory committees "are frequently a useful and beneficial means of furnishing expert advice, ideas, and diverse opinions"[95] to the FAA, but "Congress and the public should be kept informed with respect to the number, purpose, membership, activities, and cost of advisory committees[.]"[96] The FACA tries to keep the agencies and their advisory committees accountable to the public. One way it does this is by requiring almost all advisory committee meetings be open for the public[97] to "attend, appear before, or file statements[.]"[98] Advisory committees do not make any laws but only advise the FAA, which is the final decision maker.[99] The Freedom of Information Act[100] allows the people to obtain advisory committee "records, reports, transcripts, minutes, appendixes, working papers, drafts, studies, agenda, or other documents which were made available to or prepared for or by each advisory committee[.]"[101] Each meeting of an advisory committee must be published in the Federal Register.[102]

Regulatory Flexibility Act

The Regulatory Flexibility Act[103] (RFA) requires the FAA to analyze the impact of a new regulation and publish in the Federal Register an initial regulatory flexibility

89. 5 U.S.C. § 551(4).
90. Substantive agency regulations have the force and effect of law which means the rule (1) affects individual rights and obligations and (2) it must be the product of a congressional grant of legislative authority, done according to any procedural requirements imposed by Congress. *See* Chrysler Corp. v. Brown, 441 U.S. 281, 282 (1979).
91. *See* Haas v. Peake, 525 F.3d 1168, 1195–96 (Fed. Cir. 2008) ("[I]nterpretive rules 'clarify or explain existing law or regulation and are exempt from notice and comment under section 553(b)(A).'" . . . "An interpretive rule "merely 'represents the agency's reading of statutes and rules rather than an attempt to make new law or modify existing law.'"), *cert. denied*, 555 U.S. 1149 (2009).
92. *See* 5 U.S.C. § 553(b)(3)(A).
93. 5 U.S.C. § 553(b)(3)(B).
94. 5 U.S.C. app. §§ 1–16.
95. 5 U.S.C. app. § 2(a).
96. 5 U.S.C. app. § 2(b)(5).
97. 5 U.S.C. app. § 10(a)(1).
98. 5 U.S.C. app. § 10(a)(3).
99. 5 U.S.C. app. § 9(b).
100. 5 U.S.C. app. § 552.
101. 5 U.S.C. app. § 10(b).
102. *See* 5 U.S.C. app. § 10(a)(2).
103. 5 U.S.C. §§ 601–612.

analysis[104] if the regulation will be a "significant economic impact on a substantial number"[105] of small businesses, small organizations, and small governmental jurisdictions.[106] "'Significant impact' refers to the cost of compliance for any entity; 'substantial number' refers to the number of small entities affected."[107] The agency is required to adopt the least restrictive alternative.[108]

The RFA also requires the FAA to determine if there are "any significant alternatives to the proposed rule which accomplish the stated objectives of applicable statutes and which minimize any significant economic impact of the proposed rule on small entities."[109] The initial analysis is to be made available for public comment at the time the notice of proposed regulation is published in the Federal Register.[110] After the regulation's notice in the Federal Register has been published, a final regulatory flexibility analysis is to be done and also published in the Federal Register.[111] The Small Business Regulatory Enforcement Fairness Act amended the RFA to allow judicial review if the agency does not follow the RFA[112] and to require the FAA to publish a compliance guide for small entities.[113] The FAA's unmanned aircraft regulation is considered subject to the RFA.[114]

President Bush and President Obama both added requirements to the RFA. President Bush issued Executive Order 13,272, Proper Consideration of Small Entities, to further add on Small Business Administration notification requirements.[115] President Obama issued a presidential "Memorandum on Regulatory Flexibility, Small Business, and Job Creation" requiring the FAA to "give serious consideration to whether and how it is appropriate, consistent with law and regulatory objectives, to reduce regulatory burdens on small businesses, through increased flexibility" and also to "explicitly justify its decision not to do so in the explanation that accompanies that proposed or final rule."[116]

104. *See* 5 U.S.C. § 603(a)–(d).
105. 5 U.S.C. § 602(a)(1).
106. *See* 5 U.S.C. § 601(6).
107. AD Manual, *infra* note 279, at 7.
108. *See* 5 U.S.C. § 602(d).
109. 5 U.S.C. § 603(c).
110. *See* 5 U.S.C. § 603(a).
111. *See* 5 U.S.C. § 604(a)–(b).
112. *See* Small Business Regulatory Enforcement Fairness Act, Pub. L. No. 104–121, § 242, 110 Stat. 857, 865 (1996) (codified as amended at 5 U.S.C. § 611(1996)).
113. *See* § 212, 110 Stat. at 858 (codified as amended at 5 U.S.C. § 601 note (1996)).
114. *See Rulemakings with "Regulatory Flexibility Analysis" Effects*, DEP'T OF TRANS. (Sept. 25, 2012), http://www.dot.gov/regulations/rulemakings-regulatory-flexibility-analysis-effects (last visited July 6, 2014).
115. *See* Exec. Order 13,272, 68 Fed. Reg. 7,990 (Feb. 19, 2003).
116. Memorandum on Regulatory Flexibility, Small Business, and Job Creation, 2011 DAILY COMP. PRES. DOC. 33 (Jan. 18, 2011).

Congressional Review Act

The Congressional Review Act[117] will also be playing a role in the unmanned air-craft rule. Before the FAA can publish the final unmanned aircraft regulation in the Federal Register, the FAA must "submit to each House of the Congress and to the Comptroller General a report"[118] including the regulation, cost benefit analysis, final regulatory flexibility analysis, and anything else required under other congressional act or executive order.[119] If the rule is considered major,[120] it cannot go into effect until 60 days have passed from Federal Register Publication or from presentment.[121] Congress has the power to overrule a final rule.[122] The unmanned aircraft regulation is not considered major by the Office of Information and Regulatory Affairs in the executive branch.[123]

Paperwork Reduction Act

The Paperwork Reduction Act as amended[124] has as one of its purposes the reduction of government paperwork burdens on the public.[125] The act established the Office of Information and Regulatory Affairs (OIRA)[126] and requires the FAA to present any proposed regulation that would require the collection of information to OIRA, who will then do a review to determine how to decrease the burden of the regulation's information collection on the public.[127] The collection of information could be a regulation requiring an unmanned aircraft operator to apply for a license or a certificate for their aircraft by filling out an application.[128] The FAA must publish in the Federal Register the proposed collection of information; one way to do so is by publishing a notice of proposed rulemaking containing the information collection requirements.[129]

Executive Orders

In addition to the statutes imposed by Congress, presidents have created requirements on federal agencies when they are issuing regulations.[130] Executive Orders (EO) are

---

117. 5 U.S.C. §§ 801–808.
118. 5 U.S.C. § 801(a)(1)(A).
119. *See* 5 U.S.C. § 801(a)(1)(B).
120. *See* 5 U.S.C. § 804(2).
121. *See* 5 U.S.C. § 801(a)(3).
122. *See* 5 U.S.C. § 802.
123. *See* Small Unmanned Aircraft Systems Rule *infra*, note 298.
124. 44 U.S.C. §§ 3501–3520.
125. *See* 44 U.S.C. § 3501(3).
126. *See* 44 U.S.C. § 3503.
127. *See* 44 U.S.C. § 3504(c).
128. *See* 44 U.S.C. § 3502(3).
129. *See* 44 U.S.C. § 3506(c)(2)(B).
130. There is no definition of executive order or presidential memoranda in the U.S. Constitution. "[T]he execution and implementation of these written instruments stems from implied constitutional and statutory authority. In the constitutional context, presidential power is derived from Article II of the U.S. Constitution[.]" Vivian S. Chu & Todd Garvey, Cong. Research Serv., RS20846, Executive Orders: Issuance,

official documents that are created by the president of the United States. EOs appear in the Federal Register.[131] These orders are binding upon executive agencies.[132] When the FAA wants to create a regulation, there are many executive orders the FAA has to satisfy. Due to the large number of EOs, only a few of the prominent EOs will be briefly mentioned where they apply to the unmanned aircraft discussion.

Executive Order 12,866, Regulatory Planning and Review,[133] is an order requiring agencies to publish a semiannual agenda of all significant regulations under development, giving a person an idea of future rulemaking. "Agencies are required to submit to the Office of Management and Budget's (OMB) Office of Information and Regulatory Affairs (OIRA) a program for periodic review of existing significant regulations to determine whether to modify or eliminate them."[134]

Executive Order 13,563[135] supplements and affirms Executive Order 12,866. It adds on the following: (1) agency regulations are to be tailored to be the least burdensome on society,[136] (2) the agency is to "seek the views of those who are likely to be affected, including those who are likely to benefit from and those who are potentially subject to such rulemaking[,]"[137] and (3) the agency is to develop how to retroactively analyze its ineffective or outdated regulations.[138]

The Office of Management and Budget

To make things even more complicated, the Office of Management and Budget (OMB) has more requirements on how the FAA creates regulations. Inside the executive branch is the OMB. Inside the OMB is the OIRA. OIRA was created under the Paperwork Reduction Act of 1980, and it reviews documents under Executive Orders 12,866 and 13,563. The OMB creates bulletins and directives for the FAA to follow.

OMB created Circular A-4[139] to give "guidance to Federal agencies on the development of regulatory analysis as required under Section 6(a)(3)(c) of Executive Order 12866[.]"[140] It goes into detail explaining the benefit-cost analysis and the

---

MODIFICATION, AND REVOCATION 2 (2014).

131. See 44 U.S.C. § 1505(a)(1); 1 C.F.R. § 2.5(a).

132. See, e.g., U.S. Const. art. II, § 1 ("The executive Power shall be vested in a President of the United States of America").

133. Exec. Order No. 12,866, Regulatory Planning and Review, 58 Fed. Reg. 51,735 (Oct. 4, 1993).

134. DEP'T OF TRANS., supra note 70, at 23.

135. Exec. Order No. 13,563, Improving Regulation and Regulatory Review, 76 Fed. Reg. 3,821 (Jan. 21, 2011).

136. See id.

137. Id. at 3,822. The FAA could be considered to have done this requirement based upon the FAA's unmanned aircraft ARC.

138. See id.

139. OFFICE OF MGMT. & BUDGET, EXEC. OFFICE OF THE PRESIDENT, OMB CIRCULAR A-4, REGULATORY ANALYSIS (2003), available at http://www.dot.gov/sites/dot.gov/files/docs/OMB%20Circular%20No.%20A-4.pdf.

140. Id. at 1.

cost-effectiveness analysis. This circular is beyond the scope of the book, but it shows that the OMB has something to say on how the FAA does rulemaking.

The Department of Transportation

The Department of Transportation (DOT) is a cabinet-level department inside the executive branch with the FAA located inside the DOT.[141] The DOT has created documents and regulations affecting the FAA rulemaking process. Only the sections of the orders or regulations pertaining to the unmanned aircraft rulemaking will be mentioned.

The DOT issued Order 2100.5,[142] which applies to DOT as well as FAA rulemaking.[143] The order requires the FAA to submit significant proposed rulemaking regulations to the secretary of the DOT for approval.[144] The order creates the Department Regulations Council,[145] which can review significant regulations; the secretary of the DOT refers to it for recommendations.[146]

The DOT has regulations on the rulemaking process;[147] however, they do not govern the FAA rulemaking process.[148]

FAA Regulations, Orders, Notices, and Policy Statements on the Rulemaking Process

The FAA layer is the last layer that needs to be discussed. The FAA has created regulations, an order, and an advisory circular on this topic.

FAA Regulations

Part 11 of the Federal Aviation Regulations (FAR) deals with the rulemaking process. Part 11 "applies to the issuance, amendment, and repeal of any regulation for which the FAA ("we") follows public rulemaking procedures under the Administrative Procedure Act (APA) (5 U.S.C. 553)."[149] Anyone interested in knowing more about the FAA rulemaking process should definitely study part 11 as well as read the final rule with explanations published in the Federal Register of part 11.[150] The rules were done in a question and answer format and were designed to be easy to understand in

141. *See A Brief History of the FAA*, Fed. Aviation Admin., http://www.faa.gov/about/history/brief_history/.
142. Dep't of Trans., Order 2100.5, Policies and Procedures for Simplification, Analysis, and Review of Regulations (1979), *available at* http://www.dot.gov/sites/dot.gov/files/docs/DOT%20Order%202100.05%20-%20Simplification%20Analysis%20and%20Review%20of%20Regulations.pdf.
143. *See id.* at 1.
144. *See id.* 8.
145. *See id.* at 4.
146. *See id.* at 5.
147. 49 C.F.R. § 5.1 app. A.
148. *See* 49 C.F.R. § 5.1(a).
149. 14 C.F.R. § 11.1.
150. General Rulemaking Procedures, 65 Fed. Reg. 50,850 (Aug. 21, 2000) (to be codified as 14 C.F.R. pt 11).

response to President Clinton's mandate of federal agencies to put their regulations in plain language.[151]

Orders and Advisory Circulars

Orders are permanent commands until they are canceled, while notices are temporary commands which normally last a year.[152] The FAA has had a rulemaking reengineering team since 1998, and the FAA issued Order 1110.153A to create the Rulemaking Management Council.[153] The council manages the FAA's rulemaking program, approves resource allocation on projects, determines rulemaking priorities, and makes decisions.[154] There is also something called the Continuous Improvement Team, which is "a team composed of managers from [Aviation Rulemaking Office], Aviation Policy and Plans, and the Office of the Chief Counsel, meet[ing] quarterly for continuous improvement of the quality of rulemaking documents and the overall rulemaking process."[155]

The FAA published an advisory circular called AC 11-2A,[156] which gives information about the notice of proposed rulemaking distribution system. This document was created in 1984 and is now almost completely useless since notices are published on www.regulations.gov.

WHAT DOES THE FAA RULEMAKING PROCESS LOOK LIKE

The rulemaking process is not started just because someone wakes up one day and feels like starting it. The rulemaking process always starts with some type of "problem." There are many problems in aviation that have been realized and still some others now starting to be understood more fully. So how does the FAA find out about these problems?

The FAA Has to Be Informed of a Problem

There are some ways the FAA can identify the need for regulations. The employees in the FAA can find out there is a need based upon FAA personnel finding a problem.

---

151. *See id.* at 50,850.

152. Fed. Aviation Admin., Order 1320.1E, FAA Directives Management (2007), *available at* http://www.faa.gov/documentLibrary/media/Order/1320.1E.pdf.

153. Fed. Aviation Admin., Order 1110.153A, Rulemaking Management Council Charter 1 (2013), *available at* http://www.faa.gov/documentlibrary/media/order/faa%20order%201110.153a.pdf.

154. *See id.*

155. *See id.* at 2.

156. Fed. Aviation Admin., Advisory Circular 11-2A, Notice of Proposed Rulemaking Distribution System (1984).

This happens when individuals submit[157] reports on failures, malfunctions, or defects to the FAA, and FAA personnel monitoring the Safety Difficulty Reporting System (SDRS) spot unsafe trends in failures, malfunctions, or defects. A good example of this is where the FAA received multiple reports on the same manufactured helicopter having the same problem, which could affect the safety of the aircraft.[158] The FAA has a congressionally required advisory committee called the Federal Aviation Management Advisory Council, which gives recommendations on "policy, spending, funding, and regulatory matters affecting the aviation industry[.]"[159] Additionally, the FAA can create an aviation rulemaking advisory committee by order,[160] "which is a formal standing committee comprised of representatives of aviation associations and industry, consumer groups, and interested individuals . . . [to deal] with specific areas and problems."[161]

Another way the FAA finds problems is from the president of the United States. President Clinton issued an executive order creating a commission[162] on aviation and security.[163] The commission came up with fifty-seven recommendations for the FAA.[164] Additionally, President Clinton issued a presidential memorandum[165] regarding the plain use of language, which the FAA responded to and issued part 11 regarding the rulemaking process in plain language.[166]

Congress also passes legislation requiring the FAA to create regulations on a particular topic. Congress passed the FAA Modernization and Reform Act of 2012 (FMRA),[167] which mandates the FAA to do a "phased-in approach"[168] to the integration of civil

---

157. *Service Difficulty Reporting Site*, FED. AVIATION ADMIN, http://av-info.faa.gov/sdrx/.

158. *See* Sikorsky AD, *supra* note 62, at 31,231.

159. 49 U.S.C. § 106(p)(1).

160. *See* FED. AVIATION ADMIN., ORDER 1110.119N, AVIATION RULEMAKING ADVISORY COMMITTEE, *available at* http://www.faa.gov/regulations_policies/rulemaking/committees/documents/media/ARAC.Order.1110.119N.20120907.pdf

161. 14 C.F.R. § 11.27.

162. *See* 3 U.S.C. § 301.

163. *See* Exec. Order No. 13,015, 61 Fed. Reg. 43,937 (Aug. 27, 1996).

164. White House Commission on Aviation Safety and Security, *available at* http://www.fas.org/irp/threat/212fin~1.html.

165. VIVIAN S. CHU & TODD GARVEY, CONG. RESEARCH SERV., RS20846, EXECUTIVE ORDERS: ISSUANCE, MODIFICATION, AND REVOCATION 2 (2014) ("The only technical difference is that executive orders must be published in the Federal Register, while presidential memoranda and proclamations are published only when the President determines that they have 'general applicability and legal effect'").

166. *See* General Rulemaking Procedures, 65 Fed. Reg. 50,850, 50,850 (Aug. 21, 2000) ("The FAA is issuing this final rule in response to President Clinton's mandate to Federal agencies to make communications with the public more understandable. The FAA is revising and clarifying its rulemaking procedures by putting them into plain language and by removing redundant and outdated material").

167. FAA Modernization and Reform Act of 2012, Pub. L. No. 112-95, 126 Stat. 11 (2012), *available at* http://www.gpo.gov/fdsys/pkg/PLAW-112publ95/pdf/PLAW-112publ95.pdf.

168. *Id.* § 332(a)(2)(C), 126 Stat. at 73.

unmanned aircraft[169] into the national airspace system based upon a comprehensive plan.[170]

Government agencies[171] inform the FAA about problems or ask the FAA for guidance on a topic. A good example is when a news chopper crashed in Brooklyn, New York, on May 2, 2004, and the National Transportation Safety Board (NTSB), an independent investigative agency, issued safety recommendations to the FAA based upon the crash.[172] The FAA, on June 22, 2006, "issued a notice of proposed rulemaking (NPRM) to adopt an airworthiness directive" and published the final rule on March 9, 2007."[173] The FAA responds to the NTSB recommendations. "Of literally thousands of safety recommendations made to the FAA, the [NTSB] has classified about 82 percent 'Closed — Acceptable Response,' and approximately 6 percent remain open in 'Acceptable' status."[174] Sometimes international regulatory agencies, such as the European Aviation Safety Agency, inform the FAA of problems and solutions because of rulemaking agreements.[175]

The FAA can be informed of a problem through judicial review.[176] The courts can declare the way the FAA did something was not according to the law and the law needs to be redone or changed. A good example of this is where the FAA had a long-standing interpretation that hunting guides were not required to follow commercial airplane operation regulations but later changed this interpretation via publication of a notice in the Federal Register.[177] The D.C. Circuit Court of Appeals held that the FAA could not change the long-standing interpretation of the regulations without following the rulemaking process.[178]

The FAA can be informed of the problem by any individual through a petition. A petition or repetition[179] for "rulemaking is a request to the FAA by an individual or entity asking the FAA to adopt, amend, or repeal a regulation."[180] "Generally, [the] FAA does not invite public comment on petitions for rulemaking."[181]

---

169. *See id.* § 331(8), 126 Stat. at 72.

170. *See id.* §§ 331–336, 126 Stat. at 72-78.

171. *See* Unmanned Aircraft Operations in the National Airspace System Policy, 72 Fed. Reg. 6,689 (proposed Feb. 13, 2007) [hereinafter "2007 Notice"] (Department of Defense and Customs and Border Protection).

172. *FAA Aviation Safety Information Analysis and Sharing*, FED. AVIATION ADMIN., http://www.asias.faa .gov/pls/apex/f?p=100:42:0::NO::AP_BRIEF_RPT_VAR:A-05-036.

173. *See id.*

174. *Fact Sheet – FAA & NTSB's "Most Wanted" Recommendations*, FED. AVIATION ADMIN., http://www .faa.gov/news/fact_sheets/news_story.cfm?newsId=11186.

175. *See* FAA and European Agreement, *infra* note 237.

176. *See* 5 U.S.C. §§ 701–706.

177. *See* Alaska Prof'l Hunters Ass'n, Inc. v. F.A.A., 177 F.3d 1030, 1031–33 (D.C. Cir. 1999).

178. *See id.* at 1033–34.

179. *See* 14 C.F.R. § 11.101.

180. 14 C.F.R. §§ 11.17, 11.39(c).

181. 14 C.F.R. § 11.75

The FAA Finds the Solution to the Problem

The FAA uses expert resources to get advice on how to solve the problem prior to the rulemaking process. The FAA has available many special groups and experts. These groups are either (1) FAA created committees or (2) private industry organizations that are asked to help the FAA or have offered to help the FAA.

The FAA Can Create a Committee to Give Advice on an Issue

There are two types of committees the FAA can create: (1) an Aviation Rulemaking Advisory Committee (ARAC) and (2) an Aviation Rulemaking Committee (ARC). The FAA has a number of ARCs and ARACs.[182] The members of these committees cannot be registered lobbyists.[183]

The Comparing of ARCs and ARACs

The best way to study these two different types of committees is to study them side by side to see their differences and similarities. Table 4.1 is adapted from the FAA aviation rules committee manual.[184]

Table 4.1 ARAC versus ARC

	ARAC	ARC
Purpose	**Advisory Committee**	**Rulemaking Committee**
Features	"[P]rovides the FAA with information, advice, and recommendations, concerning rulemaking activity, such as aircraft operations, airman and air certification, airworthiness standards and certification, airports, and noise." The FAA can ask an ARAC to review a petition for rulemaking.[1]	"[P]rovides information, advice and recommendations to the FAA. . . . [It is] somewhat more flexible. ARCs are formed on an ad hoc basis, for a specific purpose, and are typically of limited duration."

182. *Advisory and Rulemaking Committees*, FED. AVIATION ADMIN., http://www.faa.gov/regulations_policies/rulemaking/committees/documents/.

183. OFFICE OF RULEMAKING, FED. AVIATION ADMIN., ARM COMMITTEE MANUAL (2013), *available at* http://www.faa.gov/regulations_policies/rulemaking/committees/documents/media/Comm_001_015.pdf.

184. *See* 2 U.S.C 1605; *see also* Final Guidance on Appointment of Lobbyists to Federal Boards and Commissions, 76 Fed. Reg. 61,756 (Oct. 5, 2011).

Purpose	ARAC **Advisory Committee**	ARC **Rulemaking Committee**
Reasons to Choose	Public participation is necessary on potential rulemaking activities. Public review of the products and recommendations is appropriate.	Rulemaking is underway, and the team needs industry to examine an issue. Requires involvement from several FAA offices, and it is appropriate to have more than one FAA official. The FAA has a specific membership composition it wants based on the technical subject being considered.
FACA	Must follow.[2]	Does not follow.[3]
APA	Follows during rulemaking.	Follows during rulemaking.
FOIA	Yes, unless an exception applies.	Yes, unless an exception applies.[4]
Federal Register	All information (tasks, meeting[2] announcements, and recommendations) must be published.	There is no requirement to publish any ARC information.
Decision Making Governing Body	ARAC is the industry-led governing body that makes decisions on taskings from the FAA, recommendations from its working groups, and submits its recommendations to the FAA.	An ARC is a standalone group that governs itself. There is no industry-led governing body to make decisions on tasks or recommendations. Those decisions are made by the FAA sponsoring office of the charter.
Charter	There is one charter for ARAC. It is renewed every two years. Published in the Federal Register.	Each ARC has its own charter. Each ARC charter is limited by scope and time to address issues. The charter expires on average six to twenty-four months after issuance. The charter may be extended or renewed for a short period of time to complete the tasks or address additional related tasks assigned by the FAA. The charter is not required to be published in the Federal Register.
Leader	Industry leads ARAC, subcommittees, and working groups.	Both industry and the FAA colead the ARC.
FAA Participation	Provides guidance as a nonmember.	Provides guidance as a nonmember. Active role as a member.
Recommendations	Working groups submit recommendation to ARAC, which in turn submits to the FAA.	Submitted to the sponsoring office of the charter.

1. *See* 14 C.F.R. § 11.73(d).
2. 5 U.S.C. app. 2. § 9–10.
3. "The Federal Advisory Committee Act (5 U.S.C. App.) does not apply to the [Management Advisory] Council, the Air Traffic Services Committee, or such aviation rulemaking committees as the Administrator shall designate." 49 U.S.C. § 106(p)(5).

4. *See* FED. AVIATION ADMIN., infra note 259, at 40.

5. "All ARAC (and subcommittee) meetings will be open to the public, except as provided under Section 10(d) of FACA, as implemented by 41 CFR § 101-6.10, the Government in the Sunshine Act (5 U.S.C. § 522b(c)), 41 CFR Part 102–3, and Department of Transportation (DOT) Order 1120.3B." *See id.* Fed. Aviation Admin., Order 11110.119N.

The ARAC Working Group on Unmanned Aircraft

The FAA established an ARAC as a way for the aviation public to make its inputs in the safety rulemaking process.[185] In 1991, the FAA created a subcommittee on this ARAC for air traffic, which created a working group on unmanned aerospace vehicle operations[186] tasked with developing "operating and certification standards for unmanned aerospace vehicles [including] minimum qualifications or standards for the operators of these vehicles."[187] This working group actually developed and presented to the FAA in 1996 four different proposed advisory circulars for unmanned aircraft maintenance, pilot training and qualification, aircraft design, and operations.[188]

Unmanned Aircraft ARCs

The FAA also created two ARCs to solve the unmanned aircraft integration problem. The first ARC was created on April 10, 2008, and its task was to focus on small unmanned aircraft integration.[189] The first ARC presented the FAA with recommendations on regulations a year later[190] and was disbanded.[191]

The FAA, on June 17, 2011, created another ARC, but this time it was focused not on small unmanned aircraft.[192] This second ARC is assisting the FAA by developing a plan, dealing with comments during the rulemaking process, developing and recommending updates to FAA documents on unmanned aircraft operation, and making rulemaking recommendations.[193] The second ARC has created a working group to

---

185. *See* Notice of aviation rulemaking advisory committee establishment, 56 Fed. Reg. 2190-02 (Jan. 22, 1991). The ARAC gets renewed by FAA order. *See* FED. AVIATION ADMIN., *supra* note 156.

186. *See* Notice of Establishment of Unmanned Aerospace Vehicle Operations Working Group, 56 Fed. Reg. 55,520 (Oct. 28, 1991) [hereinafter "1991 ARAC"], *available at* http://www.faa.gov/regulations_policies /rulemaking/committees/documents/media/ATuavoT1-102891.pdf.

187. *Id.* at 55,520.

188. *See* Letter from James L. Crook, Chairman of the Air Traffic Issues Group, to Chris A. Christie, Executive Director of the Aviation Rulemaking Advisory Committee (Aug. 8, 1996), *available at* http://www.faa.gov /regulations_policies/rulemaking/committees/documents/media/ATuavoT1-102891.pdf.

189. *See* FED. AVIATION ADMIN., Order 1110.150, SMALL UNMANNED AIRCRAFT SYSTEM AVIATION RULEMAKING COMMITTEE (2008), *available at* http://www.faa.gov/documentLibrary/media/Order/1110.150.pdf.

190. *See* SMALL UNMANNED AIRCRAFT SYSTEM AVIATION RULEMAKING COMMITTEE, COMPREHENSIVE SET OF RECOMMENDATIONS FOR sUAS REGULATORY DEVELOPMENT 1 (2009) [hereinafter "2008 ARC Recommendations"], *available at* http://www.modelaircraft.org/faa/recommendations.pdf.

191. *See* FED. AVIATION ADMIN., MEMORANDUM CANCELLATION OF FAA ORDER 1110.150: SMALL UNMANNED AIRCRAFT SYSTEM AVIATION RULEMAKING COMMITTEE (2013), *available at* http://www.faa.gov /documentLibrary/media/Order/Cancellation_Memo_FAA_Order_1110.150.pdf.

192. *See* FED. AVIATION ADMIN., CHARTER OF UNMANNED AIRCRAFT SYSTEMS AVIATION RULEMAKING COMMITTEE 1 (2011), *available at* http://www.suasnews.com/wp-content/uploads/2011/11/ARC2.0.pdf.

193. *See id.* at 3.

recommend changes to the 14 C.F.R. 91.113 see and avoid[194] requirements to enable unmanned aircraft operations.[195] Interestingly, though the charter says the committee "will be balanced in points of view, interests . . . [and e]ach member or participant on the committee should represent an identified part of the aviation community" such as "aviation associations, industry operators, manufacturers, employee groups unions, other Government entities, and other aviation industry participants[,]"[196] the second ARC does not have any small unmanned aircraft organizations on it.[197]

The FAA Can Use Private Organizations to Help Find a Solution

There are many different outside groups fulfilling a role in helping the FAA solve a problem. These groups are made up of subject matter experts, engineers, and industry representatives. These groups make recommendations on standards to the FAA. The FAA sometimes takes those standards and puts them into a regulation.[198]

In the context of this book, the integration of unmanned aircraft is the problem. The FAA wants to integrate them, but the problem is determining what standards are to be placed on unmanned aircraft operations. Only the groups that have worked on unmanned aircraft will be discussed below. This section is only meant to make readers aware of the groups currently working with the FAA and is not meant to be an in-depth discussion of each one.

ASTM International Committee F-38

The American Society for Testing and Materials International (ASTM) is a standards development organization (SDO) which signed a memorandum of understanding in April 2010 with the FAA regarding developing unmanned aircraft standards for the FAA.[199] F-38 is the name of the committee working on unmanned aircraft standards; they have published at least seven standards for unmanned aircraft.[200] "[T]he FAA is currently evaluating the standards with the objective of recognizing them for use in certification of small unmanned aircraft."[201]

---

194. Seeing and avoiding gives people the idea of when these regulations were first crafted. The use of detecting equipment was not even practicable other than the detecting equipment, our eyes, God gave us. The term is being changed to sense and avoid.

195. *See* Ted Lester et al., *USAF Airborne Sense and Avoid (ABSAA) Airworthiness and Operational Approval Approach*, MITRE, 15 (2014), http://www.mitre.org/sites/default/files/publications/usaf-airborne-sense-avoid-13-3116.pdf.

196. *Id.* at 5.

197. Such as the Academy of Model Aeronautics or the Remote Control Aerial Platform Association which were both on the first ARC.

198. *See* 14 C.F.R. § 36.6(c)(2).

199. *See* Ted Wierzbanowski, *ASTM International, in* 2014 RPAS Yearbook : The Global Perspective 112 (12th ed. 2014), *available at* http://uvs-info.com/index.php?option=com_flippingbook&view=book&id=19&page=1&Itemid=874.

200. *See id.*

201. sUAS NEWS, 2014 sUSB Expo Jim Williams at 10:11, YouTube (May 13, 2014), https://www.youtube

SAE AS-4 and G-10U

The Society of Automotive Engineers International has two groups working on unmanned aircraft problems. One group is called AS-4. The "primary goal of AS-4 is to publish standards that enable interoperability of unmanned systems for military, civil and commercial use through the use of open systems standards and architecture development."[202] AS-4 is comprised of four subcommittees and an executive committee, which have published over eight documents on unmanned aircraft.[203] The second committee is SAE G-10 Aerospace Behavioral Engineering Technology Committee, which has a subcommittee focusing on unmanned aircraft.[204]

RTCA SC-203 and SC-228

Radio Technical Commission for Aeronautics (RTCA) is an organization providing recommendations on minimum performance standards to the FAA of which, in 2012, "the FAA issued or updated twelve Technical Standards Orders and Advisory Circular invoking RTCA documents."[205] The RTCA is utilized as an advisory committee.[206] The RTCA created a special committee called SC-203 in 2004 on unmanned aircraft standards, and it was later deactivated in June 2013.[207] The RTCA created another special committee in May 2013 called SC-228, which hopes to build[208] upon the work done[209] by SC-203 with a much narrower scope. SC-203's scope was to develop standards for operations in classes A, G, and E airspace except (1) surface and terminal operations at public-use airports within E and G airspace and (2) E airspace inside a Mode-C veil,[210] while SC-228's scope is for standards on operating civil unmanned aircraft in class A airspace under IFR flight rules.[211]

.com/watch?v=98LF5azVxLg.

202. SAE, *SAE AS-4 Technical Committees – Unmanned Systems*,1 http://www.sae.org/exdomains/ standardsdev/global_resources/InteractiveAeroOrgChart.pdf .To access the AS-4 fact sheet, click on the AS-4 link and the Word document will be downloaded.

203. *Id.*

204. *See* SAE, *SAE G-10 Aerospace Behavioral Engineering Technology Committee*, http://www.sae.org/ exdomains/standardsdev/global_resources/InteractiveAeroOrgChart.pdf. To access the G-10 fact sheet, click on the G-10 link and the Word document will be downloaded.

205. *Committees*, RTCA, http://www.rtca.org/content.asp?admin=Y&contentid=33.

206. *See* FED. AVIATION ADMIN., ORDER 1110.77U, RTCA, INC. (UTILIZED AS AN ADVISORY COMMITTEE) (2013).

207. *See Sunsetted Committees*, RTCA, http://www.rtca.org/content.asp?pl=108&sl=33&contentid=121.

208. *See* Patrick Egan, *RTCA SC-203 Folds Up*, sUAS NEWS (June 5, 2013), http://www.suasnews.com /2013/06/23191/rtca-sc-203-folds-up/.

209. SC-203 created four documents on unmanned aircraft. *See Online Store - Unmanned Aircraft Systems (UAS...)*, RTCA, http://www.rtca.org/store_category.asp?id=76.

210. *See Terms of Reference Special Committee (SC) 203 Minimum Performance Standards for Unmanned Aircraft Systems*, RTCA, 2 (2010), *available at* http://www.rtca.org/Files/Terms%20of%20Reference/SC-203 %20Terms%20of%20Reference%20-%20Rev.%202%20%20Apr%202010.pdf.

211. *See SC-228 Minimum Operational Performance Standards for Unmanned Aircraft Systems*, RTCA, http://www.rtca.org/content.asp?pl=108&sl=33&contentid=178.

NASA

The National Aeronautics and Space Administration (NASA) can be used to assist the FAA by doing research, tests, and investigations.[212] NASA has a long history of work on unmanned aircraft going back to 1968.[213] NASA was on the first ARC[214] and is currently on the second ARC.[215] NASA started work on unmanned aircraft integration with their Access 5 program,[216] but the program was terminated in 2006.[217] NASA is currently running the Unmanned Aircraft Systems Integration in the National Airspace System Project[218] and is also hosting an unmanned aircraft integration contest.[219] NASA is also planning on validating the RTCA standards for unmanned aircraft communications and aircraft detection and avoidance.[220] Similar to the FAA's ARACs, NASA also has an advisory council to help fulfill NASA's mission.[221] There is a subcommittee on this advisory council focusing on unmanned aircraft.[222]

RCAPA

The Remote Control Aerial Photography Association (RCAPA) was founded in 2007 and its purpose "is to share developments in hardware, data collection techniques, and safe processes as required by the use of unmanned aircraft."[223] RCAPA created operational guidelines[224] for unmanned aircraft and presented these guidelines to the 2008 FAA aviation rulemaking committee, the ASTM committee, and SC-203 because RCAPA was a member of each of the groups.[225]

---

212. 49 U.S.C. § 40113(c).
213. *See Unmanned Aircraft Systems (UAS) Integration in the National Airspace System (NAS) Project*, NASA, 3 (2012) [hereinafter "NASA Project"], *available at* https://info.publicintelligence.net/NASA-UAS-NAS.pdf.
214. *See* SMALL UNMANNED AIRCRAFT SYSTEM AVIATION RULEMAKING COMMITTEE, *supra* note 192, at 1.
215. *See* FED. AVIATION ADMIN., *supra* note , at 7.
216. *See NASA Dryden Past Projects: High-Altitude, Long-Endurance Remotely Operated Aircraft in the National Airspace System*, NASA (May 16, 2006), http://www.nasa.gov/centers/dryden/research/HALE_ROA /index.html#.U5thLXJdVIE.
217. *See Access 5 / UNITE*, UAV MARKETSPACE, http://www.uavm.com/uavregulatory/access5unite.html.
218. *See* NASA Project, *supra* note , at 1.
219. *See Unmanned Aircraft Systems Airspace Operations Challenge (UAS AOC)*, NASA, http://www.nasa .gov/directorates/spacetech/centennial_challenges/uas/index.html#.U5tmZXJdVIF; *see also* Centennial Challenges 2014 Unmanned Aircraft Systems (UAS) Airspace Operations Challenge (AOC), 78 Fed. Reg. 59,974 (Sept. 30, 2013).
220. *See* Wierzbanowski, *supra* note , at 116.
221. *See NASA Advisory Council Aeronautics Committee*, NASA, http://www.aeronautics.nasa.gov/nac _aero_cmte.htm.
222. *See* NASA Advisory Council; Aeronautics Committee; Unmanned Aircraft Systems Subcommittee; Meeting, 78 Fed. Reg. 38,076 (June 25, 2013).
223. *RCAPA—What We Are and from Whence We Came*, RCAPA, http://rcapa.net/who-we-are/.
224. *See RCAPA Recommended Operational Guidelines*, RCAPA, http://rcapa.net/guidelines/.
225. *See* Patrick Egan, *The RCAPA Proposed Guidelines*, sUAS NEWS (Jan. 8, 2012), http://www.suasnews .com/2012/01/11038/the-rcapa-proposed-guidelines/.

Solving the Problem by Changing the Classification

The FAA could potentially solve some of the unmanned aircraft integration problems by classifying certain types of the unmanned aircraft as "vehicles" and excepting them from the part 91 requirements. The FAA's 2007 policy statement on unmanned aircraft said,

> The FAA has undertaken a safety review that will examine the feasibility of creating a different category of unmanned "vehicles" that may be defined by the operator's visual line of sight and are also small and slow enough to adequately mitigate hazards to other aircraft and persons on the ground. The end product of this analysis may be a new flight authorization instrument similar to AC 91-57, but focused on operations that do not qualify as sport and recreation, but also may not require a certificate of airworthiness. They will, however, require compliance with applicable FAA regulations and guidance developed for this category.[226]

This seems similar to the approach the FAA took with designating a narrow group of "aircraft" as ultralight vehicles and providing them their own section in the FARs.[227]

To try and figure out how the FAA is maybe moving forward, we need to look back at ultralight vehicles. "The FAA, in § 1.1 of 14 CFR, broadly defines an aircraft as 'a device that is used or intended to be used for flight in the air.' The FAA, however, has excepted the operation of ultralight vehicles from Part 91 under provisions of § 91.1(a)."[228] Also, the terms ultralight or vehicle are nowhere defined in § 1.1.[229] Ultralight vehicles have their own self-contained part and are vehicles intended to be operated in the air, by one person, for recreation or sport.[230] If the aircraft is unpowered, it must be below 155 pounds, but if it is powered, it must be below 254 pounds, must contain no more than five gallons of fuel, cannot travel faster than 55 knots calibrated airspeed, and must have a power off stall speed not greater than 24 knots calibrated airspeed.[231] No airworthiness certificate or registration is required for the aircraft, and no pilot's license, medical, or aeronautical knowledge for the operator is required.[232] "Those vehicles which exceed the above criteria will be considered aircraft for purposes of airworthiness certification and registration, and their operators

---

226. *See* 2007 Notice, *supra* note 171, at 6,690.

227. *See* 14 C.F.R. § 103.

228. FAA Legal Interpretation to Barbara Parisi from Rebecca MacPherson, Acting Assistant Chief Counsel (April 2, 2006), *available at* http://www.faa.gov/about/office_org/headquarters_offices/agc/pol_adjudication/agc200/interpretations/data/interps/2006/parisi-uscpsc%20-%20(2006)%20legal%20interpretation.pdf.

229. *See* 14 C.F.R. § 1.1.

230. *See* 14 C.F.R. § 103.1(a)–(b).

231. *See* 14 C.F.R. § 103.1(d)–(e).

232. *See* 14 C.F.R. § 103.7.

will be subject to the same certification requirements as are aircraft operators."[233] The reason for this "hands-off" part is:

> The FAA has chosen not to promulgate Federal regulations regarding pilot certification, vehicle certification, and vehicle registration, preferring that the ultralight community assume the initiative for the development of these important safety programs. The ultralight community is expected to take positive action to develop these programs in a timely manner and gain FAA approval for their implementation. Should this approach fail to meet FAA safety objectives, further regulatory action may be necessary.[234]

The history about the need for ultralight vehicle regulation and the need for unmanned aircraft regulation is strikingly similar (see Table 4.2). This brings to mind the proverb "What has been is what will be, and what has been done is what will be done, and there is nothing new under the sun."[235]

Table 4.2 Ultralight Vehicles versus Unmanned Aircraft

Ultralight Vehicles	Unmanned Aircraft
"On March 24, 1981, an MU-2 flew between two ultralights operating off the end of the runway at Winter Haven, Florida."[1]	"A Federal Aviation Administration official said on May 8 that an American Airlines Group Inc. jet in March nearly hit a model aircraft around 2,300 feet above Tallahassee, Fla."[2]
"[S]uspected violations are prompted by reports received from pilots, air traffic controllers, citizens, and other sources."[3]	"Many times, the FAA learns about suspected commercial UAS operations via a complaint from the public or other businesses. The agency occasionally discovers such operations through the news media or postings on internet sites."[4]
"The vehicles are routinely operated, without authorization, into regulated airspace, such as airport traffic areas, terminal control areas, positive control areas, and prohibited and restricted areas."[5]	"The FAA recognizes that people and companies other than modelers might be flying UAS with the mistaken understanding that they are legally operating under the authority of AC 91-57."[6]
"The midair collision potential presented by unauthorized operations is contrary to the FAA responsibility of ensuring the safety of all airspace operations including air carrier aircraft."[7]	"The FAA is working aggressively to ensure the safe integration of unmanned aircraft systems into the national airspace,"[8]
"Many operations have also taken place over congested areas and spectators. . . ."[9]	"Unmanned aircraft Hits Spectators Watching the Running of the Bulls (in Virginia)."[10]

---

233. Ultralight Vehicles; Operating Requirements, 47 Fed. Reg. 38,770 (proposed Sept. 2, 1982) (codified at 14 C.F.R. § 103), *available* at http://www.usua.org/Rules/faa103.htm.
234. *Id.*
235. *Ecclesiastes* 1:9 (English Standard Version).

Ultralight Vehicles	Unmanned Aircraft
"The increasing performance capabilities of these [ultralight] vehicles, and their greatly increased number. . . ."[11]	"The one thing [unmanned aircraft] have in common is that their numbers and uses are growing dramatically."[12]
"On April 11, 1981, a Western Airlines 727 captain reported a near-miss with an ultralight vehicle in the vicinity of Phoenix, Sky Harbor Airport."[13]	"The pilot of an Alitalia jet reported spotting what he described as an unmanned aircraft on Monday afternoon, as he approached New York's JFK airport for landing."[14]

1. Ultralight Vehicles; Operating Requirements, 47 Fed. Reg. 38,770 (proposed Sept. 2, 1982) (codified at 14 C.F.R. § 103).

2. Jack Nicas, *Drone-Passenger Jet Collision? Mystery Clouds a Near Miss*, WALL STREET JOURNAL, June 5, 2014, http://online.wsj.com/articles/drone-passenger-jet-collision-mystery-clouds-a-near-miss-1402014014. While the FAA has cited this as evidence of the need for regulation, there are some questions remaining as to whether the unmanned aircraft was being flown by the military instead of a civilian.

3. *Id.* at 38,772.

4. *Busting Myths about the FAA and Unmanned Aircraft*, FED. AVIATION ADMIN., http://www.faa.gov/news/updates/?newsId=76240 (*see* Myth #4).

5. *Id.* at 38,770.

6. *See* 2007 Notice, *supra* note 171, at 6,690.

7. *Id.*

8. *First commercial unmanned aircraft license granted to oil giant BP*, RT, June 11, 2014, http://rt.com/usa/165184-faa-approves-commercial-unmanned aircraft-license/.

9. *Id.*

10. Alexis C. Madrigal, *Drone Hits Spectators Watching the Running of the Bulls (in Virginia)*, THE ATLANTIC, Aug. 26, 2013, http://www.theatlantic.com/technology/archive/2013/08/drone-hits-spectators-watching-the-running-of-the-bulls-in-virginia/279040/.

11. *Id.*

12. 2007 Notice, *supra* note , at 6,689.

13. *Id.*

14. Alex Davies, *An Alitalia Pilot Reported Spotting a 'Drone' Over Brooklyn*, BUSINESS INSIDER, Mar. 5, 2013, http://www.businessinsider.com/an-alitalia-pilot-reported-spotting-a-drone-over-new-york-2013-3.

The FAA Works Alongside International Regulatory Bodies

This section is beyond the scope of this book, but readers should be aware that the United States is not an island. Congress mandated:

> The [FAA] shall promote and achieve global improvements in the safety, efficiency, and environmental effect of air travel by exercising leadership with the [FAA]'s foreign counterparts, in the International Civil Aviation Organization and its subsidiary organizations, and other international organizations and fora, and with the private sector.[236]

The FAA is actively working with other international regulatory agencies to solve common problems. The FAA has an arrangement with the European Aviation Safety Agency in rulemaking efforts which says the objective of the agreement is

236. 49 U.S.C. § 40104(b) ("International Role of the FAA").

to (1) exchange rulemaking plans and "to align as much as possible their respective rulemaking programs; [(2)] Identify rulemaking initiatives of common interest that through regulatory collaboration would allow the FAA and EASA to: (i) avoid unnecessary divergence and duplication of work, (ii) maximize available resources, and (iii) further harmonization."[237]

WHAT HAPPENS INSIDE THE FAA BEFORE A NOTICE IS PUBLISHED

This section is only meant to give a brief overview of what happens internally and is not exhaustive, see Figure 4.1. Anyone interested in a more in-depth study should read the FAA's ARM Committee Manual.[238] Listed below is a simplified process of what goes on inside the FAA. The list assumes an office or council approves the document; otherwise, the document would go back and be revised and the process would be repeated again.

1. The office of primary responsibility (OPR) determines if there is a need for rulemaking.
2. OPR then determines if they want an ARC or an ARAC and sends a Committee Request Document (CRD) to the Office of Rulemaking (ARM) for approval.
3. The ARM approves the CRD and then sends the request on to the Rulemaking Management Council.[239]
4. The Rulemaking Management Council approves and sends the CRD to the ARM who will then prepare a folder to be circulated up to either:
   a. If an ARAC, six different people in the OPR and ARM; or
   b. If an ARC, ten different people in the OPR, ARM, Office of Assistant Chief Counsel, Deputy Chief Counsel, Associate Administration for Aviation Safety, and Office of Deputy Administrator.
5. The folder gets passed around and eventually signed by the Administrator of the FAA.
6. If the document creates an:
   a. ARAC, then ARM-20 must get approval from ARAC members for approval and also ARM-1 approval to then publish a notice in the Federal Register.
   b. ARC, then ARM sends a copy to OPR.

---

237. *Agreement on Rulemaking Cooperation Guidelines for the Federal Aviation Administration and the European Aviation Safety Agency*, U.S.-Eur., June 13, 2013, http://easa.europa.eu/system/files/dfu/rulem aking-docs-procedures-and-work-instructions-FAA-EASA-Rulemaking-Cooperation-Guidelines_signed-text _13-June-2013_Paris.pdf.
238. Fed. Aviation Admin., *infra* note 239.
239. *See* Fed. Aviation Admin., Order 1110.153A, Rulemaking Management Council Charter (2013), *available at* http://www.faa.gov/documentlibrary/media/order/faa%20order%201110.153a.pdf.

Figure 4.1

COMMITTEE FLOWCHART

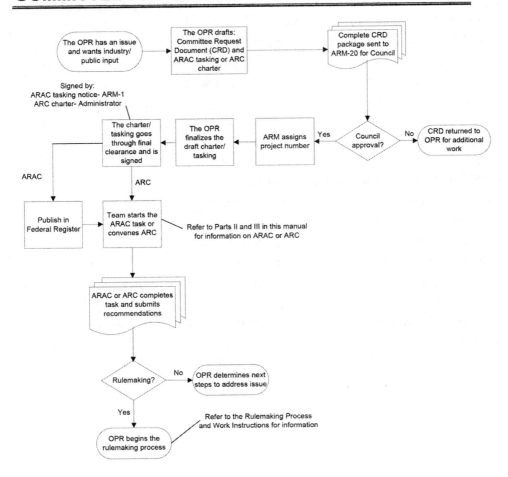

Internal FAA Rulemaking Process[240]

The FAA Must Publish a Notice of Proposed Rulemaking

There are three types of notices the FAA publishes: (1) the notice of proposed rule-making (NPRM), (2) the advanced notice of rulemaking (ANPRM), and (3) the supplemental notice of proposed rulemaking (SNPRM).

The NPRM is the most common type of notice. It "proposes FAA's specific regulatory changes for public comment and contains supporting information. It includes proposed regulatory text."[241]

---

240. FED. AVIATION ADMIN., ARM-001-015, ARM COMMITTEE MANUAL 7 (2013), *available at* http://www.faa.gov/regulations_policies/rulemaking/committees/arac/media/Comm_001_015.pdf.

241. 14 C.F.R. § 11.5.

An ANPRM "tells the public that FAA is considering an area for rulemaking and requests written comments on the appropriate scope of the rulemaking or on specific topics. An advance notice of proposed rulemaking may or may not include the text of potential changes to a regulation."[242]

An SNPRM is issued when the FAA has already issued an NPRM and the "FAA may decide that it needs more information on an issue, or that [it] should take a different approach than [it] proposed. Also, [the FAA] may want to follow a commenter's suggestion that goes beyond the scope of the original proposed rule. In these cases, [the] FAA may issue a supplemental notice of proposed rulemaking . . . to give the public an opportunity to comment further or to give [it] more information."[243]

The FAA Must Wait for Federal Register Comments

The APA requires the FAA to give some time for anyone[244] to comment, but the APA does not say how long the comment period has to be.[245] Federal agencies typically have a comment period between 30 and 60 days, but there are occasional exceptions of periods up to 180 days.[246] Executive Order 12,866 tells agencies significant rules should be given a comment period of 60 days;[247] therefore, since the unmanned aircraft rule is considered significant,[248] the comment period will most likely be at least 60 days. See Figure 4.2 for the location of the public comment period in the rulemaking process.

---

242. 14 C.F.R. § 11.3.
243. 14 C.F.R. § 11.7.
244. *See* 14 C.F.R. § 11.41.
245. *See* 5 U.S.C. § 553(c).
246. *A Guide to the Rulemaking Process*, OFFICE OF THE FED. REGISTER 5, *available at* https://www.federalregister.gov/uploads/2011/01/the_rulemaking_process.pdf.
247. "In addition, each agency should afford the public a meaningful opportunity to comment on any proposed regulation, which in most cases should include a comment period of not less than 60 days." Exec. Order No. 12,866, Regulatory Planning and Review, 58 Fed. Reg. 51,735 (Oct. 4, 1993).
248. sUASNEWS, *supra* note 225, at 27:20.

Figure 4.2

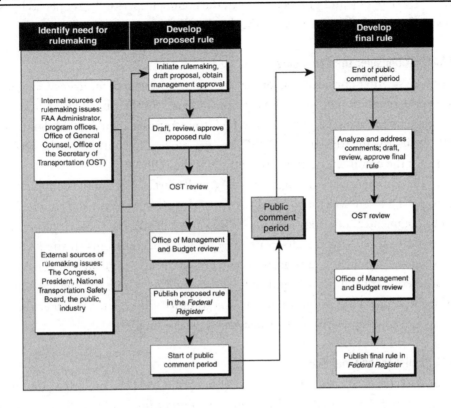

The FAA Rulemaking Process[249]

During the comment period, the DOT and FAA want outside comments to be directed at the rulemaking docket because the FAA is not to have ex-parte[250] contact with anyone outside of the government before the final rule is published.[251] However, the FAA can be requested to hold a public meeting regarding the NPRM when the FAA needs "more than written comments to make a fully informed decision."[252] The "public meeting is a non-adversarial, fact-finding proceeding conducted by an FAA representative. Public meetings are announced in the Federal Register. We invite interested persons to attend and to present their views to the agency on specific issues."[253] "When the substance of a proposed rule is significantly changed as a result of such an [ex-parte

---

249. U.S. Gov't Accountability Office, *infra* note 295, at 3.
250. One-sided contact.
251. 14 C.F.R. § 11 app. 1 (Numbers 3–5).
252. 14 C.F.R. § 11.51.
253. 14 C.F.R. § 11.53.

contact], DOT policy and practice requires the comment period be reopened by issuing a supplemental NPRM in which the reasons for the change are discussed."[254]

The FAA Must Consider the Comments

The APA says, "After consideration of the [comments] presented, the agency shall incorporate in the rules adopted a concise general statement of their basis and purpose."[255] The comments provided can prompt the FAA to reconsider their NPRM. Sometimes the FAA might want to issue an SNPRM to get more information.[256] The FAA can also extend the comment period[257] or withdraw the NPRM.

Once the comment period is open, the FAA will start analyzing the comments and start preparing to answer them. The FAA will "identify significant substantive issues raised by commenters in response to the NPRM and will give the agency's response."[258] It is important the FAA carefully craft responses to the comments. If the FAA does not answer the significant substantive issues raised in the comments, the FAA could have problems from judicial[259] and political review.[260] "Where the change between proposed and final rule is important, the question for the court is whether the final rule is a 'logical outgrowth' of the rulemaking proceeding."[261]

The FAA Publishes the Final Rule

There are two types of final rules: (1) a direct final rule and (2) a final rule after notice (FRAN). Only FRANs will be discussed here. Direct final rules will be discussed elsewhere.

A FRAN will take effect no less than 30 days[262] from publication. The final rule may contain new or modified requirements and may have had previous requirements removed based upon input during the comment period.[263] A FRAN must "also identify significant substantive issues raised by commenters in response to the NPRM and will give the agency's response."[264]

---

254. 14 C.F.R. § 11 app. 1.
255. 5 U.S.C. § 553(c).
256. *See* 14 C.F.R. § 11.7.
257. *See* 14 C.F.R. § 11.47.
258. 14 C.F.R. § 11.9.
259. 5 U.S.C. §§ 702, 706(2).
260. *See* 5 U.S.C. § 801.
261. United Steelworkers of Am. v. Marshall, 647 F.2d 1189, 1221 (D.C. Cir. 1980).
262. *See* 5 U.S.C. § 553(d).
263. *See* 14 C.F.R. § 11.9.
264. *Id.*

Where Will the FAA Put the New Regulation and What Number Should the Regulation Be?

The FARs are broken up into descending order of volume/chapters, subchapters, parts, subparts, sections, and paragraphs dealing with particular things.[265] The FAA publishes parts and sections in odd numbers so the FAA does not have to renumber the parts if they have to add more. The FAA can reserve parts and sections[266] for future use. Almost every part has for the first section an "applicability" section to give the reader a "heads-up" on what is subject to the section.[267]

With this in mind, one can somewhat accurately predict where the future unmanned aircraft regulations will end up. Furthermore, the FAA gave a clue in their unmanned aircraft integration roadmap[268] that the regulation would be 14 C.F.R. § 107. The reason for the unmanned aircraft regulation being put in section 107 is because subchapter F (parts 91–106) deals with air traffic and general operating rules. Parts 101, 103, and 105, all located within subchapter F, all deal with things that fly in the air that are kind of "out-of-place" air traffic. It is kind of like that "other" drawer in the kitchen with rubber bands, clips, ties, and an unknown key. Part 107 follows the pattern of providing "breathing room" by keeping part 106 and part 108 empty for future regulations and also keeping in theme with the previous three parts. Moreover, part 107 will likely follow the pattern of many of the other parts by having section 107.1 as an applicable section. This is not to say other parts will not be touched by the oncoming unmanned aircraft regulations. Many other parts will most likely be touched such as part 1, part 21, part 23, part 43, part 61, section 91.1(a),[269] and section 91.113.[270]

OTHER RULEMAKING SCENARIOS

There will only be brief mentions of some other types of ways the FAA can go about creating regulations. These other ways are not as frequently used compared to the informal rulemaking process previously discussed.

---

265. *See* 1 C.F.R. § 21.11.
266. *See* 1 C.F.R. § 21.12; *see also* 14 C.F.R. §§ 91.27–91.99.
267. *See generally* 14 C.F.R. § 91.1.
268. *See* Fed. Aviation Admin., Integration of Civil Unmanned Aircraft Systems (UAS) in the National Airspace System (NAS) Roadmap 58–59 (2013) [hereinafter "FAA Roadmap"], *available at* http://www.faa.gov/about/initiatives/uas/media/uas_roadmap_2013.pdf.
269. The FAA could classify some of the smaller unmanned aircraft as vehicles and exempt them from part 91 requirements like the FAA did with ultralight vehicles. *See* FAA Legal Interpretation to Barbara Parisi from Rebecca MacPherson, Acting Assistant Chief Counsel, *supra* note 228.
270. *See* Lester et al, *supra* note 195, at 15.

Formal Rulemaking

When rules are required by statute to be made on the record after opportunity for an agency hearing, sections 556 and 557 of the APA[271] applies. Without getting into great detail as to when exactly this requirement is triggered,[272] sections 556 and 557 deal with what is called formal rulemaking.[273] Formal rulemaking somewhat resembles a trial.[274] Parties are entitled to present their case "by oral or documentary evidence, to submit rebuttal evidence, and to conduct such cross-examination[.]"[275]

Direct Final Rulemaking

The normal approach to rulemaking is noticing, commenting, and then publishing the rule. Publishing a direct final rule, which skips the notice step, appears to violate the APA; however, the APA allows the FAA to issue a direct final rule without any notice when the FAA has good cause.[276] Good cause is when the rulemaking process is "impracticable, unnecessary, or contrary to the public interest."[277] The FAA issues final rules in these three good-cause situations.[278]

Generally, a direct final rule will take effect 60 days after publication in the Federal Register, unless the FAA receives an adverse comment, which is a comment showing the rule is inappropriate, ineffective, or unacceptable.[279] If an adverse comment is received, the FAA may withdraw the direct final rule and publish another direct final rule incorporating the comment or publishing an NPRM.[280]

Airworthiness Directives (ADs) are subject to the rulemaking process as described elsewhere in this chapter. The FAA has an Airworthiness Directives Manual,[281] which explains these three good-cause exceptions that will now be discussed.

When Notice and Comment Is Impracticable

"This exception can be used when an urgent and unsafe condition exists that must be addressed quickly, and there is not enough time to carry out Notice and Comment

---

271. 5 U.S.C. §§ 551–559.

272. For a better understanding of when formal rulemaking is triggered, *see* United States v. Florida E. Coast Ry. Co., 410 U.S. 224, 241 (1973).

273. *See* 5 U.S.C. § 553(c).

274. *See* 5 U.S.C. § 556(c)–(d).

275. 5 U.S.C. § 556(d).

276. *See* 5 U.S.C. § 553(b)(3)(B).

277. *Id.*

278. The FAA explains that it issues direct final rules in two situations, but I'm using the APA's three good-cause exceptions, which are compatible with the FAA sections. *See* 14 C.F.R. § 11.29(a)–(b).

279. *See* 14 C.F.R. § 11.31(a).

280. *See* 14 C.F.R. § 11.31(c).

281. Fed. Aviation Admin., FAA-IR-M-8040.1C, Airworthiness Directives Manual (2010) [hereinafter "AD Manual"], *available at* http://rgl.faa.gov/Regulatory_and_Guidance_Library/rgOrders.nsf/0/66ddd8e1d2e95db3862577270062aabd/$FILE/FAA-IR-M-8040_1C.pdf.

procedures without compromising safety."[282] The manual goes on to say the urgency must be explained, and the time to give individuals to comply with the AD must reflect the urgency.[283] "For example, it would make little sense to say immediate action is necessary to prevent a landing gear failure and then allow 60 days compliance time to resolve the unsafe condition. Also, the AD should be issued quickly to be consistent with the determination of 'impracticability.'"[284]

When Notice and Comment Is Unnecessary

This type of direct final rule is in effect a "final rule with request for comments. [The FAA's] reason for issuing [this type of] direct final rule without an NPRM is that [the FAA] would not expect to receive any adverse comments, and so an NPRM is unnecessary."[285] The FAA plans "the comment period to end before the effective date," so if there are any adverse comments, it can withdraw the final rule and issue an NPRM.[286] If the FAA publishes a rule, but a legitimate adverse comment comes up, the FAA will publish in the Federal Register a notification of withdrawal, part or whole, of the previous direct final rule.[287] The FAA can then either publish a new direct final rule with the comments taken into account or publish an NPRM.[288]

Other unnecessary situations are when (1) no one in the United States would be affected by the regulation and (2) the FAA makes "minor corrections, clarifications, and editorial changes."[289]

When Notice and Comment Are Contrary to the Public Interest

Generally, this exception is coupled with either the impracticable or unnecessary exception. This exception's purpose "is to excuse an agency from the Notice requirement if providing advance Notice would defeat the purpose of the agency action. For example, issuing advance Notice that the government is contemplating financial controls could cause public reactions so excessive that the financial system could be placed in jeopardy."[290]

---

282. *Id.* at 15.
283. *See id.*
284. *Id.*
285. 14 C.F.R. § 11.13.
286. *Id.*
287. *See* 14 C.F.R. § 11.31(c).
288. *See id.*
289. AD Manual, *supra* note 279, at 15.
290. *Id.*

Negotiated Rulemaking

The FAA has the power to create[291] an ARAC to negotiate a regulation. This is called negotiated rulemaking.[292] This is helpful for the FAA because certain regulations are hotly contested during the typical notice and comment period but can be more effectively negotiated with open dialog between both sides. The FAA has used this successfully[293] in the past with negotiating a regulation involving pilot duty times when two previous NPRMs failed because of opposition.[294] If unmanned aircraft integration efforts stall because of industry and public opposition, the FAA can use this method.

Persons Can Petition the FAA to Repeal the Rule

After the final rule has been published, individuals can petition the FAA to amend, repeal, or add to a current regulation.[295] If the repeal is unsuccessful, the individual affected should seek a waiver, deviation, or exemption from the regulation.

THE ILLUSORY UNMANNED AIRCRAFT REGULATION

The FAA has the problem of trying to fit a square peg in a round hole. The FAA has three ways to approach the integration of unmanned aircraft into the regulations. The first is for the FAA to operate as if unmanned aircraft are regulated based upon the broad definition of "aircraft" in the FARs.[296] This would subject unmanned aircraft to all the regulations that are currently in place for the certification of manned aircraft. This is currently how the FAA is operating, but this creates many burdens for unmanned aircraft to where it is almost cost prohibitive to buy a certified unmanned aircraft. The second scenario is where the FAA creates a specific place in the FARs dealing with unmanned aircraft only. This seems to be the approach the FAA is moving toward as evidenced from the previous discussion about part 107. The third scenario is where the FAA would go through all of the FARs and carefully dissect them so as to weave unmanned aircraft throughout the regulations. This would require many amendments to current regulations to go through the rulemaking process. This scenario is extremely time consuming and will likely never happen.

---

291. *See* 5 U.S.C. § 563(a).
292. *See* 5 U.S.C. §§ 561–570a.
293. *See* Flight Time Limitations and Rest Requirements, 50 Fed. Reg. 29,306 (July 18, 1985) (to be codified at 14 C.F.R. part 121 and part 135).
294. *See* Henry H. Perritt, Jr., *Negotiated Rulemaking Before Federal Agencies: Evaluation of Recommendations by the Administrative Conference of the United States*, 74 GEO. L.J. 1625, 1667 (1986).
295. *See* 14 C.F.R. § 11.61.
296. 14 C.F.R. § 1.1 ("Aircraft means a device that is used or intended to be used for flight in the air").

The FAA has crafted a small UAS (sUAS) regulation which has been bouncing around government offices more than a pinball at an arcade; hence, the reason for the delay in getting the rule out.

> In August 2011, FAA provided the Secretary of Transportation with its draft NPRM for the first time. Since then, the Office of the Secretary has provided several rounds of comments to FAA to further refine the NPRM. FAA expected to publish the NPRM in late 2011, but FAA officials told us in August 2012 that the Office of the Secretary of Transportation was still reviewing the draft and that FAA does not expect to publish it in the Federal Register before the end of [2012].[297]

Some things are known about the unmanned aircraft NPRM. Executive Order 12,866[298] and the Regulatory Flexibility Act[299] both require the DOT to publish twice a year regulatory agendas describing regulations currently being worked on. In addition to this, the DOT publishes monthly a report on significant rulemakings. Both the DOT monthly report[300] and DOT unified agenda[301] give information regarding the illusive sUAS rule. In the DOT monthly report and DOT unified agenda, the abstract about the new rule says,

> This rulemaking would adopt specific rules for the operation of small unmanned aircraft systems (sUAS) in the national airspace system. These changes would address the classification of small unmanned aircraft, certification of their pilots and visual observers, registration, approval of operations, and operational limits in order to increase the safety and efficiency of the national airspace system.[302]

Executive Order 12,866 requires a cost-benefit analysis to be performed by the FAA on rules considered significant by the Office of Information and Regulatory Affairs.[303] The unified agenda shows the total cost[304] of the regulation on the government, businesses,

---

297. U.S. Gov't Accountability Office, GAO-12-981, Unmanned Aircraft Systems 28 (2012).

298. *See* Exec. Order No. 12,866, Regulatory Planning and Review, 58 Fed. Reg. 51,735 (Oct. 4, 1993).

299. 5 U.S.C. § 602(a).

300. *Small Unmanned Aircraft Systems Rule*, Office of Info. and Regulatory Affairs, http://www.reginfo.gov/public/do/eAgendaViewRule?pubId=201404&RIN=2120-AJ60.

301. Dep't of Trans., June 2014 Internet Report, Report on DOT Significant Rulemakings (2014), *available at* http://www.dot.gov/sites/dot.gov/files/docs/JUNE%202014%20Internet%20Report.docx.

302. *Id.* at 11.

303. *See* Exec. Order No. 12,866, Regulatory Planning and Review, 58 Fed. Reg. 51,735, § 6(a)(3)(C) (Oct. 4, 1993) (For the reader's ease, I have cited the sections in the PDF and not the Federal Register Pages), *available at* http://www.archives.gov/federal-register/executive-orders/pdf/12866.pdf.

304. *See id.* at § 6(a)(3)(C)(ii).

and the economy is estimated at $168.7M and the total benefit[305] is estimated at $342.8M.

The regulation identifier number (RIN) is 2120-AJ60,[306] which is the way citizens can track the progress of the regulation as it goes through the rulemaking process. The rulemaking process was started on July, 28, 2009, and has since slowed down because of "[u]nanticipated issues requiring further analysis."[307] The head of the FAA's unmanned aircraft systems integration office, Jim Williams, spoke at the sUAS News' Small Business Expo and said,

> Congress has passed many different laws which require different types of analyses to be conducted before a rule can go into effect. This is to protect the public from overregulation; so it slows down the process. There are a lot of people involved along the way who can all hold up their hand and say "No, we don't agree with your analysis. You've got to go back and redo it." I know it sounds like I'm making excuses, but I'm really not. That is the process we have to work with and that is why it takes so long to get regulations out. . . . Congress didn't exempt me from the laws that they themselves had passed that govern the regulatory process.[308]

Later Mr. Williams said since this rule is considered significant by the OMB, the rule would take seven to ten years to complete.[309] It is not surprising that it could take this long for the FAA to accomplish the rulemaking process. In 2001, before the U.S. House of Representatives Sub-Committee on Aviation, Dr. Dillingham testified on the FAA's rulemaking efforts in response to congressional mandates or NTSB recommendations between fiscal year 1995 and fiscal year 2000.[310] He said that after the FAA published an NPRM, the "FAA took a median time of approximately 2-½ years to complete the rulemaking, although 20 percent of the rules took 10 years or longer to complete."[311]

While it is not surprising a significant rule might take a long time to develop, the FAA has had the need for unmanned aircraft certification/regulation on their "radar" for a long time. Simply blaming the lack of regulation on the rulemaking process and all the congressional and executive "hoops" the FAA has to jump through does not

---

305. *See id.* at § 6(a)(3)(C)(i).

306. *See id.*

307. *Id.*

308. sUAS NEWS, *2014 sUSB Expo Jim Williams* at 8:28, YOUTUBE (May 13,2014), https://www.youtube.com/watch?v=98LF5azVxLg.

309. *See id.* at 27:20.

310. U.S. GOV'T ACCOUNTABILITY OFFICE, GAO-01-950T, INCOMPLETE IMPLEMENTATION IMPAIRED FAA'S REFORM EFFORTS 1, 3 (2001).

311. *Id.* at 3.

account for lack of progress when the FAA had four different advisory circular proposals for unmanned aircraft operations, pilot training and certification, design, and maintenance back in 1996[312] and a proposal from the 2008 ARC.[313]

The DOT Office of Inspector General did an audit in 2014 on the FAA's UAS integration. It brought to light Congress actively putting on more restrictions while the FAA tries to comply with the requirements that Congress and the Executive branches have put on it. The DOT report said, "FAA officials indicated that privacy concerns have been the primary contributor to this recent delay. In the fiscal year 2014 Omnibus Appropriations Act, Congress directed FAA to conduct a study of the impact of UAS integration on individual privacy and submit a report on its findings."[314]

Lastly, the "ping-ponging" of the rule can be seen in Table 4.3, adapted from the DOT monthly report.[315]

Table 4.3 Rule Ping-Ponging of the UAS Integration

Milestone	Originally Scheduled Date	New Projected Date	Actual Date
To OST	01/24/2011	07/28/2014	08/29/2011
Returned to Mode			12/27/2011
Resent to OST		12/30/2011	12/30/2011
Resubmitted to OST/2		03/09/2012	03/07/2012
Returned to Mode/2			03/05/2013
Resubmitted to OST/2		06/30/2014	07/02/2014
To OMB	02/03/2011	07/28/2014	10/23/2014
OMB Clearance	03/07/2011	10/27/2014	
Publication Date	03/10/2011	11/04/2014	
End of Comment Period	07/14/2011	01/05/2015	

OST = Office of the Secretary of Transportation

OMB = Office of Management and Budget

---

312. *See* 1991 ARAC, *supra* note 186; *see also* Letter from James L. Crook, *supra* note 188.

313. *See* 2008 ARC Recommendations, *supra* note 190.

314. OFFICE OF INSPECTOR GEN., DEP'T OF TRANS., AV-2014-061, AUDIT REPORT 15 (2014) (footnote omitted), *available at* http://www.oig.dot.gov/sites/dot/files/FAA%20Oversight%20of%20Unmanned%20Aircraft%20Systems%5E6-26-14_0.pdf.

315. DEP'T OF TRANS., *supra* note 299, at 11.

CONCLUSION

Hopefully, the readers of this chapter will understand the complexity of this area and the enormous task the FAA is undertaking. The layers and layers of burdens placed on the FAA have slowed down the creation of regulations addressing the operation of unmanned aircraft. One cannot purely fault the FAA even though they started the process late. The FAA is trying to craft regulations, but anywhere along the way through this bureaucratic maze, one person saying "stop" will cause the whole process to halt.

There are also different "cultures" of individuals along the way that slow down progress. It is easier for bureaucrats to say "stop" than to say "go" because if the proposed regulations get approved by them, and something goes wrong such as a crash, they are to blame. How does saying "go" benefit them? It is far easier to say "stop" than to risk their job, promotion, reputation, and so on because government bureaucrats do not stand to gain any additional pay for any additional risk, unlike the private sector. On top of this, political climates change with new presidencies and Congresses who want to have a say. Congressional and executive politicians also put into place new agency heads who most likely share the same political views.

In addition to the bureaucrats having their say, there are private industry stakeholders who are lobbying and trying to influence the process in their favor.

Private industry stakeholders fall on both sides of the fence regarding integration. For example, manned aircraft organizations such as the Air Line Pilots Association are pushing for stricter regulations, while the Small UAV Coalition is taking the opposite side. In conclusion, the FAA has a long way to go before the final regulations go into effect.

CHAPTER

5

Unmanned Aircraft in the National Airspace

A Legal Primer

Cameron R. Cloar

Since the arrival of the very first aircraft, the United States and its laws have been forced to continuously evolve in order to accommodate one of the single most important industries and drivers of the nation's economy. In just one century, developments in the field of aviation have resulted in countless legal questions that range from ownership rights of airspace to the safe and efficient integration of new technology, both in terms of how to manage air traffic and in terms of new systems of operation. As this chapter will introduce, federal policies and laws have and will continue to play a central role in the development and regulation on what is now commonly referred to as our National Airspace System (NAS).

Designed, overseen, and regulated by the FAA, the NAS represents the entire environment for the safe operation of all aircraft within U.S. borders. It is a complex collection of systems, procedures, facilities, aircraft, and people. On average, it encompasses more than 100,000 flights per day, including airliners, general aviation, and military aircraft. Considered one of the most saturated and complex airspace systems in the world, upward estimates suggest there are approximately 18,000 commercial aircraft and 230,000 general aviation aircraft that operate within the United States, which vary in size, shape, function, and purpose.

Today, U.S. skies and its laws are in the midst of yet another historical transformation. Signed into law by President Obama in February 2012, the FAA Modernization and Reform Act of 2012 requires the Department of Transportation and the FAA to fully integrate UAS, often referred to as unmanned aircraft, into the NAS by September 2015. By some estimates, this may result in an additional 30,000 pilotless aircraft—ranging in size from the palm of your hand to as large as a commercial jetliner—that could eventually fill the nation's airspace.

This chapter introduces the National Airspace System, from legal inception to its most current form. As it illustrates, evolution in aircraft technology has necessarily been accompanied by necessary changes to law and regulation. It is also evident that a central re-occurring theme exists throughout this evolution: The FAA and, in general, the National Airspace System are very slow in adapting to new advances in aviation technology. Most technological innovations have led to increased regulatory oversight, oft accompanied by piecemeal additions and changes to the legal framework that has existed in its current form (or very close to it) for many decades. As of the date of publication for this book, it is an ongoing question of whether the integration of disruptive UAS technology will have a similar effect on the NAS or if it will help to usher in a new structure that reflects the unique nature and important benefits of this technology.

HISTORY OF THE NATIONAL AIRSPACE SYSTEM AND THE REGULATORY ENVIRONMENT

To comprehend the complexities associated with the integration of UAS into today's National Airspace System, it is first necessary to understand the development and evolution of the laws and regulations that now govern flight within our borders. In the early twentieth century, before the introduction of the modern-day aircraft, the predominant legal theory of airspace, and an individual's right to own, occupy, or possess it, could be boiled down to the Roman Law maxim *cujus est solum ejus est usque ad coelom*, which means whoever owns the land possesses all the space above the land extending upwards into the heavens.[1] The belief was adopted into English common law and eventually established itself in the United States.[2]

It remained a commonly held legal principle until the advent of the aircraft, when early aviation pioneers first began to realize that a federal policy and associated law and regulation were needed to accommodate and sustain the new industry. During

---

1. Colin Cahoon, *Low Altitude Airspace: A Property Rights No-Man's Land*, 56 J. Air L. & Com. 157, 161 (1990).
2. *See* R. Wright, The Law of Airspace 11–30 (1968).

its early beginnings, the airplane and the individuals and organizations that were designing this new technology were without any uniform federal safety standards or regulations. The fledgling aviation industry was plagued with numerous mishaps and fatal accidents. As a result, national policy and law covering aviation was focused squarely on developing and maintaining national safety standards to calm the fears that the general public had with early airplanes and to help the technology reach its full commercial and economic potential.

Questions of Early Authority

In 1926, Congress enacted the first piece of federal legislation, known as the Air Commerce Act, which began the development of the aviation industry toward its current self.[3] The act placed significant focus on testing and licensing of pilots, setting rules and the means to enforce those rules, certifying aircraft, guaranteeing aircraft airworthiness via certificates, more comprehensive investigations of aviation accidents, and, on a federal level, ensuring that aircraft were maintained properly. The act also spurred the development of air navigation aids, along with improved radio standards and procedures to aid in communications between pilots and air traffic controllers. The U.S. Secretary of Commerce was tasked with implementing the act's many new requirements. A new Aeronautics Branch in the Department of Commerce was created, and it assumed primary responsibility for aviation oversight and to fulfill these new important requirements.

Not long after, Congress enacted the 1938 Civil Aeronautics Act.[4] Both laws contained provisions providing that "to the exclusion of all foreign nations, [the U.S. has] complete sovereignty of airspace" over its borders.[5] Congress also established a "public right of freedom of transit in air commerce through the navigable airspace of the United States."[6] Such bold new pronouncements of law conflicted with the previously unchallenged idea that the traditional landowner held the rights to all airspace directly over the surface of the owned property. From a practical standpoint (that we now take for granted), this meant that there could be no common law right to travel in the nation's navigable airspace without constantly trespassing in private property. Not surprisingly, the nation's courts were soon required to settle this significant legal dispute caused by the rapid technological advances in aviation, determine the reach of the newly created federal rules, and balance the growing demand for unobstructed air travel with the common law rights of private property owners. In *United States v. Causby*, the Supreme Court of the United States was ultimately tasked with deciding

---

3. Air Commerce Act of 1926, P.L. 69-254, 44 Stat. 568, 572.
4. Civil Aeronautics Act of 1938, P.L. 75-706, 52 Stat. 973.
5. Codified as amended at 49 U.S.C. § 40103 (2012).
6. Codified as amended at 49 U.S.C. § 40101 (2012).

the issue.[7] Although its outcome seems simple today, at the time the case was heard in 1948, it presented an important issue of first impression for the nation's highest court: Who exactly owns the airspace located directly above private property.

Mr. and Mrs. Causby owned a three-acre chicken farm near a military airport just outside Greensboro, North Carolina.[8] One of the airport's runways was situated just far enough from the Causby land that numerous aircraft would often fly as low as 80 feet over the farm while departing and arriving several times per day.[9] The aircraft came close enough "at times to barely miss the tops of the trees as to blow the old leaves off," and the farm was lit up at night from the lights of the airplane traffic.[10] The noise of the aircraft frightened the chickens, and 150 of the animals were killed from flying into walls of the building where they were kept. Production on the farm plummeted; the Causby family grew increasingly nervous and was eventually forced to close their commercial chicken business. The family filed suit against the federal government claiming a violation of the Fifth Amendment Takings Clause, which provides that private property will not "be taken for public use, without just compensation." The lower court agreed finding that the United States had taken an easement over, and destroyed use of, the property.[11]

On appeal to the Supreme Court, the federal government relied heavily on the Air Commerce Act of 1926 and the Civil Aeronautics Act of 1938 to argue it had complete and sole sovereignty in the nation's airspace and that when flights are made within navigable airspace without physical invasion of private landowner property, there is no taking under the Fifth Amendment.[12] The Court ultimately found for the plaintiffs and held that "the landowner owns at least as much space above the ground as he can occupy or use in connection with the land."[13] Thus, the Court concluded that landowners own enough airspace over the surface necessary to use and enjoy the land; invasions of such space "are in the same category as invasions of the surface."[14]

Airspace above that defined area, the Court found, remains part of the public domain. Although it declined to draw a clear line on where ownership changes hands, it nevertheless concluded that the military flights over the Causby farm were a takings in the form of a servitude on the land based on the interference with the family's use

---

7. 328 U.S. 256 (1946).
8. *Id.* at 258.
9. *Id.*
10. *Id.* at 259.
11. *Id.*
12. *Id.* at 260.
13. *Id.* at 264.
14. *Id.* at 265.

and enjoyment of their property.[15] The flights resulted in a diminution in value to the land because it could no longer be used for its primary purpose as a chicken farm.[16]

The case is important for any number of reasons, particularly regarding the nation's airspace and airports and the negative impact they often have on the value of nearby privately owned land. The single most transcendent portion of the opinion, however, may be the Court's outright rejection of the long-held common law theory on land-owner rights when confronted with new technological advances in aviation. In fact, the Court appeared to do so with ease:

> It is ancient doctrine that at common law ownership of the land extended to the periphery of the universe—*Cujus est solum ejus est usque ad coelum*. But that doctrine has no place in the modern world. The air is a public highway, as Congress has declared. Were that not true, every transcontinental flight would subject the operator to countless trespass suits. Common sense revolts at the idea. To recognize such private claims to the airspace would clog these highways, seriously interfere with their control and development in the public interest, and transfer into private ownership that to which only the public has a just claim.[17]

The Court also recognized that "[t]he airplane is part of the modern environment of life, and the inconveniences which it causes are normally not compensable under the Fifth Amendment."[18] The opinion underscores a now fundamental point of law that the federal government has sole authority to control the nation's airspace. Although perhaps not readily apparent in the immediate outcome of the case, the Court's clear recognition on the effect aviation and rapidly advancing technology have on the nation's well-being provide important historical context as new aviation technology is designed and brought to market. It also has interesting parallels to the issues that have emerged from the widespread introduction of UAS technology, including the legal authority to regulate aircraft operating at very low altitudes, and further refinement of what it means to be in "navigable airspace."

During that same time period, the Supreme Court further discussed the breadth of federal authority over the nation's airspace and the individuals and aircraft operating within it. In *Northwest Airlines, Inc. v. Minnesota*, 322 U.S. 292, 303 (1944) (Jackson, J., concurring), the Supreme Court addressed the extent to which the states could impose a personal property tax on an airline's fleet of aircraft and thereby regulate air commerce within its own borders. In a concurring opinion filed by Justice Jackson,

---

15. *Id.* at 266.
16. *Id.* at 266–67.
17. *Id.* at 260–61.
18. *Id.* at 266.

he recognized the infancy of the airline industry at the time and compared it to the maritime and steamship industry that was introduced in the prior century. In the evolution of laws and rules pertaining to that industry, local and state governments were permitted to exercise control of navigable waters touching on their borders, alongside those laws and regulations of a federal nature. Justice Jackson identified that subjecting a national transportation industry to such a legal framework only led to conflicting standards and a substantial burden on the nation's commerce.

Only through a purely federal set of rules and regulations for air commerce could a repeat of those problems experienced by the maritime industry be avoided. Justice Jackson also recognized that the law must adapt to advances in technology in order to obtain the important benefits and opportunities it will bring:

> The ancient idea that landlordism and [local] sovereignty extended from the center of the world to the periphery of the universe has been modified. Today the landlord no more possesses a vertical control of the air above him than a shore owner possesses horizontal control of all the sea before him.[19]

Combined, these two cases illustrate the importance of a comprehensive and basic federal regulatory scheme to the aviation industry and how a flexible and adaptive approach is necessary to realize the countless technological advances that the industry has and will continue to produce.

The Jet Age and Beyond

In 1958, Congress ratified the Federal Aviation Act of 1958, which abolished the Civil Aeronautics Administration in favor of a new agency called the Federal Aviation Agency.[20] Passage of the 1958 Act was prompted by the arrival of another dramatic advancement in aviation technology: the jet aircraft. The general public again began to fear that such a dramatic leap in aviation technology, combined with an associated large increase in air travel, posed a serious new threat to safety. That fear only heightened after a series of catastrophic accidents involving commercial airliners rattled the nation and highlighted several safety issues in the regulation of air traffic.

The 1958 Act thus took a more comprehensive approach to the role the federal government serves both in fostering and regulating the national aviation industry. The Federal Aviation Agency was assigned to provide for the "regulation of air commerce

---

19. *Id.* at 302–303.
20. Federal Aviation Act of 1958, Pub. L. No. 85-726, 72 Stat. 731; *see* THERESA L. KRAUS, THE FEDERAL AVIATION ADMINISTRATION: A HISTORICAL PERSPECTIVE, 1903–2008, at 9 (2008) (detailing the history of the FAA); *A Brief History of the Federal Aviation Administration*, FED. AVIATION ADMIN. (FAA), http://www.faa .gov/about/history/brief_history (last updated Feb. 1, 2010).

in such manner as to best promote its development and safety and fulfill the requirements of national defense"; the "promotion, encouragement, and development of civil aeronautics"; and, "safety in air commerce." The agency was also tasked with further developing the comprehensive National Airspace System that outlines and governs the operation of aircraft:

> The [FAA] is authorized and directed to develop plans for and formulate policy with respect to the use of the navigable airspace; and assign by rule, regulation, or order the use of the navigable airspace under such terms, conditions, and limitations as he may deem necessary in order to insure the safety of aircraft and the efficient utilization of such airspace. [It] may modify or revoke such assignment when required in the public interest.[21]

The law was also significant in that it was the first to centralize responsibility and create a uniform set of regulations for the nation's airspace, recognizing that "aviation is unique among transportation industries in its relation to the federal government—it is the only one whose operations are conducted almost wholly within federal jurisdiction...."[22] The agency began an increased push to improve air safety by, among other things, creating and installing state-of-the-art radar and computer systems, increasing pilot certification requirements, and developing a human factors analysis for use in accident investigations. By the early 1960s, the FAA consisted of more than 40,000 employees working to promote and ensure the safety of the nation's rapidly growing airspace system.

During this time, the introduction of the jet aircraft resulted in rapid growth of the aviation industry and, as a result, the National Airspace System. Congestion at the nation's airports and in the skies became commonplace. For decades, responsibility for the various modes of transportation was spread out over several different agencies, with uncoordinated policies. President Johnson began to understand the need for a national transportation policy that could coordinate all modes of transportation efficiently—aviation, highway, rail, marine, and pipeline. In late 1966, he signed the Department of Transportation Act. The law brought thirty-one previously scattered elements and agencies—including the FAA—under the gambit of a single cabinet-level department known as the Department of Transportation (DOT). The Federal Aviation

---

21. Public Law 85-726, § 307(a); 72 Stat. 737 (1958).
22. S. Rept. 1811, 85th Cong., 2d Sess. (1958).

Agency was also renamed the Federal Aviation Administration. Among other things, the new DOT was given the following responsibilities:

- Ensure the coordinated, effective administration of the transportation programs of the federal government.
- Encourage cooperation of federal, state, and local governments, carriers, labor, and other interested parties toward the achievement of national transportation objectives.
- Stimulate technological advances in transportation.
- Provide general leadership in the identification and solution of transportation problems.

The 1966 law also created a five-member National Transportation Safety Board (NTSB) subsumed within the DOT. The NTSB was established to determine the probable cause of transportation accidents and to report on the facts, conditions, and circumstances that resulted in the accidents. Moreover, the NTSB was charged with reviewing, on appeal, any suspension, amendment, modification, revocation, or denial of a certificate or license issued by the secretary or by an administrator. Unlike the FAA and other agencies within the DOT, the NTSB was designed as an agency independent from the secretary and the other DOT offices and officers.[23]

Over the next several decades, the National Airspace System expanded at an exponential pace, particularly in regard to commercial traffic that continued to significantly increase following the Airline Deregulation Act of 1978 and several rapid technological advances in aircraft design. In contrast, the national airspace and air traffic control systems had evolved very little. Then, in December 2003, President Bush signed into law the long awaited Vision 100–Century of Aviation Reauthorization Act.[24] Among its many initiatives, the act created the Next Generation Air Traffic System, or what is more commonly referred to as NextGen. Introduced to create an air transportation system for the year 2025 and beyond, NextGen will expand airspace capacity to relieve congestion, prevent airborne aircraft gridlock, and essentially reform much of how the National Airspace System operates. In particular, the FAA intends to transform the currently ground-based air traffic control system to a satellite-based system. Goals of the program include easing air traffic delays at the nation's largest airports while simultaneously reducing carbon emissions.[25] However, the agency has been

---

23. Although it was originally intended that the NTSB would remain free from political influence of the DOT, the NTSB maintained close ties to the DOT until the ratification of the Independent Safety Act of 1974.
24. Public Law 108-176.
25. *See* WHY NEXTGEN MATTERS at https://www.faasafety.gov/files/notices/2014/Jul/WhyNextGen.pdf

working on this project for well over a decade, and implementation is way behind schedule and over budget.

A Note on International Law and the Chicago Convention

During the 1900s, the United States was obviously not the only nation developing an aviation industry and rules to govern it. Several technological advances in aircraft design resulted from World War II: Essentially out of necessity, several countries developed aircraft that were larger, safer, and flew increased payloads at faster speeds.[26] Shortly after the war ended, representatives of fifty-two countries from around the world convened in Chicago to meet and decide on the governing international aviation principles of sovereignty and responsibility over a country's airspace. During the meeting, the participating countries created an international organization to manage the safety and security of civil aviation for the world, known as the International Civil Aviation Organization (ICAO).[27] A written document called the Convention on International Civil Aviation, or the Chicago Convention, was also drafted to formalize the guiding principles for regulation and oversight of each participating country's national airspace system.[28] Today, ICAO consists of 191 member countries or states, and it is part of the United Nations.[29]

The standards and recommended practices for governing civil aviation developed by ICAO over many decades are reflected in the laws and regulations of many countries.[30] This is due in large part to the fact that an individual country's rules pertaining to air navigation, or with respect to standards for issuing certificates and licenses to individuals, registering aircraft, and issuance of certificates of airworthiness for aircraft, must meet the required minimums set by ICAO, otherwise other member countries need not recognize those certificates and licenses within their borders.[31] The rules and requirements for civil aviation in the United States are thus largely premised on the underlying principles of the Chicago Convention and set by ICAO.

---

26. *See generally* RAY BONDS, THE ILLUSTRATED DIRECTORY OF A CENTURY OF FLIGHT 156–235 (2003).

27. The ICAO was established in November 1944 to manage the safety and security of the world's civil aviation. Convention of International Civil Aviation, Dec. 7, 1944, 61 Stat. 1180, 15 U.N.T.S. 295, arts. 1–10, 43–79 (hereinafter "Chicago Convention").

28. In fact, Article 1 of the Chicago Convention provides the general principle that "every State has complete and exclusive authority over the airspace above it territory." Chicago Convention, art. 1.

29. *See* INT'L CIV. AVIATION ORG., http://www.icao.int/about-icao/Pages/default.aspx (last visited November 3, 2014).

30. Paul Stephen Dempsey, *Compliance & Enforcement in International Law: Achieving Global Uniformity in Aviation Safety*, 30 N.C.J. Int'l L. & Com. Reg. 1, 20–22 (2004).

31. Chicago Convention, *supra* note 28, art. 33.

LAWS AND REGULATIONS THAT DEFINE TODAY'S COMPLEX NATIONAL AIRSPACE SYSTEM

The National Airspace System is one of the world's most complex aviation systems, and it requires extensive oversight and regulation. As defined by the FAA, the National Airspace System is "[t]he common network of U.S. airspace; air navigation facilities, equipment services, airports or landing areas; aeronautical charts, information and services; rules, regulations and procedures, technical information, and manpower and material. Included are system components shared jointly with the [U.S.] military."[32] It is well beyond the scope of this chapter to describe in great detail the countless components, rules, and specific framework of the NAS. Instead, this chapter introduces the NAS with a focus on the rules and regulations that may be most undermined by the introduction of UAS technology.

The Federal Aviation Act

The Federal Aviation Act (the "Act"), Title 49, Subtitle VII, Part A, contains the general provisions governing the Federal Aviation Administration and its oversight of air commerce and safety throughout the NAS. The purpose of the Act is twofold: to promote safe air travel and to protect lives and property of people on the ground and in the air.[33] The Act is subdivided into four subparts: (I) General Provisions; (II) Economic Regulation; (III) Safety; and (IV) Enforcement and Penalties. From even a cursory review of the Act, it is evident that an overwhelming emphasis is put on safety in air commerce.[34] It also sets forth a policy to develop and maintain a strong and extensive regulatory framework to ensure the viability of the aviation industry.[35]

Pursuant to the Act, the FAA is afforded the exclusive authority to enact those regulations and govern the use of airspace.[36] There are two more notable highlights from these enabling statutes. First, the law guarantees that all citizens have a right of public transit through "navigable airspace."[37] Second, it specifies that the FAA is the federal administrative agency that must develop plans and policy for the nation's navigable airspace and regulate that airspace to ensure both the safety of aircraft as well as the maximum and efficient use of navigable airspace.[38] "Navigable airspace"

---

32. Fed. Aviation Admin., Pilot/Controller Glossary, in Aeronautical Info. Manual: Official Guide to Basic Flight Info. & ATC Procedures (2006), available at http://www.faa.gov/ATpubs/PCG/PCG .pdf.
33. *See* Bullwinkel v. F.A.A., 23 F.3d 167, 169 (7th Cir. 1994) ("The Federal Aviation Act was enacted to promote air traffic safety").
34. 49 U.S.C.A. § 40101(a)(1),(a)(3).
35. 49 U.S.C.A. § 40101(a)(6),(a)(7),(a)(10),(a)(12).
36. 49 U.S.C. § 40103
37. 49 U.S.C. § 40103(a)(2)
38. 49 U.S.C. § 40103(b).

is defined as "airspace above the minimum altitudes of flight prescribed by regulations under this subpart and subpart III, including airspace needed to ensure safety in the takeoff and landing of aircraft."[39]

As alluded to above, the introduction of UAS technology—particularly smaller UAS under 55 pounds and which operate at low altitudes—into the NAS has challenged the definition of "navigable airspace" and the underpinnings of the legal authority given to the FAA several decades ago. There is also an argument that the Act was not intended to address anything other than aviation safety with respect to aircraft with people or passengers on board. In the years ahead, the meaning of navigable airspace and the overarching purpose of the Act itself may need to change in order to keep pace with rapidly evolving UAS technology. This is particularly true with small UAS, which can operate at lower altitudes that were not previously possible with manned aircraft and hold benefits to society.

Under the statutory authority and to carry out its mission, the FAA promulgates regulations, the Federal Aviation Regulations (FARs), to ensure the safety of the NAS, prosecutes enforcement actions to ensure compliance with those regulations, and assigns and manages the use of airspace, among several other things.[40] In establishing the regulations on the use and operation of the National Airspace System, the FAA considers the significant issues of navigating, protecting, and identifying aircraft; protecting individuals and property on the ground; using the navigable airspace efficiently; and preventing mid-air collisions of aircraft and other airborne objects.[41] Those regulations are located in Title 14 of the CFR and cover all facets of the National Airspace System, from airports to aircraft, navigation aids, operators, and pilots. They establish classes of airspace; standards for certifying pilots, flight attendants, air carriers, and airports; along with requirements for the design and manufacture of aircraft, among many others.[42]

Enforcing the Rules and Regulations of the National Airspace System
The Act sets forth the authority and general mechanisms to enforce air safety rules and regulations of the FAA.[43] It permits individuals to submit written complaints to the DOT about any person, organization, or entity that allegedly violates any of the rules.[44] Where reasonable grounds of a violation exist, the FAA may on its own accord initiate and conduct an investigation into any alleged violation.[45] The Act provides

---

39. 49 U.S.C. § 40102(a)(32).
40. *What We Do*, FAA, http://www.faa.gov/about/mission/activities/.
41. 49 U.S.C. § 40103(B)(2)(A)–(D).
42. 14 C.F.R. Parts 71, 73, 77.
43. 49 U.S.C. §§ 46101–111.
44. 49 U.S.C. § 46101.
45. 49 U.S.C. § 46101.

the general parameters by which such investigations and proceedings are conducted, including service of process, evidentiary standards, jurisdiction of the federal courts, and the like.[46] Penalties for violations under the Act include, but are not limited to, civil penalties and fines, liens on aircraft, and criminal penalties, such as incarceration.[47] In situations where the FAA seeks to penalize individual pilots, mechanics, or others for infractions, the individual must be provided with a notice of the charges and an opportunity for a hearing.[48]

The regulations supplement the enforcement-enabling statutes in numerous respects. For example, the regulations cover, among other things, administrative actions, legal enforcement actions, rules of practice for FAA hearings and proceedings, and rules of practice for federally assisted airport enforcement proceedings. Through its statutory authority, the FAA may issue subpoenas, require the production of documents and things that are relevant to an investigation or enforcement action, and take evidence and depositions.[49] An individual or the FAA may appeal an adverse decision to the National Transportation Safety Board and from there obtain judicial review in federal district court.[50] Moreover, federal district courts have original jurisdiction of civil actions that involve certain penalties imposed by the FAA, such as where the amount in controversy exceeds $50,000.[51]

The Federal Aviation Regulations

The Federal Aviation Regulations (FARs) are set forth in parts 1 through 199 of Title 14 of the Code of Federal Regulations (CFR). The regulations provide the requirements for registration,[52] airworthiness certification,[53] licensing and certification of pilots and personnel,[54] and the air traffic and general operating rules of flight, among many others.[55] The FAA also publishes advisory circulars,[56] orders, notices to airmen or pilots (NOTAMs),[57] and temporary flight restrictions.[58] These items have the force and effect of law, but provide the FAA with the important flexibility to regulate aircraft under rapidly changing conditions and without having to follow the customary

---

46. 49 U.S.C. §§ 46102–111.

47. 49 U.S.C. §§ 46301–46319. The FAA bears the burden to establish the appropriateness of a civil penalty and may rely on its nonbinding Sanction Guidance Table, which is found in Appendix B to FAA Order No. 2150.3B.

48. 49 U.S.C. § 46301.

49. 14 C.F.R. § 13.3; *see* 49 U.S.C. §§ 40113, 44709, 46101.

50. 49 U.S.C. § 46301.

51. 49 U.S.C. § 46301.

52. 14 C.F.R. §§ 45.1–49.63.

53. *Id.* §§ 21.1–43.17.

54. *Id.* §§ 61.1–67.415.

55. *Id.* §§ 71.1–105.49.

56. FAA, Advisory Circulars, http://www.faa.gov (follow "Advisory Circulars (ACs)" hyperlink).

57. FAA, FAA Order 7930.2J, Notices to Airmen (February 2004).

58. FAA, Temporary Flight Restrictions Notices, http://tfr2.faa.gov/tfr/list.jsp.

rulemaking process required under the Administrative Procedures Act. As this section introduces, some of the most important regulations for much of the unmanned aircraft technology industry, and small UAS operations in particular, are those related to design and manufacture, pilots and operator training and certification, and general operating rules for aircraft and pilots.

Aircraft and Component Part Designers and Manufacturers

Aircraft and component part manufacturers must design and build aircraft in accordance with extremely specific requirements set out in the regulations. Such requirements can vary depending on size, weight, propulsion source, and operational use of the aircraft. While it is beyond the scope of this chapter to discuss in depth the requirements placed on manufacturers, it is important to understand two more fundamental points. When the FAA is satisfied that a proposed "aircraft, aircraft engine, propeller, or appliance is properly designed and manufactured, performs properly, and meets the regulations and minimum standards prescribed," the FAA issues what is called a "type certificate."[59] A "production certificate" is then issued once the FAA is satisfied that duplicates of a type certified aircraft or component will be produced in conformity with the type certificate.[60] To grant a type certificate, the FAA makes an exhaustive inspection of the design features, while the production certification process examines the manufacturing and quality-control system of approval for the mass production of a product.

Most small airplanes are certified under Part 23 of the FARs. Airplanes certified under Part 23 include, for example, the basic four-seat Cessna 172 and the more complex Embraer Phenom 300 small business jet.[61] Larger transport category airplanes, such as the iconic Boeing 737 and Airbus A380, are certified under Part 25.[62] Most rotorcraft, or helicopters, are certified under Part 27.[63] Historically, small aircraft design and certification requirements were drafted under a long-held assumption that small aircraft are simple, slow, and generally less complex than large transport category aircraft.[64] However, the industry has seen significant technological advancements in small aircraft design over the last several decades, and the rapid improvements in technology for unmanned aircraft only serves to further undermine those historical assumptions that size somehow dictates complexity.

---

59. 49 U.S.C. § 44704(a)(1).
60. 49 U.S.C. § 44704(c).
61. 14 C.F.R. §§ 23.1, 3.
62. 14 C.F.R. § 25.1.
63. 14 C.F.R. § 27.1. Transport category helicopters are certified under Part 29. 14 C.F.R. § 29.1.
64. Federal Aviation Administration, Part 23 – Small Airplane Certification Process Study 6, 16, 20 (2009), *available at* http://www.faa.gov/about/office_org/headquarters_offices/avs/offices/air/directorates_field/small_airplanes/media/CPS_Part_23.pdf.

With regard to small aircraft, the FAA has begun a move toward a more flexible approach to their certification to keep up with the advances in technology.[65] As those are implemented with manned aircraft, small UAS manufacturers are likely to see similar nimble design and certification requirements established for the industry.

General Operating Rules

The general operating rules of flight are contained within Part 91 of Title 14 of the CFR and apply to aircraft that operate within U.S. airspace, which generally reach from approximately 3 to 12 nautical miles off the coast.[66] Importantly, "aircraft" is defined broadly by the FAA to mean "a device that is used or intended to be used for flight in the air."[67] These general operating rules are designed to ensure the safe transit of aircraft through United States airspace. They include several requirements and conditions under which aircraft may operate, including the following:

- Operational rules and responsibility of the pilot in command[68]
- Rules for aircraft operating under visual flight rules (VFR) and instrument flight rules (IFR)[69]
- Abnormal flight rules or emergency rules for aircraft through notices to airmen (NOTAM)[70]
- Aircraft maintenance requirements[71]

These rules range in complexity and breadth. Some of the more general requirements provide that no person may operate an aircraft unless it is in an airworthy condition[72] and prohibit an individual from operating an aircraft in a careless or reckless manner.[73]

---

65. For example, in 2011, the FAA created a rulemaking committee to transform its recommendations into new regulations under Part 23 that it envisions may double the current level of safety while cutting in half the certification costs for small airplanes and associated systems. FAA 14 C.F.R. Part 23 Reorganization Aviation Rulemaking Committee, ARC Charter (Aug. 15, 2011), *available at* http://www.faa.gov/regulations_policies/rulemaking/committees/documents/media/Part23Reorg.ARC.Cht.8-15-2011.pdf.

66. *Id.* §§ 91.1, 91.101, 91.701, 91.801.

67. 14 C.F.R. § 1.1.

68. These requirements are several and include just a few of the following: FAR 91.3 (pilot in command bears ultimate responsibility for the safe operation); 91.7 (pilot in command responsible for determining aircraft in condition safe for flight); 91.103 (pilot must familiarize him or herself with conditions of flight); 91.113 (see and avoid other aircraft).

69. VFR flights must meet certain minimum weather conditions, FAR 91.155, and require fuel onboard for the aircraft to reach its first destination and then fly for an additional 30 or 45 minutes after that during the day or night, respectively, FAR 91.151. IFR flight rules include similar fuel requirements, but subject the pilot to additional operating rules. *See, e.g.,* 91.173, 91.183.

70. NOTAMs are issued for any number of reasons, including for new and permanent and/or temporary flight rules, for temporary flight restrictions, and for various unusual flight conditions. *See, e.g.,* 14 C.F.R. § 91.137–139.

71. The owner or operator is responsible for the maintenance of the aircraft. Required inspections for the aircraft depend on which Part the aircraft operated under, *e.g.* 91, 121, or 135.

72. 14 C.F.R. § 91.7.

73. 14 C.F.R. § 91.13.

In contrast, some of the more specific rules dictate the maximum speed aircraft may operate at different altitudes[74] and set forth the highly specific conditions necessary for an aircraft to land in marginal and poor weather.[75]

It is also important to understand that an aircraft entering the NAS must abide by one of two different types of air traffic rules: (1) visual flight rules (VFR), where the pilot visually looks outside the aircraft for navigation purposes and to see and avoid other aircraft and obstacles; and (2) instrument flight rules (IFR), where the pilot navigates the aircraft solely through flight instruments located inside the aircraft and with instruction and separation provided by air traffic control facilities along the route of flight.[76] In IFR operations, a pilot must file a flight plan—which includes items such as the destination, route of flight, and expected altitudes and speeds of the flight—and obtain a clearance to conduct the proposed flight from air traffic control before departure. Air traffic control then separates the aircraft from other air traffic throughout the route of flight, from takeoff to touchdown.[77]

Again, it is beyond the scope of this chapter to provide all of the details and law concerning air traffic control procedures in the United States. For purposes of brief background, however, the role of the air traffic controller has oft been described as one of surveillance, ensuring that the aircraft follows its assigned clearance and to separate the aircraft from other traffic within the NAS.[78] There are several different types of air traffic control facilities that separate an aircraft along its route of flight, typically by using radar systems that update the position of the aircraft every few seconds. In larger airports, the air traffic control tower controls the aircraft from taxi to takeoff and then transfers responsibility for the aircraft to a Terminal Radar Approach Control (TRACON), or, in instances where there is no TRACON, responsibility is transferred to an Air Route Traffic Control Center (ARTCC).[79] Many smaller airports do not have control tower facilities on site, in which case the aircraft provides its own traffic separation until contacting the TRACON or ARTCC shortly after takeoff. The ARTCC provides air traffic separation while the aircraft is in route between airports,

---

74. *E.g.,* 14 C.F.R. § 91.117.

75. 14 C.F.R. § 91.175.

76. *See* 14 C.F.R. § 91.155. Generally speaking, the rule to determine the application of either VFR or IFR rules depends on the class of airspace an aircraft will operate in and the weather conditions existing over the route of flight. With some exceptions, pilots may operate under VFR rules so long as they do not enter clouds, reduce visibility, and/or remain a minimum distance away from clouds. *Id.* Moreover, an aircraft may not take off or land under VFR rules if there are less than 3 statute miles visibility and less than a 1,000 foot ceiling (most often the base of the lowest layer of clouds). *Id.,* § 91.155(c)–(d).

77. Anthony C. Darienzo, *A Discussion of the Proposed Privatization of the Air Traffic Control System,* 9 AIR & SPACE LAW 9 (1995).

78. *Id.*

79. Coordination and responsibilities of various air traffic control facilities are detailed in letters of agreement between the facilities. J. Scott Hamilton, *Allocation of Airspace as a Scarce National Resource,* 22 TRANSP. L.J. 251, 280 (1994).

most often at higher altitudes. Responsibility is then transferred to the local TRACON and air traffic control tower as the aircraft approaches its destination.

Airmen, Mechanics, and Other Individuals Operating within the National Airspace System

The regulations also mandate the training and certification requirements for individuals operating within the NAS, including pilots and aircraft mechanics.[80] Certification for pilots is divided into rules for student pilots,[81] recreational pilots,[82] sport pilots,[83] private pilots,[84] commercial pilots,[85] and airline transport pilots.[86] Each level of pilot certification requires the individual applicant to possess varying levels of knowledge, skill, and experience.[87] As you might expect, airline transport pilot and commercial pilot certification requirements require more knowledge and experience than do individuals certified as recreational and/or private pilots. Pilots must undergo regular medical evaluations and obtain medical certificates.[88] Similar to the pilot certification requirements, medical certificates are organized into three classes based on the safety risk associated with the pilot certificates they correspond to—for example, airline transport pilots must undergo a more stringent medical evaluation more frequently than an individual holding a private pilot certificate.[89]

These increasing certification requirements are consistent with the general underlying policy that the FAA imposes greater requirements on commercial operators and pilots than on general aviation and pilots that do not operate for hire. Indeed, the Federal Aviation Act itself, which directs the FAA to issue pilot certifications considering "(A) the duty of an air carrier to provide service with the highest possible degree of safety in the public interest, and (B) differences between air transportation and other air commerce."[90] It must also classify a pilot certificate "according to air transportation and other air commerce."[91]

---

80. The FAA also issues certificates for aircraft, air carrier operating certificates, airport operating certificates, air agency certificates, and several others that hold less relevance specific to unmanned aircraft technology and are therefore not discussed here. *See* 49 U.S.C. § 44702.
81. 14 C.F.R. §§ 61.81–61.95.
82. 14 C.F.R. §§ 61.96–61.101.
83. 14 C.F.R. §§ 61.301–61.329.
84. 14 C.F.R. §§ 61.102–61.120.
85. 14 C.F.R. 61.120–61.141.
86. 14 C.F.R. §§ 61.151–61.171.
87. For more specific requirements for pilot certificates, established by law, see 49 U.S.C. § 44703.
88. 14 C.F.R. § 61.23.
89. *See* 14 C.F.R. §§ 67.1–67.415.
90. 49 U.S.C. § 44702(b)(1).
91. 49 U.S.C. § 44702(b)(2).

Additional provisions of the regulations require other individuals operating in the NAS to undergo continuing certification and training. This includes mechanics and repairmen,[92] air traffic control specialists, and flight engineers and navigators.[93]

PHYSICAL CONTOURS OF THE NATIONAL AIRSPACE SYSTEM

In the United States, as in many countries, the actual airspace is divided into a system of classes. The regulations provide for seven different classes or categories of airspace: Classes A, B, C, D, E, G, and Special Use Airspace.[94] Each category is comprised of varying altitudes, location, and makeup and consists of different operating requirements and restrictions. Combined, the categories touch on all phases of flight and are likely the most recognizable features of the National Airspace System.

Class A ranges from 18,000 feet mean sea level (MSL) to about 60,000 feet.[95] The airspace is occupied almost exclusively by traffic operating under instrument flight rules, and regulations require aircraft to receive air traffic control clearance before entering Class A airspace.[96]

Class B, C, and D airspaces overlay and surround airports of varying sizes. These three airspace classes are designed to safely transition aircraft to and from the airport environment, with a specific emphasis on ensuring appropriate vertical and horizontal separation between airspace occupants. The nation's largest and busiest airports are located in Class B airspace. Clearance from the air traffic control facility overseeing the airspace, typically a Terminal Radar Approach Control Facility, or TRACON, is required before entering Class B airspace, and the pilot must possess a private pilot certificate or a very specific student pilot endorsement.[97] Aircraft must also be equipped with certain equipment like a Mode C transponder.[98] Classes C and D airspace are reserved for medium to less busy airports, and operating requirements are less onerous than those of Class B. To enter and operate within such airspace, pilots must establish and maintain two-way radio contact with the appropriate air traffic control facility.[99]

Class E airspace essentially represents all other controlled airspace. Near airports, Class E airspace often extends to the ground, and regulations require pilots to establish two-way radio communication with the appropriate air traffic control facility.[100]

92. 14 C.F.R. §§ 65.71–65.95, 65.101–65.107.
93. 14 C.F.R. §§ 63.31–63.43, 63.51–63.61.
94. *See* 14 C.F.R. Parts 71, 91.
95. 14 C.F.R. § 71.33.
96. 14 C.F.R. § 91.133.
97. 14 C.F.R. § 91.131.
98. *Id.*
99. 14 C.F.R. §§ 91.129, 130.
100. 14 C.F.R. § 91.127.

Near federal airways, Class E airspace generally extends upwards from 700 or 1,200 feet above ground level. It also includes the airspace from 14,500 feet up to the Class A airspace boundary in addition to all airspace above 60,000 feet.[101]

Uncontrolled airspace, known as Class G airspace, takes up the remainder of the NAS. It generally begins at the surface and extends to 1,200 feet above the ground, but can reach as high as 14,500 feet. Class G airspace has little traffic; however, pilots are still required to adhere to some limited operating regulations.[102]

Another classification of airspace, known as special use airspace, is used for specific flight operations that must be confined for different reasons or where limitations must be imposed on aircraft operations that are not part of those specific flight operations. For instance, this includes prohibited and restricted areas. Prohibited areas consist of airspace defined by dimensions identified by an area on the surface of the earth extending to an altitude where flights are prohibited for national security or other welfare interests, for example, areas in and around Washington D.C., over power plants, and near military installations. Restricted areas, on the other hand, consist of defined dimensions of airspace where flight operations are wholly restricted or limited because of hazards to nonparticipating aircraft, like artillery firing, unusual military operations, or guided missiles.

As discussed and shown graphically in Figure 5.1, airspace Classes B, C, and D encompass airspace surrounding airports. It represents airspace that has the largest potential for mid-air collisions. Airspace Classes A, E, and G relate to altitude and flight operations that typically occur between airports (although some smaller airports without air traffic control facilities lie within Classes E and G). Commercial and air carrier traffic operate most often in Class A airspace.

LIMITATIONS ON REGULATION OF THE CURRENT NATIONAL AIRSPACE SYSTEM WITH NEW UAS TECHNOLOGY

Currently, the National Airspace System of the United States represents several decades of regulations focused entirely on manned aircraft and the intricacies and challenges such technology poses for air transportation and commerce. Requirements for pilots, aircraft designers, and manufacturers, and even the general operating rules for aircraft that transverse our skies, all rest on the most basic and fundamental concept that people *onboard* the aircraft bear ultimate responsibility for its operation. Naturally, unmanned aircraft dispose of that idea, and, in many instances, UAS technology may replace manned aircraft operations altogether. The widespread deployment of UAS

---

101. 14 C.F.R. § 71.71.
102. 14 C.F.R. §§ 91.125, 91.155.

Figure 5.1

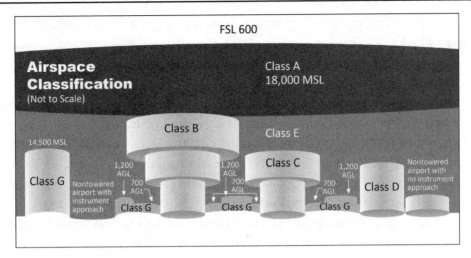

The National Airspace (Diagram by Cameron R. Cloar)

technology thus offers great promise to innovations in numerous industries, while at the same time it radically disrupts current utilization and operations in the NAS.

As a result, there is an ongoing debate across the aviation industry concerning how much the NAS must change to accommodate this technology, if at all. One of most significant questions is whether, and to what extent, the FAA will require UAS technology to conform to the current rules and regulations of the NAS. While current rules and regulations of the NAS make good sense for manned aircraft, they may not necessarily prove useful or even relevant to UAS technology. In fact, application of the existing regulations to UAS technology—especially, small UAS—is almost impossible. For instance, many of the rules either state explicitly or assume indirectly that they govern operations where an individual is onboard and controlling the aircraft.[103] Likewise, a read of other regulations reveals that it would be nonsensical to apply their requirements to unmanned aircraft.[104]

Moreover, challenges for integrating the subset of smaller UAS are illustrative of the problem. The benefits of this technology are several and include uses like search-and-rescue, mapping and surveying, infrastructure and facility inspections, agricultural inspection and analysis, cinematography, aerial photography, and environmental monitory, just to name a few. Small UAS are relatively light in weight and operate closer

---

103. *See* 14 C.F.R. § 91.1 ("This part applies to each person on board an aircraft being operated under this part, unless otherwise specified").

104. 14 C.F.R. §§ 91.11 ("No person may assault, threaten, intimidate, or interfere with a crewmember in the performance of the crewmember's duties aboard an aircraft being operated"); 91.107 ("No pilot may take off a U.S. registered civil aircraft.... Unless the pilot in command of that aircraft ensures that each person on board is briefed on how to fasten and unfasten that person's safety belt and, if installed, shoulder harness").

to the ground. Their operation, and any resultant risk to the safety and efficiency of the NAS, poses far different challenges than manned aircraft or even large UAS technology, which can carry increased payloads and operates at much higher altitudes. In other words, a small UAS simply does not pose the same risk or hazard to safety as a full-size aircraft or UAS.

However, should regulators treat small UAS the same, their operation may become much more burdensome, and it could stifle innovation. Pilot certification for small UAS operating for purposes like simple photography or facility inspections could be impractical and hinder many industries from realizing the true potential of this exciting technology. Likewise, airworthiness design and certification requirements may prove overly time consuming and costly.

It would severely undercut the practical benefits of the small and nimble technology rendering it useless. Cinematography and other similar operations, moreover, may encounter difficulty in adhering to the varying operational requirements of the different airspace classes, particularly when conducting flights in more dense population centers that often sit in or near Class B, C, and D airspace. Requiring this technology or its operators to contact air traffic control facilities may also overburden an already saturated system.

CONCLUSION

Are we trying to fit a square peg into a round hole? Should different requirements and standards be developed for UAS, which serve many new and unique purposes? These and many other questions must and will be answered in the years ahead. UAS technology has the potential to revolutionize the aviation industry and catapult the nation's economy in a way not seen since the dawn of the jet age and the social change spawned by the advent of large aircraft powered by turbine engines. However, integrating the technology may require some large changes to the National Airspace System and the rules governing it. As is discussed in more detail throughout the remaining chapters of this book, countless important legal questions must also be addressed, both in the short term and for many years to come.

CHAPTER

6

Grounded in the Law

Commercial UAV Rules

Timothy M. Ravich

Rarely do innovators in emerging industries seek out regulators to oversee their activities. For starters, legal regimes are typically reactionary and ill-equipped to anticipate, let alone grasp, the technical underpinnings of a new technology. Additionally, lawmakers historically fear and resist new inventions, including airplanes, air conditioning, antibiotics, automobiles, chlorine, the measles vaccine, open-heart surgery, radio, refrigeration, the smallpox vaccine, and X-rays.[1] So it goes with the developing commercial unmanned aerial vehicle (UAV), and yet industry stakeholders are starved for clear regulatory guidance that encourages rather than squelches operation.

The number of UAVs is projected to be 15,000 by 2020,[2] and pent-up demand exists domestically for UAV operations in the arenas of agriculture, energy, geology, and insurance. Nevertheless, commercial operation of unmanned aircraft is prohibited under current U.S. law. While the wisdom of such a policy decision is the source of various scholarship and public debate,[3] this chapter's purpose is to present the rules and policies that offer a path for UAV manufacturers, owners, and operators to follow to obtain the required authorization for civilian UAV use. Indeed, while the ban on commercial unmanned aircraft imposed by the Federal Aviation Administration

---

1. *See, e.g.,* DANIEL KAHNEMAN, THINKING, FAST AND SLOW 350 (2011).
2. FED. AVIATION ADMIN., FAA AEROSPACE FORECAST: FISCAL YEARS 2010–2030, at 48, http://www.flytheline.com/FAA2010%20Forecast%20Doc.pdf.
3. *See, e.g.,* Timothy M. Ravich, *Commercial Drones and the Phantom Menace,* J. INT'L MEDIA AND ENTERTAINMENT L. (forthcoming 2014).

(FAA) stands apart from more liberal regulations abroad, private stakeholders and public authorities have worked together to formulate an incremental, phase-based framework in which UAVs may operate for civil and business purposes domestically.

True, the FAA's default rule is that commercial UAVs are banned from operation, but Congress has directed the FAA to integrate civil unmanned aerial systems into the national airspace (NAS) not later than September 2015. In the meantime, parties interested in permissible commercial UAV operations should understand the various paths to lawful flight, including decisional law establishing the ways in which regulators approach the national airways, the FAA's guidance respecting model aircraft operation, the eligibility and substantive requirements for obtaining a Certificate of Authorization or Waiver (COA) or Special Airworthiness Certificate—Experimental Category (SAC-EC), and opportunities to obtain an exemption from existing FAA rules and regulations.

Along this path, the analytical line authorities have drawn between allowable flights for airplanes and helicopters and banned commercial UAV operations (particularly operation of small unmanned aerial vehicles (sUAVs) is blurry and requires careful attention to both the letter and spirit of the law governing autonomous and remotely piloted aviation. In this context, this chapter presents the foundational concepts, court decisions, statutory laws, and policies that inform evolving UAV operations in the United States.

COMMON LAW AND THE CONSTITUTION IN THE UNMANNED AIRCRAFT AGE

The reluctance of modern aviation regulators to fully integrate UAVs into the NAS (at least initially) is traceable to the regulatory climate that existed at the beginning of manned commercial aviation. Common law notions of trespass and privacy, coupled with Constitutional concerns about private property rights and searches and seizures, also explain the cautious approach lawmakers have taken with respect to unmanned aviation technologies. Indeed, introducing unmanned aerial systems and remotely piloted aviation assets into the national airspace system harkens back to the earliest days of manned flight (via balloon) when jurists were first confronted with the challenge of harmonizing ground-based rights with air rights.

Traditional Tort Principles and Early Unmanned Aviation

In *Guille v. Swan*,[4] a property owner in the early 1800s sued after the operator of an air balloon crash-landed into his garden in New York City. "When the balloon descended [the balloonist called for assistance and] more than two hundred persons broke into [the] garden through the fences, and came onto the premises [to his rescue], beating down [the garden's] vegetables and flowers."[5] The damages at issue in *Guille* were unremarkable measured against modern aviation tragedies, and yet the law and logic developed by the court in that case typified an early view of aviation as an ultra-hazardous activity involving unproven and potentially uncontrollable technologies for which manufacturers and owners were strictly liable. Indeed, the trial judge in *Guille* decided that the balloonist was liable because his trespass and resultant damages caused to the landowner's garden were foreseeable as a matter of law:

> Ascending in a balloon is not an unlawful act . . . , but, it is certain, that the aeronaut has no control over its motion horizontally; he is at the sport of the winds and is to descend when and how he can; his reaching the earth is a matter of hazard. He did descend on the premises of the plaintiff below, at a short distance from the place where he ascended. Now, if his descent, under such circumstances, would, ordinarily and naturally, draw a crowd of people about him, either from curiosity, or for the purpose of rescuing him from a perilous situation; all this he ought to have foreseen, and must be responsible for.[6]

The trepidation expressed by jurists more than a century ago in regard to new aviation applications has re-emerged in contemporary discourse about UAVs. Unmanned aviation not only presents traditional tort principles and safety concerns[7] but also raises novel questions about airspace management itself, namely where UAVs can or should be permitted to fly.

The National Airspace System: Constitutional Gravity

Aviation—manned or unmanned—implicates two important Constitutional concerns: one centered on property rights and the other derived from concerns about government surveillance. First, the Fifth Amendment's assurance against the government's

---

4. 19 Johns. 381 (N.Y. Sup. Ct. 1822).

5. *Id.*

6. *Id.*

7. Some research suggests military UAV accidents are disproportionality higher than the rate of accidents for other type of aircraft. *See, e.g.*, Brendan McGarry, *Drones Most Accident-Prone U.S. Air Force Craft: BGOV Barometer*, BLOOMBERG, June 18, 2013, *available at* http://www.bloomberg.com/news/2012-06-18/unmanned aircraft-most-accident-prone-u-s-air-force-craft-bgov-barometer.html ("The Global Hawk has an accident rate of 15.16 per 100,000 flight hours, almost three times that of the aircraft it's designed to replace, the Cold War-era U-2 spy plane").

taking of private property without just compensation was tested in the 1940s with the advent of modern military and commercial aviation. Until that time, the Roman doctrine of *cujus est solum ejus usque ad coelom*—"whoever owns the soil, it is theirs up to Heaven"—controlled air and property rights. That changed when the Supreme Court of the United States decided *United States v. Causby*.[8] There, a North Carolina farmer sued the federal government under the Fifth Amendment of the United States Constitution for inverse condemnation. Essentially, the landowner contended that Army and Navy bombers and fighter airplanes flying repeatedly at low altitudes above his barn deprived him of his right to enjoy his land and, as important, commercial activities stemming from his private property rights.[9] Indeed, the farmer averred that light and noise from military airplanes frightened his family and caused his chickens to kill themselves, resulting in the destruction of the use of his property as a commercial chicken farm.[10] The case required the court to consider the concept of an avigational easement.

In defending the flights giving rise to the dispute in *Causby*, government lawyers relied on the Air Commerce Act of 1926.[11] Under that law, Congress vested the national government with "complete and exclusive national sovereignty in the air space," reserving to American citizens "a public right of freedom of transit in air commerce through the navigable air space of the United States."[12] In this context, "navigable air space" included "airspace above the minimum safe altitudes of flight prescribed by the [Federal Aviation Administration]."[13] On the basis of the Air Commerce Act, the federal government argued that the military flights at the center of the farmer's lawsuit were merely an exercise of the right of travel through the airspace within the minimum safe altitudes for flight. The flights could not and did not effect a taking, government lawyers argued, because the flights occurred within the navigable airspace without any physical invasion of the farmer's property.[14] At most, then, only incidental damage occurred as a consequence of authorized air navigation, the government concluded.

While the Supreme Court of the United States sided with the farmer by agreeing that a taking had occurred, it remanded on the issue of damages and required a precise determination of the quality and nature of the taking, including whether it was temporary or permanent. In doing so, the Court abandoned historical notions of air and land rights, leaving unambiguous the lawfulness of modern aviation. Justice William O.

---

8. 328 U.S. 256, 261 (1946).
9. *Id.* at 258.
10. *Id.* at 259.
11. 44 Stat. 568, 49 U.S.C. §171 *et seq.*, as amended by the Civil Aeronautics Act of 1938, 52 Stat. 973, 49 U.S.C. § 401 *et seq.*
12. *Causby*, 328 U.S. at 260.
13. *Id.*
14. *Id.* at 260.

Douglas, writing for the *Causby* majority, reasoned that "[t]he airplane is part of the modern environment of life" where ancient doctrines of airspace ownership such as *ad coelom* "ha[d] no place in the modern world. The air is a public highway . . . Were that not true, every transcontinental flight would subject the operator to countless trespass suits."[15] *Causby* thus marked a reboot of entrenched property law doctrines, incorporating and accepting as routine the concept of machines flying in the sky.

In addition to Fifth Amendment considerations, aviation—and UAVs particularly—agitate Fourth Amendment principles. Given the remarkable competencies of UAVs for intelligence, surveillance, and reconnaissance (ISR), public debate and scholarship reflect a fear of "drones" as robot instigators of warrantless searches and seizures in contravention of the Constitution and in violation of common law conceptions of personal privacy.[16] Afraid of imagined abuses of UAV technology, state lawmakers around the nation have enacted substantive laws outlawing or restricting UAV operations for all purposes, including some law enforcement missions. North Carolina and Virginia, for example, have imposed general moratoria on public UAVs until July 1, 2015.[17] Other states have enacted rigid anti-unmanned aircraft legislation, too, that is more populist than potent,[18] including Florida,[19] Idaho,[20] Illinois,[21] Montana,[22] North Carolina,[23] Oregon,[24] Tennessee,[25] Texas,[26] and Virginia.[27] Curiously, this jaundiced attitude toward UAVs is incongruent to the way in which the law has treated aerial surveillance more generally.

In the seminal case of *Florida v. Riley*,[28] for example, the Supreme Court considered whether a search under the Fourth Amendment had occurred when a police helicopter flew 400 feet above a residential greenhouse to observe marijuana plants through a small break in the roof.[29] The Supreme Court of Florida decided that helicopter surveillance at 400 feet constituted a search for which a warrant was required, but the

---

15. *Id.* at 259.

16. *See generally* Benjamin R. Farley, *Drones and Democracy: Missing Out on Accountability*, 54 S. Tex. L. Rev. 385, 417 (2012) ("Employing unmanned aircraft allows policymakers . . . to act contrary to the law without judicial sanction and it allows them to obfuscate the formal rules governing use of force").

17. *See* Act of Jul. 26, 2013, ch. 360, 2013 N.C. Sess. Laws 360 § 7.16(e); Act of Apr. 3, 2013, ch. 755, 2013 Va. Acts 755 sec. 1, § 1.

18. *See generally* Timothy M. Ravich, *Anti-Drone Law Unlikely to Promote Privacy, Security*, Daily Bus. Rev., June 25, 2013, at A8, *available at* http://www.scribd.com/doc/150944459/Anti-Unmanned aircraft-Law-vs-Privacy-and-Security.

19. Freedom from Unwarranted Surveillance Act, 2013 Fla. Laws 33.

20. Act of Apr. 11, 2013, ch. 328, 2013 Idaho. Sess. Laws 328.

21. Freedom from Drone Surveillance Act, Pub. Act No. 98-569, 2013 Ill. Laws 569.

22. Act of May 1, 2013, ch. 377, 2013 Mont. Laws 377.

23. Act of Jul. 26, 2013, ch. 360, 2013 N.C. Sess. Laws 360.

24. Act of Jul. 29, 2013, ch. 686, 2013 Or. Laws 686 (2013).

25. Freedom from Unwarranted Surveillance Act, ch. 470, 2013 Tenn. Pub. Acts 470.

26. Texas Privacy Act, ch. 1390, 2013 Tex. Gen. Laws 1390.

27. Act of Apr. 3, 2013, ch. 755, 2013 Va. Acts 755.

28. 488 U.S. 445, 448 (1989).

29. *Id.*

Supreme Court of the United States disagreed. Justice Byron White wrote that "[t]he Fourth Amendment simply does not require the police traveling in the public airways at this altitude to obtain a warrant in order to observe what is visible to the naked eye."[30]

The holding in *Riley* was based in part on the precedence of *California v. Ciraolo*,[31] an aerial surveillance case in which the Supreme Court of the United States concluded that, "[i]n an age where private and commercial flight in the public airways is routine, it is unreasonable . . . to expect that marijuana plants were constitutionally protected from being observed with the naked eye from an altitude of 1,000 feet."[32] While *Riley* and *Ciraolo* would seem to allow law enforcement missions by UAVs, the invitation to extend the holding of decisions involving manned aerial surveillance to robotic surveillance has been resisted. In any case, the FAA is statutorily charged with promoting both air commerce and air safety and so lacks the organizational competence to smooth over social concerns about privacy and surveillance. As it turns out, the FAA also has struggled to keep pace with the commercial appetite for UAV technology in terms of rulemaking.

PATHS FORWARD, OR INTO, THE AMAZON: R/C MODELS, COAS, SAC-EC, AND SECTION 333

Amazon created quite a buzz when it broadcast on *60 Minutes* its ability to deliver more than 80 percent of its entire inventory via fully automated GPS-guided UAVs.[33] Even if possible, such commercial UAV activity is disallowed under the law because current aviation regulations prohibit any person from operating an aircraft below 1,000 feet above any congested area or below 500 feet above the surface.[34] The FAA has been consistent that

> [t]oday, unmanned aircraft are flying in the NAS under very controlled conditions, performing border and port surveillance by the Department of Homeland Security, helping with scientific research and environmental monitoring by NASA

---

30. *Id.*
31. 476 U.S. 207 (1986). *See also* Dow Chemical Co. v. United States, 476 U.S. (1985) (Environmental Protection Agency's use of a commercial aerial photographer, and standard floor-mounted, precision aerial mapping camera, to take photographs of a chemical company's industrial complex within the navigable airspace, at altitudes of 12,000, 3,000, and 1,200 feet was not a search prohibited by the Fourth Amendment).
32. Riley, 488 U.S. at 450. *See generally* Alexis Madrigal, *If I Fly a UAV Over My Neighbor's House, Is It Trespassing?*, THE ATLANTIC, Oct. 10, 2012, *available at* http://www.theatlantic.com/technology/archive/2012/10/if-i-fly-a-uav-over-my-neighbors-house-is-it-trespassing/263431/.
33. *60 Minutes: Amazon's Jeff Bezos Looks to the Future* (CBS television broadcast Dec. 1, 2013), *available at* http://www.cbsnews.com/news/amazons-jeff-bezos-looks-to-the-future/.
34. 14 C.F.R. § 91.119(b)–(c).

and NOAA, supporting public safety by law enforcement agencies, helping state universities conduct research, and supporting various other missions for public (government) entities. Operations range from ground level to above 50,000 feet, depending on the specific type of aircraft. However, UAS operations are currently not authorized in Class B airspace, which exists over major urban areas and contains the highest density of manned aircraft in the National Airspace System.[35]

In addition to prohibiting UAVs from operating near population centers, the FAA has also gone to (and created) considerable trouble to differentiate UAVs from other types of airplanes, including "model airplanes" and to further segment UAVs into categories, i.e., "public" or "civil." The legal distinctions are critical to understand if FAA enforcement action is to be avoided.

UAVs versus "Model Airplanes"

A preliminary distinction that is important for UAV operators to appreciate involves remote control or "model" airplanes. "Modelers" and aviation enthusiasts do not need to get approval from the FAA to fly a model aircraft for recreation.[36] "FAA guidance says that model aircraft flights should be flown a sufficient distance from populated areas and full scale aircraft, should be kept within visual line of sight of the operator, should weigh under 55 lbs. unless certified by an aeromodeling community-based organization, and are not for business purposes."[37] This putatively clear guidance is the subject of a pending controversial case.

On June 27, 2013, the FAA penalized Raphael "Trappy" Pirker $10,000 for operating a powered glider around the University of Virginia in October 2011 in violation of a rule that prohibits the careless or reckless operation of an aircraft.[38] According to the FAA, the glider was an "aircraft" and was operated for compensation.[39] Pirker countered that the FAA was without legal authority to regulate model aircraft flight operations. The FAA argued that it had the power to regulate all "aircraft" and that "model aircraft" fell within the scope of the term "aircraft." Judge Patrick Geraghty of the National Transportation Safety Board (NTSB), sitting as the administrative law judge (ALJ), disagreed.

---

35. FED. AVIATION ADMIN., UNMANNED AIRCRAFT SYSTEMS at https://www.faa.gov/uas/.

36. Recreational use of airspace by model aircraft is covered by FAA Advisory Circular 91-57, which generally limits operations to below 400 feet above ground level and away from airports and air traffic. In 2007, the FAA clarified that AC 91-57 only applies to modelers and specifically excludes individuals or companies flying model aircraft for business purposes. *See* http://www.faa.gov/documentLibrary/media/Advisory_Circular/91-57.pdf.

37. *Id.* at https://www.faa.gov/uas/faq/.

38. *See* Decisional Order, Fed. Aviation Admin. v. Pirker, FAA Docket No. 2012EA210009, NTSB Docket No. CP-217 (Mar. 6, 2014), at 1–2. *available at* http://droninglawyer.com/2014/04/16/make-war-or-make-ru les-faa-appeals-pirker-unmanned aircraft-case/.

39. *Id.* at Attachment 1, Order of Assessment (June 27, 2013), ¶¶ 2, 5–6.

In his order, the ALJ ruled that the FAA had historically considered "aircraft" and "model aircraft" as two different things. As a result, the ALJ rejected the FAA's argument that its power to regulate "aircraft" included regulation of "model aircraft." To believe otherwise would be to entertain the "risible argument that a flight in the air of, *e.g.*, a paper aircraft, or a toy balsa wood glider, could subject the 'operator' to the regulatory provisions of the FAA."[40] The ALJ also recognized as illegitimate the FAA's attempt to regulate UAVs as "model" aircraft where the FAA had not formally enacted any rule allowing it to regulate "model" aircraft as "aircraft"—

> [The FAA] has not issued an enforceable [Federal Aviation Regulation ("FAR")] regulatory rule governing model aircraft operation; has historically exempted model aircraft from the statutory FAR definitions of "aircraft" by relegating model aircraft operations to voluntary compliance with [existing FAA guidance]. [Thus, Pirker's] model aircraft was not subject to [federal aviation] regulation and enforcement.

Also significant for the ALJ was the fact that the FAA had not followed the proper rulemaking procedures for enacting valid UAS regulations. The FAA had published various notices and policy statements respecting UASs, but such policy statements are for internal FAA use and not binding upon the general public.[41] To create a valid rule for UAV operation, the FAA was required to publish a Notice of Proposed Rulemaking, but it had not done so.[42] Thus, "there was no enforceable FAA rule or FAR Regulation applicable to model aircraft or for classifying model aircraft as a UAS."[43]

The FAA appealed the ALJ's decision within a day to the full NTSB.[44] In a press release announcing its appeal, the FAA expressed a concern "that this decision could impact the safe operation of the national airspace and the safety of people and property on the ground."[45] In addition, with its appeal pending, the FAA issued policy guidance that all but called Amazon out by name and grounded commercial unmanned aircraft

---

40. *Id.*
41. *Id.* at 5.
42. *Id.* at 6.
43. *Id.* at 8.
44. *See* Fed. Aviation Admin. v. Pirker, Administrator's Appeal Brief, Docket No. CP-217 (Apr. 7, 2014), *available at* http://droninglawyer.com/2014/04/16/make-war-or-make-rules-faa-appeals-pirker-unmanned aircraft-case/.
45. Press Release, Fed. Aviation Admin, FAA Statement (Mar. 7, 2014), *available at* http://www.faa.gov/news/press_releases/news_story.cfm?newsId=15894. Putatively to allow testing of UAVs in a controlled environment, the Federal Aviation Administration announced, on December 30, 2013, its selection of six UAV research and test site operators across the country at the University of Alaska, the State of Nevada, New York's Griffiss International Airport, North Dakota Department of Commerce, Texas A&M University – Corpus Christi, and Virginia Polytechnic Institute and State University. "Across the six applicants, the FAA is confident that the agency's research goals of System Safety & Data Gathering, Aircraft Certification, Command & Control Link Issues, Control Station Layout & Certification, Ground & Airborne Sense & Avoid, and Environmental Impacts will be met." *See* http://www.faa.gov/news/fact_sheets/news_story.cfm?newsId=14153.

operations with near certainty without articulating clear standards or analytical tools for operators to assess their own operations in a multitude of situations that do not fall neatly within hobby or recreation operations. Instead, UAV users were provided this tabular guidance (see Table 6.1):

Table 6.1 Hobby or Recreational Flights vs. Disallowed Operations

Hobby or Recreation	*Not* Hobby or Recreation
Flying a model aircraft at the local model aircraft club.	Receiving money for demonstrating aerobatics with a model aircraft.
Taking photographs with a model aircraft for personal use.	A realtor using a model aircraft to photograph property that he is trying to sell and using the photos in the property's real estate listing. A person photographing a property or event and selling the photos to someone else.
Using a model aircraft to move a box from point to point without any kind of compensation.	Delivering packages to people for a fee.
Viewing a field to determine whether crops need water when they are grown for personal enjoyment.	Determining whether crops need to be watered that are grown as part of commercial farming operations.

FAA Modernization and Reform Act of 2012

In 2012, Congress enacted legislation designed to promote safety and commerce for UAS assets. Under the "FAA Modernization and Reform Act of 2012" (FMRA),[46] Congress directed the FAA to produce comprehensive UAV regulations to "safely accelerate the integration of civil unmanned aircraft systems into the national airspace system."[47] The FMRA specifically requires the FAA to implement a plan to integrate UAVs into the NAS "not later than" September 30, 2015. The FMRA also directs the FAA to prepare recommendations and projections on the rulemaking that will define the acceptable standards for operation and certification of civil UAVs, ensure that any civil UAV has sense-and-avoid capability, and establish standards and requirements necessary to achieve the safe and routine operation of civil UASs in the NAS.[48] The FMRA allows for a "phased-in" approach for civil UAV integration, but it also establishes target dates or ranges, *i.e.*, August 2014 for the publication of a final rule governing operations for sUAS.

---

46. Pub. L. 112-95 (2012), § 331 *et seq.* [hereinafter FMRA].
47. *See, e.g.*, Pub. L. 112-95 (2012), § 332(a)(1). Congress has considered amending the FMRA to address privacy-related concerns arising from unmanned aircraft operations. *See, e.g.*, Drone Aircraft Privacy and Transparency Act of 2013, H.R. 1262, 113th Cong. (1st Sess. 2013). *See also* Preserving American Privacy Act of 2013, H.R. 637, 113th Cong. (1st Sess. 2013).
48. *Id.* at § 332(a)(2) (2012).

In September 2013, selected federal authorities jointly released a comprehensive plan ("Plan") called for in the FMRA.[49] The Plan set out several strategic goals for the phased-in integration of UAVs into the NAS, giving priority to "public" UAVs while laying the framework for eventual "civil" UAV integration by 2015.[50] The Plan anticipated that sUAVs with visual line-of-sight would operate in the NAS without special authorization by 2015, with "routine" UAV operations by 2020.[51] In addition to the goals of studying acceptable levels of automation for UAV in the NAS and harmonizing UAV operations under international UAV protocols, the Plan also addressed important "non-safety related issues" such as privacy and national security (including cyber and communications security). To that end, the Plan initiated a program for the establishment of UAV test ranges to "help inform future rulemaking activities and other policy decisions related to safety, privacy, and economic growth."[52]

Six test sites around the nation now serve as a test bed for the FAA to further its research goals of systems safety and data gathering, aircraft certification, command and control link issues, control station layout and certifications, ground and airborne sense and avoid, and environmental impacts. The Plan also projected the release of a Notice of Proposed Rulemaking for sUASs in early 2014 and an Integration Roadmap laying out a rolling five-year plan for implementing UAS operations into the NAS.[53] On November 7, 2013, the FAA released its "Integration of Civil Unmanned Aircraft Systems (UAS) in the National Airspace (NAS) Roadmap" ("Roadmap").[54] The Roadmap anticipated an evolutionary transition from "accommodating" UAVs to "integrating" the technology within the NAS. It also outlined a broad timeline for implementation of the actions mandated by the FMRA.

The Roadmap expressly contemplated sUAV use in the media and entertainment industry by recognizing UAV applications in "commercial photography, aerial mapping and charting, and advertising" as potential civil UAS applications. The Roadmap did not go so far as to authorize commercial UAS use, however. For now, no person may operate a commercial UAV in the NAS without first obtaining specific authority from the FAA in one of two ways.[55]

---

49. *See* JOINT PLANNING AND DEVELOPMENT OFFICE, UNMANNED AIRCRAFT SYSTEMS (UAS) COMPREHENSIVE PLAN: A REPORT ON THE NATION'S UAS PATH FORWARD (Sept. 2013).

50. *Id.*

51. *Id.* at 9, 16.

52. *Id.* at 7, 15, § 2.4.

53. *Id.* at 17.

54. FED. AVIATION ADMIN., INTEGRATION OF CIVIL UNMANNED AIRCRAFT SYSTEMS (UAS) IN THE NATIONAL AIRSPACE (NAS) ROADMAP, *available at* http://www.faa.gov/about/initiatives/uas/media/UAS_Roadmap_2013.pdf.

55. *See* FED. AVIATION ADMIN., ORDER 8130.34, NATIONAL POLICY: AIRWORTHINESS CERTIFICATION OF UNMANNED AIRCRAFT SYSTEMS (Mar. 2008), *available at* http://www.faa.gov/about/office_org/headquarters _offices/ato/service_units/systemops/aaim/organizations/uas/coa/faq/media/Order_8130.34.pdf.

Certificate of Authorization or Waiver (COA)

The operator of a UAV (but not of an airplane model) should recognize that the legality of UAV flight turns on a characterization of the operator itself as "public" or "civil." A public aircraft is one that is owned and operated by a governmental institution, and a civil aircraft is other than a public aircraft. As the FAA puts it, "[a] public aircraft is one that is only for the United States government or owned and operated by the government of a state, the District of Columbia, or a territory or possession of the U.S. or a political subdivision. Operators of public aircraft include DOD, DOJ, DHS, NASA, NOAA, state/local agencies and qualifying universities. Civil aircraft means other than a public aircraft."[56] The difference in definition between a public aircraft and a civil aircraft is simple, but also critical. Only UAV that are "public aircraft" can fly in the NAS, and "there are no means to obtain authorization for commercial UAS operations in the NAS. [Rather], manufacturers may apply for an experimental certificate for the purposes of R&D, market survey and crew training."[57] Because "civil" operation of a UAV is outlawed, UAV operators have but two options to fly lawfully: (1) to arrange to fly as a public entity and to obtain a Certificate of Authorization or Waiver (COA) (sometimes pronounced *koh-a*) from the FAA; or (2) to obtain a special airworthiness certificate from the FAA in the experimental category.[58]

Under current regulations, "[o]btaining an experimental airworthiness certificate for a particular UAV is currently the only way civil operators of unmanned aircraft are accessing the NAS. Experimental certificate regulations preclude carrying people or property for compensation or hire, but do allow operations for research and development, flight and sales demonstrations, and crew training."[59] Obtaining a special airworthiness certificate is thus viable for training and research purposes but effectively is not an option for commercial UAS operators and owners given its limited issuance and inherent limitations. Accordingly, the best option is to obtain a COA.

A COA, according to the FAA, "is an authorization issued by the Air Traffic Organization to a public operator for a specific UA activity."[60] Obtaining a COA follows

---

56. 14 C.F.R. § 1.1. *See also* 49 U.S.C. § 40102.
57. *See* FAA Unmanned Aircraft Systems Frequently Asked Questions *at* https://www.faa.gov/uas/faq/#qn5.
58. According to aviation authorities, "[a] civil UAS cannot be operated in air commerce in the National Airspace System unless there is an appropriate and valid airworthiness certificate issued for that UAS. U.S. registration is a prerequisite for the issuance of an airworthiness certificate." Fed. Aviation Admin., Special Airworthiness Certification—Certification for Civil Operated Unmanned Aircraft Systems (UAS) and Optionally Piloted Aircraft (OPA), at https://www.faa.gov/aircraft/air_cert/airworthiness_certification /sp_awcert/experiment/sac/. Eligible individuals may apply for the following: (a) type certificate for special class aircraft and a 21.183 standard airworthiness certificate for special class aircraft; (b) type certificate for restricted category aircraft and a special airworthiness certificate in the restricted category; (c) special airworthiness certificate in the experimental category for the purposes of research and development, crew training, and market survey; or (d) special flight permit for the purpose of production flight testing new aircraft.
59. http://www.faa.gov/news/fact_sheets/news_story.cfm?newsId=14153.
60. Fed. Aviation Admin., Certificates of Waiver or Authorization (COA), at https://www.faa.gov /about/office_org/headquarters_offices/ato/service_units/systemops/aaim/organizations/uas/coa.

an application process involving "a comprehensive operational and technical review. If necessary, provisions or limitations may be imposed as part of the approval to ensure the UA can operate safely with other airspace users. In most cases, FAA will provide a formal response within 60 days from the time a completed application is submitted."[61] Stated more expansively, a COA authorizes an operator to use defined airspace and includes special provisions unique to the proposed operation:

> For public operation, the FAA issues a Certificate of Authorization or Waiver (COA) that permits public agencies and organizations to operate a particular UA, for a particular purpose, in a particular area. The FAA works with these organizations to develop conditions and limitations for UA operations to ensure they do not jeopardize the safety of other aviation operations.
>
> The objective is to issue a COA with parameters that ensure a level of safety equivalent to manned aircraft. Usually, this entails making sure that the UA does not operate in a populated area and that the aircraft is observed, either by someone in a manned aircraft or by someone on the ground. Common uses today include law enforcement, firefighting, border patrol, disaster relief, search and rescue, military training, and other government operational missions.
>
> Applicants make their request through an online process. After a complete application is submitted, FAA conducts a comprehensive operational and technical review. If necessary, provisions or limitations may be imposed as part of the approval to ensure the UA can operate safely with other airspace users. In most cases, FAA will provide a formal response within 60 days from the time a completed application is submitted.
>
> The COA allows an operator to use a defined block of airspace and includes special provisions unique to the proposed operation. For instance, a COA may require flying only under Visual Flight Rules (VFR) and/or only during daylight hours. COAs usually are issued for a specific period—up to two years in many cases. Most COAs require coordination with an appropriate air traffic control facility and may require a transponder on the UAS to operate in certain types of airspace.
>
> Because UAS technology cannot currently comply with "see and avoid" rules that apply to all aircraft, a visual observer or an accompanying "chase plane" must maintain visual contact with the UAS and serve as its "eyes" when operating outside airspace restricted from other users.

---

61. *Id.*

To facilitate the COA process, the FAA has deployed a web-based application system (see Figure 6.1) through which UAV operators, after obtaining an account, can specify the conditions of their operation:

Figure 6.1

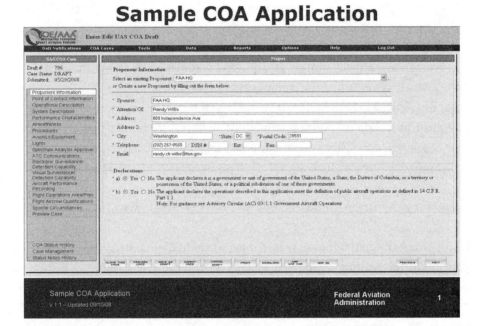

Sample COA Application

The "333" Exemption

In addition to establishing September 2015 as the deadline by which the FAA must integrate civil UAVs into the NAS, Congress also empowered the FAA to exempt UAV operators from the blanket ban on private and/or commercial UAV operations in cases where the authority was satisfied that safe operations could be assured. So-called "Section 333" of the FMRA specifically provides:

> **SEC. 333. SPECIAL RULES FOR CERTAIN UNMANNED AIRCRAFT SYSTEMS.**
> (a) IN GENERAL. Notwithstanding any other requirement . . . the Secretary of Transportation shall determine if certain unmanned aircraft systems may operate safely in the national airspace system before completion of the plan and rule-making required by [the FMRA].

(b) ASSESSMENT OF UNMANNED AIRCRAFT SYSTEMS. In making the determination under subsection (a), the Secretary shall determine, at a minimum –

(1) which types of unmanned aircraft systems, if any, as a result of their size, weight, speed, operational capability, proximity to airports and populated areas, and operation within visual line of sight do not create a hazard to users of the national airspace system or the public or pose a threat to national security;

(2) whether a certificate of waiver, certificate of authorization, or airworthiness certification . . . is required for the operation of unmanned aircraft systems identified under paragraph (1).

(c) REQUIREMENTS FOR SAFE OPERATION. If the Secretary determines under this section that certain unmanned aircraft systems may operate safely in the national airspace system, the Secretary shall establish requirements for the safe operation of such aircraft systems in the national airspace system.[62]

In its own words, the FAA understands Section 333 as follows:

Recognizing the demand to expedite integration of Unmanned Aircraft Systems (UAS) into the National Airspace System (NAS), the FAA continues efforts to develop the regulatory framework for safely integrating small UAS into routine NAS operations. . . . While these efforts continue, the FAA is also working to leverage the authority granted under Section 333 of the FAA Modernization and Reform Act of 2012 (FMRA) to establish an interim policy that bridges the gap between the current state and NAS operations as they will be once the small UAS rule is finalized.

Section 333, "Special Rules for Certain Unmanned Aircraft Systems," provides flexibility for authorizing safe civil operations in the NAS by granting the Secretary of Transportation the authority to determine whether airworthiness certification is required for a UAS to operate in the NAS. Specifically, Section 333 authorizes the Secretary to determine:

1. If certain unmanned aircraft systems, if any, as a result of their size, weight, speed, operational capability, proximity to airports and populated areas, and operation within visual line of sight do not create a hazard to users of the national airspace system or the public or pose a threat to national security; and

---

62. FMRA, *supra* note 42.

2. Whether a certificate of waiver, certificate of authorization, or airworthiness certification under section 44704 of title 49, United States Code, is required for the operation of unmanned aircraft systems identified under paragraph (1).

This framework will provide operators who wish to pursue safe and legal entry into the NAS a competitive advantage in the UAS marketplace, thus discouraging illegal operations and improving safety. It is anticipated that this activity will result in significant economic benefits, and the FAA Administrator has identified this as a high priority project to address demand for civil operation of UAS for commercial purposes.[63]

Importantly, a UAV manufacturer could not use Section 333 to exempt commercial operations conducted by its customers (who would need to apply in their own name). Rather, Section 333 only applies to the UAV operator itself (which, in some cases, could be the manufacturer itself). Additionally, Section 333 does not replace the COA process, and Section 333 petitioners must also apply for and obtain a COA for any civil operations allowed under Section 333.

CONCLUSION

Stakeholders in the burgeoning UAV industry are generally unsatisfied with the pace and substance of regulators in authoring clear rules for operation. However, a path toward the integration of UAVs into the NAS exists for the responsible commercial UAV manufacturer, owner, and operator. True, the rules, regulations, processes, and regulatory guidance in place is in the nature of work-around; the FAA has presented incremental solutions that derive a solution without squarely addressing the central question itself of how to incorporate the modern unmanned or optionally manned aviation technologies into the highways in the sky. While the law does not yet answer this question clearly, a review of Section 333 petitions in the public record and COAs already issued by the FAA makes clear that regulators are more likely to accommodate commercial UAV interests that present a sound safety case, demonstrating reliable flight characteristics of autonomous or automated machines that will not jeopardize life, property, or national security where loss-link, line-of-sight, or accidents might occur.

63. https://www.faa.gov/uas/legislative_programs/section_333/.

7

Considerations of a Legal Framework for the Safe and Resilient Operation of Civilian Autonomous Unmanned Aircraft

Donna A. Dulo and Cameron R. Cloar

"In flying I have learned that carelessness and overconfidence are usually far more dangerous than deliberately accepted risks."

—Wilbur Wright

Aviation industry analysts project the market for Unmanned Aircraft Systems (UAS), commonly referred to as unmanned aircraft, may reach almost $15 billion in annual worldwide sales within the current decade, and they foresee exponential growth after that. They are destined to perform an unprecedented variety of tasks once the aircraft are integrated into our airspace, as set out in the Federal Aviation Administration (FAA) Modernization and Reform Act of 2012. These systems will perform search and rescue, survey rugged terrain, deliver pizza, photograph the world in a wide range of media, battle forest fires, and perform other tasks that stretch the limits of the imagination. The extent of innovation for UAS is seemingly limitless. Yet, within this futuristic vision emerges an essential issue that cannot be ignored: safety.

It is a paramount concern that all UAS must have significant safety systems to ensure inherent resilience in the event of system failure or an external mishap. However, one potential subset of this new fledgling industry that presents unique safety challenges is autonomous UAS. Currently, many aerial systems operate under mostly human control; however, some segments of their operation can and will soon undoubtedly be done autonomously. For example, in the event of lost communications with the human operator, otherwise known as a lost link, or in a near collision that can trigger an automatic response in some systems, the UAS could be thrust into a total autonomous mode to alleviate the potential emergency.

Still other UAS on the market now and next are designed to operate under complete autonomy from takeoff to touchdown. In short, the spectrum for aerial robots operating autonomously is broad and increases by the day. The rapidly advancing technology raises numerous potential safety issues for all aircraft operating in the National Airspace System (NAS), as well as for everyone occupying the ground below.

For now, the FAA has indicated that even when UAS are integrated into the NAS, its legal framework will not permit the use of autonomous technology. Foreclosing the use of such technology may stifle or end investment in some of the most promising and beneficial UAS platforms. Although challenging, the FAA should work to develop a legal framework that allows for the use of autonomous UAS technology. Legal rules for this UAS subset must account for many factors such as the underlying software, algorithms and mathematics that drive the robotic systems, the interface between the robotic systems and potential human operators, if any, the interface between the robotic system and the collision avoidance system, as well as all inherent onboard authority systems.

With this chapter, the authors hope to begin the important discussion on developing a unified set of legal principles that may serve as the foundation to someday permit the operation of autonomous UAS. A legal framework will ensure that designers and manufacturers have the freedom of invention and innovation while having a defined set of rules with which to develop their aerial robotic systems to ensure safe, resilient, autonomous and semi-autonomous operations in the national airspace. It will ensure that operators understand the bounds with which their vehicles must operate safely in the NAS. As importantly, such a framework assists legal practitioners and the judicial system in defining areas of product liability, operator liability, as well as areas of negligence and potential criminal culpability.

Our discussion is informed by the "UAS Autonomy Spectrum," a visual system developed by the authors. While initially prepared for application to autonomous UAS, our ideas may be adaptable to other related new technology, including unmanned underwater robots, self-driving land vehicles, and any type of robotic vehicle that has varying degrees of autonomous capabilities. It touches upon the regulatory framework for aircraft under the Federal Aviation Regulations, with a particular emphasis on the new consensus-driven standards that are envisioned to reshape the design and certification of small general aviation aircraft. While our discussion is by no means complete, nor intended to serve as a final set of legal rules that can govern autonomous aerial technology, we hope that it will serve as a guide for stakeholders and help to ensure that unmanned aerial robots become the safe and resilient transformative innovations that they are destined to be.

THE MODERNIZATION AND REFORM ACT OF 2012

Unmanned Aircraft Systems (UAS), or unmanned aircraft, are not new technology. In fact, unmanned aerial technology has existed since the Wright brothers.[1] However, its access to airspace across the globe has been severely limited or proscribed altogether. In the United States, the Federal Aviation Administration currently prohibits the commercial use of UAS, while requiring public agencies, universities, and researchers to obtain specific authorization to use the technology.[2] That will soon change. A law passed in 2012 paves the way for public and commercial use of UAS in the United States. The wide-scale use of this technology is likely the most significant change to the aviation industry since the introduction of the jet aircraft many decades ago. Today, the NAS consists of more than 100,000 manned aircraft flights each day, and more than 18,000 commercial aircraft and 230,000 general aviation aircraft.[3] Integration of UAS technology thus presents countless challenges for federal regulators and to the NAS, already the world's most busy and complex airspace.

Signed into law by President Obama in February 2012, the FAA Modernization and Reform Act of 2012 (the "2012 Act") requires the Department of Transportation (DOT) to integrate UAS into the NAS by September 2015.[4] Specifically, it requires the DOT to "develop a comprehensive plan to safely accelerate the integration of civil

---

1. RUSSELL FREEDMAN, THE WRIGHT BROTHERS: HOW THEY INVENTED THE AIRPLANE 31 (1991).
2. In February 2007, the FAA published a "policy statement" that exists to this day and prohibits UAS operations without specific authority from the agency. *See* Unmanned Aircraft Operations in the National Airspace System, Docket No. FAA-2006-25714; Notice No. 07-01, 72 Fed. Reg. 29 at 6689 (Feb. 13, 2007). A recent decision by an NTSB administrative law judge finds that this "policy statement" is not controlling law. The FAA has appealed that decision. Decisional Order, Administrator v. Raphael Pirker, NTSB Docket No. CP-217 (March 6, 2014).
3. U.S. GEN. ACCOUNTABILITY OFFICE, UNMANNED AIRCRAFT SYSTEMS, MEASURING PROGRESS AND ADDRESSING POTENTIAL PRIVACY CONCERNS WOULD FACILITATE INTEGRATION INTO THE NATIONAL AIRSPACE SYSTEM (2012), at 4–5.
4. FAA Modernization and Reform Act of 2012, Pub. L. 112-95, § 332(a).

unmanned aircraft systems into the national airspace system."[5] The plan must include the necessary rulemaking to be conducted, thus mandating that the FAA promulgate specific regulations concerning the unique issues and challenges that the operation of UAS presents to the NAS.[6] The 2012 Act also requires that the plan consist of standards for certification, registration, and operation of civil UAS, standards for operators and pilots, and ensure that all civilian-operated UAS have an acceptable sense-and-avoid capability to avoid mid-air collisions.[7]

By the 2012 Act, the FAA was required to select six test ranges for UAS. Although late in doing so, in December 2013, the FAA fulfilled that obligation through the selection of six sites to address research, development, and operational questions that will aid in the development of regulations and standards for UAS operations.[8] Test sites in Nevada, Texas, Virginia, Alaska, New York, and North Dakota each have unique goals that should eventually provide regulators with valuable information.[9] The New York site, for example, will work on research surrounding the sense-and-avoid questions, including developing test procedures and assisting with a plan to manage UAS operating in the congested skies over the northeast corridor of the United States.[10]

As also required by the 2012 Act, in November 2013, the FAA unveiled its UAS Comprehensive Plan, which outlines the necessary steps to safely integrate UAS into the National Airspace System (the "Plan"). At the time, the FAA also released its Civil Unmanned Aircraft Systems (UAS) in the National Airspace System (NAS) Roadmap (the "Roadmap").[11] For many stakeholders, these documents indicate that the FAA plans to integrate UAS slowly over a lengthy period of time, which will include protracted research, testing, and federal rulemaking. For potential commercial operators of medium-to-large size UAS, final authorization to operate these aircraft may take a decade or longer.

As explained by the FAA, one goal of the Roadmap is to "guide aviation stakeholders in understanding operational goals and aviation safety and air traffic challenges when considering future investments."[12] Scattered among the broad goals that the FAA hopes will shape investment of UAS are a number of requirements and assumptions that will likely govern future operations, including that UAS comply with existing

5. *Id.*
6. *Id.* The 2012 Act required the Department of Transportation to present its comprehensive plan, including the necessary rulemaking, within one year of enactment.
7. 2012 Act at 332(a)(1)-(2).
8. FAA, *FAA Selects Six Sites for Unmanned Aircraft Research*, Press Release, December 30, 2013, *available at* http://www.faa.gov/news/updates/?newsId=75399.
9. *Id.*
10. *Id.*
11. The FAA also released a third document accompanying the Plan and Roadmap, titled "Notice of Final Privacy Requirements for UAS Test Sites." All three of the documents are available on the FAA website: http://www.faa.gov/about/initiatives/uas/.
12. Roadmap at 6.

operating rules or procedures, the need for an airworthiness certificate, a requirement to operate under an Instrument Flight Rules (IFR) flight plan (like certain manned aircraft operations), the use of a transponder, and air traffic separation capabilities, just to name a few.[13]

The FAA also makes crystal clear that it will *not* permit autonomous UAS operations; instead, each UAS must have a "flight crew" that includes a pilot-in-command who "has full control, or override authority to assume control at all times during normal UAS operations."[14] The Roadmap suggests that UAS weighing less than 55 pounds (sUAS) may avoid some of these rules, provided that they operate *exclusively* within visual line-of-sight of the flight crew.[15]

THE IMPACT OF UNMANNED TECHNOLOGY ON LEGISLATION

It is important to understand UAS and associated technology to appreciate the legal challenges that they pose on the current regulatory landscape. Most UAS are one of four different types of airframes, or a variation on the four: (1) fixed-wing airplane design; (2) rotary-wing design; (3) tilt-rotor airframe; and (4) a lighter-than-air model type. Each design offers different capabilities and benefits in terms of speed, range, and maneuverability. Generally, these are the main factors that go into choosing the technology best suited for use in a given operation.

The advantages that UAS offer over their manned counterparts are significant. As an engineer for the U.S. Navy working on that organization's UAS program commented: "There's . . . persistence and endurance. So where a manned pilot can only go for a certain number of hours before human fatigue sets in, [UAS] can keep going and keep going and keep going until it runs out of fuel. Once we demonstrate aerial fueling, we're talking about mission endurance that goes well beyond 20, 40 hours before it has to come back for maintenance." In fact, one manufacturer rumored to be in talks for acquisition by Facebook, Titan Aerospace, has developed a UAS that can carry up to 250 pounds in payload and remain airborne for as long as five years.[16]

---

13. Roadmap at 33–35.

14. Roadmap at 34. Importantly, the Roadmap also states that "At the core of these policies is the concept that each aircraft is flown *by a pilot* in accordance with required procedures and practices." Roadmap at 9 (emphasis added). The document also identifies one goal to establish certification requirements for pilots of UAS weighing less than 55 pounds ("sUAS"), including medical requirements and training standards. *Id.* at 52. In sum, these statements suggest that the FAA will at least initially attempt to regulate UAS operations very similar to their manned counterparts, requiring ground-based pilots who have undergone specific training, passed an FAA-mandated pilot exam, and who are medically qualified by an FAA-qualified medical examiner.

15. Roadmap at 34.

16. Alan Mark De Luzuriaga, *Facebook Drone: Mark Zuckerberg and Facebook Buy Titan Aerospace for $60 M to Blanket Areas with Wi-Fi; Trounce's Google's Balloons and Amazon's Drone*, The Bitbag, March 12, 2014, *available at* http://www.thebitbag.com/facebook-drone-mark-zuckerberg-facebook-buys-titan-aerospace-60-m

Aside from the more obvious range and endurance benefits, UAS can operate in spaces that manned aircraft cannot, or it is unsafe for them to do so. UAS are also less expensive to design and manufacture, and have the potential for fewer operational expenses, though the FAA's plan to require certified flight crews may lessen that upside.

Generally speaking, each UAS platform is developed for a specific operation and/or application. Often that includes some form of data collection, e.g., audio, video, photography, and remote sensing. Put simply, such systems operate much like a personal computer with data processing capabilities that are controlled remotely via radio devices or, as this chapter addresses, autonomously and/or through preprogrammed flight.

The exact payload and data handling capabilities that UAS can carry depends on the design and operational needs. In many instances, the user may want streaming data and onboard data backup should something interrupt that stream. That requires advanced data collection and storage, which itself may allow for the live streaming of data in the form of videos, photographs, and other information gathered from onboard equipment. Given the modern storage devices on the market, large onboard data retention is possible at a relatively small payload weight.

UAS may be custom configured to perform specific in-flight functions as required by each operator. Payloads can be adjusted to fit on various UAS airframes, and each flight may have a different configuration and/or data communication method. In data streaming applications, UAS can transmit real-time video or data to a ground unit and on to points across the globe. In advanced configurations, UAS often have Internet connectivity through an Inmarsat satellite and may therefore transmit data directly over the Internet.

Much of this UAS technology is available today. It can be outfitted on UAS that weigh as little as several ounces and which can operate at very low altitudes.[17] Most typical civilian applications consist of a small, inexpensive UAS often controlled by a smartphone or tablet. The mobile device contains a custom application developed by the aircraft manufacturer or the operator that is downloaded onto the mobile device for use. In many cases, the UAS and the application together can cost as little as $300. There are numerous potential uses of this small and lightweight UAS technology, including photography and video, research and data collection, flight and aviation training, search-and-rescue, agricultural and meteorological analysis, mapping and geographic surveying, infrastructure inspection and repair, among others.

-blanket-areas-wi-fi-trounces-googles-balloons-amazons-drone/71247; Sarah Perez & Josh Constine, *Facebook Looking into Buying Unmanned Aircraft Maker Titan Aerospace*, TC NEWS, March 3, 2014, *available at* http://techcrunch.com/2014/03/03/facebook-in-talks-to-acquire-drone-maker-titan-aerospace/.

17. Megan Treacy, *Insects Inspire World's Smallest Autonomous Flapping Unmanned Aircraft*, THE TREEHUGGER, February 26, 2014, *available at* http://www.treehugger.com/gadgets/insects-inspire-worlds-smallest-autonomous-flapping-unmanned aircraft.html.

Many of the more cutting-edge new UAS designs, most notably of the rotor design, call for the use of autonomous technology for navigation and other in-flight purposes. This technology promises still more benefits for end users. In certain operations, for instance, autonomous UAS are better suited to identify and maneuver around airborne or ground-based obstacles, as opposed to UAS controlled by an individual from a remote location.

Most of these uses fall outside of the line-of-sight and prohibition on autonomous operations requirements that the FAA insists will eventually become law. As a result, the FAA's proposed regulatory framework may actually stifle or end investment into the smallest and most beneficial UAS platforms. Other UAS developers may move their operations overseas. To prevent such results, the FAA should develop a legal framework that accounts for the unique opportunities and benefits presented by autonomous UAS.

MUCH OF THE CURRENT REGULATORY STRUCTURE AND LIABILITY FRAMEWORKS ARE ILL-SUITED FOR AUTONOMOUS UAS TECHNOLOGY

Thus far, the FAA has offered only mixed messages to the UAS and aviation industries on how it will eventually regulate the technology. On one hand, the FAA has stated that it will attempt to develop rules, regulation, and guidance that allow for and support evolving and efficient UAS technology and operations.[18] The agency also understands that it is difficult to apply existing FAA regulations and guidance to the UAS industry.[19] However, the Roadmap states that a baseline requirement will be for UAS to operate under existing flight and operating rules, and they will be required to have a ground-based flight crew and pilot-in-command.[20] Adding to the confusion, in 2011, the FAA in fact initiated legal action against an operator of a small UAS claiming that he violated regulations that apply to pilots of traditional manned aircraft.[21]

The existing Federal Aviation Regulations (FARs) were never intended to apply to unmanned aircraft. For instance, Part 91 of the regulations, which set forth the general operating and flight rules,[22] apply "to each person on board an aircraft being

---

18. Roadmap at 5.
19. *Id.* at 6.
20. For example, the Roadmap states that "UAS will also need to be flown by a certified pilot in accordance with existing, revised, or new regulations and required standards, policies and procedures." Roadmap at 10. For more, *see* Roadmap at 33.
21. Administrator v. Raphael Pirker, NTSB Docket No. CP-217 (July 18, 2013).
22. For flight and operating rules that govern air carrier and other similar operations, see 14 C.F.R. Parts 121 and 135.

operated under this part, unless otherwise specified" (14 C.F.R. § 91.1). Not surprising then is the fact that many of the regulations contained within Part 91 make no sense when applied to UAS. Courts interpreting the regulations have similarly understood that they apply to manned aircraft. In *Elassaad v. Independence Air, Inc.*, 613 F.3d 119 (3d Cir. 2010), the Third Circuit Court of Appeals scrutinized the meaning of 14 C.F.R. § 91.13(a), prohibiting the reckless or careless operation of an aircraft:

> [T]he statutory and regulatory definitions of "operate" state that a plane is only being operated, within the meaning of § 91.13(a), when it is being "use[d]" for "navigation," and the Aviation Act's definitions of "navigate aircraft" and "air navigation facility" demonstrate that the term "navigation" principally applies to the takeoff and landing of an aircraft, and the "piloting" that occurs during the flight. These definitions contemplate a flight crew's interaction with an aircraft and with passengers who are on the aircraft.[23]

The framework for liability that arises from aviation mishaps is grounded on similar assumptions that fault lies with pilot error, technical failure, an external condition such as terrorism, or a combination thereof—all involving human interaction and/or error. Civil liability arising from aviation accidents or incidents most often sound in tort and include theories of liability that range from negligence, strict liability, and products liability. Briefly, to successfully bring a negligence lawsuit, the claimant must prove that another party failed to take reasonable care in preventing the risk that led to the injury. Strict liability, on the other hand, can be established without proving fault by simply showing that the individual or entity was engaged in the activity. An injured party may also bring a product liability lawsuit alleging a manufacturing defect, a design defect, a breach of warranty, and/or a failure to warn.

For aircraft operations, regulations and liability principles have historically rested on the pilot-in-command principle, which the Roadmap states will remain in effect for UAS operations.[24] Pursuant to the FARs, the pilot-in-command of an aircraft is directly responsible for, and acts as the final authority as to, the operation of the aircraft.[25] The FARs generally define pilot-in-command as the person who (1) has the final authority and responsibility for the safe operation of the flight; (2) has been

---

23. Elassadd, 613 F.3d at 130. *See also* Abdullah v. American Airlines, Inc., 181 F.3d 363, 368 (3d Cir. 1999) ("Congress's purpose in enacting the FAA was to promote safety in aviation and thereby protect the lives of persons who travel on board aircraft.") (citation and internal quotation marks omitted).

24. As the D.C. Circuit has stated, the "ultimate decision is the pilot's since he knows the condition of his aircraft, its capabilities and must deal with the unusual and unexpected during flight." Neff v. United States, 420 F.2d 115, 120 (D.C. Cir. 1969).

25. 14 C.F.R. § 91.3(a).

designated as the pilot-in-command before or during the flight; and (3) holds the appropriate certification and ratings for the conduct of the flight.[26]

Similarly, federal regulations mandate that it is the pilot's responsibility to see and avoid other aircraft.[27] Courts have echoed this requirement that pilots use all available means to avoid other aircraft, while on the ground and in the air.[28] These rules and principles are also important for purposes of liability because in many jurisdictions a violation of the FARs is evidence of negligence.[29]

The FAA also regulates the design and manufacture of aircraft through the FARS, again grounded on the basis that all aircraft will consist of at least one pilot operator. Most small airplanes and commuter airplanes with a maximum takeoff weight of less than 19,000 pounds are certified under Part 23 of the FAR.[30] Aircraft certified under Part 23 include, for example, the basic four-seat Cessna 172, the nineteen-seat Beechcraft 1900D turboprop airliner, and small business jets.[31] It is possible that regulators may attempt to fold UAS airworthiness, certification, and design rules into Part 23, or they may attempt to create an entirely new set of rules specific to UAS design and certification. Although the Roadmap suggests that the FAA may use both some new and existing certification regulations, it also suggests that the proposed regulatory framework may be much more burdensome than UAS developers had hoped for.

Currently, Part 23 consists of highly specific areas of test, verification, and inspection, many of which are relevant only to manned aircraft.[32] In fact, it includes over 360 different areas that manufacturers and designs must satisfy before a new aircraft is certified as airworthy. As is discussed in more detail, *infra*, that has become a barrier to manufacturing small aircraft with modern equipment. One estimate pegs the cost to develop a small airplane in the range of $100 million from start to finish.[33]

This broadly summarizes the legal and regulatory framework that exists for much of the aviation industry today. It also helps to explain why the FAA is not ready to

---

26. 14 C.F.R. § 1.1.

27. 14 C.F.R. § 91.113(b).

28. PanAm v. Port Authority, 787 F. Supp. 312, 318 (E.D.N.Y. 1992); Spaulding v. United States, 455 F.2d 222 (9th Cir. 1972) (flight crew members have a continuing duty to be aware of dangers which they can perceive with their own eyes); *See* Aircraft Disaster at John F. Kennedy Int'l Airport on June 24, 1975, 635 F.2d 67, 74 (2d Cir. 1980) (pilots cannot fail to use their own eyes and ears to be aware of danger; United States v. Schultetus, 277 F.2d 322 (5th Cir. 1960) ("[A] clearance issued by a tower . . . either by radio or visual signal is permissive in nature and does not relieve the pilot from exercising a reasonable degree of caution in executing the provisions of the clearance); Thinguldstad v. U.S., 343 F. Supp. 551, 557 (S.D. Ohio 1972) (flight crew members have a continuing duty to be aware of the dangers which they can perceive with their own eyes").

29. *See, e.g.,* Texasgulf Inc. v. Colt Electronics Co., 615 F. Supp. 648, 660 (S.D.N.Y. 1984).

30. 14 C.F.R. §§ 23.1, 3.

31. Larger transport category airplanes, like the Boeing 737 and Airbus A380, are certified under Part 25. 14 C.F.R. § 25.1.

32. For example, Part 23 includes topics on oxygen and pressurization systems and seat construction. 14 C.F.R. § 23.

33. *Washington Report: FAR Part 23 Rewrite*, Air Facts, Nov. 13, 2012, *available at* http://airfactsjournal .com/2012/11/washington-report-far-part-23-rewrite/.

upend the legal and regulatory framework that has been constructed around the concept of manned aircraft. The introduction of the UAS—and the autonomous UAS, in particular—complicates these long-standing principles. Without an individual operator in the air or on the ground, for example, the list of potential parties at fault for an accident or incident may change. Such a list might include the operator or owner of the platform, the UAS manufacturer, the automator, and the programmer, just to name a few. In short, there are countless regulatory and liability issues that demand early attention so that they will not prevent the many benefits promised by the use of autonomous UAS.

THE UAS AUTONOMY SPECTRUM

Simply put, the mandate of all UAS operators is to fly the aircraft in a safe manner. This of course applies to manned aircraft as well. To do so effectively requires strict adherence to aerodynamic principles. These principles apply to pilot control as well as autonomous control and all varying degrees in between. Thus, there is a spectrum of autonomy that lies between total pilot control and total autonomous control.

In this chapter, the spectrum shall be called the "UAS Autonomy Spectrum." Figure 7.1 depicts the Autonomy Spectrum with full pilot control represented on the right and full system control represented on the left, with varying degrees depicted in the central portion converging on a central point which represents equal aircraft control by both entities. This point shall be called the "control ball."

Figure 7.1

The UAS Autonomy Spectrum[34]

Pilot control, system control, or a blending of both on the Autonomy Spectrum provide the foundation for the safe flight of the aircraft. The operation of a UAS requires that the aircraft maintain aerodynamic lift while retaining stability and control in a safe and reliable manner. Stability is the aerodynamic behavior of an aircraft to remain in its current state in time at rest or in motion regardless of the disturbances such as wind, turbulence, or friction that act upon it. A UAS must be stable if it is to maintain safe flight. Stability indicates that the aerodynamic forces of lift, drag, thrust,

---

34. All diagrams in this chapter by Donna A. Dulo, 2014.

and weight are all in relative balance and if disturbed will be quickly restored to the original state of stable equilibrium.

Control, on the other hand, is maintaining the balance of the aircraft on its respective axes while in flight. The axes are pitch, roll, and yaw. The aircraft must be in a state of control as aligned through its control surfaces, which vary depending on the particular UAS design, but in terms of general fixed-wing aircraft, they are elevator, aileron, and rudder control.

The stability and control as well as the overall operation of the UAS will be a blend of pilot control and system control, or one of the two extremes on the Autonomy Spectrum. The location of the control ball on the spectrum diagram represents the degree of control present in the current scenario.

Pilot Control

Pilot control reflects full pilot operator control of the aircraft and is represented on the UAS Autonomy Spectrum in Figure 7.2. It means that the operator is in full control of all three axes of the aircraft: the roll axis, the pitch axis, and the yaw axis.

Figure 7.2

Full Pilot Control

Pilot control also means that the pilot is fully controlling the means of stabilizing the aircraft, such as controlling thrust by maintaining control of the propulsion system, maintaining lift, and maintaining the equilibrium of the airframe as it operates against opposing forces. It also means that the pilot is controlling various systems in the aircraft such as navigation systems, communication systems, payload systems, sensor systems, and so forth.

The term "pilot" is actually a general term with unmanned systems, as there can be many individuals involved with the control of the aircraft, especially complex UAS systems with advanced payloads:

- **Pilots:** human operators that control or partially control the aircraft from a distance
- **Payload Specialists:** personnel that control and operate the payloads of the aircraft to ensure optimal performance

- **Safety Personnel:** personnel that monitor operations to ensure safety in all areas of UAS operations including spotting and collision avoidance
- **Launch and Recovery Personnel:** personnel that provide support for safe launch and recovery operations
- **Operations Supervisors:** personnel that provide overall supervision to the UAS evolution
- **Navigation and Communication Specialists:** personnel that direct and control communications and navigation operations.

At any one time, several of these individuals may be in control of the aircraft or directing control of the aircraft. Thus legal liability may rest on a number of individuals in the event of a mishap or incident. However, for general discussion purposes and simplicity, the term "pilot" will be used on the Autonomy Spectrum and will encompass all of the operators that are in control of the aircraft.

Autonomous Control

Autonomous control reflects that the control of the aircraft is maintained through the aircraft hardware and software systems. In a UAS, this control is maintained by the onboard computer system which is fed information by onboard sensors, actuators, controllers, GPS and navigational signals, as well as complex software algorithms which all together maintain the operations, stability, and control of the UAS in all aspects of its flight. In a fully autonomous flight, all of these systems are working in tandem to ensure a safe, reliable flight to perform the mission of the UAS. Fully autonomous flight is depicted in Figure 7.3.

Figure 7.3

System Control · · · · · · · · · Pilot Control

Full Autonomous System Control

Autonomous control means that the UAS as a complex system is in full control of the roll, pitch, and yaw axes of the aircraft. It also means that the UAS internal computer system is fully controlling the means of stabilizing the aircraft: propulsion control, lift maintenance, equilibrium maintenance, as well as internal systems operations control of the payload, navigation system, sensors, and so forth. With full autonomous control, the internal computer, guided by external stimuli and navigation inputs, is controlling the aircraft.

The degree of control can be relatively fixed in the computer algorithms, where the source and destination locations are programmed into the system by the operators, and general sensor inputs control the altitude, attitude, and airspeed of the aircraft. The degree of control can also be more flexible with more artificially intelligent algorithms programmed into the computer allowing the UAS to make decisions during its operation in addition to its general autonomous control capabilities. The degree of complexity of these artificial intelligence capabilities varies considerably depending on the scope and mission of the UAS.

Migrating from Pilot to Autonomous Control

The operation of a UAS will cause the control ball in the Autonomy Spectrum to continually shift from right to left in varying degrees throughout flight operations. The degree to which the pilot depends on the UAS system to control the flight will greatly depend on the sophistication and complexity of the aircraft. In general, automatic flight control systems within a UAS have several degrees of autonomous system control:

- **Throttle Control:** Maintains control of the propulsion system to control the UAS airspeed
- **Altitude Control:** Maintains lift to fly at a designated altitude
- **One-Axis Control:** Controls the roll axis, usually through ailerons on fixed-wing aircraft
- **Two-Axis Control:** Controls the roll axis and the pitch axis, through the ailerons and elevators on fixed-wing aircraft
- **Three-Axis Control:** Controls the roll, pitch, and yaw axes, through the ailerons, elevators, and rudders on fixed wing aircraft

The pilot has the capability to vary the control of the aircraft between full pilot control and one-, two-, and three-axis control. The pilot can also determine the degree of throttle control and altitude control. Handing over three-axis control combined with full throttle control and altitude control to the UAS would be giving the aircraft full autonomous control of its flight operations. The pilot has the flexibility to vary the autonomy throughout the flight with perhaps no autonomy during takeoff and landing operations and full autonomy during midflight. With the pilot in full control, the degree of autonomy, if any, is at the discretion of the pilot in command.

Voluntary Autonomy

The scenario where the pilot has full control of the autonomy of the aircraft is deemed voluntary autonomy. In this scenario, the pilot is free to take full control of the aircraft or shift control to the UAS system in varying degrees, depending on the specific needs and requirements of the pilot in the current situation. The degree of autonomy is fully controlled by the pilot, and autonomy can be revoked at any point in time for any reason by the pilot.

In some scenarios, the UAS can be set into fully autonomous mode from launch to recovery, but this is considered voluntary, even if the system strays off of its intended path, since the operator has set the system as autonomous from mission initiation. This voluntary mode requires careful considerations of the limitations of the internal navigation and computational systems of the aircraft to ensure that the aircraft does indeed complete its flight according to the predetermined waypoints.

Involuntary Autonomy

Involuntary autonomy arises when the pilot loses control of the aircraft through means external to pilot control. This instance can come about instantaneously or gradually over time through a cascading effect of systems failures.

One way to invoke involuntary autonomy is through a lost link. This is when the communications of the ground station are lost with the UAS, and the aircraft is forced to fly fully autonomously. Lost link can be caused by weather, terrain, communications systems failures, electrical systems anomalies, and many other factors. The internal algorithms and systems of the UAS will determine how the aircraft responds to this situation.

In response to a lost link, the aircraft can hover or circle and attempt to reconnect the communications link. It can attempt an auto-land. It can maintain its current heading and attempt a communications reconnect. The varieties of lost link algorithmic recoveries are vast, depending on the complexity and sophistication of the computational system within the aircraft. In some lower end systems, a lost link will mean a certain crash of the aircraft.

A second method of involuntary autonomy is the result of a system failure. In this event, the pilot loses one-, two-, or three-axis control or throttle control or altitude control. The pilot may have partial control of the aircraft or none at all depending on the extent of the damage of the aircraft. Some advanced UAS systems have an auto-land feature which can help mitigate this situation, if it is indeed functional after the systems failure. Other systems have no methodology, and the aircraft will thus become fully or partially autonomous with or without full aerodynamic stability and control of the airframe. With this type of involuntary autonomy, the loss of control can have catastrophic consequences if measures are not built into the system by the manufacturer or if specified operations are not put in place by the operator to handle the situation expeditiously and judiciously.

A final issue to mention is the loss of pilot control through malicious means, such as GPS spoofing or viruses and malware. With GPS spoofing, a UAS could be hijacked and crashed or set into autonomous mode by spoofing its live GPS signal. Viruses and malware can cause the internal computer system to execute unscripted commands, relinquishing pilot control and forcing the system into autonomous control. Malicious means can also give a third-party access to the controls of the UAS, resulting in loss of pilot control and internal autonomous control.

Malicious third-party intervention in UAS operations has a dangerous and chilling effect in the safe operations of unmanned aircraft in the national airspace. As such, both manufacturers and operators must ensure that safeguards are in place to avoid these scenarios, since malicious control or malicious involuntary autonomy can lead to catastrophic consequences both in the air and on the ground.

UAS AUTONOMY SPECTRUM AS A GUIDE FOR A LEGAL FRAMEWORK

The UAS Autonomy Spectrum is a visual guide for a legal framework to assist lawmakers in visualizing the degree of pilot and system control in an unmanned aircraft. Through this visualization, regulations can be developed to ensure the safe and reliable operation of the UAS in the NAS. It is important to remember that the point of control is continually changing in flight operations, and thus it may be difficult to determine the actual degree of autonomy in the system at any given time. Therefore, the UAS Autonomy Spectrum should only be used as a point of reference and not as a definitive measure of autonomous control in terms of actual system operations.

It is vital for lawmakers and legal professionals to understand the autonomous systems in an unmanned aircraft, and their impacts on the aircraft through stability and control to craft effective legislation to regulate UAS. A lack of understanding of this technology can lead to misguided laws, resulting in confusion both in manufacturing and in the operational side of unmanned systems, which can have a negative cascading effect on the safe operations of unmanned systems. As such, the UAS Autonomy Spectrum is a critical tool to help orientate and educate legal professionals on the autonomous capabilities and systems of UAS and the varying degrees of autonomy that can be present in a UAS at any one time during flight operations.

Broad Considerations that Should Be Taken into Account in Any Legal Structure for Autonomous UAS

The mere fact that UAS will be flying in the NAS means that some of the aircraft will be flying in an autonomous mode at any given point in time regardless of the current regulations. This does not mean that operators are trying to bypass the law. As demonstrated in the Autonomy Spectrum discussion, an unmanned system may be thrust unexpectedly into fully autonomous mode. This will place the operator and the manufacturer into a nebulous liability situation, if laws and regulations are not in place to handle the situation, and force the courts to make the legal decisions on this highly technological matter.

Operators and corporations, too, will be pushing the envelope on autonomous unmanned aircraft for the delivery of their product, for the hosting of their aerial Wi-Fi clouds, and for uses only the future can dream up. The reality is that if UAS are permitted into the national airspace in large numbers, operators will continually push the control ball left in the UAS Autonomy Spectrum slowly and under the proverbial legal radar until fully autonomous systems are operating in the norm, with the regulatory system left in the dust. This is what historically happens in the technological world where the law lags behind by many years or decades. Unfortunately, with unmanned aircraft flying in the midst of manned aircraft in the NAS, UAS law cannot afford to repeat this historic trend.

Therefore, the UAS Autonomy Spectrum must be considered when crafting laws and regulations regarding UAS autonomy and the varying degrees of UAS autonomy. In conjunction with the UAS Autonomy Spectrum, the following broad considerations should be considered as guide points for analyzing the structure and purpose of UAS laws to ensure the safe, reliable operation of unmanned systems and to ensure that all entities involved in their manufacture and operation understand their roles and responsibilities in maintaining a safe national airspace. These considerations are purposely broad to ensure that they cover salient points while not being too overbearing with details as to distract from the purpose of the chapter, which is to give a broad overview of the myriad issues that permeate the field of unmanned aircraft integration into the national airspace.

Human-Systems Interdependence Considerations

Will self-sufficient and autonomous UAS mean less liability for their human operators? This is one of the most logical considerations for operators of all autonomous machines, not just UAS. Self-sufficient UAS may lead to human operators with decreased capability to observe and understand the autonomous operations, and it will become a taxing legal concern. This becomes a problem of interaction between humans and machines. Moreover, it is conceivable that full autonomous UAS may not communicate effectively so as to allow for human interdependence.

An operator that is unable to understand what the autonomous UAS is doing, why it is doing it, or when it will finish will be much less likely to take on risk of liability for the autonomous activity. This is both a design concern and a legal concern. In fact, one outcome may be that increased knowledge requirements and skill demands are imposed on operators through regulation and/or standards of liability. A regulatory framework should require autonomous UAS to have the capability to communicate effectively and work interdependently with human operators.[35]

As the control ball moves left toward systems control, the human operator becomes more of an observer or monitor of the system than an operator, as shown in Figure 7.4. UAS operation thus becomes a human factors situation, which has many training and skill implications that are quite different from basic piloting skills. It also has a different set of responsibilities that must be reflected in laws and regulations.

Figure 7.4

Human-System Interdependence Considerations

In larger UAS operations, two or more personnel perform these functions, one as the pilot, and one as the observer. However, in many situations, the tasks will be performed by a single human. Given the complexities of flight, this dual nature of operator and observer can inject risks into the unmanned aircraft operations. Thus considering the UAS as a human-in-the-loop system is important for a regulatory framework. The fields of Human Factors Engineering and Human Computer Interaction (HCI), as well as their related fields, therefore, must be considered when crafting UAS regulations. These fields are constantly changing and improving, so specialists in these respective fields should be consulted by lawmakers on a regular basis to ensure that the latest research and analysis is reflected in UAS law and regulations.

---

35. For more on this concept, see M. Johnson, et al., *Autonomy and Interdependence in Human-Agent-Robot Teams*, IEEE Intelligent Systems, Vol. 27, No. 2 (2011), at 43–51.

Uncommanded/Involuntary Autonomy Considerations

What about automation surprises—new features, options, and modes that create new demands, types of errors, and paths toward failure? Uncommanded, involuntary, full autonomy must be a situation that is carefully considered in a regulatory framework as it is an inevitable scenario that will be played out continually in the national airspace as more and more UAS permeate the sky.

Systems failures cause the control ball in the UAS Autonomy Spectrum to suddenly and unexpectedly shift hard to the left, making the pilot an instant unwitting observer, and in many cases extracting all operator control from the pilot instantaneously, as depicted in Figure 7.5. This sudden shift of the control ball can have catastrophic consequences, especially if the pilot is unable to regain partial control of the aircraft to enable a controlled crash or to initiate an auto-land of the system.

Figure 7.5

Uncommanded/Involuntary Autonomy Considerations

UAS have demonstrated a high accident rate in the Air Force as compared to the manned aircraft fleet. The Bloomberg BGOV Barometer statistics indicate that Northrop's Global Hawk and General Atomic's Predator and Reaper have a combined 9.31 accidents for every 100,000 hours of flying time, which is the highest rate of any aircraft of any category and more than triple the Air Force fleet-wide average of 3.03 accidents for every 100,000 hours.[36]

This high accident rate is indicative of the need to focus civilian regulations on the safe manufacture of unmanned aircraft to prevent uncommanded and involuntary autonomy. The systems failures in Figure 7.5 give a clear initial indication of which areas of the UAS systems to focus upon in these regulations, although more detailed studies over time across a wide variety of unmanned aircraft models would be most beneficial to lawmakers. However, the point being that studies like the one mentioned above coupled with informed and accurate statistics of UAS failure rates, manufacturer specifications of UAS model performance and designs, as well as the results of crash

---

36. B. McGarry, *Drones Most Accident-Prone U.S. Air Force Craft: BGOV Barometer* (June 17, 2012). http://www.bloomberg.com/news/articles/2012-06-18/drones-most-accident-prone-u -s-air-force-craft-bgov-barometer.

tests and risk mitigation studies on the various aircraft are vital to the legislative and regulatory decision-making process in the area of unmanned systems.

Sense-and-Avoid Considerations

Sense-and-avoid: Is an operator/owner liable for the sense-and-avoid actions of the UAS? The FAA has specific national goals for sense-and-avoid capabilities. In the Integration of Civil Unmanned Aircraft Systems (UAS) in the National Airspace System (NAS) Roadmap First Edition-2013,[37] the FAA targets an Airborne Sense and Avoid (ABSAA) certification for the national airspace in four stated goals:

- **Goal 1:** Initial FAA certification of ABSAA that facilitates UAS operations without the requirement for a visual observer by 2016–2020.
- **Goal 2:** Installation and certification of ABSAA developed to meet industry standards for use by the DoD and other public and civil entities that provide the SAA functions required in the NAS for Classes A, E, and G airspace, and operations approved without the requirement for a visual observer or a COA.
- **Goal 3:** DoD or other public entity certification of initial ABSAA systems that enable the DoD and other public entities to safely operate ABSAA-equipped UAS in all NAS airspace classes without the need for a COA.
- **Goal 4:** Installation and certification of ABSAA systems for use by the DoD and other public and civil entities that provide the SAA functions that facilitate integrated operation of manned and unmanned aircraft in all NAS airspace classes.

The goals are broad and ambitious but lack specificity as to the desired actions of the aircraft during the sense-and-avoid operations. This is deliberate as the Roadmap is of a high level. However, in the details of the laws that are developed from this roadmap, the conditions of autonomy that may be initiated must be a part of the regulatory scheme for several reasons.

During a sense-and-avoid operation, one or both of the aircraft will be diverted to an alternate path that most likely will be independent of pilot control. As such, the pilot will be in the position of an observer rather than an operator, which will shift the control ball on the UAS Autonomy Spectrum to the left. This may be an unexpected event, and if the pilot is caught unaware, the pilot may counteract the sense-and-avoid commands of the aircraft causing even more disruption to the already diverted flight path.

---

37. FAA, INTEGRATION OF CIVIL UNMANNED AIRCRAFT SYSTEMS (UAS) IN THE NATIONAL AIRSPACE SYSTEM (NAS) ROADMAP FIRST EDITION-2013 (2013), http://www.faa.gov/about/initiatives/uas/media/uas_roadmap _2013.pdf.

The degree of sense-and-avoid may in fact correspond to the degree of autonomy in the system, as depicted in Figure 7.6, which is another way to ensure safety, but is another way to facilitate fully autonomous systems in the national airspace. Sense-and-avoid algorithms may be programmed into the UAS to correspond to the current level of automation in the UAS at the time, thus if the pilot is in full control, the sense-and-avoid systems will send a warning to the pilot to divert. If the system is in autonomous mode or in a higher degree of autonomy than pilot control, the sense-and-avoid system architecture will trigger fully autonomous collision avoidance.

Figure 7.6

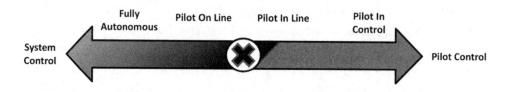

Sense-and-Avoid Considerations

The matching of the degrees of sense-and-avoid and the Autonomy Spectrum are depicted in Figure 7.6. The degrees of automation in relation to sense-and-avoid are as follows:

- **Pilot in Control:** The pilot directly commands the stability and control of the aircraft on all axes including throttle and altitude control.
- **Pilot in Line:** The unmanned aircraft follows a preprogrammed flight, but the pilot can take full control of the aircraft at any time in a sense-and-avoid situation.
- **Pilot on Line:** The unmanned aircraft follows a preprogrammed flight, but the pilot can only take over the navigation control (set inputs as headings or waypoints only). The pilot cannot take over the aviation function of the aircraft even in a sense-and-avoid situation; the aircraft systems are relied upon fully during sense-and-avoid scenarios.
- **Fully Autonomous:** The unmanned aircraft controls all stability and control functions including throttle and altitude control during a sense-and-avoid situation.

The degree of autonomy, thus the position of the control ball on the UAS Autonomy Spectrum, will play a major part in rulemaking. Aircraft systems that are highly automated will need more safe and reliable sense-and-avoid subsystems than those unmanned systems that rely primarily on pilot control. Lawmakers must be cognizant of this fact and create a stratified sense-and-avoid regulatory scheme, not a one-size-fits-all set of laws.

The actions of the unmanned aircraft in the sense-and-avoid system will be dependent on the algorithmic programs developed by the manufacturer, which will be dependent on the regulations that are based upon the FAR §91.113. An aviation rulemaking committee of the FAA is currently evaluating FAR §91.113, which prescribes aircraft right of way rules to accommodate UAS sense-and-avoid systems so that they can avoid aircraft collisions.[38]

The FAA has stated that it expects sense-and-avoid standards to be published in the future.[39] Hopefully, these standards will reflect the real, not theoretical, needs of the UAS industry and will consider the current and future autonomy requirements to ensure that as UAS inch closer to fully autonomous control, the sense-and-avoid standards and regulations will accommodate them without the need for disruptive and time-wasting revision.

Malicious Control Considerations

Malicious Takeover: What is the extent of liability if a third party takes over the aircraft, through autonomous means or direct control; what measures should have been in place to prevent liability?

Malicious control is a major threat to the UAS industry as a whole. The field of Information Assurance is expansive in the computer and information fields, and this logically extends to unmanned systems as the control and operations of unmanned systems are extremely data- and communications-intensive. However, information assurance and information security seem to be on the backburner to safety, yet they are the possible, direct, first-line causes of malicious takeovers or loss of control that can cause safety issues in the first place.

An unmanned aircraft is not merely an aircraft that flies by itself, but in systems-engineering terms, it is a "system of systems" consisting of the aircraft, the ground station, the GPS satellite constellation, the communication infrastructure (L-Band and C-Band or radio-controlled, for example), the launch-and-recovery infrastructure, the personnel, and so on. All aspects of these systems must be secured and maintain information assurance, as data is constantly transmitted in the form of information and commands.

---

38. *See* B. Clarey, *FAA Plans Unmanned 'Sense and Avoid' Rule in 2016*, AIN AIR TRANSPORT PERSPECTIVE (July 22, 2013), http://ainonline.com/aviation-news/ain-air-transport-perspective/2013-07-22/faa-plans-unmanned-sense-and-avoid-rule-2016.

39. *Id.*

UAS operations have computational and communicational complexity, giving rise to increasing risk to information assurance threats. Attacks can occur in embedded UAS systems, software, hardware, or any combination of them, as depicted in Figure 7.7.

Figure 7.7

Malicious Control Considerations

Embedded systems security is a major concern for UAS as well as manned aircraft and satellite systems. Embedded systems tend to have generic hardware and software, which in many cases do not have a development process with mandatory security protocols. This can result in built-in vulnerabilities in the chips (integrated circuit hardware) and the software that drives the chips. The interconnectivity of the system of systems makes these vulnerabilities pervasive throughout the entire system. Example: A virus in a UAS chip can spread to the ground station or a networked UAS.

Malicious software in embedded systems such as Integrated Circuits (IC) or Programmable Logic Controllers (PLC) can inflict physical as well as informational damage in a UAS. Controllers are real-time computer chips that have the potential to manipulate electrical outputs based on the programming conditions within the controller or integrated circuit. The chips or controllers are connected to electrical devices such as pumps, motors, sensors, or other electromotive devices which have a specific electrical purpose controlled by the chip or circuit. Through what is called ladder logic (because program control diagrams resemble a ladder), the laws of physics, as well as the laws of information technology, enable the fusion and functionality of the controller, the computational logic, the software, and the UAS electronics to operate in a viable manner.

An embedded cyberattack act impedes the physical processing of the controllers; this is what makes it dangerous and deadly. Malicious manipulations of the controllers can lead to logic issues resulting in software corruption or, in the worst-case scenario, physical damage to the hardware of the system due to erroneous electrical impulses in the physical manifestations of the logic carried out in the electronics attached to the controllers. The result is damage to the UAS and possibly catastrophic failure or malicious control of the UAS from rearranged logic signals. The overall result is an unexpected shift into nonpilot control either through failure (fully autonomous mode) or through a malicious third party (third-party control).

Viruses, worms, and other forms of software-based malware are critical threats for UAS systems—both aircraft and ground stations. These forms of malicious software are particularly dangerous even though they are often dismissed as issues in unmanned systems.

A final malicious issue to mention is GPS spoofing. GPS civilian signals are an open standard, with free accessibility signals. This transparency and predictability has created a major weakness—the ability to be spoofed, which means it can be replicated easily. This means that the GPS signal can literally be faked to an unmanned system causing it to follow fake GPS coordinates, which means that the malicious third-party "spoofer" can gain control of the aircraft. There are various technological ways to conduct GPS spoofing, and the equipment is not very expensive, thus this vulnerability remains a considerable threat to unmanned systems in the national airspace.

Lawmakers and legal professionals must take information security and information assurance as seriously as they do safety, as there is a direct correlation between security and safety, as mentioned above. A maliciously hijacked unmanned aircraft is a danger to everyone in the national airspace and on the ground, and an infected autonomous aircraft fares no better.

Regulations and laws governing UAS must place mandates on the minimum levels of information assurance and security that are built into unmanned systems as well as policies and procedures that are followed in unmanned systems operations. Failure to do so places the entire national airspace at risk, and we do not want to wait until a maliciously controlled UAS flies into the engine of a passenger-filled jetliner to get the idea of creating information security regulations. Security must be at the forefront of UAS regulations and laws, right up there with safety.

Regulatory Considerations

The development of a regulatory framework that is easily adaptable to technological change and innovation is key. One of the most significant problems for aircraft manufacturers and designers has been the large regulatory burden that prevents the introduction of innovative technology. The small airplane design and certification requirements of Part 23 were drafted under a long-held assumption that small airplanes are simple, slow, and generally less complex than large transport airplanes.[40]

For several decades, Part 23 offered a basic and efficient process to design, certify, and produce small airplanes. But that is no longer true. Technological advances in manned aircraft and the aviation industry, more generally, have skyrocketed over the last several decades. And, some of the most innovative technological advances are being implemented in UAS products.

Despite the rapidly evolving airplane design advancements, few significant changes have been made to the certification process for small aircraft. The FAA has instead implemented countless piecemeal rule changes to Part 23. The practice effect of those changes has resulted in crushing oversight and complex certification specifications for many small aircraft manufacturers. The costs to comply with the myriad requirements have become a barrier to producing small airplanes with modern safety equipment, and they are one of many reasons that the United States is at a fifty-year low for certified private pilots.

The FAA is in the process of reworking Part 23, and the agency should use what it has learned there to develop certification requirements for UAS, particularly the autonomous UAS. Rigid and quickly outdated rules should be discarded for certification requirements set by consensus-driven industry panels comprised of consumers, manufacturers, and other key stakeholders.

Regulators plan to reorganize Part 23 on these principles, and a similar process is already now in use for aircraft certified under the light sport aircraft category. For that new sector of the aviation industry, the consensus-driven certification model has resulted in significant benefits.[41] The bottom line is that the FAA must not let technological advances outpace the regulatory framework. Nor should it foreclose some of the newest autonomous UAS technology from seeing the light of day because it is not prepared to handle their operation.

CONCLUSION

Pilot versus autonomous control is a vital issue that must be considered when crafting legislation for unmanned systems in the national airspace. While the FAA has indicated that it will prohibit autonomous control of UAS in the national airspace, it is inevitable that fully autonomous aircraft will emerge whether the aircraft are in that state on a voluntary or involuntary basis. The issue is not if but when, and therefore

---

40.   FEDERAL AVIATION ADMINISTRATION, PART 23 – SMALL AIRPLANE CERTIFICATION PROCESS STUDY 6, 16, 20 (2009), *available at* www.faa.gov/about/office_org/...offices/.../CPS_Part_23.pdf.

41.   Robert Goyer, *Certification Rules that Make Sense*, FLYING MAGAZINE, July 2013, at 12.

a system of regulations to delineate liability must be developed to assist manufacturers, operators, and legal professionals in understanding the limits of civil liability when unmanned systems are involved in civil actions. The proposed framework considerations, based on the presented UAS Autonomy Spectrum, is an initial proposal to start the discussion in this critical area of jurisprudence. With the emerging pervasiveness of unmanned systems in the national airspace, a proactive stance in this area is mandatory to ensure that all participants in the operation and development of unmanned systems understand their roles and responsibilities in keeping the national airspace safe for everyone.

3

Unmanned Aircraft Safety, Security, and Information Assurance Regulation and Technology in the National Critical Infrastructure

CHAPTER

8

Information Assurance, Cybersecurity, and Legislation Relating to Unmanned Aircraft in the National Critical Infrastructure

Donna A. Dulo

"There is no security on this earth. Only opportunity."

—Douglas MacArthur

The purpose of this chapter and the following chapter is to discuss the information assurance[1] and cybersecurity[2] of civilian unmanned aircraft operating within the

---

1. Information Assurance is the field of protecting data and managing the risks of data in all three states of the data. Data can be in three states: storage, transit, and processing in an information system. Protecting data in all three states is critical, and information assurance encompasses the software, the hardware, the personnel, and the physical security and the organizational policies and procedures that are used to process, store, and move data.

2. "Cybersecurity" is a term that encompasses all of the technologies, policies, and procedures in protecting

national critical infrastructure.[3] Unmanned aircraft systems, which comprise the aircraft, the ground station, the payloads, the communication systems with satellite constellations, etc., are considered to be part of the industrial control infrastructure in the United States, particularly in the transportation sector. The transportation sector is one of the sixteen critical infrastructure sectors as defined by the United States government in various federal documents including Presidential Policy Directive 21 of February 2013. Industrial Control Systems (ICS)[4] in general are a part of the foundational cyber infrastructure for many industrial systems sectors such as electric power, water, manufacturing, chemical development, research and manufacturing, mining, petrochemicals, transportation, food processing, and many other systems in the critical national infrastructure. Proper information assurance is vital for these systems to ensure the safe, functional performance of these "system of systems[5]" and their corresponding processes.

Unmanned aircraft, as with manned aircraft, are an integral part of the national cyber infrastructure due to their heavy reliance on industrial control systems/embedded systems in their computers, integrated circuits, electronics, and communications systems. Unmanned aircraft are purposefully engineered to have significant computational, networking, and communications processes, and these processes rely on both hardware and software, intricately connected and coupled, to perform their aerial operations. These aerial systems subsequently pose inherent safety and security risks to the national critical infrastructure. As a result, unmanned systems have a definitive position in the national transportation infrastructure as well as in the national airspace and must be managed and operated with the high degree of safety and security standards as are manned aircraft.

---

information assets, data, networks, communication systems, human resources, and cyber infrastructure. Information assurance is a subset of cybersecurity. In the information technology domain, the term "security" is synonymous with "cybersecurity."

3. The Department of Homeland Security describes the critical infrastructure as follows: "Critical infrastructure is the backbone of our nation's economy, security and health. We know it as the power we use in our homes, the water we drink, the transportation that moves us, and the communication systems we rely on to stay in touch with friends and family. Critical infrastructure are the assets, systems, and networks, whether physical or virtual, so vital to the United States that their incapacitation or destruction would have a debilitating effect on security, national economic security, national public health or safety, or any combination thereof." http://www.dhs.gov/critical-infrastructure.

Federal law specifically defines the term "critical infrastructure" as "systems and assets, whether physical or virtual, so vital to the United States that the incapacity or destruction of such systems and assets would have a debilitating impact on security, national economic security, national public health or safety, or any combination of those matters." 42 U.S. Code § 5195c (e).

4. The term "Industrial Control System" is a generic term for the computational processes and components that control cyber-physical systems and infrastructures as aircraft, transportation systems, industrial production systems, water treatment plants, nuclear power plants, and so forth in a distributed, networked manner to ensure safe, precise, centralized, and controlled operations.

5. "System of Systems" is a systems engineering term referring to the overall primary system that is composed of and is driven by its components and subsystems.

According to the United States Industrial Control System Cyber Emergency Response Team (ICS-CERT),[6] U.S. companies that had ICS as part of their infrastructure reported a significant increase in the number of ICS-related cybersecurity incidents between 2009 and 2013. The ICS-CERT was founded in 2009, and in that year 9 incidents were reported to the response team.[7] In 2010, that number increased to 38,[8] and in 2011 it increased again to 140; in 2012, 197 incidents were reported, and in 2013, 257 incidents were reported to ICS-CERT.[9] While not all of the reported incidents were of a major cybersecurity concern, the increasing number and magnitude of these events in industrial control systems was alarming.[10]

Currently, US-CERT has issued many warnings about increasing threats to ICS, including an alert in May 2013 concerning blended threat elements[11] that are increasing the risk of control systems attack. These threats include newer and more sophisticated exploit tools targeting programmable logic controllers (PLC) and supervisory control and data acquisition systems (SCADA)[12] which could use simple tools such as Internet search engines as shortcuts to finding the vulnerable PLC or SCADA targets.[13] Manned aircraft systems use embedded PLC and SCADA systems to various degrees, as well as other vulnerable electronic components, and unmanned systems follow suit with PLC and SCADA components in their aircraft systems, networking, communications, and ground control stations. In fact, the network and wireless-communication-based

---

6. ICS-CERT materials and reports are vital to the management and operation of industrial control systems and can be found at https://ics-cert.us-cert.gov/.

7. ICS-CERT, ICS-CERT INCIDENT RESPONSE SUMMARY REPORT 2009–2011, (2012), http://ics-cert.us-cert .gov/sites/default/files/ICS-CERT%20Incident%20Response%20Summary%20Report%20%282009-2011 %29.pdf.

8. ICS-CERT, ICS-CERT INCIDENT RESPONSE SUMMARY REPORT 2012 (March, 2013), https://ics-cert.us-cert .gov/sites/default/files/documents/Year_in_Review_FY2012_Final.pdf

9. ICS-CERT, ICS-CERT INCIDENT RESPONSE SUMMARY REPORT 2013 (February, 2014), https://ics-cert .us-cert.gov/sites/default/files/documents/Year_In_Review_FY2013_Final.pdf.

10. ICS-CERT, (2012). *Id.*

11. A blended threat is a threat that has multiple attack vectors designed to inflict maximum damage in a minimal amount of time.

12. A programmable logic controller (PLC) is a type of digital computational device that uses logic to control real-time systems such as cyberphysical systems, of which an unmanned system is an example. PLCs are useful due to their immunity to electronic noise, their ruggedness in various temperatures and states of vibration, and their ability to be used in multiple systems using both analog and digital inputs. Supervisory control and data acquisition systems (SCADA) are centralized control systems, which usually manage an entire system of systems and contain many components including PLCs. They manage data throughout the system of systems and contain databases of information about the system and can provide autonomous control of the overall system while monitoring for safety of the overall system's operation. The danger of these types of controllers is that they control actual physical hardware, so that a security threat can inflict physical damage to a system by moving the actuators or physical components controlled by the controllers. This causes a higher dimension of damage to a system than traditional data type threats, which manipulate, steal, or reduce access to data. In an aircraft, for example, a malicious third party can take control of the aircraft through its cyberphysical control systems, resulting in a hostile takeover of the physical aircraft.

13. ICS-CERT, ICS-ALERT - 12-046-01A INCREASING THREAT TO INDUSTRIAL CONTROL SYSTEMS (UPDATE A) (May 8, 2013), http://ics-cert.us-cert.gov/alerts/ICS-ALERT-12-046-01A.

nature of unmanned aircraft and their reliance on remote communications and signals make them particularly vulnerable targets in the air.

In their original implementations, industrial control systems (ICS) and embedded systems were only vulnerable to local threats, but the threat horizon has greatly expanded due to the fact that many systems are now connected by data and communication networks, as well as the Internet. This trend in system connectivity has increased the vulnerability of industrial control systems as they are increasingly connected to potential external threats, many of them worldwide. External threats can range from amateur hackers to international crime rings and rogue nations. In addition, particularly with unmanned systems that use wireless communications, there are increased threats from malicious entities which are relatively close to or in the wireless range of the operational aircraft and ground control systems. These entities do not need to have direct access to the physical systems to cause damage, creating a high vulnerability envelope within the entire wireless range of operations.[14] ICS and embedded systems threats are thus local and worldwide including "hostile governments, terrorist groups, disgruntled employees, malicious intruders, complexities, accidents, natural disasters, as well as malicious or accidental actions by insiders."[15]

The increase in threats to cyberphysical systems[16] has been increasing worldwide, however several factors have contributed specifically to the escalation of risks specific to industrial control systems, including "the (1) adoption of standardized technologies with known vulnerabilities, (2) connectivity of control systems to other networks, (3) constraints on the use of existing security technologies and practices, (4) insecure remote connections, and (5) widespread availability of technical information about control systems."[17]

Industrial control systems are by necessity distributed systems[18] with complex and highly automated processes, networks, and ancillary computing assets. ICS implementations are increasingly vulnerable to information assurance and cyberthreats. The increasing complexity of the engineering structure of industrial control systems compounds these vulnerabilities, increasing exposure to potential attackers

---

14. NIST, SPECIAL PUBLICATION 800-82 REVISION 1. GUIDE TO INDUSTRIAL CONTROL SYSTEMS (ICS) SECURITY (May, 2013), http://dx.doi/org/10.6028/NIST.SP.800-82r1.

15. *Id.*

16. Cyberphysical systems are hardware systems that are heavily controlled by computational processes and software and are generally found in networked configurations. This networking of the systems distinguished cyberphysical systems from traditional computational electronic embedded systems. Unmanned aircraft are considered cyberphysical systems due to their hardware and software systems control through wireless networks and communication systems.

17. GAO, CRITICAL INFRASTRUCTURE PROTECTION CHALLENGES IN SECURING CONTROL SYSTEMS, GAO-04-140T (October, 2003).

18. A distributed system is a computational system where software and hardware components are disbursed in different locations, in many cases globally, but communicate efficiently with each other in a networked manner to solve computational problems through unified goals and the independence of each component in the overall system.

and unintentional errors in use. The increase in threats to all types of ICS has been "acknowledged across the federal government, including the National Institute of Standards and Technology (NIST), the Department of Homeland Security (DHS), the Department of Energy (DOE), and the Federal Energy Regulatory Commission (FERC)."[19]

Integrity, availability, and confidentiality are foundational ICS and information assurance concepts that will be discussed throughout this chapter and are central to ICS cybersecurity programs and related regulations and legislation. These three concepts are therefore vital to mitigating blended threats and reducing system-wide vulnerabilities in ICS sectors and sector components such as unmanned aircraft in the transportation sector. Efforts by the U.S. Government in conjunction with the efforts of U.S. industries and research by academia together form a vital set of tools to combat such threats including those in the unmanned aviation domain.

However, the area of unmanned aircraft security and information assurance is in its early developmental state. As such, the full integration of unmanned aircraft into the national airspace challenges the overall security of the transportation sector and increases the safety challenges correspondingly. Therefore, laws and technology in the unmanned aircraft domain must be fully developed and reflective of each other to treat unmanned aircraft as vital security-centric entities and participants in the national transportation system to ensure that unmanned aircraft flying in the national airspace are safe and secure throughout their flight operations. The goal of this chapter and the next is to present foundational security concepts and the concepts of industrial control systems in the context of current legislative acts to demonstrate the critical nature of the fusion of unmanned aircraft security, information assurance technology, and the law.

UNITED STATES CRITICAL INFRASTRUCTURE LEGISLATION

Only since 9/11 have critical infrastructures of the United States been recognized as potential targets for cyberattacks. However, during this time the government has acted, albeit very slowly, to ensure that the national critical infrastructure is adequately protected as a national security concern. This section briefly discusses the legislation and acts meant to protect the nation's industrial control systems from cyberattacks.

---

19. NIST, NISTIR 7628, GUIDELINES FOR SMART GRID CYBER SECURITY: VOL. 1, SMART GRID CYBER SECURITY STRATEGY, ARCHITECTURE, AND HIGH LEVEL REQUIREMENTS (August, 2010).

Presidential Decision Directive 63

In 1998, President Bill Clinton signed Presidential Decision Directive 63 (PDD 63) to "swiftly eliminate any significant vulnerability to both physical and cyber-attacks on our critical infrastructures, including especially our cyber systems."[20] PDD 63 states that the United States "shall achieve and maintain the ability to protect the nation's critical infrastructures from intentional acts that would significantly diminish the abilities of:

- The Federal Government to perform essential national security missions and to ensure the general public health and safety;
- State and local governments to maintain order and to deliver minimum essential public services;
- The private sector to ensure the orderly functioning of the economy and the delivery of essential telecommunications, energy, financial, and transportation services."[21]

PDD 63 states the president's intent to assure the continuity and viability of United States critical infrastructures, particularly cyberdriven and cyberphysical infrastructures. This directive also places forth a strong plan to reduce cyber vulnerabilities by:

- Assessing the vulnerabilities of the sector to cyber or physical attacks
- Recommending a plan to eliminate significant vulnerabilities
- Proposing a system for identifying and preventing attempted major attacks
- Developing a plan for alerting, containing, and rebuffing an attack in progress
- Reconstituting minimum essential capabilities in the aftermath of an attack[22]

In essence, PDD 63 was a major step forward in the initial development of a national plan for the protection of the critical infrastructure of the United States, of which industrial control systems are a major part. Additionally, it was one of the first legislations to expand on the threat of cyberattacks to the nation's critical infrastructure, which set the stage for a national cybersecurity program.

The Critical Infrastructures Protection Act of 2001

The Patriot Act, signed into law by President George W. Bush in October of 2001, specifically addressed the critical infrastructure of the United States in Title X, Sec.1016

---

20. THE WHITE HOUSE, PRESIDENTIAL DIRECTIVE PDD/NSC-63, CRITICAL INFRASTRUCTURE PROTECTION, WASHINGTON, DC (May 22, 1998).
21. *Id.*
22. *Id.*

(e) which was codified as 42 USC § 5195c, and is known as "The Critical Infra-structures Protection Act of 2001"[23] (CIPA). The CIPA of 2001 states the following congressional findings, which bear a direct impact upon industrial control systems:

- The information revolution has transformed the conduct of business and the operations of government as well as the infrastructure relied upon for the defense and national security of the United States.
- Private business, government, and the national security apparatus increasingly depend on an interdependent network of critical physical and informational infrastructures including telecommunications, energy, financial services, water, and transportation sectors.
- A continuous national effort is required to ensure the reliable provision of cyber and physical infrastructure services critical to maintaining the national defense, continuity of government, economic prosperity, and the quality of life in the United States.
- The national effort requires extensive modeling and analytic capabilities for the purposes of evaluating appropriate mechanisms to ensure the stability of these complex and interdependent systems, and to underpin policy recommendations, so as to achieve the continuous viability and adequate protection of the critical infrastructure of the Nation.[24]

The CIPA of 2001 further states that it is the policy of the United States

1. that any physical or virtual disruption of the operation of the critical infra-structures of the United States be rare, brief, geographically limited in effect, manageable, and minimally detrimental to the economy, human and government services, and national security of the United States;
2. that actions necessary to achieve the policy stated in paragraph (1) be carried out in a public-private partnership involving corporate and non-governmental organizations; and
3. to have in place a comprehensive and effective program to ensure the continuity of essential Federal Government functions under all circumstances.[25]

The CIPA of 2001 was a second vital step forward in the development of founda-tional infrastructure protection for the national assets with cyberprotection being

---

23. Critical Infrastructures Protection Act of 2001, 42 U.S.C. § 5195c.
24. *Id.*
25. *Id.*

front and center, paving the way for increased research and development of modern protective measures.

National Strategy for the Physical Protection of Critical Infrastructures and Key Assets

The third major act of the government was in February 2003 when President George W. Bush released the National Strategy for the Physical Protection of Critical Infrastructures and Key Assets, hereinafter the "National Strategy." The National Strategy aligned very closely with PDD 63 and the Critical Infrastructures Protection Act, and addressed the protection of several critical components of the national critical infrastructure, including many Industrial Control Systems such as the chemical industry, manufacturing, water, transportation, and the energy industry.[26]

The National Strategy was developed in light of the attacks of September 11, 2001, which demonstrated the nation's vulnerability to terrorist attacks. The strategic objectives of the National Strategy include the following:

- Identifying and assuring the protection of those infrastructures and assets deemed most critical in terms of national level public health and safety, governance, economic and national security, and public confidence consequences;
- Providing timely warning and assuring the protection of those infrastructures and assets that face a specific, imminent threat; and
- Assuring the protection of other infrastructures and assets that may become terrorist targets over time by pursuing specific initiatives and enabling a collaborative environment in which federal, state, and local governments and the private sector can better protect the infrastructure and assets they command.[27]

The National Strategy provides more specifics than PDD 63 and the CIPA of 2001 and is the first document to identify critical infrastructure areas that need specific protection, such as the transportation sector. This document is the foundational document to the establishment of the sixteen critical infrastructures that are currently in place today.

Presidential Policy Directive 21

The Presidential Policy Directive PPD-21 signed into law on February 12, 2013, entitled "Critical Infrastructure Security and Resilience" advanced a "national unity of effort to strengthen and maintain secure, functioning, and resilient critical infrastructures."[28]

---

26. THE WHITE HOUSE, NATIONAL STRATEGY FOR THE PHYSICAL PROTECTION OF CRITICAL INFRASTRUCTURES AND KEY ASSETS, Washington, D.C. (February, 2003).

27. *Id.*

28. THE WHITE HOUSE, PRESIDENTIAL POLICY DIRECTIVE 21: CRITICAL INFRASTRUCTURE SECURITY AND RESILIENCE, Washington, DC (February 12, 2013).

This directive seeks three specific strategic imperatives that will drive the federal approach to strengthen the security[29] of the critical infrastructure:

- Refine and clarify functional relationships across the federal government to advance the national unity of effort to strengthen the critical infrastructure security and resilience;
- Enable effective information exchange by identifying baseline data and systems requirements for the federal government; and
- Implement an integration and analysis function to inform planning and operations decisions regarding critical infrastructure.[30]

The PPD-21 is much more extensive and comprehensive than its predecessors and is also more information technology specific in its plans and policies, noting that major protections of critical infrastructure come from the cyber end of the spectrum. This was a major step forward in protecting critical infrastructure from cyberattacks.

It is also important to note in PPD-21 the emphasis of resilience.[31] "Resilience" is a term that has been emerging in the engineering literature over the past decade. The seminal researchers of resilience engineering state that resilience is a paradigm for safety management that "focuses on how to help people cope with complexity under pressure to achieve success . . . A resilient organization treats safety as a core value, not a commodity that can be counted . . . one way to measure resilience is the ability to create foresight—to anticipate the changing shape of risk, before failure and harm occurs."[32]

Resilience is thus the ability to cope with change in real time to mitigate issues of safety, security, and risk before they escalate into catastrophic issues. Resilience engineering is a complementary process, not a competing process, with traditional safety and security engineering. Resilience engineering systems such as software systems aid in the prevention or mitigation of system errors missed by normal safety and security engineering and testing cycles. Thus, resilience engineering transcends traditional engineering processes and presents new methods to ensure system safety and security through the elimination or management of failure states in a system.[33] It is a well-suited concept for critical infrastructure protection.

---

29. PPD-21 defines security as "reducing the risk to critical infrastructure by physical means or defense cyber measures to intrusions, attacks, or the effects of natural or man-made disasters."

30. The White House (February 12, 2013). *Id.*

31. PPD-21 defines resilience as "the ability to prepare for and adapt to changing conditions, and withstand and recover rapidly from disruptions. Resilience includes the ability to withstand and recover from deliberate attacks, accidents, or naturally occurring threats or incidents."

32. E. HOLLNAGEL, D. WOODS, & N. LEVESON, RESILIENCE ENGINEERING: CONCEPTS AND PRECEPTS (Ashgate) (2006).

33. D. Dulo, *Resilience Engineering in Critical Long Term Aerospace Software Systems: A New Approach*

The PPD-21 places a significant emphasis on research and development of security for critical infrastructure, particularly the cyber infrastructure. The directive states that the Director of Homeland Security in conjunction with other agencies shall provide activities that seek to strengthen and promote and strengthen the security and resilience of the nation's critical infrastructure including:

- Promoting research and development to enable the secure and resilient design and construction of critical infrastructure and more secure accompanying cybertechnology;
- Enhancing modeling capabilities to determine potential impacts on critical infrastructure of an incident or threat scenario, as well as cascading effects on other sectors;
- Facilitating initiatives to incentivize cybersecurity investments and the adoption of critical infrastructure design features that strengthen all hazards security and resilience; and
- Prioritizing efforts to support the strategic guidance issues by the Secretary of Homeland Security.[34]

Note the increased emphasis on cybersecurity as compared to the earlier laws and directives concerning critical infrastructure. Reviewing the directive, one cannot help but notice a distinct emphasis on cybersecurity placing industrial control systems at the forefront of the protection of the critical infrastructure protection of the United States.

The PDD-21 further develops sixteen critical infrastructure sectors and assigns oversight of these sectors to a federal agency or set of federal agencies. Table 8.1 describes these sectors and their sector-specific agency.

Table 8.1 The Critical Infrastructure Sectors[35]

Critical Infrastructure Sector	Sector Specific Agency
Chemical	Department of Homeland Security
Commercial Facilities	Department of Homeland Security
Communications	Department of Homeland Security
Critical Manufacturing	Department of Homeland Security
Dams	Department of Homeland Security
Defense Industrial Base	Department of Defense

to Spacecraft Software Safety, JOURNAL OF THE BRITISH INTERPLANETARY SOCIETY. Vol. 67. No. 4. (April 2014).
   34. The White House (February, 2003). *Id.*
   35. *Id.*

Critical Infrastructure Sector	Sector Specific Agency
Emergency Services	Department of Homeland Security
Energy	Department of Energy
Financial Services	Department of the Treasury
Food & Agriculture	Departments of Agriculture and Health & Human Services
Government Facilities	Department of Homeland Security & General Services Administration
Healthcare and Public Health	Department of Health and Human Services
Information Technology	Department of Homeland Security
Nuclear Reactors, Materials, and Waste	Department of Homeland Security
Transportation Systems	Department of Homeland Security and Department of Transportation
Water and Wastewater Systems	Environmental Protection Agency

The transportation sector is overseen by both the Department of Homeland Security and the Department of Transportation due to the intensive safety aspect of the sector. Safety is highly dependent on the security of a system, and as a result, the critical infrastructure of transportation systems requires the collaboration of both agencies to ensure the safety of the sector.

According to the Department of Homeland Security, the transportation sector, as related to aviation, "includes aircraft, air traffic control systems, and approximately 450 commercial airports and 19,000 additional airports, heliports, and landing strips. This mode includes civil and joint use military airports, heliports, short takeoff and landing ports, and seaplane bases."[36] These numbers will certainly rise with the addition of unmanned aircraft heliports and airfields, as well as mobile launch sites.

The information assurance and cybersecurity of unmanned aircraft in the national critical infrastructure relies heavily on three of the critical infrastructure sectors: the transportation sector, the information technology sector, and the communications sector. All three sectors provide vital information assurance and cybersecurity as well as physical security structures for the safe and secure operation of unmanned aircraft in the national airspace. Each sector provides critical functional foundations, strategies, and plans to ensure comprehensive intersector operations and security management. The sector plans serve as annexes to the overall National Infrastructure Protection Plan.

---

36. DEPARTMENT OF HOMELAND SECURITY (2014), http://www.dhs.gov/transportation-systems-sector.

National Infrastructure Protection Plan

The National Infrastructure Protection Plan (NIPP 2013)[37] is an evolved document that stems from the original 2006 version that was developed in response to Title II of the Homeland Security Act of 2002 (as amended)[38] and revised in 2009. NIPP 2013 was streamlined and adapted to current national security risk, policy, and strategic environment and fulfills the requirements of PPD-21. The plan was developed with leaders and stakeholders of all sixteen critical infrastructure sectors, by leaders from all fifty states, and from leaders and experts from all levels of government and private industry, making it a comprehensive document reflective of universal needs and requirements of members and organizations in the national critical infrastructure.

The NIPP 2013 was updated as required by PPD-21 and is consistent with Executive Order 13636, *Improving Critical Infrastructure Cybersecurity*,[39] which "directs the Federal Government to coordinate with critical infrastructure owners and operators to improve information sharing and collaboratively develop and implement risk-based approaches to cybersecurity."[40] NIPP 2013 also aligns with the National Preparedness System called for in Presidential Policy Directive 8 (PPD-8), *National Preparedness*.[41] In addition, the NIPP 2013 aligns with two other policy documents: the president's *Climate Action Plan*[42] and the *National Strategy for Information Sharing and Safeguarding (NSISS)*.[43]

The vision of NIPP 2013 is "[a] Nation in which physical and cyber critical infrastructure remain secure and resilient, with vulnerabilities reduced, consequences minimized, threats identified and disrupted, and response and recovery hastened."[44] Its corresponding mission is to "[s]trengthen the security and resilience of the Nation's critical infrastructure, by managing physical and cyber risks through the collaborative

---

37. DEPARTMENT OF HOMELAND SECURITY (2013), NATIONAL INFRASTRUCTURE PROTECTION PLAN, PARTNERING FOR CRITICAL INFRASTRUCTURE SECURITY AND RESILIENCE, WASHINGTON D.C., http://www.dhs.gov/sites/default/files/publications/National-Infrastructure-Protection-Plan-2013-508.pdf.

38. HOMELAND SECURITY ACT OF 2002. PUBLIC LAW 107-296, 107TH CONGRESS, (November 25, 2002), https://www.dhs.gov/xlibrary/assets/hr_5005_enr.pdf.

39. OFFICE OF THE PRESIDENT OF THE UNITED STATES, EXECUTIVE ORDER 13636, IMPROVING CRITICAL INFRASTRUCTURE CYBERSECURITY, WASHINGTON D.C. (February 19, 2013), http://www.gpo.gov/fdsys/pkg/FR-2013-02-19/pdf/2013-03915.pdf.

40. DEPARTMENT OF HOMELAND SECURITY (2013). *Id.*

41. PRESIDENTIAL POLICY DIRECTIVE PPD-8: NATIONAL PREPAREDNESS, WASHINGTON D.C. (March 30, 2011), http://www.dhs.gov/presidential-policy-directive-8-national-preparedness.

42. THE WHITE HOUSE, THE PRESIDENT'S CLIMATE ACTION PLAN, WASHINGTON D.C. (June, 2013), http://www.whitehouse.gov/sites/default/files/image/president27sclimateactionplan.pdf.

43. THE WHITE HOUSE, NATIONAL STRATEGY FOR INFORMATION SHARING AND SAFEGUARDING, WASHINGTON D.C. (December, 2012), http://www.whitehouse.gov/sites/default/files/docs/2012sharingstrategy_1.pdf.

44. DEPARTMENT OF HOMELAND SECURITY (2013). *Id.*

and integrated efforts of the critical infrastructure community."[45] The NIPP 2013 has seven core tenants that align closely with its vision and mission:

1. Risk should be identified and managed in a coordinated and comprehensive way across the critical infrastructure community to enable the effective allocation of security and resilience resources.
2. Understanding and addressing risks from cross-sector dependencies and interdependencies is essential to enhancing critical infrastructure security and resilience.
3. Gaining knowledge of infrastructure risk and interdependencies requires information sharing across the critical infrastructure community.
4. The partnership approach to critical infrastructure security and resilience recognizes the unique perspectives and comparative advantages of the diverse critical infrastructure community.
5. Regional and SLTT[46] partnerships are crucial to developing shared perspectives on gaps and actions to improve critical infrastructure security and resilience.
6. Infrastructure critical to the United States transcends national boundaries, requiring cross-border collaboration, mutual assistance, and other cooperative agreements.
7. Security and resilience should be considered during the design of assets, systems, and networks.[47]

Overall the NIPP 2013 is the foundational and core document for the protection of the national critical infrastructure, presenting strategies, policies, procedures, and plans to serve as the central tenants for the plans of the individual sectors within the national critical infrastructure. The individual critical infrastructure sector plans are considered annexes to the NIPP 2013. Thus, the operation of unmanned aircraft in the national critical infrastructure would be informed by the NIPP 2013 and the relevant sector specific plans.

Of the sixteen critical infrastructure sectors, the three most relevant to the operation of unmanned aircraft in the national airspace are the transportation sector, the information technology sector, and the communications sector, as shown in Figure 8.1. These are discussed in detail below.

---

45. *Id.*
46. SLTT means state, local, tribal, and territorial governments.
47. Department of Homeland Security (2013). *Id.*

Figure 8.1

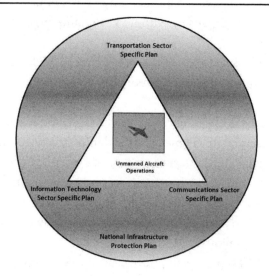

The Context of the National and Sector Specific Plans (Photo courtesy of Donna Dulo)

Homeland Security Presidential Directive 7 and the Transportation Sector Specific Plan

The Homeland Security Presidential Directive 7 (HSPD-7) was enacted on December 17, 2003, and is the basis for the transportation sector's specific plan for critical infrastructure protection.[48] It established a "national policy for Federal departments and agencies to identify and prioritize United States critical infrastructure and key resources and to protect them from terrorist attacks."[49] For the transportation sector, it specifically states that "The Department of Transportation and the Department (of Homeland Security) will collaborate on all matters relating to transportation security and transportation infrastructure protection. The Department of Transportation is responsible for operating the national air space system. The Department of Transportation and the Department (of Homeland Security) will collaborate in regulating the transportation of hazardous materials by all modes (including pipelines)."[50]

Both the Department of Homeland Security and the Department of Transportation department heads and corresponding agency heads, according to HSPD-7, are "responsible for the identification, prioritization, assessment, remediation, and protection of their respective internal critical infrastructure and key resources. Consistent with the Federal Information Security Management Act of 2002, agencies will identify

---

48. HDPD-7 was superseded by PPD-21; however, its verbiage and influence on the Transportation Specific Plan is cited in the current Transportation Specific Plan, which was published before PPD-21.

49. HOMELAND SECURITY PRESIDENTIAL DIRECTIVE 7, CRITICAL INFRASTRUCTURE IDENTIFICATION, PRIORITIZATION, AND PROTECTION (December 17, 2003), http://www.dhs.gov/homeland-security-presidential-directive-7.

50. *Id.*

and provide information security protections commensurate with the risk and magnitude of the harm resulting from the unauthorized access, use, disclosure, disruption, modification, or destruction of information."[51]

The Transportation Sector Specific Plan: An Annex to the National Infrastructure Protection Plan[52] (the "Plan") is the strategic plan for the transportation sector which fulfills the requirements of Homeland Security Presidential Directive 7: Critical Infrastructure Identification, Prioritization, and Protection, and the requirements of the Intelligence Reform and Terrorism Prevention Act of 2004 (as amended) for the National Strategy for Transportation Security.[53]

The vision of the transportation sector, according to the Plan, is "[a] secure and resilient transportation system, enabling legitimate travelers and goods to move without significant disruption of commerce, undue fear of harm, or loss of civil liberties." And its mission is to "continuously improve the risk posture of transportation systems serving the Nation."[54] The sector has developed four goals to help fulfill its mission:

- **Goal 1:** Prevent and deter acts of terrorism using, or against, the transportation system;
- **Goal 2:** Enhance the all-hazard preparedness and resilience of the global transportation system to safeguard U.S. national interests;
- **Goal 3:** Improve the effective use of resources for transportation security; and
- **Goal 4:** Improve sector situational awareness, understanding, and collaboration.[55]

The Plan notes the critical nature of cross-section critical dependencies between the various sectors and stresses that all sectors must work with full cooperation and coordination to ensure critical infrastructure protection. For example, the Plan states, in part, that:

- The Communications Sector co-locates much of its networking equipment (routers, fiber-optic cable, etc.) along existing transportation routes (rail lines, highway tunnels, and bridges), the destruction of which may impact service availability

---

51. *Id.*
52. DEPARTMENT OF HOMELAND SECURITY, THE TRANSPORTATION SECTOR SPECIFIC PLAN: AN ANNEX TO THE NATIONAL INFRASTRUCTURE PROTECTION PLAN, WASHINGTON D.C. (2010), http://www.dhs.gov/xlibrary/assets/nipp-ssp-transportation-systems-2010.pdf.
53. 49 U.S.C. 114 (s), as enacted by the Intelligence Reform and Terrorism Prevention Act, P.L. 108-458 § 4001, (2004), as amended by the Implementing Recommendations of the 9/11 Commission Act, P.L. 110-53 § 1202 (2007).
54. DEPARTMENT OF HOMELAND SECURITY (2010). *Id.*
55. *Id.*

in wide geographic areas and complicate response efforts in the event of a major incident.

- The transportation network's efficient operations are increasingly dependent upon functions, products, and services provided by Communications Sector and IT Sector entities. Producers and providers of these services, such as the IT and Communications Sectors, have unique roles in cybersecurity, and responsibilities in enhancing the security and resiliency of their cyber infrastructure.
- The Emergency Services Sector depends on the resilience of the transportation network to respond effectively to emergencies.
- All sectors rely on transportation service for access, supplies, and emergency services.[56]

This cross-functional critical set of dependencies is important, noting the reliance of transportation systems, such as information technology driven cyberphysical manned and unmanned aircraft on the communication, information technology, and emergency sectors, among others. The reliance goes both ways as well, making the critical infrastructure a highly complex, interdependent system. As a result, all entities within the critical infrastructure have an inherent responsibility to the overall system itself. The security requirement of these systems, therefore, is self-evident.

Overall, the Plan ensures the fulfillment of The President's Guiding Principles for Homeland Security:

> Ensuring the resilience of our critical infrastructure is vital to homeland security. Working with the private sector and government partners at all levels, we will develop an effective, holistic, critical infrastructure protection and resiliency plan that centers on investments in business, technology, civil society, government, and education. We will invest in our Nation's most pressing short- and long-term infrastructure needs, including modernizing our electrical grid; upgrading our highway, rail, maritime, and aviation infrastructure; enhancing security within our chemical and nuclear sectors; and safeguarding the public transportation systems that Americans use every day.[57]

Additionally, the Plan sets forth specific models and risk management frameworks for the secure and resilient operation of the transportation sector as a whole, ensuring that all entities within the system are safe with the highest degree of security possible.

---

56. *Id.*
57. *Id.*

The Information Technology Sector Specific Plan

The information technology sector is central to the safe operations of the transportation sector and plays a significant role in the information assurance and cybersecurity of the transportation sector. Therefore, it is vital that both sectors are understood in tandem along with the communications sector, which provides the glue for the safe and secure operation of the overall transportation infrastructure. The Department of Homeland Security states that the Information Technology Sector is "central to the nation's security, economy, and public health and safety. Businesses, governments, academia, and private citizens are increasingly dependent upon Information Technology Sector functions. These virtual and distributed functions produce and provide hardware, software, and information technology systems and services, and—in collaboration with the Communications Sector—the Internet. The sector's complex and dynamic environment makes identifying threats and assessing vulnerabilities difficult and requires that these tasks be addressed in a collaborative and creative fashion."[58]

As with the transportation sector, the information technology sector has a published plan, the Information Technology Sector Specific Plan: An Annex to the National Infrastructure Protection Plan (the "Plan").[59] The Plan has six critical function areas:

1. Provide IT products and services;
2. Provide incident management capabilities;
3. Provide domain name resolution services;
4. Provide identity management and associated trust support services;
5. Provide Internet-based content, information, and communication services;
6. Provide Internet routing, access, and connection services.[60]

The Plan focuses on the aggregate of all information technology: the owners, operators, hardware, software, systems, communications, and services in conjunction with systems development, integration, operations, and overall communications and security. This holistic approach provides a comprehensive safety, security, and operational posture for the sector to serve its constituent sectors in a proactive manner. Since the transportation sector is highly reliant on information systems, the understanding and application of the Plan and its contents as well as the services of this sector are vital.

Unmanned aircraft operators are immersed in information technology, from local wireless clouds to satellite-provided Internet services. This wide scope of networking

---

58. DEPARTMENT OF HOMELAND SECURITY (2014), http://www.dhs.gov/information-technology-sector.

59. DEPARTMENT OF HOMELAND SECURITY, INFORMATION TECHNOLOGY SECTOR SPECIFIC PLAN, WASHINGTON D.C. (2010), http://www.dhs.gov/sites/default/files/publications/IT%20Sector%20Specific%20Plan%202010.pdf.

60. *Id.*

and connectivity places a burden on unmanned aircraft operators to provide proper security as a member of the transportation sector and as a customer of the information technology sector, coupled with the communication sector. The Plan provides guidance, and the information technology sector provides support for these operations. An inspection of the goals of the sector as provided in the Plan make it clear of the sector's importance to unmanned aircraft operators:

- **Goal 1**: Identify, assess, and manage risks to the IT Sector's critical functions and international dependencies.
- **Goal 2**: Improve situational awareness during normal operations, potential or realized threats and disruptions, intentional or unintentional incidents, and crippling attacks (cyber or physical) against IT Sector infrastructure, technological emergencies and failures, or presidentially declared disasters.
- **Goal 3**: Enhance the capabilities of public and private sector partners to respond to and recover from realized threats and disruptions, intentional or unintentional incidents, and crippling attacks (cyber or physical) against IT Sector infrastructure, technological emergencies or failures, or presidentially declared disasters, and develop mechanisms for reconstitution.
- **Goal 4**: Drive continuous improvement of the IT Sector's risk management, situational awareness, and response, recovery, and reconstitution capabilities.[61]

The Plan presents the sector's functionally driven top-down approach to risk management which maps well to and is a critical part of information assurance in all sectors. This approach focuses on two levels, the individual enterprise level, which is the level of the organizations within the sector, and the sector/national level. At the individual enterprise level, the information technology sector focuses on cybersecurity initiatives and best practices for the organization. At the sector and national level, the risk management is mapped to the six critical function areas as described above.

With unmanned operations, the enterprise level initiatives of risk management would focus on individual operators and their unmanned systems infrastructure including all aircraft, ground control stations, communications equipment, networking equipment, and related computational systems within the organization. However, the sector and national level focus would be utilized as well since the unmanned aircraft would be flying in the national airspace under the management of air traffic control systems and infrastructure, making the information technology sector a central and holistic influence on unmanned systems information assurance and cybersecurity. Since unmanned aircraft operating in the national airspace pose dangers to other air

---

61. *Id.*

traffic and those on the ground, both risk management level approaches would be paramount and would be required to work in tandem to ensure full spectrum information assurance and security.

The Communications Sector Specific Plan

The Communications Sector Specific Plan: An Annex to the National Infrastructure Protection Plan (the Plan)[62] is a foundational sector that, like the Information Technology Sector, supports many of the other sectors in the critical infrastructure. According to the Department of Homeland Security, "The Communications Sector is an integral component of the U.S. economy, underlying the operations of all businesses, public safety organizations, and government. Presidential Policy Directive 21 identifies the Communications Sector as critical because it provides an 'enabling function' across all critical infrastructure sectors.[63]"

Since communications is central to almost all transportation sector functions, whether in the skies, on the water, in space, or on the ground, the communications sector and its infrastructure protection are central to the safety and security of the transportation sector. The Plan of the sector is similar in design and scope to the other plans. The Plan's vision statement is clear: "The United States has a critical reliance on assured communications. The communications sector strives to ensure that the Nation's communications networks and systems are secure, resilient, and rapidly restored in the event of disruption."[64] This statement reflects the foundational and central role of the communications sector in the national critical infrastructure, as it supports many of the other sectors in their basic operations. The Plan has three goals for the sector:

- **Goal 1**: Protect and enhance the overall physical and logical health of communications.
- **Goal 2**: Rapidly reconstitute critical communications services in the event of disruption and mitigate cascading effects.
- **Goal 3**: Improve the sector's national security and emergency preparedness (NS/EP) posture with federal, state, local, tribal, international, and private sector entities to reduce risk.

The communication sector, as a central part of the national critical infrastructure, places a high value on risk management and the security of the national communications

---

62. Department of Homeland Security, Communications Sector Specific Plan, Washington D.C. (2010), http://web.archive.org/web/20141107223442/http://www.dhs.gov/xlibrary/assets/nipp-ssp-communications-2010.pdf.

63. Department of Homeland Security, Communications Sector (2014), http://www.dhs.gov/communications-sector.

64. Department of Homeland Security, Communications Sector Specific Plan (2010). *Id.*

infrastructure. With critical communications down, whether ground, air, sea, or space based, other sectors may become partially or completely paralyzed. This emphasizes the vital functional nature of the communications sector and its central role in national security and in the security of sectors such as the transportation sector. As with the other critical sectors that affect unmanned aircraft operations, the communications sector serves to protect all unmanned aircraft systems assets in operation in the national airspace. Correspondingly, operators of unmanned aircraft must clearly understand the communications sector and the risks involved with the safe, reliable, and resilient operation of communications systems within the sector.

CONCLUSION

The federal government, over the past decade and a half, has been developing laws and directives to protect the national critical infrastructure. Increasingly, these laws and directives are becoming more cyberspecific as the critical nature of industrial control systems security has moved to the forefront of critical infrastructure security. With unmanned systems increasingly permeating the skies and with the highly integrated cyberphysical nature of them, protection of the national airspace is vital for the safety and security of those flying in the national airspace or residing under it as well as those affected by the data and communications of unmanned system operations.

It is imperative that unmanned aircraft operators become familiar with the national critical infrastructure and the methods of safety and security that are required to operate within it. The next chapter describes, at a high level, the information assurance and cybersecurity foundations of operating cyberphysical systems in the national airspace and the technologies and concepts that surround these concepts. Along with the theme of the book, technology and the law need to be coupled partners, and as such, understanding the technology of information assurance is important to enable the sound compliance with the regulations of the systems that are being operated. The following chapter provides these foundations.

9

Technological Context of Cybersecurity and Unmanned Aircraft in the National Critical Infrastructure

Donna A. Dulo

"I know there's a proverb which says 'To err is human,' but a human error is nothing to what a computer can do if it tries."

—Agatha Christie, *Hallowe'en Party*

This chapter continues the discussion on critical cybersecurity issues in the context of aircraft-based industrial control systems (ICS) information assurance in the critical infrastructure, as related to the transportation sector and unmanned aircraft. It is important to map the technology with the regulations to ensure that proper fusion of the two takes place to ensure compliance, safety, and security. A basic understanding of industrial control systems and information technology systems is necessary to ensure that safety and security processes are followed and enforced in accordance with the regulations.

THE CIA TRIAD AND UNMANNED AIRCRAFT INFORMATION ASSURANCE

As a part of the national critical infrastructure, unmanned aircraft and the industrial control systems/embedded systems within their structures are at risk for security issues during both their operational and nonoperational phases. A primary security issue for any integrated control system such as an unmanned aircraft is the prevention of unauthorized access to the sensitive control systems through third-party and noncontrolled external systems. As such, integrity is the most critical security requirement. Another security issue is the availability of the systems, assuring continued availability throughout the operational cycle. Additionally, a critical security concern is confidentiality of the system data controls. These issues, coupled with the complex "system of systems" nature of unmanned aircraft, make the information assurance of unmanned systems in the national airspace a significant engineering and operational endeavor that must be reflected in corresponding security, information assurance, and operational laws and regulations.

The integrated architecture of modern aircraft ICS and embedded systems mandates that security paradigms of traditional information technology systems be applied to ICS, in a whole or modified form. This integration is in addition to the ICS specific security paradigms. The integration must facilitate a holistic approach to security, with the traditional separation or isolation of the ICS no longer applicable due to modern networking and distributed systems.

All information technology systems, whether traditional or industrial control based, employ the "CIA" best practice model: confidentiality, integrity, and availability. The CIA model is comprised of the following components:

- **Confidentiality:** how the system or data is accessed
- **Integrity:** the accuracy or completeness of the data
- **Availability:** the reliability of accessing the system or data

In traditional information technology systems, the order of importance is confidentiality, integrity, and availability. The placement of rigorous end user access controls and data encryption processes provide confidentiality for critical information. Integrity is of second but vital importance, followed by the availability of the system.[1]

Industrial control systems require the "CIA" model (see Figure 9.1) but must follow a modified order of importance of the components of the model. "The primary security issue is preventing unauthorized access to the sensitive control systems through

---

1. J. WEISS (2008). *Id.*

Figure 9.1

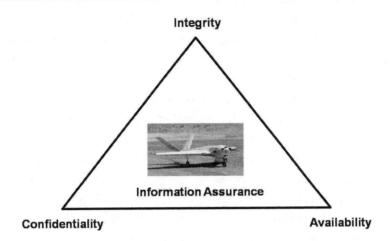

Unmanned Aircraft Information Assurance Concepts (Photo courtesy of Donna Dulo)

non-control systems. As such, integrity is the most critical security requirement."[2] As stated previously, industrial control systems including specific types such as SCADA systems inherently must be continuously live, and as a result, there are security related consequences if the systems are offline, suffer a security breach, or go down. This makes availability the second component of the model.

Traditional information technology systems aim to consolidate and centralize to achieve optimal economies of scale for lower operational costs for the overall system. Integrated control systems are by nature and necessity distributed systems that must ensure the reliability and availability of the system and the system's controls. This translates to the fact that all sites, remote and local, rely on the availability of the industrial control system. With unmanned aircraft, distributed systems are central with the aircraft, ground control stations, communication stations, and the like consistently being remote from each other. Remote sites, therefore, and thus remote access are often available directly from field devices which may reduce the effectiveness of security firewalls[3] at central demilitarized zones,[4] which places added burdens on protecting the availability of the ICS at these points. The challenge of availability

---

2. NIST, NISTIR 7628, Guidelines for Smart Grid Cybersecurity: Vol. 1, Smart Grid Cyber Security Strategy, Architecture, and High-Level Requirements (August, 2010).

3. A firewall is a hardware- and software-based network device that controls the traffic between the external organization or network and the internal network or organization.

4. A demilitarized zone in information technology is a security technique where a zone or subnetwork is established around information technology assets to buffer the assets from attack, so that the attacker winds up in the demilitarized zone, not on the critical assets.

is quite formidable in industrial control systems[5] and equally challenging in the highly mobile unmanned aircraft network and communication systems.

Confidentiality is also a critical component of the model but is third in importance compared to the other three components. This brings up an important distinction between traditional information technology systems and ICS. In a traditional IT system, the end user is typically a live person, while in an ICS, the "end user" is generally a computer or an intelligently controlled device, such as an autonomous or semi-autonomous unmanned aircraft. This distinction lies at the center of why confidentiality can be the third in importance in the model, since the computational "end user" devices are less likely by far to instigate a security issue than a human end user, and also the security is programmed into these devices when the ICS is developed, making confidentiality preprogrammed into the system, making it more controllable than with traditional information technology systems.[6]

Therefore the model for industrial control systems security is "IAC" rather than "CIA." However, for the purposes of industry standard, the term "CIA Triad" will continue to be used with the understanding of the unique nature of the model as applied to industrial control systems. To gain a more clear understanding of the CIA Triad, legal definitions are presented below with precise definitions:

1. Information Security
The term "information security" means protecting information and information systems from unauthorized access, use, disclosure, disruption, modification, or destruction in order to provide . . . integrity . . . confidentiality . . . availability. [44 U.S.C., Sec. 3542 (b)(1)]
2. Integrity
"Guarding against improper information modification or destruction, and includes ensuring information non-repudiation and authenticity." [44 U.S.C., SEC. 3542 (b)(1)(A)]
3. Confidentiality
"Preserving authorized restrictions on information access and disclosure, including means for protecting personal privacy and proprietaryinformation." [44 U.S.C., Sec. 3542 (b)(1)(B)]
4. Availability
"Ensuring timely and reliable access to and use of information." [44 U.S.C., SEC. 3542 (b)(1)(C)]

---

5. J. WEISS (2008). *Id.*
6. *Id.*

Impact levels, which are more precise breakdowns of the concepts of the CIA Triad, are based upon the expected adverse effects of a security breach on "organizational operations, organizational assets, or individuals."[7] The impact level definitions are derived from FIPS 199.[8] The impact levels are used in the selection of security requirements for each logical interface category of the system. This example, while based on an example of an ICS within a power grid system, can serve as an example impact table (see Table 9.1) for many industrial control systems including those used in manned and unmanned aircraft due to the pervasive nature of the security requirements of operations, assets, and personnel in all industrial control systems.

Table 9.1 CIA Triad Impact Levels[9] [10]

	Low Impact	Moderate Impact	High Impact
Confidentiality	The unauthorized disclosure of information could be expected to have a limited adverse effect on organizational operations, assets, or individuals.	The unauthorized disclosure of information could be expected to have a serious adverse effect on organizational operations, assets, or individuals.	The unauthorized disclosure of information could be expected to have a severe or catastrophic adverse effect on organizational operations, assets, or individuals.
Integrity	The unauthorized modification or destruction of information could be expected to have a limited adverse effect on organizational operations, assets, or individuals.	The unauthorized modification or destruction of information could be expected to have a serious adverse effect on organizational operations, assets, or individuals.	The unauthorized modification or destruction of information could be expected to have a severe or catastrophic adverse effect on organizational operations, assets, or individuals.

   7. NIST, NISTIR 7628 (August, 2010). *Id.*

   8. FIPS Pub 199, Standards for Security Categorization of Federal Information and Information Systems, Department of Commerce (2004), http://csrc.nist.gov/publications/fips/fips199/FIPS-PUB-199-final .pdf. "The Federal Information Processing Standards Publication Series of the National Institute of Standards and Technology (NIST) is the official series of publications relating to standards and guidelines adopted and promulgated under the provisions of Section 5131 of the Information Technology Management Reform Act of 1996 (Public Law 104-106) and the Federal Information Security Management Act of 2002 (Public Law 107-347). These mandates have given the Secretary of Commerce and NIST important responsibilities for improving the utilization and management of computer and related telecommunications systems in the federal government. The NIST, through its Information Technology Laboratory, provides leadership, technical guidance, and coordination of government efforts in the development of standards and guidelines in these areas."

   9. NIST, NISTIR 7628 (August, 2010). *Id.*

   10. FIPS, FIPS 199: Standards for Security Categorization of Federal Information and Information Systems (February, 2004). *Id.*

	Low Impact	**Moderate Impact**	**High Impact**
Availability	The disruption of access to or use of information or an information system could be expected to have a limited adverse effect on organizational operations, assets, or individuals.	The disruption of access to or use of information or an information system could be expected to have a serious adverse effect on organizational operations, assets, or individuals.	The disruption of access to or use of information or an information system could be expected to have a severe or catastrophic adverse effect on organizational operations, assets, or individuals.

As demonstrated in the above section, integrity, availability, and confidentiality are critical components of an aircraft ICS. Careful consideration must be paid to each of these with special consideration to integrity and availability, as ICSs must be fully operational and structurally sound at all times to maintain their information assurance. The pervasiveness of industrial control systems in the national arena is evident. The security risk to these systems is also quite evident as they become intertwined with traditional information systems architectures requiring an integrated approach to security. The traditional CIA triad must be revised to IAC to accommodate the unique nature and requirements of ICSs, with integrity as the most critical aspect of security followed by availability. This CIA-IAC security model is becoming the paradigm of modern aircraft ICSs as they are becoming increasingly integrated into the traditional information technology architectures.

THE DIFFERENCE BETWEEN ICS SECURITY AND GENERAL INFORMATION ASSURANCE

Industrial control system information assurance differs from traditional information assurance due to the cyberphysical nature of system structures, communications, computational processes, and operations. An unmanned aircraft, for example, is a physical system comprised of hardware that is highly controlled by the cyber aspects of the system such as software, networks, and communications. Industrial control systems differ from the traditional information technology network systems in that the generic information technology network uses "physics to manipulate data" while the ICS uses "data to manipulate physics." This has many potential safety consequences to the public. "Compromised ICS systems have led to extensive cascading power outages, dangerous toxic chemical releases, and explosions. It is therefore important to implement an ICS with security controls that allow for reliable, safe, and flexible performance."[11] A compromised unmanned aircraft, for example, can result in many types of incidents such as mid-air collisions, collisions with ground objects and people, intercepted data, and many more issues that have potential catastrophic effects for the general public.

In essence, the difference is explicit: many of the critical differences between industrial control systems and information technology systems originate from the fact that the computational logic executing in ICSs has a direct and systematic effect on the physical world. ICSs have specific and unique performance and reliability requirements and often use software and operating systems as well as applications that may be considered unconventional to typical information technology operations.[12] When referring to industrial control systems, many embedded components/systems are involved such as:

1. Supervisory Control and Data Acquisition Systems (SCADA)
2. Programmable Logic Controllers (PLC)
3. Automated Control Systems (ACS)
4. Distributed Control Systems (DCS)
5. Remote Terminal Units (RTU)
6. Intelligent Electronic Devices (IED)
7. Critical infrastructure networking systems
8. Inclusive computational systems

When discussing an ICS, there is a distinct difference in an ICS from an information technology (IT) network system in terms of information assurance. The purpose of IT enterprise security is to protect organizational data from attack. The purpose of ICS security is "to protect the ability of the facility to safely and securely operate, regardless of what may befall the rest of the network."[13] In other words, an industrial control system such as an unmanned aircraft system and its corresponding network must not be breached, as a system failure can cause the aircraft in the sky to cease operations, crash, fly off course, or operate in an unintended manner. Note the emphasis on safety and security, as systems controlled by industrial control systems involve life safety operations as opposed to general information systems in organizations that only process business or organizational data. Unmanned aircraft industrial systems, for example, have a definitive life safety issue, and therefore must be treated with

11. J. Weiss, *Assuring Industrial Control System Cyber Security,* CENTER FOR STRATEGIC & INTERNATIONAL STUDIES (2008). http://csis.org/files/media/csis/pubs/080825_cyber.pdf.
12. NIST, SPECIAL PUBLICATION 800-82 REVISION 1, GUIDE TO INDUSTRIAL CONTROL SYSTEMS (ICS) SECURITY (May, 2013), http://dx.doi.org/10.6028/NIST.SP.800-82r1.
13. J. Weiss (2008). *Id.*

the highest information assurance and computer security levels possible, given their ICS-based architecture.

Modern industrial control systems, however, are being upgraded with newer technologies that are on par with current IT networking technologies. According to the Department of Homeland Security, "While a high dependence on legacy ICS still exists, critical infrastructure systems are migrating to new communications technologies. As a result, common communications protocols and open architecture standards are replacing the diverse and disparate proprietary mechanics of ICS."[14] This has both positive and negative consequences.

The positive aspects allow asset owners efficient methods of communications and robust data, system interoperability, quicker time to marker, ease of operation, and standardized technology, which facilitates ease of maintenance, upgradability, and systems operations. Hence, the advent of advanced unmanned aircraft technologies and the availability of these technologies to general civilian users.

The negative aspects of robust data and communication flows are that new risks are introduced into the system including new cyber vulnerabilities that did not exist when ICSs were isolated or technologically inferior.[15] The increased interdependence of ICS systems and the new protocols and communications standards that provide the increased interoperability are, in fact, the same technologies that have been exploited on the Internet domain ad in the traditional corporate network domains. The problem is that "the migration from older legacy-type architectures to modern operating systems and platforms can force ICS to inherit many cyber vulnerabilities, with some of these vulnerabilities having countermeasures that often cannot be deployed in automation systems."[16]

SCADA and ICS systems inherently must be continuously live, and as a result, there are security consequences. For example, a flying unmanned aircraft must not fail in the air, otherwise it may crash or cause unforeseen damage. Thus, it must be continuously live during aerial operations to avoid serious consequence. Since SCADA and ICS systems require high availability, any type of interface that integrates with non-control systems "should ensure that interactions with these and other systems do not compromise the high reliability requirement."[17]

In the context of industrial control systems, vulnerabilities of traditional information technology systems are inherited into the system, but the security countermeasures may not be applicable in many cases. Additionally, the operational postures of ICS differ

---

14. Department of Homeland Security, Recommended Practice: Improving Industrial Control Systems Cybersecurity with Defense-in-Depth Strategies, Washington, D.C. (October, 2009).

15. *Id.*

16. *Id.*

17. NIST, NISTIR 7628, Guidelines for Smart Grid Cybersecurity: Vol. 1, Smart Grid Cybersecurity Strategy, Architecture, and High Level Requirements (August, 2010).

from traditional information technology and therefore the information assurance posture must differ as well. In essence, ICS requires a new set of security paradigms as well as technologies to assure that the system is not compromised. As a result, unmanned aircraft operators must adhere to both ICS critical infrastructure protection and the traditional security protection of information technology equipment and networks. This is a daunting task given that most information technology security professionals are not well versed in industrial control system security paradigms and procedures.

Industrial control system security has historically been defined as "the level of reliability of the system to operate safely and efficiently."[18] The complete isolation of the ICS from the external network in the past permitted the organization to reduce threats to those associated with personnel having physical access to the facility or plant floor, which required only limited security oversight. In this closed environment, all communications were trusted, and all trusted operators had access to the system.

Industrial controls systems once existed in isolated contexts which provided an inherent level of protection for the systems including the proverbial "air gap,"[19] which was a separation of the system from external networks. This is no longer the case in many instances, as modern ICSs, such as an aircraft ICS, as discussed above, are increasingly converged with modern networks as well as the Internet.[20] This convergence and increased interconnectivity is causing increased security issues in the industrial control systems domain due to many factors, including the following:

- Increased dependency on automation
- Insecure connectivity to the Internet and external networks
- Use of common technologies with known vulnerabilities creating previously unseen risks in the ICS domain
- Lack of a qualified cybersecurity business case for ICS environments
- Administrator lack of awareness of security capabilities of security technologies
- Absence of basic security functionality in standard communications protocols as applied to ICS
- A considerable amount of open-source information that is available regarding ICS, their operations, and security vulnerabilities[21]

---

18. Department of Homeland Security, Recommended Practice: Improving Industrial Control Systems Cybersecurity with Defense-in-Depth Strategies, Control Systems Security Program, National Cybersecurity Division of the Department of Homeland Security (October, 2009).

19. An "air gap" is a physical separation of one network and another, making it physically impossible to transfer information security threats unless the threat is physically carried and intentionally placed onto the network on the other side of the gap.

20. Civilian unmanned aircraft can be controlled through the Internet through satellite Internet services that allow over the horizon control of the aircraft.

21. *Id.*

In an in-depth study of ICS security, McAfee researchers found that ICSs are highly vulnerable despite an enhanced focus on their security. The threats to ICSs have accelerated, but the responses to those threats have not, creating a widespread security issue for all ICSs. In fact, according to an industry-wide survey by McAfee researchers, there have been only modest improvements in security in ICSs over the past few years while threats have grown exponentially.[22] This is not a good trend for the transportation sector as unmanned aircraft become integrated into the national airspace. As a result of unmanned aircraft integration, the issues of the transportation sector protection will become even more pervasive as well as complex as the additional aircraft, controlled remotely, enter the national skies.

UNMANNED AIRCRAFT AND INDUSTRIAL CONTROL SYSTEM ATTACKS

Cyberattacks may be complex and protracted or relatively small and rapid and may target high visibility, high impact infrastructure assets of aircraft industrial control systems. Attacks against ICSs may be against programmable logic controller (PLC), integrated circuit (IC), or supervisory control and data acquisition (SCADA) systems on a large scale to inflict physical as well as informational damage to the aircraft or ground control station. Controllers are real-time computer chips or systems that have the potential to manipulate electrical outputs based on the programming conditions within the controller or integrated circuit.

The chips or controllers are connected to electrical devices within the aircraft such as pumps, motors, sensors, or other electromotive devices which have a specific electrical purpose controlled by the chip or circuit. Through ladder logic, or in more recent systems, advanced forms of logic, the laws of physics as well as the laws of information technology enable the fusion and functionality of the controller, the computational logic, the software, and the electronics to operate in a viable manner.

Cyberattacks impede the physical processing of the airborne or ground-based controllers; this is what makes them dangerous and deadly. Malicious manipulations of the controllers can lead to logic issues resulting in software corruption or in the worst-case scenario physical damage to the hardware of the system due to erroneous electrical impulses in the physical manifestations of the logic carried out in the electronics attached to the controllers. The results, if programmed correctly, can be catastrophic. The Stuxnet[23] threat, which is considered the world's first cybermissile,

---

22. S. Baker, N. Filipiak, & K. Timlin, McAfee Corporation and the Center for Strategic & International Studies: In the Dark—Crucial Industries Confront Cyberattacks (2011), www.mcafee.com.

23. For an in-depth treatment of the Stuxnet threat, *see* Symantec Corporation (2011), W32.Stuxnet

caused major physical damage to Iranian nuclear power plants. It set the example of the immense damage that a computer software code can do to the corresponding control system hardware.

The key to cyberattacks of this nature is the physical as well as the informational damage. The long-term cyberwarfare strategy of potential attackers must be to take down physical as well as informational systems: damage the economy, the information systems, as well as the infrastructure. This will impose psychological impacts on an exponential scale on the population. Thus attacks on aircraft ICSs can have short-term or lasting effects based on the nature of the attacks and the damage from the attacks. The attacks can be localized or have long-term widespread ramifications on the local, regional, or even national population.

Unmanned Aircraft Control Systems Attack Vectors

The growth of ICSs in complexity will give rise in the growth of the complexity of defense-in-depth strategies. An aircraft or ground control station ICS has a wide set of attack vectors that can target multiple resources on the control system which can be executed asynchronously and over a long period of time targeting multiple vulnerabilities in the unmanned aircraft system's environment.[24]

Thus one or two countermeasures will not be adequate to properly secure the aircraft ICS in either the short term or the long run. Therefore, an aggregate of security measures must be deployed to disseminate risk in a defense-in-depth strategy in the event of the failure of any one or more security mechanisms.

An effective defense-in-depth strategy involves a thorough analysis and understanding of the possible attack vectors that pose threats to the aircraft and ground control system ICS environment. These attack vectors include the following:

- Backdoors and holes in the wireless or communications network perimeter
- Vulnerabilities in ground station computers, control systems, or communications
- Attacks on aircraft systems and avionics
- Ground station database attacks

Dossier at https://www.symantec.com/content/en/us/enterprise/media/security_response/whitepapers/w32_stuxnet_dossier.pdf.

24. Department of Homeland Security, Recommended Practice: Improving Industrial Control Systems Cybersecurity with Defense-in-Depth Strategies, Control Systems Security Program, National Cybersecurity Division of the Department of Homeland Security (October, 2009).

- Communications hijackings and GPS spoofing[25]
- Man-in-the-middle attacks[26]

Attack vectors are continuously changing and must be continually evaluated as new technologies and new protocols are integrated into the aircraft or ground control station ICS. As such, vigilance is required to carefully monitor all attack vectors for new and emerging threats and possible zero-day attack[27] methodologies.

DEFENDING UNMANNED AIRCRAFT INDUSTRIAL CONTROL SYSTEMS THROUGH OFFENSIVE AND DEFENSIVE POSTURES

The critical safety and security nature of industrial control systems requires that a clear understanding of security challenges be present and appropriate security countermeasures be applied. Countermeasures may be defenses as a part of a defense-in-depth strategy or may be offensive such as a cyber deterrence strategy. A holistic approach is most beneficial combining defensive and offensive postures to ensure that the availability and integrity of the system be maintained. This ensures an aggregated security posture to defend against all threats and to minimize vulnerabilities that may be exploited by those threats.

This section presents a two-pronged approach to defending aircraft and ground control station industrial control systems: defensive and offensive. The defensive strategy combines defensive measures in an aggregated manner to ensure system security in a flexible and useable framework through a multilayered approach. The offensive strategy involves deterring the potential attackers of the system through specific offensive cyber techniques. All techniques should follow federal, state, and other legal and regulatory guidelines for information assurance.

Defensive Posture: Defense-in-Depth

The security in unmanned aircraft system industrial control systems should be provided in layers with at least one security measure being applied at each layer. This is the foundation of the concept of defense-in-depth. The objective of defense-in-depth

---

25. GPS spoofing is an attack on the unmanned aircraft where false GPS coordinates are injected into the aircraft systems causing the aircraft to fly off course or in a programmed manner that is deviant from its intended course. This results in an uncontrolled or third-party controlled aircraft that can cause safety and security issues to the surrounding environment.

26. A man-in-the-middle attack is a cyberattack where the attacker has the ability to intercept, inject, or change network communication messages, unbeknownst to the parties or systems on either side of the communication.

27. A zero-day-attack is a new type of attack that targets a specific vulnerability in a system where a security fix or patch is non-existent at the time of the attack.

Figure 9.2

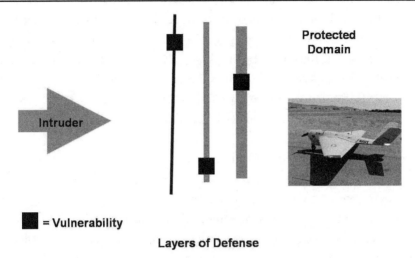

Defense-in-depth (Photo courtesy of Donna Dulo)

is "to mitigate the risk of one component of the defense being compromised or circumvented."[28]

A defense-in-depth approach focuses on defending information assets, systems, communications, and information technology infrastructures through layered defenses. Since there is a wide variety of communications methods as well as characteristics of these methods, including the quality of defensive systems, there is no single security measure that can provide effective countermeasures to all types of threats to the system. Thus multiple levels of security must be implemented to counter all possible threats.[29]

In graphical form, defense-in-depth can be viewed as a series of security measures, represented by various lines, as shown in Figure 9.2. Each method has a vulnerability that can be exploited by an attacker. "Cyber security, from a defense-in-depth perspective, is not just about deploying specific technologies to counter certain risks. An effective security program for an organization will depend on its adherence and willingness to accept security as a constant constraint on all cyber activities. Implementing an effective defense-in-depth strategy will require taking a holistic approach and leveraging all of an organization's resources in order to provide effective layers of protection."[30]

---

28. NIST, NISTIR 7628 (August, 2010). *Id.*
29. *Id.*
30. DEPARTMENT OF HOMELAND SECURITY (October, 2009). *Id.*

The Department of Homeland Security Strategic Security Framework for Defense-in-Depth

The Department of Homeland Security provides a strategic framework for cyber defense-in-depth for industrial control systems. This framework is a multilevel but integrated framework that must be employed throughout the ICS organization in order to be effective and viable. This DHS framework is specific to industrial control systems' security challenges, infrastructure, and unique risks.[31] The DHS Strategic Security Framework centers around six basic tenants:

1. Know the risks that an organization faces
2. Quantify and qualify the risks
3. Use key resources to mitigate security risks
4. Define each resource's core competency and identify overlapping areas
5. Abide by existing or emerging security standards for specific controls
6. Create and customize specific controls that are unique to an organization[32]

The framework starts with the basic understanding of the risks to the organization that oversees the ICS. The risks are best understood by understanding the specific threats and vulnerabilities that face ICSs throughout their operations in both normal and abnormal conditions. This risk is understood by a rigorous risk assessment that covers all aspects of the organization. Risk assessments are key to define, understand, and plan remediation efforts against specific organizational and ICS threats and vulnerabilities and are constantly updated at regular intervals.[33]

A cross-functional team must be developed that understands the ICS, its operations, cybersecurity, and the technology of the entire system. This team should include executive-level managers as well as cybersecurity personnel and engineers. This team must be fully aware of the present and future cybersecurity challenges facing the ICS infrastructure as well as the ICS within the structure of the integrated organizational network architecture.

The team will be responsible for the fourth layer of the framework including the development of policies and procedures, product procurement, training and awareness, as well as the cybersecurity aspects of the framework. "Sound guidance for an industrial control system will need to address all the operational requirements first.[34] This ensures that new policies do not affect the availability of the industrial control system. Once the operational requirements are built, an operational security (OPSEC) program can be built and implemented within the framework guidance. This program

31. Department of Homeland Security (October, 2009). *Id.*
32. *Id.*
33. *Id.*
34. *Id.*

rests on security standard controls as well as corporate specific controls, which round out the bottom layer of the strategic security framework for the ICS.[35]

Architectural Zones

The Department of Homeland Security ICS defense-in-depth strategy consists of dividing the common control systems architectures into zones, which assists security personnel in creating clear boundaries so that they can effectively apply defense-in-depth strategies. This includes critical network segmentation methodologies including best practices leveraging:[36]

- Single, Multi-homed, Dual, and Cascading Firewalls
- Network Routers with Access Control Lists
- Configured Switches
- Static Routes
- Network Routing Tables
- Dedicated Communications Media

Using the above network segment technologies and methodologies, the industrial control system information architecture is divided into five basic function zones. The architectural zones have specific features that are segmented to bolster security within the ICS and organizational network. The zones have the following basic functions:[37]

1. **External Zone:** an area that connects to the Internet, any peer locations, and remote offsite locations. This is a site that is usually considered an untrusted point of connectivity. For industrial control systems:
   - Least amount of priority
   - Highest variety of risks
2. **Corporate Zone:** an area for corporate connectivity. This is where e-mail, DNS, and Web servers reside. For industrial control systems:
   - Higher priority than external zone
   - Lower priority than rest of zones
   - Wide variety of risks
   - Mature security posture
   - Redundancy of systems
3. **Manufacturing/Data Zone:** the area where the majority of monitoring and control takes place and is therefore a critical area for continuity and management of

---

35. *Id.*
36. *Id.*
37. *Id.*

the control networks. This zone contains engineering and management devices as well as data servers. For industrial control systems:

- High priority zone
- Risks are associated with direct connectivity to external and corporate zones
- Central to operation of the corporate zone

4. **Control/Cell Zone:** the area that has connectivity to physical devices such as programmable logical controllers, actuators, sensors, and other such devices. For industrial control systems:

- High priority zone
- Zone has support for TCP/IP
- Lower risks

5. **Safety Zone:** this zone has devices that control the safety level of the end devices automatically. For industrial control systems:

- Highest priority zone
- Risk is lower as many devices are only connected to end devices

Each architectural zone has a unique security focus; therefore, a defense-in-depth strategy would be to secure each of the core zones with a defensive strategy with depth and then introduce cascading countermeasures into the overall architecture in a manner that will not impede the functionality of the system. This system, while generic, can be readily applied to unmanned aircraft systems and their control and communication networks. The key is the proper application of the framework and architectures and the consistent application of security principles and information assurance to the system with a distinct focus not just on the information technology but with a focus on the aircraft and ground station industrial control systems.

Defense-in-Depth Strategy and Structure

In addition to maintaining architectural zones, a proper defense-in-depth strategy for an unmanned aircraft system industrial control system would have the following elements:

1. Firewalls
2. Demilitarized Zones
3. Intrusion Detection Systems
4. Policies and Procedures

Firewalls

Firewalls are key to a solid defense-in-depth strategy for any information technology structure or architecture, and they are critical for unmanned aircraft networks and information technology structures. General rules for ICS firewalls are as follows:[38]

- Inbound traffic to the control system should be blocked.
- Access to devices inside the control system should be through a DMZ.
- Outbound traffic through the control system firewall should be limited to essential communications only.
- All outbound traffic from the control network to the corporate network should be source and destination restricted by service and port.

Additionally, firewalls should be configured with carefully structured outbound filtering to stop forged IP packets from leaving the control network. This is to prevent the control network from being the source of spoofed communications such as Denial of Service attacks or GPS Spoofing.

Demilitarized Zones

Demilitarized zones (DMZ) should be created to provide protection for industrial control systems and their supporting networks. This is particularly relevant in unmanned aircraft ground and communication stations. Firewalls should be the devices used to create the DMZ that protects the control network. All connections through the unmanned aircraft system's ICS network should be routed through the ICS firewall without exception, and no connection should ever circumvent the firewall.[39]

Multiple DMZs should be used across the organizational architecture. The understanding of the flow of data in and out of networks monitored and protected by DMZs is critical, and security personnel must understand these data flows at all times. "Having multiple DMZs protects the information resources from attacks using virtual LAN hopping and trust exploitation, and is a very good way to enhance the security posture and add another layer to the defense-in-depth strategy."[40]

Intrusion Detection Systems

An intrusion detection systems (IDS) monitors events on a network, for example, traffic patterns, and can also monitor a system and log entries or file access with the

---

38. NIST, SPECIAL PUBLICATION 800-82 REVISION 1, GUIDE TO INDUSTRIAL CONTROL SYSTEMS (ICS) SECURITY (May, 2013), http://dx.doi.org/10.6028/NIST.SP.800-82r1.

39. DEPARTMENT OF HOMELAND SECURITY, RECOMMENDED PRACTICE: IMPROVING INDUSTRIAL CONTROL SYSTEMS CYBERSECURITY WITH DEFENSE-IN-DEPTH STRATEGIES, CONTROL SYSTEMS SECURITY PROGRAM, NATIONAL CYBERSECURITY DIVISION OF THE DEPARTMENT OF HOMELAND SECURITY (October, 2009).

40. *Id.*

intent of identifying an intruder breaking into the system. An IDS ensures that unusual activity out of the norm such as unusual traffic patterns, changes to operating system files, the opening of new ports, etc., is brought to the attention of specifically identified personnel such as security personnel.[41] There are two basic types of intrusion detection systems used with industrial control systems networks:[42]

1. **Network-Based IDS**: These IDSs monitor network traffic and generate alarms when attacks are identified.
2. **Host-Based IDS**: These IDSs are software monitors that monitor a characteristic of a system, such as system configuration changes, log file entries, and access to sensitive data, and respond with an alarm or countermeasure when a security breach occurs.

With an ICS, both methodologies are used with network-based IDSs deployed between the control network and the corporate network in conjunction with the firewall. Host-based IDSs are usually deployed on the systems that use general-purpose operating systems and applications such as SCADA servers and engineering workstations.[43]

"Current IDS products are effective in detecting and preventing well known Internet attacks but until recently they have not addressed ICS protocol attacks."[44] IDS vendors are now beginning to address this issue, and work is being done in both the research and vendor communities in collaboration to create a number of signatures for IDSs that are specific to aircraft and ground control station ICSs and can be used to monitor for specific attacks that target aircraft systems specifically.

Policies and Procedures

Policies and procedures is a pivotal cornerstone in an organization's defense-in-depth strategy. Policies and procedures must be well documented and reviewed periodically, preferably on an annual basis. Policies for information assurance should follow federal guidelines, and, in particular, unmanned aircraft systems networks, communication, ground stations, and aircraft should follow the national critical infrastructure plans, regulations, and guidelines, as appropriate and as practical. Several policies and

---

41. NIST (2013). *Id.*
42. *Id.*
43. *Id.*
44. *Id.*

procedures that provide sound defense-in-depth for most information technology-based systems support are as follows:[45]

1. Log and Event Management: Central consoles provide unified monitoring of logs and events with filtering capabilities.
2. Security Policies: These policies are the first step to a secure ICS network. They must be specific to ICSs and also apply to the traditional network structures.
3. Patch Management: A systematic approach to patch management must be followed. Specifically for ICSs, regression testing is advised, and offline testing should be done before applying to online ICS systems.
4. Media Protection: Removable media provide specific threats to ICSs and as such must have specific, enforced policies applied to them at all times including policies for labeling, transportation, erasing, and destruction.
5. Training and Education Policies: Training and education are a critical part of ICS security. Training and education programs must be established and enforced, including control system specific training, awareness training, physical process training, and incident prevention.

Defense-in-Depth Defensive Posture Conclusion

Defense-in-depth is a major concept that must be applied rigorously to industrial control systems to ensure a robust security architecture. A defense-in-depth architecture is complex and must be developed with careful consideration to the data flows, functions, and control mechanisms of the systems as well as the risks and capabilities of the personnel implementing the security program.

With a solid, viable defense-in-depth program in place, industrial control systems networks and infrastructures are well equipped to face the information assurance and security challenges of the modern integrated architecture of the unmanned aircraft system ICS. Though complex, a defense-in-depth architecture is dynamic and flexible to adapt to the changing security environment to ensure that unmanned aircraft navigate in the national airspace in a safe and secure manner.

Offensive Posture: Cyber Deterrence

Deterrence is a theory that runs counter to a purely defensive posture, such as the previous defense-in-depth posture for industrial control systems. Cyberdeterrence is the prevention of an external entity or organization from conducting future cyberattacks by proactively attacking their technology to deny them the freedom of cyberspace to attack one's assets.

---

45. DEPARTMENT OF HOMELAND SECURITY (October, 2009). *Id.* and NIST (2013). *Id.*

In the world of ICS and critical infrastructure security, this essentially means attacking the attacker's attack capabilities to prevent them from conducting attacks. Thus, if an entity attacks an industrial control system, a counterattack can be launched to deter the attack from continuing or from happening in the future. Additionally, an attack can be launched against a potential attacker based on that attacker's actions against another entity or system.

Deterrence Basics

There is no single theory of cyberdeterrence, and the application to ICSs must be adapted to the current situation. However, in this chapter a general theory will be applied to ICS to demonstrate the value of this posture for critical systems such as the transportation critical infrastructure as well as the entities in that infrastructure such as individual unmanned aircraft systems. There are eight elements of cyberdeterrence:[46]

1. An interest that needs to be protected
2. A deterrent declaration that is credible and reassuring
3. Denial measures that consist of prevention and futility
4. Penalty measures that consist of retaliation, interdependency, and counter-productivity
5. Credibility that the deterrence declaration is believable
6. Reassurance that if the entity does not attack it will not suffer consequences
7. Fear of the denial or penalty measures
8. Cost-benefit calculations to ensure viability of the deterrence

The interest that is to be protected is the ICS. In the case of national ICS assets, a group of assets can be protected using a single cyberdeterrence strategy against a single entity. The deterrent declaration can be made by the federal government of jurisdiction of the ICS or group of ICSs. Denial measures must be swift and effective as well as continuous to prevent further attacks on the ICS. Penalties must be consistent and credible and launched swiftly to ensure deterrence. The attacker must be persuaded that attacking the ICS is counterproductive and that punitive measures will be enacted. The entire deterrence system must be cost effective and viable for both the ICS entity and the government sponsoring the deterrence, if applicable.

An issue that is not listed in the above is attribution. Launching a deterrence strategy against an entity that is not targeting the ICS is counterproductive, costly, and dangerous. Attribution is critical to the success of deterrence, and a strategic focus on

---

46. W. Goodman, *Cyber Deterrence: Tougher in Theory than in Practice?* US AIR FORCE AIR UNIVERSITY STRATEGIC STUDIES QUARTERLY, Fall, 2010, at 102–135.

attribution identification methods should be a major part of a cyberdeterrence capability of a nation that is sponsoring deterrence of its ICSs. Concerted efforts toward developing improved attribution methods and capacities through technological and other means are time and money well spent.[47]

Planners must stop treating "cyber" as a discrete and homogenous category when planning a deterrence campaign. The threats spread across a wide spectrum, and deterrence doctrines and red lines must be established in many ICS security areas to deter these threats.[48] There is a three-prong approach to cyberdeterrence in complex systems:[49]

1. Defense: the first step in protecting against the vast majority of aggressors and dissuading some from attacking at all (defense-in-depth strategy)
2. Attribution: for maintaining credibility and ensuring legitimacy
3. Retaliation: the willingness and capability to retaliate against any attack from any source under any circumstances must be assured

The scope of cyberdeterrence is quite large with a large architecture to protect the ICS and a numerous set of technological requirements that must not interfere with the operation of the ICS. The models that must be engaged are also numerous and complex. This makes cyberdeterrence a challenging problem at the strategic, operational, and technological levels.[50]

Retaliatory Deterrence

Retaliation is the third area in the cyberdeterrence strategy and is applicable to industrial control systems when defense-in-depth strategies are not sufficient to deter potential attackers, especially state run attackers with intentions of cyberwar aimed at a nation's industrial complex and areas such as the transportation system. This is the situation where ICSs require the added protection of cyberdeterrence.

In many cases, retaliation-based cyberattacks are only useful for deterrence, as they are incapable of disarming the attacker, and thus if cyber retaliation does not build deterrence, then nothing will.[51] However, the traditional strategic models of deterrence do not apply to cyberspace; traditional deterrence is bipolar while cyber-

---

47. F. Cilluffo, S. Cardash, & G. Salmoiraghi, *A Blueprint for Cyber Deterrence: Building Stability through Strength*, Military and Strategic Affairs, Vol. 4. No. 3., December 2012, at 3–22.

48. S. Weiner, *Searching for Cyber Deterrence*, Center for Strategic and International Studies (November 26, 2012), http://csis.org.

49. C. Haley, *A Theory of Cyber Deterrence*, Georgetown University Journal of International Affairs, February 6, 2013.

50. T. Mowbray, Solution Architecture for Cyber Deterrence (The SANS Institute) (April 12, 2010).

51. M. Libicki, Cyberdeterrence and Cyberwar (Rand Corporation) (2009).

deterrence is governed potentially by a number of asymmetrical, multilateral, and bilateral relationships, all of which are in a constant state of flux.[52]

Another problem is the identification of the attacker and other potential opponents to engage in retaliatory deterrence. In the worst-case scenario, too, the attacker may not be persistent and may disband after the initial round or a few rounds of attacks. Also, an attacker may attack an ICS in another's name, further complicating the identification problem.[53]

Retaliatory cyberdeterrence is a dangerous endeavor if the target of the retaliation does not wish to continue in the cyberdomain or does not have the capability to continue in that domain. "Retaliation has a high likelihood of collateral damage,"[54] meaning that the threat or action of cyber retaliation may mean the launching of an attack in an entirely new domain. This issue places cyberdeterrence in a sensitive category; thus, defending ICS through offensive measures must be a well-planned and well thought out strategy that complements defense-in-depth strategies and is only used in highly sensitive scenarios.

Deterrence Disadvantages

There are several disadvantages of deterrence in the industrial control system defensive strategy. The first is contestability, which is caused by three mutually reinforcing factors: anonymity, asymmetry, and super-empowerment, which all pose great difficulty for deterrence in cyberspace. Another set of disadvantages is scalability and temporality. Scalability creates problems for establishing deterrence thresholds. Temporality refers to the instantaneous nature of cyberattacks. Combined they form a treacherous force against cyberdeterrence strategies.[55]

Finally a lack of reassurance is a major disadvantage of cyberdeterrence. Few international laws define the norms in cyberspace; thus, there is no defined acceptable or unacceptable behavior, which means that a targeted enemy cannot rest assured that they will not be targeted if they refrain from targeting. This creates a cyber guessing game that can lead to catastrophic consequences if an ICS's security controlling entity's guard is let down.[56]

---

52. E. Sterner, *Retaliatory Deterrence in Cyberspace*, US AIR FORCE AIR UNIVERSITY STRATEGIC STUDIES QUARTERLY (Spring, 2011) at 62–80.

53. *Id.*

54. *Id.*

55. W. Goodman, *Cyber Deterrence: Tougher in Theory than in Practice?* US AIR FORCE AIR UNIVERSITY STRATEGIC STUDIES QUARTERLY (Fall, 2010) at 102–135.

56. *Id.*

Coordination of Private Sector and Government

A final issue with the offensive nature of cyberdeterrence is the need of the private sector to coordinate with the government because of the potential cyberattack dimensions of the deterrence strategy. The cyberwarfare domain is a new domain of warfare, and any attack through the deterrence guise may spawn a counterattack requiring the assistance of the forces of the government.

The United States government must provide cyberdefenses to private sector critical infrastructure organizations to prevent cyberattacks if the strategy of cyberdeterrence it utilizes is part of a comprehensive defense through offense strategy. This strategy should include[57]

- Policy and regulation fostering a robust logical cyberinfrastructure
- Government investment in cyberdefenses
- Diversity of international and domestic connections
- Domestic availability of DNS resolution through root servers to lessen dependence on more exposed international connections, if any
- Fostering the growth of a collaborating community of security professionals with the critical infrastructure sectors
- Improving the ability to intercede inventively to restore connections in the event of a cyberconflict or other type of cyberattack
- Improving the ability to conduct incident forensic collection and analysis

As discussed in the first section of this chapter, major strides have been made in the policies and legislation of the federal government concerning the protection of the civilian critical infrastructure. The policy and use of cyberdeterrence should be an added tool within those directives, as deterrence is a viable methodology for a strategic offensive defense.

Deterrence Conclusion

Cyberdeterrence is major consideration for a nondefensive strategy for an industrial control system. In today's world of cyberespionage, cyberterrorism, and cyberwar, prevention may be the best medicine. The only issue is at what cost is an entity willing to go to defend its cyberassets to deter potential attackers in light of the serious issue of attribution. Deterrence is a viable strategy that needs to be explored but in a strategic, operational, and tactical manner all within the technological capabilities of

---

57. R. Stapleton-Gray & B. Woodcock, *National Internet Defense: Small States on the Skirmish Line*. ACM Queue, January 19, 2011.

an ICS security complex. In most cases, cyberdeterrence will be conducted for ICSs by the nation of the ICS for critical ICS systems such as nuclear power.

Defending Unmanned Aircraft Industrial Control Systems through Offensive and Defensive Postures Conclusion

Defense is a major concern for the operations of industrial control systems. For all ICS organizations, defense-in-depth is absolutely critical and must be implemented throughout the ICS architecture. For some national industrial control systems such as nuclear power systems or those that are part of the military industrial complex, or even critical power or water systems, added defensive posturing may be necessary. Thus the use of cyberdeterrence may be used in conjunction with defense-in-depth as a means to protect the ICS from attack. The decision to use cyberdeterrence is a major decision, as it requires considerable resources and comes with considerable risk as well. However, for critical ICS organizations and complexes, this may be a vital defensive posture, especially in a time of war or high vulnerability.

CONCLUSION

The integration of unmanned aircraft into the national airspace also integrates them into the national critical infrastructure. This not only increases the complexity and traffic in the national airspace but also adds more entities that need to be protected into the transportation sector of the national critical infrastructure. Operators of unmanned aircraft and their supporting systems need to be cognizant of the inherent security risks associated with the operation of unmanned aircraft, especially those whose cyber architecture contains industrial control systems.

Awareness of the national critical infrastructure laws, plans, and architectures, as well as the security principles that go along with those plans and architectures, is vital to all unmanned aircraft operators. Through awareness and proactive security and information assurance management, focused on traditional information assurance and the special principles of security revolving around industrial control system-based assets, operators can contribute to the safety and security of their aircraft in the skies as well as the safety and security of others, as the national airspace becomes pervasively shared.

4

Constitutional Issues of Unmanned Aircraft in the National Airspace

CHAPTER

10

Unmanned Aircraft and the Media

First and Fourth Amendment Issues in a Technological Framework

Donna A. Dulo

"Our liberty depends on the freedom of the press, and that cannot be limited without being lost."

—Thomas Jefferson

The United States Department of Transportation by authorization of the Congress has mandated that the Federal Aviation Administration (FAA) integrate unmanned aircraft (UA, UAS, UAV, or drones)[1] into the United States National Airspace in accordance with the FAA Modernization and Reform Act of 2012.[2] The integration of unmanned aircraft into the national airspace will open up a broad array of diverse uses for the media industry. These uses will expand the reach and speed of the media

---

1. The media industry utilizes several terms for unmanned aircraft, often incorrectly. In general, "UA" refers to unmanned aircraft. "UAS" refers to unmanned aerial/aircraft system. "UAV" refers to unmanned aerial/aircraft vehicle. "Drone" is an informal term handed down throughout aviation history referencing the worker bees of the queen bee, and has been a term denoting remote controlled aircraft since the early days of aviation. Unmanned aircraft have been in use since the first decade of manned aviation but have gained prominence in the past two decades due to modern technology and increased usability in both military and civilian applications.

2. FAA Modernization and Reform Act of 2012, P.L. 112-95, 126 Stat. 11.

into newsworthy domains. They will also revolutionize news-gathering paradigms inso-
far as increasing the personal safety of media crews by eliminating complex manned
news-gathering operations and significantly reducing the costs of news-gathering by
providing more cost-effective, rapid, three-dimensional, compact, aerial applications.

Conversely, the advantages of unmanned aircraft could likely be eclipsed by legal
issues if the media does not appropriately integrate the use of unmanned aircraft into
the national airspace. Accordingly, media organizations face daunting challenges in
an uncertain environment that is rife with vague and untested government regulations, multifaceted legal issues, and rapidly changing payload and airframe technology.
Moreover, given there are few major unmanned aircraft cases to provide legal precedent and few currently being litigated in the court system,[3] the current relevant
legal precedent is based solely on manned aviation and somewhat analogous cases
involving technologies that can reasonably be applied to unmanned aircraft situations. Consequently, media organizations attempting to operate UA in the current
ambiguous legal environment are in a tenuous position due to the combination of
underdeveloped FAA regulations—which are nebulous or non-existent—and the lack
of relevant legal precedent.

First and Fourth Amendment issues are of concern to media organizations regarding the use of unmanned aircraft. These competing amendments will likely be central
points of contention between the media and the general public it serves. The First
Amendment rights of the media to use unmanned aircraft may be challenged by individuals whose privacy rights are potentially being infringed. If the media is jointly
involved with law enforcement, it may be violating the Fourth Amendment rights of
individuals as well. The constitutional questions regarding the locations and dimensions of aerial planes of privacy surrounding a dwelling or structure, as well as the
temporal issues of hovering and technological persistence of the UA in the air during
news-gathering operations, will be of utmost concern to media UA operators.
Additionally, the technology dimension may likely be a factor weighing in the First
Amendment equation wherein the depth and penetration agility of the aircraft combined with its subsequent payload sensing and photographic capabilities could tip
the scales toward a privacy tort. This First Amendment "freedom of the press" continuum will require that media organizations properly balance the extent of UA use
with the privacy rights of the public.

---

3. The most prominent case currently in the courts is Huerta v. Pirker, NTSB CP-217.

Figure 10.1

A Fixed-Wing Sentry Unmanned Aircraft (Photo courtesy of Donna Dulo)

The responsibility of maintaining the proper balance between UA (see Figure 10.1) use and invasiveness into privacy will fall squarely on media organizations in order for them to retain the privilege of unmanned aerial operations. Hence, the legal risk and results will be borne by media entities venturing outside of the scope of regulation—knowingly or unknowingly.

The Fourth Amendment arises as an issue when the media acts as a joint participant or actor wherein media organizations assist the police with information and media products resulting from their news-gathering operations. This evidentiary assistance against private citizens could manifest through deliberate or unintentional actions, especially where the media organization has superior aerial technology or greater access to such technology than its law enforcement counterparts. Accordingly, conducting aerial media operations, which garner evidentiary information, places the media in the untenable situation of balancing the public's right to the news regarding matters of public concern with a citizen's reasonable expectation of privacy. Here again, the legal consequences will be borne by media entities venturing outside of the scope of regulation.

Due to the uncertainty of current UA laws and regulations, which place the difficult burden of compliance on media UA operators, a legal-technological framework has been developed to serve as a basic guide for media organization UA operators to navigate the relatively uncharted regulatory environment while the regulators, legislators, and courts work to expand and resolve civilian unmanned aircraft laws and regulations. Accordingly, this framework serves to broaden the scope of relevant legal precedent as it groups cases from both aerial vantage points and technological points of reference rather than merely Constitutional Amendment categorization. Subsequently, as technology develops and emerges, media operators will have a more understandable legal frame of reference on which to base their operations.

The legal-technological framework presented in this chapter serves as an initial awareness guide for media unmanned aircraft operations. The continued long-term effectiveness of the framework's legal baseline will expand as legislators and regulators enact new UA laws and as unmanned aircraft and other technological and Constitutional issues emerge and are litigated. The overall intent of the framework is to serve as a center of awareness that media organizations can reference to help ensure that all unmanned aircraft operations do not exceed their Constitutional protections and limitations. The framework will guide media operators toward effective delivery of news to the public while protecting the public's right to privacy, in essence properly balancing the privacy tort–First Amendment continuum.

THE FIRST AMENDMENT AND FREEDOM OF THE PRESS

The First Amendment states in part that "Congress shall make no law . . . abridging the freedom of speech, or of the press. . . ."[4] This amendment is a foundation of American ideology, which supports the right of society to receive news from the press that is unobstructed by the government.

Although the First Amendment provides constitutional protections to the press, the freedom of the press is not an absolute right. The United States Supreme Court has held that the media's First Amendment freedom of speech rights are limited, and as such the government has the power to enact regulations that restrict the media's invasion into another's privacy and prohibit tortious conduct by the media.

The Federal Regulatory Authority
The primary administrative agencies affecting the use of unmanned aircraft are the Federal Aviation Administration (FAA) under the authority of the Department of Transportation (DOT), which has been tasked by the DOT to integrate unmanned aircraft into the national airspace, and the Federal Communications Commission (FCC),

---

4. U.S. Const. amend. I.

which is currently creating the communications regulations for unmanned aircraft radio, command, and control operations. Both the FAA and the FCC have significant authority over the operation of unmanned aircraft by all operators, including the media. Despite the fact that current UA regulations range from the non-existent to the underdeveloped in a continually evolving regulatory environment, all unmanned aircraft operators are required to comply with published regulations, and breach of such regulations—whether deliberate or mistaken—may result in civil and/or criminal penalties.[5]

Media unmanned aircraft operators will be subject to all laws and regulations including the new rules of unmanned aviation and may lose their First Amendment right of free speech via unmanned aircraft if they do not comply with FAA and FCC mandates. The right to restrict the media's free speech rights has been addressed by the United States Supreme Court. The Court's ruling in *National Broadcasting Co. v. United States* states that:

> The right of free speech does not include . . . the right to use the facilities of radio without a license. The licensing system established by Congress in the Communications Act of 1934 was a proper exercise of its power over commerce. The standard it provided for the licensing of stations was the "public interest, convenience, or necessity." Denial of a station license on that ground, if valid under the Act, is not a denial of free speech.[6]

Although the Court's ruling as to the constitutionality of FCC license regulations was based on the Communications Act of 1934, the justices acknowledged that they deferred to the First Amendment in their reasoning stating, "The question here is simply whether the Commission, by announcing that it will refuse licenses to persons who engage in specified [broadcast] network practices . . . , is thereby denying such persons the constitutional right of free speech."[7] Accordingly, their ultimate ruling rested on the argument that "Unlike other modes of expression, radio inherently is not available to all. That is its unique characteristic, and that is why, unlike other

---

5. A nationwide increase in arrests for unmanned aircraft operators who were attempting to photograph events and sites from small unmanned aircraft systems has necessitated the banning of UA at national parks and various professional sporting events and venues. . . . For instance, in September 2014, a man was arrested for flying an unmanned aircraft close to the US Open, *see* http://nypost.com/2014/09/04/man-arrested-for-flying-unmanned-aircraft-outside-us-open/. Also, in September 2014, a man was sentenced to probation and banned from Yellowstone National Park for crashing an unmanned aircraft into the Yellowstone hot springs while filming a documentary, *see* http://rt.com/usa/190040-yellowstone-unmanned aircraft-crash-ban/. Additionally, a man was detained for flying an unmanned aircraft over an NFL game. . . . Currently unmanned aircraft are banned at national parks and NFL games, *see* http://www.charlotteobserver.com/2014/08/26/5130873/unmanned aircraft-buzzes-panthers-chiefs-game.html#.VCJaMvldUkM.

6. 319 U.S. 190 (1943).

7. *Id.*

modes of expression, it is subject to governmental regulation."[8] Notably, *National Broadcasting Co. v. United States* established the foundational administrative law that granted administrative agencies more expansive powers to regulate broadcast media.

Conversely, unlike the extensive regulation of the broadcast media, the government's regulation of the print media has been minimal. There have been very few legislative acts in the United States regulating the newspaper industry. Likewise, even the most salient regulation of newspapers does not curtail their First Amendment rights. Correspondingly, the *Newspaper Preservation Act of 1970*[9] provides an exemption to antitrust laws allowing for two newspapers to merge operations if one is close to the brink of failure, which actually enhances a newspaper's First Amendment rights.

Although there is currently minimal First Amendment regulation of the print media, both the reasoning and holding in *National Broadcasting* may aptly apply to the print media in conjunction with unmanned operations. Consequently, despite the media's First Amendment protection, the freedom of the press is not an absolute right; hence, all media enterprises and media UA operators will be subject to FAA and FCC regulations based on "public interest, convenience, or necessity,"[10] and the press may be limited in their use of unmanned aircraft through further government regulation—despite flawed presumptions of absolute First Amendment protections.

The Non-Absolute Rights of the First Amendment

A long line of cases reject the absolute free speech rights of the press, and many of these cases uphold the privacy rights of the individual over the First Amendment rights of the press. Although privacy is a central issue in many of these cases, the concept of the right of privacy is a relatively new area of jurisprudence in the United States as the first substantive mention of the right of privacy was in an 1890 *Harvard Law Review* article.[11] The article describes Samuel D. Warren's and Louis D. Brandeis' seminal interpretation of the right of privacy and the "evil of the invasion of privacy by the newspapers."[12] Remarkably, their description and interpretation of an individual's privacy rights relative to the press's invasion of such privacy are applicable to the current domain of unmanned aircraft use by the media—despite the fact that the article was written over 120 years ago.

Warren and Brandeis argue that "Recent inventions . . . call attention to the next step which must be taken for the protection of the person . . . [including]

---

8. *Id.*
9. 15 U.S.C. § 1802(2) (1970).
10. Communications Act of 1934.
11. *The Right To Privacy*, HARVARD LAW REVIEW, 193 (1890). This article is foundational to privacy tort law in the United States and is considered the seminal legal writing in privacy tort law.
12. *Id.* 15 U.S.C. § 1802(2) (1970).

numerous mechanical devices. . . ."[13] Moreover, they state that "instantaneous photographs . . . have invaded the sacred precincts of private and domestic life. . . ."[14] Furthermore, they argue that "The press is overstepping in every direction the obvious bounds of privacy and decency"[15] and that the privacy of the individual must be protected "from invasion either by the too enterprising press, the photographer, or the possessor of any other modern recording devices for recording. . . ."[16] While Warren and Brandeis could not have foreseen the use of unmanned aircraft by the media, their admonishments to the media for using modern mechanical devices and inventions to photograph or record the private individual apply directly to the media's use of unmanned aircraft. Principally, their article sets forth the foundations of privacy law that can be applied to nearly all areas of the invasion of privacy through technological means by the media.

Modern cases reflect the concerns of Warren and Brandeis regarding the media's invasion of privacy and other tortious conduct as they relate to the First Amendment right providing freedom of the press. A prime case is *Galella v. Onassis*.[17] In *Galella*, the Second Circuit Court of Appeals stated that regarding the right to privacy ". . . legitimate countervailing social needs may warrant some intrusion despite an individual's reasonable expectation of privacy and freedom from harassment. However the interference allowed may be no greater than that necessary to protect the overriding public interest."[18] Accordingly, the court balanced the right to privacy and the freedom of the press stating that the defendant's "action went far beyond the reasonable bounds of news-gathering. When weighed against the de minimis public importance of the daily activities of the defendant, Galella's constant surveillance, his obtrusive and intruding presence, was unwarranted and unreasonable."[19]

Galella's argument focused on his belief in an absolute "wall of immunity" that protects the media under the First Amendment right to freedom of the press; however, he did not dispute the court's finding of tortious conduct. In response to Galella's "wall of immunity" argument, the court countered that "There is no such scope to the First Amendment right."[20] Accordingly, the court shattered his argument based on the media's obligation to follow the law as "Crimes and torts committed in news gathering are not protected. . . . There is no threat to a free press in requiring its agents to act within the law."[21]

---

13. *Id.*
14. *Id.*
15. *Id.*
16. *Id.*
17. 487 F.2d 986 (1973).
18. *Id.*
19. *Id.*
20. *Id*
21. *Id.*

The Connecticut Superior Court in *Rafferty v. Hartford Courant Co.*[22] addressed the tortious invasion of privacy at a private event. A reporter and a photographer attended a private celebration and thereafter published the photographs they had taken during that celebration. The issue was whether they were invited guests (ordinary citizens) or members of the press. The court ruled that the media has "no greater right to intrude to obtain information than each citizen."[23]

The New York case of *Anderson v. WROC-TV*[24] involved the intrusion of media entities into the house of a private citizen during an animal rights investigation. The media was called in by an animal rights investigator who requested that the media be present during the investigation. The media subsequently entered the residence despite objections by the occupant during the investigation. The Supreme Court of Monroe County, New York, ruled that "news people do not stand in any favored position with respect to news-gathering activity. The United States Supreme Court has repeatedly held that the First Amendment right to speak and publish does not carry with it the unrestrained right to gather information. News people have no special First Amendment immunity or special privilege to invade the rights and liberties of others."[25]

Finally, in *Dietemann v. Time,*[26] investigative media entities utilized subterfuge to enter a private dwelling and took secret photographs and recordings of the plaintiff, then published them. The defendant claimed that "the First Amendment immunizes it [his media company] from liability for invading plaintiff's den with a hidden camera and its concealed electronic instruments because its employees were gathering news and its instrumentalities 'are indispensable tools of investigative reporting.'"[27] The Ninth Circuit Court did not agree, stating:

> We agree that news-gathering is an integral part of news dissemination. We strongly disagree, however, that the hidden mechanical contrivances are "indispensable tools" of news-gathering. Investigative reporting is an ancient art; its successful practice long antecedes the invention of miniature cameras and electronic devices. The First Amendment has never been construed to accord newsmen immunity from torts or crimes committed during the course of news-gathering. The First Amendment is not a license to trespass, to steal, or to intrude by electronic means into the precincts of another's home or office. It does not

22. 36 Conn. Supp. 239, 416 A.2d 215 (Super. Ct. 1980).
23. *Id.*
24. 109 Misc. 2d 904 (1981).
25. *Id.*
26. 449 F.2d 245 (9th Cir. 1971).
27. *Id.*

become such a license simply because the person subjected to the intrusion is reasonably suspected of committing a crime.[28]

The media's absolute First Amendment right to freedom of the press and free speech, as demonstrated in the above cases, is a fallacy, and media entities must not fall into the luring realm of tortious actions with the utilization of unmanned aircraft. The public's current infatuation with privacy makes the challenge even greater for the media, as the awareness of the potential use of unmanned aircraft by the media is growing exponentially. Media operators must be consciously aware of their place within the law when utilizing unmanned aircraft or any other innovative technology, and they should exercise cautious restraint despite the temptations of this new dimension in news-gathering.

The First Amendment as the Court's Last Resort

The ultimate question is whether the courts will utilize First Amendment doctrine in unmanned aircraft cases when other nonconstitutional pathways are available. It appears that courts often attempt to avoid citing the Constitution in favor of alternative legal grounds. In *Lyng v. Nw. Indian Cemetery Protective Ass'n*, the Supreme Court stated:

> A fundamental and longstanding principle of judicial restraint requires that courts avoid reaching constitutional questions in advance of the necessity of deciding them. This principle required the courts below to determine, before addressing the constitutional issue, whether a decision on that question could have entitled respondents to relief beyond that to which they were entitled on their statutory claims. If no additional relief would have been warranted, a constitutional decision would have been unnecessary and therefore inappropriate.[29]

The court justifiably avoided using the Constitution in this case as other viable options were available. Similarly, the Ninth Circuit Court in *United States v. Sandoval-Lopez*[30] stated, "We avoid constitutional questions when an alternative basis for disposing of the case presents itself."[31] The Court cited *Ashwander v. Tennessee Valley Authority*[32] in which Justice Brandeis' concurring opinion states, "Considerations of propriety, as well as long-established practice, demand that we refrain from passing upon the

---

28. *Id.*
29. 485 U.S. 439 (1988).
30. 122 F.3d 797 (9th Cir. 1997).
31. *Id.* n.9.
32. 297 U.S. 288, 347, 56 S.Ct. 466, 483, 80 L.Ed. 688 (1936).

constitutionality of an act of Congress unless obliged to do so in the proper performance of our judicial function, when the question is raised by a party whose interests entitle him to raise it."[33]

Furthermore, undoing a constitutional ruling is difficult. The difficulty of undoing constitutional rulings is a central part of the Second Circuit Judge Pierre Leval's argument in his work on trademarks wherein he contends that invoking the First Amendment to solve trademark disputes is unnecessary and difficult to undo.[34] Leval's article provides sage advice for future courts in unmanned aircraft cases since one significant ruling may affect the entire industry, and may, in fact, dissolve the ability of operators to utilize unmanned aircraft.

Since the issue of unmanned aircraft being utilized by the media is currently in its infancy, the use of the constitution in disposing of related cases may not be in the crosshairs of the courts in the next few years. However, the Constitutional issues of unmanned aircraft must be taken seriously due to the technological nature of unmanned aviation since UA news-gathering requires considerable investment in equipment and well-trained personnel to effectively operate a safe and viable UA program.

Given the myriad projected uses of unmanned aircraft and their lawful integration into the national airspace, the probability that a constitutional case will arise in the not-so-distant future is quite high. There is a distinct possibility that a single court ruling could cause the loss of crucial unmanned programs. Therefore, the tenor and progression of unmanned aircraft cases in the courts must be closely monitored to ascertain likely court directions and rulings that could affect future uses of unmanned aircraft by media operators.

Current State of First Amendment Unmanned Aircraft Cases

Unmanned aircraft law and relevant cases involving the First Amendment are gestational, as the use of unmanned aircraft in the national airspace is currently not allowed by FAA regulation, except under special authorization by the agency.[35] Therefore, the body of case law is diminutive.

---

33. *Id.*

34. Pierre Leval, *Trademark: Champion of Free Speech*, 27 COLUM. J.L. & ARTS 187 (2004). This work discusses the increased and aggressive use of other people's trademarks and argues that there needs to be a balance between the trademark holder and the interest of expressive users to protect free speech and to also allocate the rights of trademark holders.

35. Current authorization is provided by the FAA to operators acquiring a "Certificate of Waiver or Authorization" by the agency to fly in controlled national airspace. In 2007 the FAA issued FAA Notice 07-01 stating that "operators who wish to fly an unmanned aircraft for civil use must obtain an FAA airworthiness certificate the same as any other type aircraft." 72 Fed. Reg. 6689-90 (Feb. 13, 2007). For details on COAs *see* https://www.faa.gov/about/office_org/headquarters_offices/ato/service_units/systemops/aaim/organizations/uas/coa.

One of the foremost First Amendment cases applicable to unmanned aircraft is *Streisand v. Adelman,*[36] argued in the Superior Court of the Los Angeles West District. This case involves a manned small helicopter operated by the defendant in a documentary type media project to take digital images across the coastline of California to be made available in a public forum (the Internet) to news organizations, researchers, and other interested parties free of charge for basic images or with a cost for higher quality prints.

The defendant was unaware that one of his images, Image 3850, contained a portion of the plaintiff's property. The defendant did not earn any profits from the images taken including Image 3850. Each of the defendant's over 12,000 images was the subject of the litigation, including an image of the plaintiff's property. The images were all taken by a 35mm camera with no telephoto lens despite being taken from the air. The plaintiff requested an injunction to remove the images from the project website out of concerns for her privacy and safety.[37]

The court ruled in favor of the defendant's First Amendment rights, stating that the "published image indisputably addressed issues of long-standing and current public interest; is posted in a public forum . . . and represents the exercise of [the defendant's] First Amendment rights in connection with a public issue and an issue of public interest."[38] The court continued its ruling by classifying the photographs as protected speech: "The purpose and function of the photography and its publication on the California Coastal Records Project website are examples of speech protected by the state and federal constitutions."[39]

The issues of privacy were also resolved by the court. The plaintiff argued that the photographs were an intrusion into her seclusion[40] and also violated her general rights of privacy under the California Constitution which states that "All people are by their nature free and independent and have inalienable rights. Among these are . . . pursuing and obtaining safety, happiness, and privacy."[41]

The court disagreed with the plaintiff stating that "Neither this right to be left alone, nor the wrong for which the tort principle provides a remedy is absolute . . . the intrusion must be intentional . . . and the plaintiff must establish that the defendant

---

36. Streisand v. Adelman, et al, Case No. SC 077 257 Los Angeles Superior Court (December 31, 2003).
37. *Id.*
38. *Id.*
39. *Id.*
40. The privacy tort of intrusion into seclusion is one of four privacy torts enumerated by the American Law Institute Restatement (Second) of Torts. The Restatement (Second) states in part that "The right of privacy is invaded by a) unreasonable intrusion into the seclusion of another . . . b) appropriation of the other's name or likeness . . . c) unreasonable publicity given to the other's private life . . . d) publicity that unreasonably places the other in a false light before the public. . . ."
41. Cal. Const. Art. 1 § 1 (West 2011).

'penetrated some zone of physical or sensory privacy surrounding . . . the plaintiff.'"[42] The court further argued that the "tort is not automatically established or negated based on the location at which the allegedly offending conduct occurred."[43] Additionally, the court pointed out a compelling statement in the Restatement (Second) of Torts which asserts that "Complete privacy does not exist in this world except in a desert, and anyone who is not a hermit must expect and endure the ordinary incidents of the community of which he is a part."[44]

The *Streisand* case[45] was a distinct and direct assertion of the rights of the defendant to conduct aerial photographic operations for the benefit of the general public in public navigable airspace.[46] Therefore, this case has numerous implications for the media when conducting unmanned aircraft operations relative to pursuing their First Amendment right to freedom of the press and in their defense against claims of invasion of privacy.

The court in *Streisand* established the fact that the right of privacy is not absolute. This contrasts the previous discussion of the non-absolute rights of the First Amendment. As such, a more balanced continuum of the rights of privacy of the individual and the free speech rights of the media can be envisioned by media in all manners of news-gathering, including that involving the use of unmanned aircraft.

THE FOURTH AMENDMENT AND JOINT ACTION

The Fourth Amendment states in part that "The rights of the people to be secure in their persons, houses, papers, and effects, against unreasonable searches and seizures, shall not be violated. . . ."[47] However, the Fourth Amendment is not absolute, as the Court in *United States v. Sharp* clarifies, "The Fourth Amendment is not, of course, a guarantee against all searches and seizures, but only against unreasonable searches and seizures."[48] Accordingly, the scope of the search must also be considered relative to government interests. The Supreme Court in *United States v. Place* reasoned that "We must balance the nature and quality of the intrusion on the individual's Fourth

---

42. Streisand v. Adelman.
43. *Id.*
44. Rest. 2d. Torts, sec 652D, comment c.
45. The case of Streisand v. Adelman gained notoriety for Streisand, as many in the public and media believed that this case was frivolous and hypocritical on the part of Streisand. The term "Streisand Effect" emerged as a result of the case, denoting the rich and famous as valuing their perceived personal rights of privacy over the media's freedom of speech. For more details, *see* http://www.economist.com/blogs/economist-explains/2013/04/economist-explains-what-streisand-effect.
46. Under 49 U.S. Code § 40103 - Sovereignty and use of airspace, (a)(2) "A citizen of the United States has a public right of transit through the navigable airspace."
47. U.S. Const. amend. IV.
48. United States v. Sharpe, 470 U.S. 675 (1985).

Amendment interests against the importance of the governmental interests alleged to justify the intrusion. . . . We must weigh the nature and extent of the intrusion upon the individual's Fourth Amendment rights."[49]

Standing to make a Fourth Amendment challenge for alleged unreasonable searches and seizures requires that government conduct violates an individual's reasonable expectation of privacy. Hence, standing requires that two prongs be met: First, government conduct is required in effecting the search and/or seizure; second, the challenger must have a reasonable expectation of privacy in the person or place searched and/or the person or thing seized.

Primarily, the search and seizure must be conducted by a government actor, not a private citizen or private legal entity. Alternatively, the government conduct requirement is met where a search or seizure is conducted by an individual or entity acting at the behest or direction of the government. Although a Fourth Amendment challenge cannot be made against a purely private actor or entity, a trespass or a privacy tort claim may be available to the injured party.

Although media organizations are private entities, the media faces potential liability under the Fourth Amendment in situations where a media organization acts jointly with a government entity—either intentionally or inadvertently—causing that organization to function as a state actor. The media industry's use of unmanned aircraft for news-gathering will likely expose media organizations to both intentional and unintentional joint actions with the government, wherein media UA operators may be seen as acting in conjunction with the government. An intentional action could occur where a media entity provides aerial services to law enforcement. The media could serve law enforcement in situations where the media provides UA equipment that law enforcement lacks or the media provide their aerial services to law enforcement.

An unintentional action could potentially occur in the event that data from the media's aerial observations is routed to law enforcement. Such unintended transfers of data could potentially be due to either a lack of information assurance and data security or through a third party. Consequently, to circumvent potential government entanglement and Fourth Amendment challenges, media organizations should be mindful when providing UA assistance to the government, as well as be careful with both disseminating intended transmissions and controlling unintended routing of UA gathered data to the government.

In addition to government conduct, standing to bring a Fourth Amendment challenge requires that the governmental search intrudes into a person's reasonable expectation of privacy. A reasonable expectation of privacy exists where an individual actually expects privacy and that individual's expectation is one that society as a

---

49. United States v. Place, 462 U.S. 696 (1983).

whole would deem legitimate. The expectation of privacy is crucial to distinguishing a legitimate, reasonable government search and seizure from an unreasonable one. A "search occurs for purposes of the Fourth Amendment when the Government violates a person's reasonable expectation of privacy"[50]—whether the search is by physical or technological means. Pursuant to the Supreme Courts holding in *Katz v. United States* a physical intrusion upon the actual property of the person may not be necessary for a search to have occurred. In *Katz v. United States*, the Supreme Court clarified the constitutional parameters of a search, stating that "oftentimes what seems to be a search is not a search at all. . . . What a person knowingly exposes to the public, even in his home or office, is not a subject of Fourth Amendment protection . . . but what he seeks to preserve as private, even in an area accessible to the public, may be constitutionally protected."[51]

The Supreme Court's point on public accessibility is crucial for media UA operators because the Court has held that a reasonable expectation of privacy may be found to exist in a publicly accessible area where it is a specific individual's opinion that a certain location or situation is private. Further, the court may accept this as a reasonable expectation of privacy where the individual can show they possessed a subjective expectation of privacy and it is an objective expectation of privacy that society would generally recognize.

A media unmanned aircraft operator may be involved in a Fourth Amendment search, intentional or unintentional, therefore, if the unmanned vehicle is conducting surveillance or imaging a publicly accessible location of a person, even if the unmanned aircraft is in legal navigable airspace. If the aircraft's data communication lines are not secure, a third-party entity, or even the police, may be able to intercept the data and use the information against the person unbeknownst to the media UA operator. Additionally, if the media are conducting a ride-along with the police or are a part of a reality show filming, they may be subject to Fourth Amendment liability from a search.

These potential situations and many more open up potential liability for the media organization. As such, the media needs to be aware of the Fourth Amendment issues surrounding the use of unmanned aircraft in their news-gathering operations. While this situation may not be common in the daily operations of the media, its implications for civil liability may be significant, especially if the court finds that the media was in fact a joint entity with the government.

---

50. Katz v. United States, 389 U.S. 347, 351 (1967).
51. *Id.*

The Fourth Amendment Liability of the Media

The Fourth Amendment rights of the private person and the First Amendment free speech rights of the press to report newsworthy events may clash. When a situation such as this occurs, it will be left up to the courts to decide which interest is most pervasive. Several cases provide guidance on the balancing of the two amendments in various circumstances.

The case of *Wilson v. Layne*[52] serves as an example of the media following law enforcement into a raid. In this case, law enforcement conducted a raid on a home. The suspect was not at home during the raid, but his parents were. Law enforcement invited a reporter and photographer to accompany them, but this accompaniment was not included in the warrant. Law enforcement entered the home early in the morning with the media personnel documenting the raid with photographs being taken of the police action including several photographs of the parents of the suspect in their night clothes. The photographs were never published. The plaintiff's cause of action stated that the action of law enforcement in inviting the media personnel to observe and record the attempted execution of the arrest warrant violated their Fourth Amendment rights.

The Supreme Court held that "A media 'ride-along' in a home violates the Fourth Amendment."[53] Accordingly, the Court reasoned:

> It violates the Fourth Amendment rights of homeowners for police to bring members of the media or other third parties into their home during the execution of a warrant when the presence of the third parties in the home was not in aid of the warrant's execution. The Amendment embodies centuries-old principles of respect for the privacy of the home, which apply where, as here, police enter a home under the authority of an arrest warrant in order to take into custody the suspect named in the warrant. . . . It does not necessarily follow from the fact that the officers were entitled to enter petitioners' home that they were entitled to bring a reporter and a photographer with them. The Fourth Amendment requires that police actions in execution of a warrant be related to the objectives of the authorized intrusion.[54]

Notably, the Court opined that in some circumstances third parties, such as the media, may have a constitutionally permissible right to be present during the execution of a warrant, particularly if the presence of the third party was specified in the warrant.

---

52. Wilson v. Layne 526 U.S. 603 (1999).
53. *Id.*
54. *Id.*

The case of *Lauro v. Charles*[55] involves the staging of law enforcement actions with the media documenting the situation. The issue was whether law enforcement could stage "perp walks" for the benefit of the media, with no other law enforcement interest. The court held that a "staged perp walk exacerbates the seizure of the arrestee unreasonably and therefore violates the Fourth Amendment."[56]

The Court noted, however, that "The interests of the press, and of the public who might want to view perp walks, are far from negligible."[57] The issue the court had was the artificial staging of the event for the benefit of the media. This action had no law enforcement interest, and according to the Court law enforcement "is not well served by an inherently fictional dramatization of an event that transpired hours earlier."[58]

A case soon followed that further clarified the issue of law enforcement's staging of events for the media. The case, *Caldarola v. County of Westchester*,[59] involved the law enforcement choreographing the suspects' arrests to facilitate videotaping and subsequently allowing the media to utilize the videos. The court held that the plaintiffs' Fourth Amendment rights were not violated as law enforcement has a legitimate government purpose in utilizing the media in their arrest procedures. They state "that perp walks are broadcast by networks and reprinted in newspapers at least in part for their entertainment value. Yet, perp walks also serve the more serious purpose of educating the public about law enforcement efforts. The image of the accused being led away to contend with the justice system powerfully communicates government efforts to thwart the criminal element, and it may deter others from attempting similar crimes."[60]

This holding can be distinguished from the ruling in *Lauro v. Charles* with the distinction being a staged event versus a choreographed event. The court in *Caldarola* noted that in the case of *Lauro* the suspect's rights of privacy were violated and that "legitimate state interest in accurate reporting of police activity is not well served by an inherently fictional dramatization of an event that transpired hours earlier."[61] This ruling therefore limited law enforcement's inclusion of the media in law enforcement actions to "staged" events that pose no legitimate government interest as violations of the Fourth Amendment.

The case of *Berger v. Hanlon*[62] demonstrates how a media entity can be held liable under joint action. The media in this case was held as a joint actor for their role in a

---

55. Lauro v. Charles, 219 F.3d 202 (2nd Cir. 2000).
56. *Id.*
57. *Id.*
58. *Id.*
59. Caldarola v. County of Westchester, 343 F.3d 570 (2nd Cir. 2003).
60. *Id.*
61. *Id.*
62. Berger v. Hanlon, 188 F.3d 1155 (9th Cir. 1999).

raid against the plaintiffs, where the media entity, CNN, video- and audio-taped the raid from both the ground and an aerial vantage point. CNN had negotiated their role in the raid with law enforcement, which included the audio wiring of agents in the raid. *Berger* advanced to the Supreme Court where the Court ruled that the plaintiff's Fourth Amendment rights were violated. The Court remanded the case back to the Ninth Circuit, which subsequently ruled that CNN was a joint actor and did not have a qualified immunity defense. Significantly, the court found that CNN had actively participated in the "staging" of the raid such as in *Lauro,* where the staging of a law enforcement action is a violation of the plaintiff's privacy.

The main distinguishing factor between the two cases is that in *Berger*, the media took an active role in the staging of the event, while in *Lauro*, the media had a passive role. Hence, in *Berger*, the media organization was considered a joint actor in the Fourth Amendment violation.

The trends in the cases demonstrate that when the media is actively involved in the staging of law enforcement events, they may be held liable under the Fourth Amendment as a joint actor. Yet the lines between choreographing and staging may be nebulous. With the increased mobility that unmanned aircraft have in live events, the media may be lured into using them within the context and with the acceptance and encouragement of law enforcement for the documentation of law enforcement actions. This documentation may have many purposes as stated above, such as for entertainment value, for the interest of the public in reducing crime, for the interest of protecting law enforcement, etc.

Law enforcement may rely on the media to provide their unmanned aircraft to document events and law enforcement actions in the near future. This invitation may be for many reasons including law enforcement's lack of access to unmanned aircraft technology, law enforcement's desire to demonstrate to the public their capabilities through media documentation, legal protection through video documentation, and so forth.

Media unmanned aircraft operators must exhibit caution when undertaking such activities until a thorough assessment of the facts of the proposed operation is evaluated to ensure that they do not become joint actors in the incident. Unlike law enforcement, the media may have a more difficult or impossible time gaining qualified immunity in such a case as compared to their law enforcement counterparts. As a result, if held as a joint actor, the media, with its significantly deeper pockets, may in fact become the central focus of the plaintiff's cause of action.

Current State of Fourth Amendment Unmanned Aircraft-Related Cases

There are several cases that can be directly applied to the operation of unmanned aircraft that involve the Fourth Amendment. With the increase in use of unmanned aircraft over the next few years by the media (see Figure 10.2 for a UA suitable for media operations), the probability of a joint action with law enforcement or other government entities may increase. As a result, a thorough understanding of unmanned aircraft-related cases is advantageous to media UA operators. Additionally, if the Fourth Amendment is not violated in a case, most likely a privacy tort in general will not be applicable to general media operations of the same nature, thus preserving the First Amendment rights of the media unmanned aircraft operator. While none of the prevailing Fourth Amendment cases involve unmanned aircraft directly, they do either involve manned aircraft or technology that can be installed on an unmanned aircraft as functional payload.

Figure 10.2

A Shadow Unmanned Aircraft (Photo courtesy of Donna Dulo)

The first case, *California v. Ciraolo*,[63] involves a private aircraft flown by law enforcement agents over a residential area as a direct result of a tip that marijuana was being grown at the target residence. Based on the naked-eye aerial observations by one of the officers on board the aircraft that was flying at 1,000 feet, a subsequent search warrant of the premises was obtained. The search warrant contained a photograph

---

63. California v. Ciraolo, 476 U.S. 207 (1986).

of the residence that was taken from the aircraft. The defendant moved to suppress the evidence based on a violation of his Fourth Amendment rights, since the aerial observations were not completed under a warrant.

The Supreme Court ruled that the Fourth Amendment was not violated by the naked-eye aerial observation of respondent's backyard. Their rationale was direct:

> [The] respondent's expectation of privacy from all observations of his backyard was unreasonable. That the backyard and its crop were within the "curtilage" of respondent's home did not itself bar all police observation. The mere fact that an individual has taken measures to restrict some views of his activities does not preclude an officer's observation from a public vantage point where he has a right to be and which renders the activities clearly visible. The police observations here took place within public navigable airspace, in a physically nonintrusive manner.[64]

The key points in this case are the flying of the aircraft in navigable airspace[65] and having a public vantage point. The public are authorized to fly in the nation's navigable airspace under direct authority of Federal Regulations.[66] Additionally, under Federal Regulations, the government has exclusive sovereignty of airspace of the United States.[67]

While flying, passengers and crew of aircraft have a unique visual advantage over people on the ground. This advantage is part of the aviation experience, yet may become vital in the observation of criminal activity. This is not a barrier to law enforcement activities in the air under the Fourth Amendment. The Court points out that:

> The Fourth Amendment protection of the home has never been extended to require law enforcement officers to shield their eyes when passing by a home on public thoroughfares. Nor does the mere fact that an individual has taken measures to restrict some views of his activities preclude an officer's observations

---

64. *Id.*

65. Navigable airspace is defined broadly in 49 U.S. Code § 40102 – Definitions (a)(32) in the following manner: "'navigable airspace' means airspace above the minimum altitudes of flight prescribed by regulations under this subpart and subpart III of this part, including airspace needed to ensure safety in the takeoff and landing of aircraft."

66. Under 49 U.S. Code § 40103 - Sovereignty and use of airspace (a)(2) "A citizen of the United States has a public right of transit through the navigable airspace. To further that right, the Secretary of Transportation shall consult with the Architectural and Transportation Barriers Compliance Board established under section 502 of the Rehabilitation Act of 1973 (29 U.S.C. 792) before prescribing a regulation or issuing an order or procedure that will have a significant impact on the accessibility of commercial airports or commercial air transportation for handicapped individuals."

67. 49 U.S. Code § 40103 - Sovereignty and use of airspace (a)(1).

from a public vantage point where he has a right to be and which renders the activities clearly visible.[68]

In essence, the aerial vantage point is merely an added third dimension to the normal two dimensions of observations that law enforcement has at ground level. The application of the public view doctrine therefore extends to aerial operations.

A similar case ruled in the same year as *Ciraolo* is *Dow Chemical Co. v. United States*.[69] This case involves the Environmental Protection Agency's (EPA) use of commercially generated photographs from navigable airspace at 1200, 3000, and 12,000 feet above the Dow Chemical facility. The photographs were taken by a commercial photographer. As with *Ciraolo*, the photographs were taken in lawful navigable airspace by a citizen entitled to fly in that airspace. The court ruled that it is within the EPA's authority to utilize aerial observation and photography since "For purposes of aerial surveillance, the open areas of an industrial complex are more comparable to an 'open field' in which an individual may not legitimately demand privacy."[70] This "open field" contrasts with the "curtilage" concept of a private dwelling as featured in *Ciraolo*.

The case of *Florida v. Riley*[71] has similar facts as the previous cases applied to an actual physical structure. Here, law enforcement utilized a helicopter in navigable airspace at 400 feet to see, via the naked eye, into the openings of a greenhouse, where they observed the growing of marijuana. The only difference, in essence, between this case and *Ciraolo* is that here, the observations were undertaken in a helicopter at 400 feet as opposed to a fixed-wing aircraft at 1,000 feet. An interesting comment by Justice O'Connor is relevant to unmanned and manned flight operations. She highlights the fact that reasonable expectations of privacy should be focused upon, not "compliance with FAA regulations alone," in the determination of the constitutionality of aerial observations. This opinion may re-emerge in future cases involving unmanned aircraft, particularly since many unmanned aircraft can, in many instances, be legally operated from the ground and upward during regular operations, unlike manned aircraft that are required to maintain a minimum altitude during regular operations.

These three cases demonstrate vividly the concepts of lawful navigable airspace and public view via the naked eye, setting a trend that will likely carry over into unmanned operations. The only difference with an unmanned aircraft is the fact that observations will occur through a video or aerial viewing system set up with the pilot controlling the aircraft from the ground with payload operators controlling the video or visual

---

68. California v. Ciraolo, 476 U.S. 207 (1986).
69. Dow Chemical Co. v. United States, 476 U.S. 227 (1986).
70. *Id.*
71. Florida v. Riley, 488 U.S. 445 (1989).

systems of the aircraft. The fact that unmanned aircraft observations are not directly observed by the naked eye, but through aerial imaging systems and cameras, could be an issue that may facilitate a deviation in the court's rulings from the above cases.

Several related cases revolve around the payload capabilities of the aircraft rather than the aerial vantage point of the aircraft. In *Kyllo v. United States*[72] the Supreme Court ruled that a thermal imager used by law enforcement on a home violated the Fourth Amendment. The ruling showed that when "the Government uses a device that is not in general public use, to explore details of a private home that would previously have been unknowable without physical intrusion, the surveillance is a Fourth Amendment 'search,' and is presumptively unreasonable without a warrant."[73]

The key in this case is the use of a device not in public use, one that augments the physical senses of the human observer, in essence sense-enhancing technology that in effect reduces the scope of a person's reasonable expectation of privacy. With the advent of technology and the exponential growth of technology through advanced principles of science and engineering, what is now a device unique to the government may be commonplace within a few years. A prime example is that or Moore's Law, a popular concept in the field of computer science and engineering. Moore's Law postulates that the processing power of computer chips will double every two years. This doubling in power is due to the technological advancements in chip design and materials. The computer, once thought to be a device only found in large government facilities, is now so common that almost every electronic device has one built in, including hot dog grills and cat toys.

The use of Moore's Law has shown over the years the incredible increase in processing power, resulting in faster, smarter, and cheaper technologies that are pervasive in the average American household. This calls into question the Court's use of the "not in general public use" doctrine as expressed in *Kyllo*. Justice Scalia recognizes this fact. In his opinion he states that "It would be foolish to contend that the degree of privacy secured to citizens by the Fourth Amendment has been entirely unaffected by the advance of technology. . . . The question we confront today is what limits there are upon this power of technology to shrink the realm of guaranteed privacy."[74]

United States v. Jones[75] is another case that deals with technology rather than the aerial vantage point. In this case the Supreme Court ruled that a GPS device attached to a vehicle and its use to monitor the use and movements of that vehicle violates the Fourth Amendment. The key here is the use of a technology and the temporal persistence aspects of that technology to monitor the defendant. The Court defines

---

72. Kyllo v. United States, 533 U.S. 27 (2001).
73. *Id.*
74. *Id.*
75. United States v. Jones, 615 F. 3d 544 (2012).

the vehicle as an "effect" as found in the words of the Fourth Amendment, and the government's application and use of the GPS define a "search" as the device occupied the property of the defendant. The concurrence by Justice Sotomayor contains striking words describing the relationship between the citizen and the government if the *Jones* use of GPS would be ruled constitutional:

> Awareness that the Government may be watching chills associational and expressive freedoms. And the Government's unrestrained power to assemble data that reveal private aspects of identity is susceptible to abuse. The net result is that GPS monitoring—by making available at a relatively low cost such a substantial quantum of intimate information about any person whom the Government, in its unfettered discretion, chooses to track—may "alter the relationship between citizen and government in a way that is inimical to democratic society." United States v. Cuevas-Perez, 640 F. 3d 272, 285 (CA7 2011) (Flaum, J., concurring).[76]

Again, the key concept here is the use of a technology to monitor a person in a temporal and persistent manner. The use of technology such as a GPS in a public place in essence violates the defendant's reasonable expectation of privacy.

Thus, when dealing with Fourth Amendment cases concerning aircraft or cutting-edge technology, we see two basic categorizations: aerial vantage point and temporal persistence. These categorizations will be used in a subsequent section of the chapter to build a basic framework for understanding constitutional issues of using unmanned aircraft by the media. The overarching theme is that the media must be cautious when working jointly with law enforcement or other government entity. What may seem like a reality show adventure with the police may end up being the reality that earns the media UA operator their name on a privacy tort cause of action.

HUERTA V. PIRKER

A case that requires close attention and considerable analysis by the media is the case of *Huerta v. Pirker*.[77] This is one of the first major cases revolving specifically around the issue of the use of unmanned aircraft in the national airspace and is still being resolved in the courts.[78] The rulings and motions are detailed below to indicate the

---

76. *Id.*

77. Huerta v. Pirker, NTSB CP-217 Decisional Order. Also cited as Michael P. Huerta, Administrator, Federal Aviation Administration v. Raphael Pirker.

78. Note that the rulings of the case do not adhere to the FAA Modernization Reauthorization and Reform Act of 2012 since the legislation postdates the events at issue in the case. The judge does state in his Decisional Order, however, that the "language of provisions of the 2012 Act is instructive."

complexities and uncertainties of unmanned aircraft law and the interpretations of the regulations in light of new, incomplete, or nebulous regulations concerning the operation of unmanned aircraft in the national airspace.

The respondent, Raphael Pirker, is a freelance Austrian aerial photographer. At the time of the incident in October of 2011, he was flying a remote-controlled Ritewing Zephyr,[79] a small V-shaped Styrofoam-powered glider weighing five pounds, on the grounds of the University of Virginia in Charlottesville, Virginia, to shoot a promotional video and still photographs for monetary compensation. As a result of his actions, the FAA subsequently fined Pirker $10,000 in June of 2013 for the violation of Part 91, Section 91.13(a)[80] of the Federal Aviation Regulations (FAR) for operating an aircraft in a careless and reckless manner.

Pirker filed a Motion to Dismiss, asserting that as a matter of law the FAA did not have the authority to regulate his model aircraft operations,[81] and the National Transportation Safety Board administrative Law Judge Patrick G. Geraghty, hearing the case, agreed. Judge Geraghty also ruled that the FAA did not write its commercial unmanned aircraft policy in accordance with the formal rulemaking process and did not comply with the Administrative Procedures Act, thus Pirker's motion to dismiss was granted and the FAA fine was vacated and set aside.

Particularly, the case revolved around the definition of the word *aircraft*. Pirker argued that the FAA was acting outside of the scope of law, by prohibiting commercial unmanned aircraft use based on model airplane guidelines[82] from 1981 that required only voluntary compliance.[83] The judge agreed, stating that the FAA "has not issued an enforceable FAR regulatory rule governing model aircraft operation; has historically exempted model aircraft from the statutory FAR definitions of 'aircraft' by regulating model aircraft operations to voluntary compliance. . . ."[84]

---

79. For information and specifications on the Ritewing Zephyr *see* http://www.ritewingrc.com/Zephyr_II _ARF.html.

80. Part 91, Section 91.13(a) of the FAR states: No person may operate an aircraft in a careless or reckless manner so as to endanger the life or property of another.

81. 49 U.S.C. § 40102(a)(35) defines aircraft operation: "operate aircraft" and "operation of aircraft" mean using aircraft for the purposes of air navigation, including—

(A) the navigation of aircraft; and

(B) causing or authorizing the operation of aircraft with or without the right of legal control of the aircraft.

82. The guidelines were FAA issued Advisory Circular (AC) AC 91-57, "Model Aircraft Operating Standards" published on June 9, 1981. A copy of this circular can be found at http://rgl.faa.gov/Regulatory_and _Guidance_Library/rgAdvisoryCircular.nsf/0/1ACFC3F689769A56862569E70077C9CC.

83. AC 91-57 states that "This advisory circular outlines, and encourages voluntary compliance with, safety standards for model aircraft operators." It further asserts that "Modelers, generally, are concerned about safety and do exercise good judgment when flying model aircraft. However, model aircraft can at times pose a hazard to full-scale aircraft in flight and to persons and property on the surface. Compliance with [AC 91-57] . . . standards will help reduce the potential for that hazard and create a good neighbor environment with affected communities and airspace users."

84. *Id*. Huerta v. Pirker, Decisional Order.

The FAA appealed the decision to the full National Transportation and Safety Board on the express basis of the safety of the national airspace. The FAA's appeal argues that Pirker "deliberately operated the aircraft at low altitudes over vehicles, buildings, people, streets and structure,"[85] in one case causing a person "to take immediate evasive maneuvers so as to avoid being struck by the aircraft,"[86] with the aircraft coming within 20 feet of an active road and coming within 100 feet of an active heliport. The FAA also asserted that Pirker "operated the aircraft in a careless and reckless manner so as to endanger the life or property of another,"[87] a specific violation of Part 91, Section 91.13(a).

The FAA appeal claimed that the NTSB judge erred in the interpretation of the definition of an aircraft[88] versus a model aircraft and that the judge erred in stating that the aircraft was not subject to regulation under the FAA. The FAA also claimed that the judge ignored the wording of the federal statutes, which define an aircraft, and that he imposed his own "novel interpretation"[89] of the word "aircraft."

The initial ruling of the NTSB administrative judge was cited by many in the unmanned aircraft industry as the end to the ban on the commercial use of unmanned aircraft in the national airspace. However, the fact that the FAA appealed to the full NTSB had the specific effect of staying the NTSB administrative judge's ruling until the full NTSB published its ruling on the case. Therefore, the FAA regulations and current ban on commercial unmanned aircraft use in the national airspace with a waiver was still in effect awaiting the ruling of the board.

There was, however, a twist in the case that must be noted, as *Pirker* was decided outside of the rules of operation of unmanned aircraft in the FAA Modernization Reauthorization and Reform Act of 2012 ("Act of 2012"). Under the Act of 2012, a model aircraft is defined as being "flown strictly for hobby or recreational purposes."[90] The word "strictly" is significant for potential commercial operators. Aviation hobbyists may fly a small, unmanned hobby aircraft in furtherance of their hobby interests; however, if they earn a profit, they may be classified in certain circumstances as a

---

85. Huerta v. Pirker, NTSB CP-217 Administrator's Appeal Brief.

86. *Id.*

87. *Id.*

88. Legal definitions of the word "aircraft" can be found in 49 U.S.C. § 40102(a)(6) and 14 C.F.R. § 1.1. Under 14 C.F.R. § 1.1 the word "aircraft" means a "device that is used or intended to be used for flight in the air." In contrast, for example, it defines "airplane" as "an engine-driven fixed-wing aircraft heavier than air, that is supported in flight by the dynamic reaction of the air against its wings." 49 U.S.C. § 40102(a)(6) defines "aircraft" as "any contrivance invented, used, or designed to navigate, or fly in, the air."

89. *Id.* Huerta v. Pirker, Administrator's Appeal Brief.

90. The Act defines a model aircraft in Sec. 336(c) as

(1) capable of sustained flight in the atmosphere;

(2) flown within visual line of sight of the person operating the aircraft; and

(3) flown for hobby or recreational purposes.

The Act further defines the flight of model aircraft in Sec. 336 (a)(1): "the aircraft is flown strictly for hobby or recreational use."

business under the Internal Revenue Code.[91] This classification may place them in the category of a business rather than a hobby, changing the legal classification of their aircraft from a model aircraft to a small aircraft. As such, this change of classification may ban them from operations in the national airspace under the Act of 2012 unless they have a waiver.

On November 18, 2014, the NTSB reversed the decision of the NTSB administrative judge[92] and remanded the case to the administrative judge for further proceedings consistent with their opinion and order. The board opinion stated that unmanned aircraft are properly classified as "aircraft" and cannot be operated as "an aircraft in a careless or reckless manner so as to endanger the life or property of another."[93] Further, the board noted that regulations regarding the term "aircraft," whether a model or not, are "clear on their face" and "draw no distinction between whether a device is manned or unmanned" and that an aircraft is any device that is "used for flight" and concerning definitions such as that of an aircraft, "the definitions are as broad as they are clear . . . they are clear nonetheless."[94] Thus, the board ultimately concluded that "the plain language of the statutory and regulatory definitions is clear: an 'aircraft' is any device used for flight in the air."[95]

Pirker provides critical insight on potential FAA action with regard to the safe operation of unmanned aircraft. The FAA's highest mandate is to promote safety as well as efficiency in the national airspace.[96] Media operators of unmanned aircraft can be assured that the FAA will enforce Part 91, Section 91.13(a) and fine them if they operate an unmanned aircraft in a "careless or reckless manner so as to endanger the life or property of another."[97] Thus media operators must integrate safety into their operations along with the protection of individual privacy as potential issues that may restrict their freedom of speech under the First Amendment.

91. *See* IRC § 183: Activities Not Engaged in For Profit (ATG), 26 U.S. Code § 183 - Activities not engaged in for profit.
92. NTSB Order No. EA-5730, Docket CP-217 (Nov. 18, 2014).
93. *Id.*
94. *Id.*
95. *Id.*
96. See the FAA's statement on safety: "At FAA, what drives us — through everything we do — is our mission to provide the safest, most efficient aerospace system in the world. We continually strive to improve the safety and efficiency of flight in this country." http://www.faa.gov/about/safety_efficiency/.
97. Part 91, Section 91.13(a).

FORGING A TECHNOLOGICAL LEGAL FRAMEWORK FOR UA OPERATIONS

The rulings of the courts regarding or related to unmanned aircraft revolved around key technological areas: that of the airframe of the unmanned aircraft or that of the payload. These technological areas determine the aerial vantage point of aircraft operations as well as the temporal persistence and depth of penetration through publicly unavailable technology of the aircraft's payload. As such, using these concepts, a simple framework can be established to assist in the understanding of the court rulings as applicable to the First and Fourth Amendments in future unmanned aircraft operations.

Figure 10.3

A Sentry Unmanned Aircraft during Aerial Operations (Photo courtesy of Donna Dulo)

Aerial Vantage Point in Navigable Airspace

The first technological area to consider is the airframe of the unmanned aircraft (see Figure 10.3). The airframe may have the fuselage of a fixed-wing aircraft or of a rotorcraft, in particular, a helicopter. This airframe type will impact the aerial vantage point capabilities of the unmanned aircraft. For example a fixed-wing aircraft has the capability of flying larger distances at higher altitudes and at a more rapid

Figure 10.4

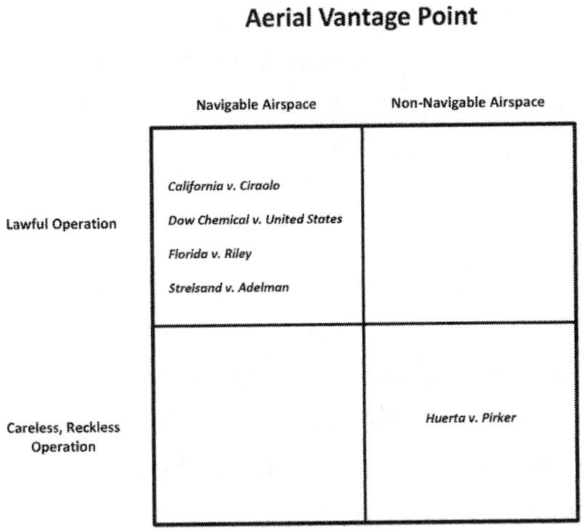

Aerial Vantage Point

	Navigable Airspace	Non-Navigable Airspace
Lawful Operation	*California v. Ciraolo* *Dow Chemical v. United States* *Florida v. Riley* *Streisand v. Adelman*	
Careless, Reckless Operation		*Huerta v. Pirker*

Aerial Vantage Point

speed than rotorcraft. A rotorcraft such as a helicopter has vertical takeoff and land-ing capabilities and can transverse vertical distances such as the face of a building. Additionally, a rotorcraft can hover and more easily maneuver close to the ground than a fixed-wing aircraft.

This aerial vantage point was a major factor in several of the aforementioned cases. In *Ciraolo*, law enforcement in a fixed-wing aircraft operating in legally navigable airspace at 1000 feet identified the growing of marijuana, avoiding the violation of the Fourth Amendment. In *Dow Chemical*, the EPA's use of photographs obtained from a photographer who took the images in legally navigable airspace at 1200, 3000, and 12,000 feet did not violate the Fourth Amendment. In *Riley*, law enforcement's use of a helicopter at 400 feet, lawful navigable airspace for a helicopter, to see into a marijuana greenhouse did not violate the Fourth Amendment.

In *Streisand*, the private photographer was in a helicopter within navigable airspace, at between 150 and 2000 feet, with his photographs ruled as not violating the privacy rights of the plaintiff, preserving his rights of free speech under the First Amendment.

On the other hand, in *Pirker*, the respondent's operation of an unmanned aircraft in airspace deemed unlawful, such as close to a heliport or a street or near persons on the ground, coupled with his reckless operation of the aircraft, may result, once the case is resolved, in the respondent's liability for his actions and potentially limit-ing his free speech rights.

Thus, aircraft operations can be categorized under an "Aerial Vantage Point" matrix(see Figure 10.4) as being either in navigable airspace or in non-navigable air-space and lawfully operated or carelessly and recklessly operated in the corresponding airspace. The cases with which the aircraft was in navigable airspace were all ruled in favor of the rights of the entities collecting the imagery, with the protection of First Amendment rights and the negation of Fourth Amendment violations. In the case where navigable airspace was violated with careless and reckless operation of the aircraft, potential free speech rights were silenced.

Payload Factors

The payload of an unmanned aircraft is essentially the primary tool for the aircraft's operations. Without the payload, the unmanned aircraft would be operated mainly for experimental purposes or for hobby or training purposes. The payload may be myriad technologies such as photographic equipment, sensors, monitors, or other types of technology. In fact, the type of airframe utilized depends highly on the type of payload required for the operation. In higher end unmanned aircraft, an imagery payload is mandatory in order to maintain visual sight in the air in addition to the operational payload.

Figure 10.5

The Payload Module of a Shadow Unmanned Aircraft (Photo courtesy of Donna Dulo)

The payload (see, for example, Figures 10.5 and 10.6) of an aircraft operated by the media, as well as its specific use, may play a significant role in maintaining the

Privacy–First Amendment continuum. For example, in *Jones*, the GPS device attached to the vehicle violated the Fourth Amendment in part because of the temporal persistence of the technology, persistence that "chills associational and expressive freedoms"[98] due to the long-term government monitoring.

In *Kyllo*, the technology used was advanced thermal imaging, the kind that is currently available on unmanned aircraft. This thermal imaging enabled law enforcement to have a depth of penetration of a structure outside the normal realm of general use technology. The Fourth Amendment was therefore violated in part because the technological device used by the government was not in public use.

Figure 10.6

Payload Module of a Sentry Unmanned Aircraft (Photo courtesy of Donna Dulo)

Thus, it can be established that the specific persistent use of the technology in the particular operation, as well as the degree of technical sophistication of the technology leading to a high degree of depth of penetration of a structure, can determine whether the operating entity violated the Fourth Amendment or privacy rights of the individual or individuals being observed or monitored.

---

98. United States v. Jones, 615 F. 3d 544 (2012) (Sotomayor concurrence).

The presence of technology not in public use due to its powerful capabilities, cost, or other factors coupled with the temporal persistence of the use of that technology can be categorized into a "Payload Penetration and Persistence" matrix (see Figure 10.7). The categories of "In General Public Use" or "Outside Public Use" are matched against long- or short-term temporal persistence.

As indicated on the matrix, the case of *Ciraolo* utilized normal technology, a camera that was available to the general public as well as a naked-eye observation, which can be considered a general public capability. The officers did not hover persistently over the property, thus the operation consisted of a short-term temporal persistence. The aerial photographer in *Dow Chemical* utilized a camera found in general public use, as did the photographer in *Streisand*, and both flights were conducted in short-term operations. Additionally, in *Riley*, naked-eye observations were used and the helicopter did not hover over the property in a long-term manner.

Figure 10.7

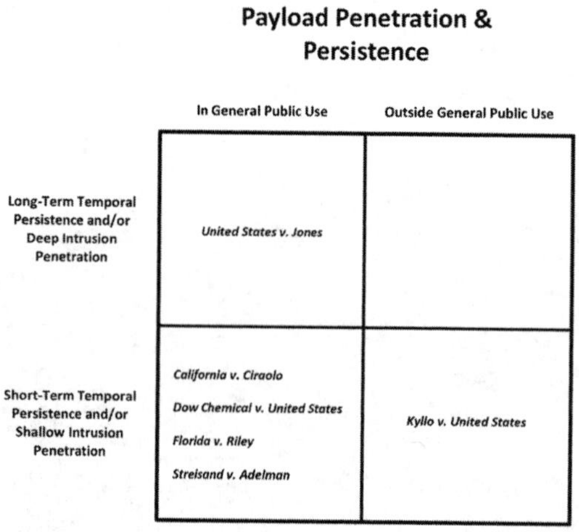

Payload Penetration and Persistence

The Overall Framework

The legal technological framework can be constructed by combining the two matrices into a single framework of reference. Unmanned aircraft cases can be matched to a specific quadrant in both of the matrices, indicating the aerial vantage point as well as the state of the payload during the operation in question to give an indication of whether the privacy rights of the operation's targets are being violated.

Figure 10.8

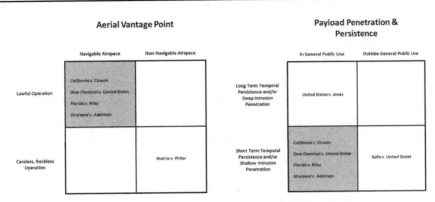

A Technological Legal Framework for Unmanned Aircraft Operations

Technological Framework

The shaded areas of the framework in Figure 10.8 indicate the "safe zones" of operations where Fourth Amendment and privacy rights are not violated and where First Amendment protections are preserved. The nonshaded quadrants indicate areas of potential concern and possible "danger zones" where unmanned aircraft use may result in the loss of First Amendment free speech protection due to privacy or Fourth Amendment violations.

While being a simple visual, the framework allows for a quick inspection of the various issues regarding privacy and the use of unmanned aircraft operations, which can assist unmanned aircraft media operators in avoiding the pitfalls associated with the utilization of aerial technology. In turn, by understanding the framework, media UA operators can attempt to avoid the "evil of the invasion of privacy of the newspapers"[99] as Warren and Brandeis admonished so eloquently back in 1890.

SUMMARY AND CONCLUSIONS

The use of unmanned aircraft by the media presents a daunting challenge in both protecting the privacy rights of the subjects of the aerial operation and in preserving the First Amendment rights of the media itself. The issue of privacy and unmanned aircraft is currently a hot button issue across the country as many citizens fear a loss of privacy as a direct result of the use of unmanned aircraft by both public and private entities.

---

99. *Id.* Harvard Law Review 193 (1890).

The opinion of a Supreme Court justice was made crystal clear on September 11, 2014. In a speech at Oklahoma City University, Justice Sotomayor pontificated sharply on the use of unmanned aircraft over private property:

> There are unmanned aircraft flying over the air randomly that are recording everything that's happening on what we consider our private property. That type of technology has to stimulate us to think about what it is that we cherish in privacy and how far we want to protect it and from whom. Because people think that it should be protected just against government intrusion, but I don't like the fact that someone I don't know . . . can pick up, if they're a private citizen, one of these unmanned aircraft and fly it over my property.[100]

The issue of privacy is front and center in the minds of many Americans, including the justice. The media needs to be cognizant of this fact when conducting aerial operations. With unclear federal regulations and laws concerning the use of unmanned aircraft and very little legal precedent, the media will be navigating uncharted waters when it integrates unmanned aircraft into its news-gathering operations.

The regulations, though, are slowly becoming clarified. On September 25, 2014, the FAA announced that it would permit six media aerial photo and visual production organizations to use unmanned aircraft. This, according to the FAA is "the first step to allowing the film and television industry the use of unmanned aircraft systems (UAS) in the National Airspace System."[101] Transportation Secretary Anthony Foxx stated that:

> Today's announcement is a significant milestone in broadening commercial UAS use while ensuring we maintain our world-class safety record in all forms of flight. . . . These companies are blazing a trail that others are already following, offering the promise of new advances in agriculture and utility safety and maintenance.[102]

The fact that the organizations selected to proceed with unmanned aircraft operations are media entities is significant. They have been granted special permissions but also have been tasked with the heavy burden of utilizing the unmanned aircraft in a safe

---

100. Justice Sonia Sotomayor, Speech to faculty and students of Oklahoma City University (Sept. 11, 2014).

101. FAA, U.S. Transportation Secretary Foxx Announces FAA Exemptions for Commercial UAS Movie and TV Production, (Press Release), http://www.faa.gov/news/press_releases/news_story.cfm?newsId=17194.

102. *Id.*

and productive manner, guarding the privacy rights of the public while delivering a viable product to them.

The First Amendment right of free speech and freedom of the press is a highly valued privilege of the media. Its loss would be a significant detriment to both the media organization losing it as well as to the industry. The use of unmanned aircraft is a direct challenge to the media to take its First Amendment rights seriously and utilize unmanned aircraft in a responsible manner that preserves both the public's right to privacy and the media's right to use this cutting-edge aerial technology.

CHAPTER 11

Sensing and Surveillance

Constitutional Privacy Issues of Unmanned Aircraft

Hillary B. Farber

Unmanned aerial systems, as compared to planes and helicopters, pose unique threats to society's expectation of privacy. The very essence of pervasive unmanned aerial surveillance enables users to track the movements of large numbers of people simultaneously, zeroing in on people and places with simple keystrokes. People can be observed on the streets, in their cars, in their backyards, and even through the open blinds in their homes. The visual imagery gathered can be stored indefinitely, just like other digital data. In contrast to surveillance by manned aircraft, unmanned aerial vehicles (UAVs) are readily portable, have the ability to hover, fly at various altitudes, and stay aloft for hours or even days at a time. Unmanned aircraft can be small enough that people on the ground are unaware that they are being watched. Moreover, the breadth and scope of the data an unmanned aircraft can capture is far greater than the capability of traditional surveillance tools. These capabilities set these devices apart from planes and helicopters, closed circuit television (CCTV), and satellite surveillance.

The aerospace and robotics industries are developing the technology faster than lawmakers and courts can regulate it. As this chapter will discuss, the Fourth Amendment does not prohibit the government from carrying out warrantless aerial surveillance of private property. Without legislative action limiting aerial monitoring by unmanned aircraft, the privacy Americans have enjoyed in their movements and activities is threatened.

In 2012, Congress passed the Federal Aviation Administration Modernization and Reform Act, which required the Federal Aviation Administration (FAA) to promulgate regulations for the integration of unmanned aircraft into the national airspace.[1] In addition, the law directs the agency to create a five-year roadmap for the introduction of civil unmanned aircraft systems into public airspace. It is estimated that by 2020, there will be as many as 30,000 unmanned aircraft systems (UAS) occupying national airspace.[2] A significant portion of these remotely piloted vehicles will be owned and operated by law enforcement. State and local police departments in Alabama, Arkansas, Colorado, Idaho, Kansas, Massachusetts, North Dakota, Ohio, Texas, Utah, and Washington have sought permission to use unmanned aircraft in U.S. airspace.[3] In 2014, New York City police commissioner William Bratton endorsed the use of UAVs as a reliable and effective means to investigate criminal activity.[4] Federal agencies including the Federal Bureau of Investigations (FBI); the Bureau of Alcohol, Tobacco, and Firearms (ATF); the Drug Enforcement Agency (DEA); and Customs and Border Protection (CBP) have deployed unmanned aircraft to patrol the U.S. border, conduct surveillance of suspected criminal activity, survey damage caused by natural disasters, and execute search and rescue missions. In June 2013, the former director of the FBI, Robert Mueller, testified before Congress that his agency has used unmanned aircraft for domestic surveillance. Records show that the CBP increased UAV flights eightfold between 2010 and 2012.

Because of the enhanced aerial perspective an unmanned system provides, law enforcement can amass large amounts of data concerning a target, as well as information on people and places about whom the police have no particularized suspicion. Rarely does law enforcement conduct dragnet-style surveillance from a manned aircraft; it is simply too costly, both in terms of operating the aircraft and paying the personnel involved. Unmanned aircraft are a far more effective and cost-efficient means of conducting pervasive surveillance and crowd monitoring. The expense of operating and maintaining unmanned aircraft is estimated at one-fifth that of operating and maintaining manned aircraft.

Interest in using unmanned aircraft in the civil and commercial arenas is also growing exponentially. Last year, Amazon, one of the largest retail companies in the United States, revealed its intention to use unmanned aircraft to deliver packages as soon

---

1. Federal Aviation Administration Modernization and Reform Act, Pub. L. No. 112-095 (2012).

2. The Future of Unmanned Aircraft in America: Law Enforcement and Privacy Considerations, Hearing Before the S. Comm. on the Judiciary, 113th Cong. 2 (2013) (statement of Sen. Patrick J. Leahy, Chairman, S. Comm. on the Judiciary).

3. *See* Jennifer Lynch, *Just How Many Unmanned Aircraft Licenses Has the FAA Really Issued*, ELECTRONIC FRONTIER FOUNDATION (Feb. 21, 2013), https://www.eff.org/deeplinks/2013/02/; Hunter Stuart, *Unmanned Aircraft List Released By FAA Shows Which Police Departments Want to Fly Unmanned Aerial Vehicles*, HUFFINGTON POST (Feb. 8, 2013, 10:36 PM), http://www.huffingtonpost.com/2013/02/08/unmanned aircraft-list-domestic-police-law-enforcement-surveillance_n_2647530.html. For a complete list *see* https://www.eff.org/sites/default/files/filenode/faa_coa_list-2012.pdf.

4. *See* Inae Oh, *NYPD Is Looking Into Using Drones for Surveillance*, HUFFINGTON POST (May 5, 2014, 11:17 AM), http://www.huffingtonpost.com/2014/05/22/nypd-drones_n_5371807.html.

as U.S. regulations permit. Film production companies, real estate agencies, farmers, and videographers are keenly interested in conducting aerial photography with unmanned systems. The FAA has slowly responded to the chorus of manufacturers and owners of unmanned aircraft systems seeking an expansion of certificates for civil and commercial use. In September 2014, the FAA announced that it would permit six media aerial photo and visual production organizations to use unmanned aircraft.[5] Similarly, in June 2014, the FAA approved the first commercial use of an unmanned aircraft system for surveying the oil fields in and around the Alaskan pipeline.[6] With few exceptions, the FAA only permits operators who have obtained a Certificate of Authorization to operate unmanned aircraft in the public airspace. Some commercial users have grown impatient waiting for the FAA to approve the use of small unmanned aircraft.[7] Instances of commercial users flying small model aircraft, classified by the FAA as UAVs, are being reported more frequently.

The FAA is at the center of the integration of unmanned aircraft in civil society, but the protection of societal expectations of privacy does not necessarily top its agenda. The FAA regulates operations within the national airspace, and its primary objective is safety. The FAA is under pressure from the private sector to approve the use of commercial unmanned aircraft. Agency officials estimate that 7,500 commercial unmanned aircraft could be in operation by 2015.[8] Because of their size, cost, and versatility, unmanned aircraft will ultimately develop into a substantial business market. The Association for Unmanned Vehicle Systems International (AUVSI) has estimated that integrating unmanned aircraft into U.S. airspace would have an economic effect worth more than $13.6 billion and create more than 70,000 jobs in the first three years.[9]

The first step is the establishment of six test sites that will lay the groundwork for the integration of UAS into the national airspace.[10] The research and flight operations

5. Press Release, Federal Aviation Administration, U.S. Transportation Secretary Foxx Announces FAA Exemptions for Commercial UAS Movie and TV Production (Sept. 25, 2014), *available at* http://www.faa.gov/news/press_releases/news_story.cfm?newsId=17194.

6. Jack Nicas, *FAA Gives Approval to BP to Use Commercial Drone*, WALL ST. J. (June 10, 2014, 9:00 AM), http://online.wsj.com/news/article_e-mail/bp-launches-landmark-drone-program-in-alaska-1402404549-lMyQjAxMTA0MDEwMDExNDAyWj.

7. On February 15, 2015, the FAA set forth a framework of regulations for small UAs (under 55 pounds) conducting nonrecreational operations. *See* http://www.faa.gov/regulations_policies/rulemaking/media/021515_SUAS_summary.pdf.

8. Michael Huerta, Fed. Aviation Admin., "UAS Roadmap": Speech at Unmanned Aircraft Systems Forum (Nov. 7, 2013), *available at* http://www.faa.gov/news/speeches/news_story.cfm?newsid=15354; *Game of Drones*, THE ECONOMIST, Dec. 21, 2013, *available at* http://www.economist.com/news/business/21591862-some-see-privacy-threats-civilian-drones-others-see-profits-game-drones.

9. Darryl Jenkins and Bijan Vasigh, *The Economic Impact of Unmanned Aircraft Systems Integration in the United States*, AUVSI, March 2013, *available at* http://qzprod.files.wordpress.com/2013/03/econ_report_full2.pdf.

10. University of Alaska; State of Nevada; Griffiss International Airport (NY); North Dakota Dept. of Commerce; Texas A&M University – Corpus Christi; Virginia Tech University.

that occur at the test sites will help the FAA to develop guidelines and regulations for future civil and commercial use of unmanned aircraft.

In response to the volume of privacy concerns expressed during the public comment period, the FAA issued a privacy policy for all the test sites. The policy requires the test sites to (1) maintain a record of all test site operations and a written plan for data use and retention; (2) comply with federal, state, and other laws protecting an individual's right to privacy; (3) establish their own privacy policy and make it publicly available; and (4) conduct an annual review of compliance with privacy practices, and share the results in a public forum that allows for public comment.[11] The test sites will operate until February 2017.[12]

The FAA policy meets minimum expectations. It is unlikely that the FAA privacy policy or the privacy policies implemented at any of the test sites will ameliorate the privacy concerns at the federal, state, or local level. The responsibility lies with lawmakers to develop comprehensive regulation on the use of unmanned aircraft to ensure privacy protections.

UNMANNED AIRCRAFT CAPABILITIES

Unmanned aircraft systems are versatile, efficient, and often are designed to be undetectable. They can be as large as a fixed-wing commercial jetliner or as small as an insect. They range in weight from tons to grams depending on their design and purpose. Some unmanned aircraft are designed to mimic birds and insects and move in all directions. An unmanned aircraft can fly over fenced-in backyards and open fields, capturing images not visible from ground level. As a result, unmanned aircraft are extremely difficult to evade when outside the confines of one's home.

The unmanned aerial vehicle is the platform for enabling persistent surveillance; the onboard instruments gather, store, and transmit the data. Most unmanned aircraft are equipped with cameras with high-powered zoom lenses and photo sensors for high-resolution imagery. Even the least expensive, commercially available, unmanned aircraft have the ability to transmit real-time video or data to the ground control unit. The more sophisticated unmanned aircraft are equipped with a variety of sense-enhancing technologies, such as global positioning systems, Wi-Fi sniffers, license

---

11. FAA, Final Privacy Requirements for the UAS Test Site Program (2013), *available at* http://www.faa.gov/about/initiatives/uas/media/UAS_privacy_requirements.pdf.

12. Office of the Inspector General released an Audit Report on June 26, 2014, noting that test site operations are behind schedule and the goals for test sites lack definition and clarity. The report notes the FAA faces significant barriers to meeting its September 2015 deadline. *See* Dept. of Transp., Office of Inspector Gen., Audit Rep. AV-2014-061, FAA Faces Significant Barriers to Safely Integrate Unmanned Aircraft Systems into the National Airspace System (2014).

plate readers, infrared sensors, night vision cameras, and facial recognition technology. Meanwhile, the military is developing radar technologies that can see through walls and ceilings, allowing for the tracking of human subjects inside a building.[13] Also in the development stage is application of artificial intelligence technologies to identify people and suspicious activity.[14] Even with the technology available today, an unmanned aircraft hovering over a location or target for fifteen to twenty minutes can amass vast amounts of information.

When you combine the payload with the platform of an unmanned aerial vehicle, the specter of how quickly these aerial observers could erode existing privacy norms is sobering. An unmanned aircraft system that hovers over a neighborhood for hours or days could reveal intimate details about its residents. Through persistent surveillance, the recreational habits, professional activities, social relationships, economic status, medical and personal hygiene, and family status could all be aggregated and retained. Currently, most state laws do not specifically regulate unmanned aircraft and ostensibly allow the government to carry out this type of surveillance surreptitiously.[15] When considered in these terms, it is understandable that the privacy concerns generated by this powerful technology are paramount in the minds of lawmakers, advocacy groups, and concerned citizens.[16] Many of these groups are pressing for legislation that will regulate the extent to which information can be gathered and retained by unmanned aircraft systems.[17] In Seattle, a city council meeting generated so much opposition to a plan to allow police departments to use unmanned aircraft for crime detection that the mayor cancelled the program.[18] Civil liberties groups in New York City have expressed concern over the prospect of the police department using unmanned aircraft

---

13. *Eyes in the Sky: The Domestic Use of Unmanned Aerial Systems, Hearing before H. Comm. on the Judiciary*, May 17, 2013 (statement of Christopher Calabrese, Legislative Counsel, ACLU).

14. *See id.*

15. Only sixteen states have enacted laws to regulate unmanned aircraft systems.

16. *See Domestic Unmanned Aerial Vehicles (UAVs) and Drones*, Electronic Privacy Info. Ctr. at http://epic .org/privacy/drones (last visited Jan. 20, 2014) ("Drones present a unique threat to privacy. Drones are designed to [maintain a constant], persistent eye on the public, to a degree that former methods of surveillance were unable to achieve. . . . The ability to link facial recognition capabilities on drone aircraft cameras [operated by DHS] to the FBI's Next Generation Identification database or DHS' IDENT database, two of the largest collections of biometric data in the world [further exacerbates the privacy risks]").

17. Civil liberties groups such as the ACLU, Electronic Frontier Foundation, and the Electronic Privacy Information Center (EPIC) have testified before Congress in support of measures to limit the scope of domestic surveillance via unmanned aircraft systems. *See* Jay Stanley and Catherine Crump, ACLU, Protecting Privacy from Aerial Surveillance: Recommendations for Government Use of Drone Aircraft (Dec. 2011), *available at* https://www.aclu.org/files/assets/protectingprivacyfromaerialsurveillance.pdf; *Future of Drones in America: Law Enforcement and Privacy Considerations: Hearing Before S. Comm. On the Judiciary*, 113th Cong. (2013) (statement of Amie Stepanovich, Dir. of the Domestic Surveillance Proj. Elec. Privacy Info. Ctr.).

18. Christine Clarridge, *Seattle Grounds Police Drones Program*, THE SEATTLE TIMES (Feb. 7, 2013), http://seattletimes.com/html/localnews/2020312864_spddronesxml.html; Martin Kaste, *As Police Drones Take Off Washington State Pushes Back,* NPR (Feb. 22, 2013), http://www.npr.org/2013/02/22/172696814/as-pol ice-drones-take-off-washington-state-pushes-back.

for widespread surveillance.[19] As unmanned aircraft proliferate in civil society and as public awareness about their capabilities increases, legislators and the FAA are hearing louder calls for regulation.[20]

FEDERAL AND STATE LEGISLATIVE ACTIVITY

Constraints on the use of these powerful aerial observers must originate from state and federal lawmakers as opposed to manufacturers and administrative agencies. On the federal level there is bipartisan concern over the potential for unmanned aircraft to erode reasonable expectations of privacy. There have been a number of hearings before Congress, but so far there has been no federal legislation regulating the use of unmanned aircraft systems.[21] Several bills have been introduced within the past two years. In 2012, Senator Rand Paul (R-KY) introduced the Preserving Freedom from Unwanted Surveillance Act, which called for a sweeping prohibition of unmanned aerial surveillance by any person or entity affiliated with the U.S. government.[22] In 2013, Senator Mark Udall (D-CO) introduced the Safeguarding Privacy and Fostering Aerospace Innovation Act, which would prohibit private individuals from deploying unmanned aircraft to conduct surveillance on other individuals.[23] The act permits an exception for surveillance of individuals who are "in a place of public use where surveillance would not be highly offensive to a reasonable person."[24]

Perhaps the most comprehensive legislation pending before Congress is the Drone Aircraft Privacy and Transparency Act (DAPTA). The bill was first introduced in March 2013 by Senator Edward Markey (D-MA) and then reintroduced in March 2015. DAPTA proscribes limits on the gathering, retention, and sharing of data collected by unmanned aircraft. It requires that certain disclosures be made as part of the flight approval process, including the identity of the aircraft operator, the flight path, the type of data to be collected, and how the data will be used. Law enforcement agencies must file a "data minimization statement," which explains how the

---

19. Tina Moore, *NYPD Considering Using Drones and Gunshot Detectors to Fight Crime*, NY DAILY NEWS (May 20, 2014), http://www.nydailynews.com/new-york/nyc-crime/nypd-drones-fight-crime-article-1.1799980.
20. *Peeping Drones: Who Should Be Allowed to Fly Drones?*, NBC NEWS, http://www.nbcnews.com/watch /nightly-news/peeping-drones-who-should-be-allowed-to-fly-unmanned aircraft-289197123831.
21. The Future of Drones in America: Law Enforcement and Privacy Considerations. Hearing Before the S. Comm. on the Judiciary, 113th Cong. 2 (March 20, 2013); The Future of Unmanned Aviation in the U.S. Economy: Safety and Privacy Considerations, Hearing before the S. Comm. on Commerce, Science, and Transportation (2014); Subject: Eyes in the Sky: The Domestic Use of Unmanned Aerial Systems, Hearing before H. Comm. on the Judiciary (2013); Using Unmanned Aerial Systems Within the Homeland: Security Game Changer? Subcommittee on Oversight, Investigations and Management, H. Comm. on Homeland Security (2012).
22. Preserving Freedom from Unwanted Surveillance Act, S. 3287, 112th Cong. (2012).
23. The Safeguarding Privacy and Fostering Aerospace Innovation Act, S. 1057, 113th Cong. (2013).
24. *Id.*

agency will minimize the collection and retention of data unrelated to the criminal investigation. All this information will be available in a publicly searchable database, including the times and location of all unmanned aircraft flights, along with disclosures of any data security breaches suffered by a licensee. Moreover, DAPTA places restrictions on how long the data will be in the possession of the agency that collected it and whether the information can be sold, leased, or otherwise provided to third parties. These measures add a layer of transparency and accountability to the deployment of unmanned aircraft.

States have responded more quickly than the federal government, all inclined toward restricting the scope and use of unmanned aircraft. At this writing, sixteen states have passed bills ranging from moratoriums on unmanned aircraft to prohibiting any government official from using an unmanned aerial vehicle without first obtaining a warrant.[25] In 2014, thirty-five states considered bills and resolutions to regulate the use of unmanned aircraft systems.[26] The momentum among state lawmakers is spurred by concern over the potential privacy intrusions resulting from use of this emerging technology.[27] Efforts to create an enforceable privacy interest are evinced in the titles of the proposed bills: Florida—Freedom From Unwanted Surveillance Act[28]; Idaho—Preserving Freedom From Unwanted Surveillance Act[29]; and Illinois—Freedom from Unmanned Aircraft Surveillance Act.[30]

Each state law requires a warrant for government surveillance, with some states allowing for exceptions, including a high risk of a terrorist attack, search and rescue missions, preventing the escape of a suspect, imminent danger to life, or serious damage to property. Other provisions in the laws include barring the use of unlawfully obtained evidence from criminal prosecution, enforcing civil penalties for noncompliance, and limiting the time period that data can be retained by law enforcement agencies. Some states go even further. Oregon creates various crimes for unauthorized use of unmanned aircraft.[31] Massachusetts prohibits facial recognition technology

---

25. *See* H.B. 255, 28th Leg. (Alaska 2014); H.B. 1349, 90th Gen Assemb. (Ark. 2015); S.B. 92, 2013 Leg., 115th Reg. Sess. (Fla. 2013); S.B. 1134, 62nd Leg., 1st Reg. Sess. (Idaho 2013); Freedom from Unmanned Aircraft Surveillance Act, S.B. 1587, 98th Gen. Assemb., 1st Reg. Sess. (Ill. 2013); H.B. 1009, 118th Gen. Assemb. (Ind. 2014); H.B. 2289, 85th Gen. Assemb. (Iowa 2014); H.B. 1029, 2014 Reg. Sess. (La. 2014); S.B. 196, 63rd Leg. (Mont. 2013); S.B. 744, 2013 Gen. Assemb. (N.C. 2014); H.B. 2710, 77th Leg. Assemb. (Or. 2013); Freedom from Unwarranted Surveillance Act, S.B. 796, 108th Gen. Assemb., 1st Reg. Sess. (Tenn. 2013); Texas Privacy Act, H.B. 912, 83rd Leg. (Tex. 2013); S.B. 167, 2014 Gen. Sess. (Utah 2014); S.B. 1331, 2013 Gen. Assemb., Reg. Sess. (Va. 2013); S.B. 196, 2013–2014 Reg. Sess. (Wis. 2014).

26. *See* http://www.ncsl.org/research/civil-and-criminal-justice/2014-state-unmanned-aircraft-systems-uas-legislation.aspx.

27. *See* Hillary B. Farber, *Eyes in the Sky: Constitutional and Regulatory Approaches to Domestic Drone Deployment*, 64 SYR. L. REV. 1, 31 (2014).

28. S.B. 92, 2013 Leg., 115th Reg. Sess. (Fla. 2013).

29. S.B. 1134, 62d Leg., 1st Reg. Sess. (Idaho 2013).

30. Freedom from Unmanned Aircraft Surveillance Act, S.B. 1587, 98th Gen. Assemb., 1st Reg. Sess. (Ill. 2013).

31. H.B. 2710, 77th Leg. Assemb. § 2 (Or. 2013).

and other forms of biometric matching technology to be used on any data collected by the unmanned aircraft, except to identify the subject of the warrant.[32] Virginia opted for a moratorium on all domestic unmanned aircraft use in all but a few limited exceptions.[33] The Massachusetts proposed law attempts to safeguard protected First Amendment activities by explicitly prohibiting governmental use of unmanned aircraft to track, collect, or maintain information about political, social, or religious activities and associations of any individual or group, unless such information relates directly to a criminal investigation.[34]

More recently, lawmakers have sought to restrict use of unmanned aircraft by private users. Among the sixteen states that have passed laws regulating unmanned aircraft, nine states include restrictions on private deployment of unmanned aircraft.[35] Moreover, approximately half of the unmanned aircraft-related legislation introduced in 2014 proposed restrictions on private use of unmanned aircraft. Tennessee recently made it a crime to use an unmanned aircraft to capture an image over certain open air events.[36] New Jersey proposes to make it unlawful for any person, except law enforcement officials, forest fire departments, an active member of armed forces, and entertainment venues, to purchase, own, or possess an unmanned aircraft system.[37]

In addition, anyone who lawfully purchases an unmanned aircraft must publicly announce the purchase in the newspaper, reporting the price paid, its size, and the supplier and manufacturer of the aircraft system.[38] Hawaii amended its privacy statute to criminalize using unmanned aircraft to conduct surveillance of another person or dwelling without the person's consent and prohibiting a person from using a UAS to photograph a person without their consent for purposes of public distribution.[39]

The National Park Service has banned unmanned aircraft systems from being used in the parks citing concerns over their interference with the public's use and enjoyment of the national parks.[40] Prior to the start of the world-class sailing race from Newport, Rhode Island, to Bermuda, Rhode Island officials declared a prohibition on unmanned aircraft vehicles flying over the Narragansett Bay, citing concern for

---

32. S.B. 1664, 188th Gen. Court § 99c(d)(2) (Mass. 2013).
33. S.B. 1331, 2013 Gen. Assemb., Reg. Sess. (Va. 2013).
34. *See* S.B. 1664, 188th Gen. Court § 99c(d)(3) (Mass. 2013).
35. H.B. 1349 90th Gen Assemb. (Ark. 2015); S.B. 1134, 62d Leg., 1st Reg. Sess. (Idaho 2013); S.B. 1587, 98th Gen. Assemb., 1st Reg. Sess. (Ill. 2013); H.B. 1009, 118th Gen. Assemb. (Ind. 2014); H.B. 1029, 2014 Reg. Sess. (La. 2014); S.B. 744, 2013 Gen. Assemb. (N.C. 2014); S.B. 796, 108th Gen. Assemb., 1st Reg. Sess. (Tenn. 2013); H.B. 912, 83d Leg. (Tex. 2013); S.B. 196 2013–14 Reg. Sess. (Wis. 2014).
36. S.B. 509, 109th Reg. Sess. (Tenn. 2015).
37. NJ Assembly Bill 2147 PL 1983, c. 135 sec 6.
38. *Id.* at § 2.
39. H.B. 609, 28th Leg. § 261 (Haw. 2015).
40. Mark Berman, *National Park Service Bans Drone Use in All National Parks*, WASH. POST (June 20, 2014), http://www.washingtonpost.com/news/post-nation/wp/2014/06/20/national-park-service-bans-drone-use-in-all-national-parks.

collisions with other air traffic and sailboats.[41] The catalyst for these prohibitions is due in large part to the increasing number of people who own unmanned aircraft. Visitors to the national parks were using unmanned aircraft to capture aerial footage of canyons, climbers, and livestock. Spectators at boat races were operating unmanned aircraft out over the waters to take photographs and videos of the boats at the start of the race. These lightweight, small, aerial vehicles with cameras and live streaming capability make for good videography but interfere with the safety and privacy interests of others. Citing the dearth of state and federal laws regulating unmanned aircraft, officials and event organizers are implementing their own bans on unmanned aircraft.

When Congress and/or the FAA does promulgate regulations on unmanned aircraft systems, some of these recently enacted state laws may be preempted. Because use of unmanned aircraft will exist largely in federal airspace, Congress has the authority to set policy over how unmanned aircraft are operated. This will undoubtedly cause disruption in terms of the enforceability of particular state statutes.

AERIAL SURVEILLANCE AND CURRENT FOURTH AMENDMENT JURISPRUDENCE

It is often said that privacy is a thing of the past. Some opine that no amount of data can be securely stored and note that when we are out in public our images are routinely recorded by surveillance cameras and our locations are persistently tracked via our cellular devices. Moreover, with our electronic devices we create a digital record of the intimacies of our daily lives. Though technology has transformed how much and how easily we are able to collect information about anyone and anything, unmanned aircraft systems pose immediate threats to privacy that most of these other emerging technologies do not. For one, UAS are already in the hands of thousands of users, from hobbyists to law enforcement personnel. Second, unmanned aircraft pose a myriad of novel legal issues that will be slow to resolve.

The Fourth Amendment guarantees "the right of the people to be secure in their persons, houses, papers, and effects, against unreasonable searches and seizures."[42] If the police unreasonably execute a search without a warrant or probable cause, the evidence derived from the illegal search will be inadmissible. Conversely, if there has been no "search" then the Fourth amendment is not implicated. In 1967 the Supreme Court in *Katz v. United States* declared that the Fourth amendment protects "people not places," a major departure from the pre-existing property rights-based

---

41. Alex Kuffner, *R.I. Airport Corp. Says Use of Drones Banned at Start of Newport Bermuda Race*, Providence J. (June 14, 2014), http://www.providencejournal.com/article/20140614/NEWS/306149988.
42. U.S. Const. amend. IV.

analysis.[43] The Court's decision transformed the way courts assess whether police conduct constitutes a search under Fourth Amendment principles. Justice Harlan's famous concurrence set forth the two-pronged "reasonable expectation of privacy" test. This doctrinal formulation makes investigatory searches by police constitutionally significant if (1) there is an actual expectation of privacy (subjective prong) and (2) the expectation is deemed one that society is willing to recognize as reasonable (objective prong).[44] Hence in *Katz*, the government agents who were electronically eavesdropping on a conversation Katz was having in a public phone booth were found to be in violation of the Fourth Amendment because Katz possessed a reasonably justifiable expectation of privacy in the booth.[45]

Some years following *Katz*, the Court applied its reasonable expectation analysis to observation from the sky. The Supreme Court decided three important aerial surveillance cases involving police-manned aircraft flying at altitudes of 400 and 1000 feet, taking pictures of private property concealed from ground observation.[46] In all three cases, the Supreme Court found no reasonable expectation of privacy because the observations were made from navigable airspace.[47] The Court reasoned that navigable airspace is the equivalent of a public thoroughfare, open to anyone who abides by the regulations governing air travel.[48] Hence, the view of one's curtilage from a public vantage point does not constitute a "search" under the Fourth Amendment.[49]

In the first of these three cases, *Dow Chemical v. United States*, the Environmental Protection Agency (EPA) was denied access to Dow's manufacturing plant for inspection.[50] Dow erected fences to obstruct view of the plant from the perimeter of the property, and the plant's operations took place inside the buildings.[51] The EPA hired a commercial photographer to take pictures of the plant from the sky.[52] The Supreme Court concluded that taking aerial photographs of an industrial plant complex from publicly navigable airspace did not constitute a search under the Fourth Amendment.[53] In reaching this conclusion, the Court considered the quality of detail revealed in the photos, the technology utilized, and the place being surveyed. Although the aerial photography captured buildings and equipment not visible from ground

---

43. Katz v. United States, 389 U.S. 347 (1967).

44. Katz, 389 U.S. at 361.

45. *Id.*

46. *See* Dow Chem. Co. v. United States, 476 U.S. 227 (1986); California v. Ciraolo, 476 U.S. 207 (1986); Florida v. Riley, 488 U.S. 445 (1989).

47. *Id.*

48. Ciraolo, 476 U.S. at 213 ("The Fourth Amendment protection of the home has never been extended to require law enforcement officers to shield their eyes when passing by a home on public thoroughfares").

49. *Id.*

50. Dow, 476 U.S. at 229.

51. *Id.*

52. *Id.*

53. *Id.* at 239.

level outside the plant's walls, the Court noted that the photographs themselves did not reveal detailed information that would rise to the level of constitutional protection.[54] Perhaps foreshadowing the inevitable advancement in aerial photography, the Court acknowledged that surveillance of private property with highly sophisticated surveillance equipment not generally available to the public might implicate Fourth Amendment protections.[55]

In *California v. Ciraolo*, police received an anonymous tip that the defendant was growing marijuana in his backyard.[56] The backyard was surrounded by a fence and was unobservable at ground level.[57] Without a warrant, police flew an airplane over the defendant's house at an altitude of 1,000 feet.[58] Without any visual aids, the police saw marijuana plants growing in the backyard. The police used this information to obtain a search warrant for the defendant's property. The issue before the Court was whether Ciraolo possessed a reasonable expectation of privacy in the curtilage of his home that police intruded upon when they flew over the backyard and observed its contents. Although the Court recognized that the defendant possessed a subjective expectation of privacy in his backyard because he had taken measures to block it from public view by erecting a fence, the Court deemed his expectation to be one society was not willing to recognize.[59] The Court explained that Ciraolo's expectation of privacy was objectively unreasonable in light of the fact that his backyard could be viewed by any member of the public from an elevated position or an aircraft in navigable airspace.[60] Importantly for unmanned aircraft privacy implications, the Supreme Court once again forewarned that aerial observation may trigger constitutional protections with the use of technologies that have the capability to reveal "intimate associations, objects or activities otherwise imperceptible to police or fellow citizens."[61]

Finally, *Florida v. Riley* presented the question whether surveillance of the interior of a partially covered greenhouse in a residential backyard constituted a search under the Fourth Amendment.[62] Police suspected defendant Riley of cultivating marijuana inside his greenhouse. Unable to observe inside the greenhouse from ground level, police flew over Riley's property in a helicopter four hundred feet above the ground.

54. *Id.* at 238 ("But the photographs here are not so revealing of intimate details as to raise constitutional concerns. Although they undoubtedly give EPA more detailed information than naked-eye views, they remain limited to an outline of the facility's buildings and equipment. The mere fact that human vision is enhanced somewhat, at least to the degree here, does not give rise to constitutional problems").

55. *Id.*
56. *Ciraolo*, 476 U.S. 207.
57. *Id.*
58. *Id.*
59. *Id.* at 211.
60. *Id.* at 213–14. "The Fourth Amendment protection of the home has never been extended to require law enforcement officers to shield their eyes when passing by a home on public thoroughfares."
61. *Id.* at 215 n.3 (quoting Brief for Petitioner 14–15).
62. Florida v. Riley, 488 U.S. 445, 449 (1989).

Some of the panels on the roof of the greenhouse were missing, exposing the inside of the greenhouse to aerial view. Looking down inside the greenhouse with the naked eye, police were able to observe marijuana plants growing inside. As was the case in *Ciraolo*, the Court found that Riley had no reasonable expectation of privacy because the interior of the greenhouse and its contents were visible to anyone passing overhead.[63] A key consideration for the Court was that the observations were made from navigable airspace and in compliance with FAA regulations.[64]

At present, constitutional protections place minimal limitation on aerial surveillance. It is well settled that people do not possess a legally recognizable expectation of privacy in public or from a public vantage point. Precedent makes clear that if police are collecting information from navigable airspace, they are not required to get a warrant or have any particularized suspicion to justify their surveillance. Regardless of the steps one takes to protect one's privacy at ground level, there is no hiding from an unmanned aircraft hovering overhead. An unmanned aircraft will be able to see, capture, and store data around the curtilage of one's home and anywhere else it can gain an aerial perspective. The only way to counter the surveillance would be to stay indoors—but even that will not prevent visibility if the windows are not covered.

The Supreme Court addressed the constitutional relevance of sense-enhancing technology in *Kyllo v. United States*.[65] The case involved police use of a thermal imaging device. Federal agents suspecting Kyllo of using high-intensity heat lamps to grow marijuana plants inside his home used a thermal imaging device to detect the heat levels from discrete areas inside his home. An officer sat in his car at 3:30 a.m. pointing a thermal imager at Kyllo's house. Simply by pointing the device at the home from across the street, the officer was able to detect an abnormal level of heat emanating from certain areas inside the house. Coupled with other information, the police obtained a search warrant for the house and found marijuana plants growing inside. In this very close case the Court determined that sensory enhancing technology used to obtain information regarding the interior of a home that could not be detected through visual observation constitutes a search.[66] But the Court also added an important caveat, which is that the technology used was not in "general public use."[67]

---

63. · *Id.* at 450–51.

64. *Id.* at 451.

65. Kyllo v. United States, 533 U.S. 27, 33–34 (2001) ("It would be foolish to contend that the degree of privacy secured to citizens by the Fourth Amendment has been entirely unaffected by the advance of technology. [T]he technology enabling human flight has exposed to public view (and hence, we have said, to official observation) uncovered portions of the house and its curtilage that once were private. The question we confront today is what limits there are upon this power of technology to shrink the realm of guaranteed privacy").

66. Kyllo, 533 U.S. at 40.

67. At the beginning of the twenty-first century thermal imaging devices were not readily available to the general public. Kyllo, 533 U.S. at 34. They were expensive devices used by law enforcement and by engineers for civil applications. Today, one can purchase a fairly sophisticated thermal imaging device from an online retailer for under $1,000. *See*, http://www.amazon.com/Fluke-VT02-Visual-IR-Thermometer/dp/B00APPPL2W

Kyllo v. United States is an interesting case in terms of its application to unmanned aerial surveillance. One the one hand, *Kyllo* solidified the principle that the home is deserving of the greatest privacy protection under the Constitution. On the other hand, the Court based its ruling in part on the fact that the technology used by police to collect information about the inside of the home was not readily available to the public.[68] Unmanned aircraft systems and many of the technologies with which they can be equipped, by contrast, are in general public use. Although the regulations for unmanned aircraft use are still being developed, many people own and operate them today. Hobbyists and commercial users tend to own small, lightweight, aerial vehicles that range from a few hundred dollars to several thousand dollars. One of the more basic platforms is the "AR Parrot Drone 2.0," which retails for under $300 and is available at many commercial outlets. The "Parrot Drone" is equipped with live streaming video capability and a 720-megapixel camera. As the price increases, the onboard instruments get more sophisticated. The proliferation of unmanned aircraft in American society may well dilute the protections enunciated in *Kyllo*, leaving Americans vulnerable to intrusions in and around their homes by government and neighbors alike.

Prior to the revelation of the National Security Agency's phone data collection program, many people may have doubted the existence of a government program to amass data on millions of Americans for whom the government had no particularized suspicion. Today, the concern over privacy intrusions by government is far more real to millions of Americans. Dragnet surveillance may not be the intended purpose of police conducting unmanned aerial surveillance, but it may be the unavoidable result. To help illustrate this point, consider a practical application of unmanned aircraft technology by law enforcement. A suburban community is experiencing a problem with speeding motorists, particularly at high traffic periods of the day. To counteract this public safety concern, the local police department deploys an unmanned aerial vehicle to deter, monitor, and prosecute speeding motorists. It hovers at altitudes between 400 and 1,000 feet, surveying the roadways in a five-square-mile radius, eight hours per day.

The aerial vehicle is equipped with an automated license plate reader, a night vision camera, a GPS, a high-resolution megapixel camera with zoom/tilt capability, and a high-definition video camera that live streams video directly to the police department where officers monitor the traffic from a screen.[69] From its vantage point, the

---

/ref=sr_1_1?ie=UTF8&qid=1415747825&sr=8-1&keywords=thermal+imager.

68. Kyllo, 533 U.S. at 34.

69. The night vision camera will enable the system to see through dense ground fog, darkness, smoke, aerial fog, and other air anomalies which impede the photographic capabilities of the other photographic systems. Precision GPS capabilities will enable the UAV to cover small area incidents with high positional precision and rapid incident locating.

unmanned aircraft can capture images of people in their backyards, walking in the woods, traveling from discrete locations—doing errands, visiting friends, going to appointments. A seemingly benign public safety initiative that deploys an unmanned aircraft system gives the police the power to amass vast amounts of information about the daily activities of individuals.

Whether the police choose to selectively parse out data collected that does not pertain to speeding motorists is completely discretionary and unreviewable. Should the police store all the digital data for some potential use is also permissible without some regulation concerning the retention and storage of data obtained via unmanned aircraft. As the recently revealed practices of the National Security Agency have demonstrated, permitting government officials to amass data on unsuspecting civilians through covert operations is subject to abuse. A requirement that police first obtain a warrant from a neutral and detached magistrate before being allowed to conduct persistent surveillance is one way to reduce potential privacy violations.

For the time being, restraints on government use of unmanned aerial surveillance must originate in legislatures because Fourth Amendment jurisprudence does not offer protection. It is plausible that the increased power that technology affords police could prove to be a significant factor in the Court's willingness to extend the reach of the Fourth Amendment under some circumstances. The impact of technology in relationship to the Fourth Amendment was discussed by some members of the Court in *United States v. Jones*. In *Jones*, the Supreme Court considered whether the use of a GPS device to monitor Jones's movements constituted a search within the framework of the Fourth Amendment.[70] Police attached a GPS device to the undercarriage of defendant Antoine Jones's wife's car without either consent or knowledge by either party.[71] The police monitored Jones's movements in the car for a four-week period. The data revealed multiple trips to a suspected drug house.[72] Police used the location data from the GPS device, along with other intelligence, to obtain search warrants, which ultimately recovered drug paraphernalia and cash. Following his indictment, Jones moved to suppress the information gained from the GPS tracking device. The trial court denied the motion, but the Supreme Court unanimously concluded the practice violated the Fourth Amendment. The majority limited its rationale to the narrowest set of facts possible—that the global positioning system (GPS) device was impermissibly affixed to the car Jones was using.[73] Writing for the majority, Justice Scalia relied on eighteenth-century tort law to explain why the government's actions

---

70. United States v. Jones, 132 S. Ct. 945, 948–49 (2012).
71. *Id.* at 948.
72. *Id.*
73. *Id.* at 949 (majority opinion rests on finding of physical trespass).

constituted a trespass, thereby violating Jones's right to be free from unreasonable searches and seizures.[74]

In two notable concurrences, five justices expressed a willingness to reassess the legal framework for evaluating long-term electronic monitoring of a person in public.[75] Both concurring opinions recognized the "quantum of intimate information about a person" that can be obtained from a GPS device with relative ease and little expense.[76] In his concurrence, Justice Alito opined that the level of monitoring in this instance exceeded a reasonable duration, thereby unreasonably infringing on Jones' expectation of privacy.[77] But Alito refrained from defining the point at which surveillance requires a warrant.[78] We will have to wait for a future case to see if the justices are willing to recalibrate the standard for determining when surveillance crosses the line from reasonably to unreasonably intrusive.

Justice Sotomayor, for her part, expressed concern for even the short-term monitoring of a person's public activities.[79] Moreover, she warned of the limitations of the third-party doctrine in this new age of modern technology.[80] Sotomayor urged the Court in the future to think critically about the inconsistency between our modern use of technology and the expectation of privacy test. Living in modern society requires disclosure to third parties of extensive amounts of information that citizens would prefer be kept from government interference and other unintended recipients. For instance, online banking, online payment systems, renewing a driver's license or registration, making airline reservations, and paying bar dues are all necessary tasks that require disclosure of confidential information. That being the case, it is incumbent on courts to reassess how to ensure Fourth Amendment protections in the face of advancing technology to avoid unfettered access by the government to sensitive and personal information.

It is not certain whether *Jones* will apply to unmanned aerial surveillance when unmanned aircraft are not affixed to anything and travel in public airspace. But public attitudes and social conventions may influence where the Court draws the line between personal privacy and the public domain. In the 2014 case of *Riley v. California*, Chief Justice Roberts emphasized the pervasiveness of cell phones and their

---

74. *Id.*

75. *See* Jones, 132 S. Ct. at 954 (J. Sotomayor concurring); *id.* at 957 (J. Alito concurring).

76. *Id.* at 955 (J. Sotomayor concurring) ("With increasing regularity, the Government will be capable of duplicating the monitoring undertaken in this case by enlisting factory- or owner-installed vehicle tracking devices or GPS-enabled smartphones").

77. *Id.* at 964 (J. Alito concurring).

78. *Id.* ("We need not identify with precision the point at which the tracking of this vehicle became a search, for the line was surely crossed before the 4-week mark. Other cases may present more difficult questions. But where uncertainty exists with respect to whether a certain period of GPS surveillance is long enough to constitute a Fourth Amendment search, the police may always seek a warrant").

79. *Id.* at 955 (J. Sotomayor concurring).

80. *Id.*

immense storage capacity.[81] He noted how easy technology has made it to literally walk around with a cache of personal information stored in one small container. To a large extent this is why a unanimous Court held that police should not be permitted to search cell phones without a warrant or exigent circumstances.[82]

Technology has a direct impact on privacy, both in terms of what one can quickly and easily learn about a person as well as changing perceptions about what is considered "private."[83] Quite possibly we are nearing the point where technology is posing too many vexing problems for current Fourth Amendment jurisprudence. Perhaps privacy is no longer an adequate proxy for Fourth Amendment protection.[84] At this point, it seems clear that the capabilities associated with unmanned aircraft systems are too vast to allow police unfettered discretion.

Permitting police access to this all-powerful surveillance tool without any constitutional safeguards is at odds with our democratic principles. As Warren and Brandeis wrote in their famous treatise at the turn of the twentieth century, "that the individual shall have the full protection in person and in property is a principle as old as the common law; but it has been found necessary from time to time to define anew the exact nature of and extent of such protection."[85]

RECOMMENDATIONS

It is too soon to predict how the courts will approach restraints on the police use of unmanned aerial surveillance. There are, however, a number of measures that can be taken on a legislative and regulatory level to militate against public distrust and protect personal privacy. First, lawmakers should pass statutes requiring police to obtain a warrant prior to deploying unmanned aircraft systems to conduct surveillance. This requirement simply mandates the police follow the same procedures that are required for physical searches and electronic surveillance. Moreover, exceptions for exigent circumstances should be consistent with existing law, and lawmakers should be careful not to create overly broad exceptions that swallow the protections in the rule.

Information that is not related to the target of the investigation should be destroyed immediately, and no trace of the data should remain in the hands of law enforcement.

---

81. Riley v. California, 134 S. Ct. 2473, 2490 (2014) ("Now it is the person who is not carrying a cell phone, with all that it contains, who is the exception").

82. *See id.*

83. Mark Landler & Dalia Sussman, *Poll Finds Strong Acceptance for Public Surveillance*, N.Y. TIMES, May 1, 2013, at A16.

84. *See generally*, Paul Ohm, *The Fourth Amendment in a World Without Privacy,* 81 MISS. L. J. 1309 (2012); Daniel J. Solove, *Nothing To Hide: The False Tradeoff Between Privacy and Security* 114 (Yale University Press, May 2011). *See also,* Farber, *supra* note 27, at 34–42.

85. Samuel D. Warren & Louis D. Brandeis, *The Right to Privacy*, 4 HARV. L. REV. 193 (1890).

Some office equivalent to a Public Interest Advocate should be created so that when the government seeks a warrant for unmanned aerial surveillance, the public interest can be represented before the judge or magistrate.

Second, all unmanned aircraft flights should be entered into a publicly searchable database that contains information stating who will be operating the vehicle, when and where it will be flown, and the type of information it is authorized to collect. Third, law enforcement agencies should be obligated to minimize the retention of data unrelated to their investigation. As discussed, unmanned aerial surveillance has the capacity to amass data well beyond the scope and breadth of the target of an investigation. Information that is not related to the investigation and/or the warrant should be prohibited from use by the government for any purpose and destroyed immediately.

Fourth, Congress and state legislatures should enact laws to ensure that unmanned aircraft communications are safe, secure, and viable in the national airspace. Attention to information assurance will reduce the risk of hacking and data interception and would maintain confidentiality for the information traveling between the unmanned aircraft, the ground stations, and potentially other entities. With the proliferation of unmanned aircraft, the volume of communication streams in the air will rise precipitously, creating a critical need for improved information security laws. Fifth, legislation should prohibit any data collected by unmanned aerial surveillance to be sold, leased, shared, or otherwise disseminated to third parties. Sixth, facial recognition and other biometric matching technology should be prohibited from use on all data collected by the unmanned aircraft except to identify the subject of the warrant.

Seventh, some governmental body should be assigned the responsibility to maintain oversight and ensure that operators are complying with these requirements via audit procedures and other measures. An annual report compiling all the data pertaining to unmanned aircraft flights conducted within the past year, including information that was collected, should be made publicly available by the designated agency or body composed to ensure compliance.

Finally, each state should create an Oversight Board made up of lawmakers, advocacy groups, academics, and members of the robotics and aerospace industries to review and assess the impact of unmanned aircraft systems on privacy. This would be akin to the Privacy and Civil Liberties Oversight Board created in 2007 through the Implementing Recommendations of the 911 Commission Act, which has reviewed the NSA phone records collection program as well as the program that involves collecting internet communications data from service providers.

With respect to restrictions on private use of unmanned aerial vehicles, the issues are more complicated. Restrictions on private use of unmanned aircraft have the potential to conflict with First Amendment guarantees of free speech, association, and, if being used for news gathering purposes, freedom of the press.[86] Lawmakers need to be careful not to create laws that intrude upon these constitutional guarantees. Once the FAA promulgates regulations for integrating civil unmanned aircraft into the public airspace, it may legitimize many of the restrictions lawmakers seek to place on private use. Industry leaders that manufacture the platforms and the technologies for unmanned aircraft should devote resources toward developing technology that addresses privacy concerns. These efforts could go a long way toward both inspiring public confidence and advancing the economic growth of the industry.

CONCLUSION

Technology often outpaces the law, and this is certainly the case with unmanned aircraft. There are no quick paths to figuring out whether unmanned aerial surveillance constitutes a search under the Fourth Amendment. The Supreme Court is just beginning to address the vexing problems technology poses to Fourth Amendment jurisprudence. For instance, in *Riley v. California*, the Court acknowledged the capacity of modern technology to hold and to reveal the privacies of life.[87] But a physical search of a cell phone incident to a lawful arrest is just the tip of the iceberg.

---

86. *See* John Jarvis, *U.S. Drone Use Hovers on Boundaries of First, Fourth Amendments*, 44 Gateway Journalism Rev. 12 (2014).

87. Riley at 2494–5 ("Modern cell phones are not just another technological convenience. With all they contain and all they may reveal, they hold for many Americans "the privacies of life").

CHAPTER 12

Civilian Weapons on Unmanned Aircraft

Issues of the Second Amendment

Christine L. Keyzers

"A well-regulated Militia, being necessary to the security of a free State, the right of the people to keep and bear Arms, shall not be infringed."

—Second Amendment, U.S. Constitution

The Second Amendment to the United States Constitution was adopted on December 15, 1791, as part of the Bill of Rights in order to protect the right of individuals to keep and bear arms. However, the peculiar wording of the Second Amendment has traditionally given rise to much scholarly debate and historical analysis as to what is protected and what is not—especially given the technological and societal changes since the amendment was adopted. Also, there have historically been relatively few Second Amendment Supreme Court decisions.[1] Consequently, constitutional scholars have long lamented that determining the scope of the Second Amendment's protections with any precision may be impossible.

---

1. *See* Cases v. United States, 131 F.2d 916, 922 (1st Cir. 1942) ("Considering the many variable factors bearing on the question it seems to us impossible to formulate any general test by which to determine the limits imposed by the Second Amendment but that each case under it, like cases under the due process clause, must be decided on its own facts and the line between what is and what is not a valid federal restriction pricked out by decided cases falling on one side or the other of the line").

SECOND AMENDMENT KEY RULINGS

It was not until 2008—more than 200 years after its adoption—that the United States Supreme Court handed down a landmark 5–4 decision in *District of Columbia v. Heller,* 554 U.S. 570 (2008),[2] expressly holding that the Second Amendment to the U.S. Constitution protects a responsible, law-abiding citizen's right to possess an operable handgun in the home for traditionally lawful purposes such as self-defense,[3] and marked the first time the Supreme Court had clearly acknowledged a Second Amendment right not connected to service in the lawfully established militia.[4] The Court further stated that its prior precedent was not inconsistent with its interpretation, reiterating that the right is not unlimited and does not prohibit all regulation of either firearms or similar devices.[5] Thereafter, in *McDonald v. City of Chicago* (2010), the Court held that state and local governments are limited to the same extent as the federal government from infringing the substantive right as described in *Heller.*[6]

Seventy years prior to *District of Columbia v. Heller*, the Supreme Court's most recent and most extensive discussion of the Second Amendment was *United States v. Miller* (1939), wherein the Supreme Court ruled that the federal government and the states could limit any weapon types not having a "reasonable relationship to the preservation or efficiency of a well-regulated militia."[7]

In *United States v. Miller* (1939), the Court upheld the National Firearms Act against a challenge that it unconstitutionally infringed upon the Second Amendment right to bear arms where two persons were indicted for transporting an unregistered sawed-off shotgun across state lines in violation of the National Firearms Act of 1934. The court held that the Second Amendment right to keep and bear arms is not applicable in the absence of a reasonable relationship to the "well-regulated militia" provision of the Second Amendment. Accordingly, Justice McReynolds wrote, "In the absence of any evidence tending to show that possession or use of a 'shotgun having a barrel of less than eighteen inches in length' at this time has some reasonable relationship to the preservation or efficiency of a well-regulated militia, we cannot say that the Second Amendment guarantees the right to keep and bear such an instrument. Certainly it is not within judicial notice that this weapon is any part of the ordinary military

2.   District of Columbia v. Heller, 554 U.S. 570 (2008).This is the first decision since the Supreme Court decided Miller in which a federal court overturned a law regulating firearms based on the Second Amendment.

3.   Heller, 554 U.S. at 599 (stating individual self-defense is "the central component" of the Second Amendment right).

4.   *Id.* (the right vests in individuals, not merely collective militias).

5.   United States v. Miller, 307 U.S. 174 (1939). Miller was distinguished and not overturned in Heller; however, for seventy years constitutional scholars and Courts of Appeal had agreed nearly unanimously that Miller restricted the Second Amendment right to weapons linked to service in the lawfully established militia.

6.   McDonald v. City of Chicago, 561 U.S. 561 3020 (2010).

7.   United States v. Miller, 307 U.S. 178 (1939).

equipment or that its use could contribute to the common defense."[8] Consequently, "Miller should be read to approve restrictions only on weapons that have the special characteristics shared by those identified in the National Firearms Act of 1934—i.e., slight value to law abiding citizens and high value to criminals."[9] Long thereafter, in the *District of Columbia v. Heller,* the Court invalidated two District of Columbia provisions finding that the D.C. ban on handgun possession violated the Second Amendment right because it prohibited an entire class of arms favored for the lawful purpose of self-defense in the home. Similarly, the Court found that the requirement that lawful firearms be disassembled or bound by a trigger lock made it impossible for citizens to effectively use arms for the core lawful purpose of self-defense, and therefore violated the Second Amendment right.

Justice Antonin Scalia authored the majority opinion wherein the Court analyzed textual historical evidence on the meaning of the Second Amendment's operative clause, "the right of the people to keep and bear Arms, shall not be infringed," and concluded that this language guarantees "the individual right to possess and carry weapons in case of confrontation,"[10] but that this right is subject to "reasonable regulation."[11] The Court stated that the right to keep and bear arms is subject to regulation, such as concealed weapons prohibitions, limits on the rights of felons and the mentally ill, laws forbidding the carrying of weapons in certain locations, laws imposing conditions on commercial sales, and prohibitions on the carrying of dangerous and unusual weapons. It stated that this was not an exhaustive list of the regulatory measures that would be presumptively permissible under the Second Amendment.

The Court then considered the Second Amendment's prefatory clause, "[a] well-regulated Militia, being necessary to the security of a free State," and determined that, while this clause announces a purpose for recognizing an individual right to keep and bear arms, it does not limit the operative clause. Likewise, the Court found that analogous contemporaneous provisions in state constitutions, the Second Amendment's drafting history, and post-ratification interpretations were consistent with its interpretation of the amendment. Finally, the Court asserted that its prior precedent was not inconsistent with its interpretation.[12]

---

8. United States v. Miller, 307 U.S. 178 (1939).
9. *Id.* at 171.
10. United States v. Miller, 307 U.S. 178 (1939).
11. United States v. Miller, 307 U.S. 178 (1939).
12. "This meaning is strongly confirmed by the historical background of the Second Amendment. We look to this because it has always been widely understood that the Second Amendment, like the First and Fourth Amendments, codified a pre-existing right. The very text of the Second Amendment implicitly recognizes the pre-existence of the right and declares only that it "shall not be infringed." As we (the United States Supreme Court) said in United States v. Cruikshank, 92 U. S. 542, 553 (1876), "[t]his is not a right granted by the Constitution. Neither is it in any manner dependent upon that instrument for its existence. The Second amendment declares that it shall not be infringed . . ."; *available at* http://www.supremecourt.gov/opinions/07pdf/07-290.pdf.

Two years after *Heller*, the Supreme Court in *McDonald v. City of Chicago*, 561 U.S. 3020, 3050, (2010), held that the Second Amendment right recognized in *Heller* is applicable to the states through the Due Process clause of the Fourteenth Amendment, meaning that the Court ruled that the Second Amendment limits state and local governments to the same extent that it limits the federal government.[13] In so holding, the Court reiterated that "the Second Amendment protects the right to keep and bear arms for the purpose of self-defense";[14] that "individual self-defense is 'the central component' of the Second Amendment right";[15] and that "[s]elf-defense is a basic right, recognized by many legal systems from ancient times to the present day."[16]

Subsequent to the holdings in *Heller* and *McDonald*, there has been a dramatic increase in Second Amendment litigation. Accordingly, given the Court's clear instruction that the right to possess a handgun in the home for self-defense is consistent with a variety of gun laws, it's not surprising that lower courts have almost uniformly rejected Second Amendment arguments in hundreds of decisions in federal and state courts nationwide subsequent to *Heller*.[17]

Consequently, the Supreme Court Second Amendment holdings in both *Heller* and *McDonald* provide a solid framework within which to assess the prospect of armed civilian UAS. The critical statement in *Heller* suggests that the weapons' ability to be regulated is directly related to their commonness and dangerousness: Constitution protects "the individual right to possess and carry weapons in case of confrontation," but this right is subject to "reasonable regulation." The majority's opinion clearly states that the Second Amendment protects only a limited right. The Court directly stated that the amendment does not protect a "right to keep and carry any weapon

---

13. McDonald v. City of Chicago, 561 U.S. 3025 (2010).
14. *Id*. 130 S. Ct. at 3026
15. *Id*. 130 S. Ct. at 3036 (quoting Heller, 554 U.S. at 599).
16. *Id*. 130 S. Ct. at 3036 McDonald, 130 S. Ct. At 3036 (noting that Blackstone had asserted that the right to keep and bear arms was "one of the fundamental rights of Englishmen"). The Second Amendment was based partially on the right to keep and bear arms in English common-law and was influenced by the English Bill of Rights of 1689. Sir William Blackstone described this right as an auxiliary right, supporting the natural rights of self-defense, resistance to oppression, and the civic duty to act in concert in defense of the state.
17. *Significant Post-Heller Second Amendment Challenges Have Been Filed Nationwide*; Information about significant Post-Heller Litigation nationwide at http://smartgunlaws.org/post-heller-litigation-summary/. In United States v. Williams the 7th Circuit upheld the prohibition on convicted felon possession of firearms in 18 U.S.C. § 922(g) as substantially related to an important government interest. *See* United States v. Williams, 616 F.3d 685 (7th Cir. 2010). In United States v. Carter, the Fourth Circuit upheld 18 U.S.C. 922 (g) as reasonably related to substantial government interest; United States v. Carter 669 F. 3d 411 (4th Cir. 2012). In United States v. Decastro the Second Circuit held that heightened scrutiny is triggered only where a regulation substantially burdens the Second Amendment right; United States v. Decastro, 682 F.3d 169 (2d Cir. 2012). Conversely, Ezell v. City of Chicago is the only post-Heller federal Court of Appeals case that has upheld a right to arms based challenge to government action. In Ezell v. City of Chicago, the Seventh Circuit has issued a preliminary injunction against the City of Chicago, lifting a ban on firing ranges in the City of Chicago that rendered compliance with a hand gun licensing scheme requiring one hour of annual training burdensome, thereby vitiating the right to have a handgun to defend the home. In reaching its decision to enjoin the firing range ban, the Court noted that Second Amendment standards are still emerging, making it difficult for trial courts to apply the still largely undefined right with precision. *See* Ezell v. City of Chicago, CA 7 (2012).

whatsoever in any manner whatsoever and for whatever purpose" and listed several examples of presumptively constitutional regulations, including laws prohibiting firearm possession by felons and the mentally ill, forbidding guns in sensitive places such as schools and government buildings, and regulating the commercial sale of firearms.[18] Also, according to dicta uttered by Justice Scalia in *Heller* and echoed by Justice Alito in *McDonald*, the Second Amendment is consistent with laws banning "dangerous and unusual weapons" and laws "regulating the storage of firearms to prevent accidents."[19]

In *Heller* the Court expressly held that the Second Amendment limits the right of a responsible, law-abiding citizen to possess an operable handgun in the home for traditionally lawful purposes such as self-defense; however, it does not protect dangerous and unusual weapons and does not grant private parties the right to acquire military material.[20]

WEAPONS AND UNMANNED AIRCRAFT

Presently, government regulations state that UAS specifically designed for military purposes—"infrared focal plane arrays, imaging radar systems, and electronic systems or equipment specifically designed . . . for intelligence, security, or military purposes" are restricted "munitions."[21] Therefore, depending on their capabilities, unmanned aircraft, purportedly designed for civilian use that embody military technology, could be regulated under the catch-all "[a]ny article . . . which has substantial military applicability" clause in the International Traffic-In-Arms Regulations (ITAR)[22] and such designated technology would appear to be, per se, technology that is restricted so that it is "not in general public use."[23]

The FAA has current rules in place that deal with releasing anything from an aircraft, and those rules prohibit weapons from being installed on a civil aircraft, including unmanned aircraft.[24] According to James Williams of the FAA, "Over the next 10

---

18. Heller, 554 U.S. at 626–27.10.
19. Heller, 554 U.S. at 627, 632.
20. Takahashi, Timothy, *Drones and Privacy*, 72 COLUM. SCI. & TECH. L. REV. Vol. XIV, p.109 (April 7, 2012); *available at* SSRN: http://ssrn.com/abstract=2035575 or http://dx.doi.org/10.2139/ssrn.2035575 ; District of Columbia v. Heller, 554 U.S. 570, 626 (2008) (J. Scalia writing the majority holding that "[l]ike most rights, the right (to bear arms) secured by the Second Amendment is not unlimited . . . the right was not a right to keep and carry any weapon whatsoever in any manner whatsoever and for whatever purpose. . . . Nothing in our opinion should be taken to cast doubt on longstanding prohibitions on the . . . qualifications on the commercial sale of arms"). http://www.supremecourt.gov/.
21. *Id.* 22 C.F.R. § 121.1 (2011). The government, through its commerce power, regulates the development, possession, and sale of military material.
22. *Id.* 22 C.F.R. § 121.1 Category XXI(a) (2011).
23. *Id.* Kyllo v. United States, 533 U.S. 27, 40 (2001) http://www.supremecourt.gov/.
24. Jeff Schogol, *FAA: No Armed Drones in U.S. Airspace*, AIR FORCE TIMES FLIGHTLINES (February 13,

years, unmanned aircraft could fill a number of commercial and government uses here at home—but those uses don't include putting ordnance on target."[25]

Though Federal Aviation Administration regulations do not explicitly mention the use of firearms on unmanned aircraft, they do expressly forbid people from arming their private plane, and they prohibit any type of recreational flying or dropping objects from aircraft that endanger life or property. Therefore, it is unlikely that individuals will be allowed to arm an unmanned aircraft with an operable handgun for the purpose of self-defense. Furthermore, prohibiting the use of weaponry on an unmanned aircraft is consistent with laws banning dangerous and unusual weapons as a UAS could be armed with all manner of dangerous munition, explosive or chemical payloads, and remotely flown at the operator's intended target. Such designated technology would appear to be, per se, technology that is restricted so that it is not in general public use.

EXAMPLES OF CIVILIAN UNMANNED AIRCRAFT WITH WEAPONS

The following examples should illuminate the Court's holding that the right to bear arms secured by the Second Amendment is not unlimited . . . the right was not a right to keep and carry any weapon (handgun, explosive, or chemical/biological agents) whatsoever in any manner whatsoever and for whatever purpose (self-defense, criminal purpose, or terrorism). Several YouTube videos show hobbyists who have allegedly created rudimentary armed unmanned aircraft. One video shows a remote-controlled helicopter outfitted with a .45 caliber handgun. Another video shows a six-rotor helicopter that has been modified to shoot paintballs. The man who created that craft wore a bandana covering his face and used voice-modifying technology because attaching weapons to aircraft is expressly forbidden by the Federal Aviation Administration.

An online video titled "Citizen Unmanned Aircraft Warfare" posted on YouTube in December 2012 shows a hobbyist unmanned aircraft equipped with a custom-mounted paintball pistol flying over a grassy field and peppering human-shaped shooting-range targets with pellets; the video also shows footage of one of the targets splattered with three large red blotches on its head and neck area. In other footage that was not posted, Milo next used human targets in order to see if they could escape

---

2013), http://flightlines.airforcetimes.com/2013/02/13/faa-no-armed-drones-in-u-s-airspace/ (Quoting Jim Williams, the man in charge of regulating drones for the FAA).

25. Jason Koebler, *The Next Gun Debate—Armed Drones Could Be Protected by the Second Amendment*, US NEWS & WORLD REPORT (May 22, 2013), http://www.usnews.com/news/articles/2013/05/21/the-next-gun-debate-armed-drones-could-be-protected-by-the-second-amendment.

the paintball pistol equipped unmanned aircraft; they could not, and they suffered a similar paint-splattered fate.

The entire project, he said, took no more than a dozen hours and cost less than $2,000. He purchased the unmanned aircraft and the paintball gun online, downloaded open-source piloting software, and found instructions on how to get the unmanned aircraft up and running by running simple Internet searches for the terms "drones" and "DIY." He also noted that, with the unmanned aircraft's capabilities and very little extra work, he could program the unmanned aircraft on a computer to fly on a path, fire on a fixed target, and then fly home with little human intervention.[26] Another 2012 YouTube video appeared to show a homemade quad-rotor unmanned aircraft with a custom-mounted machine gun laying explosive waste to a group of mannequins. Viewed more than 15 million times, the video turned out to be a hoax, part of a viral marketing campaign for the future-warfare video game "Call of Duty: Black Ops II."

In 2004, a New Zealand engineer managed to build a miniature cruise missile for less than $5,000, a project that subsequently was shut down by the nation's government because of security concerns. In November 2012, 27-year-old Rezwan Ferdaus of Massachusetts was sentenced to seventeen years in prison for plotting to attack the Pentagon and the Capitol with a remote-controlled model aircraft rigged with explosives. Ferdaus was attempting to carry out an elaborate plot with undercover FBI agents posing as al-Qaeda operatives that involved the use of three unmanned aircraft carrying deadly explosive-packed payloads to attack and destroy the Pentagon and U.S. Capitol.[27]

According to Peter W. Singer, director of Brookings' 21st Century Defense Initiative, "With more of these unmanned aircraft in the skies, it becomes harder to tell which, if any, are malicious. As GPS technology improves, terrorists might be able to use unmanned aircraft to perform precision strikes on key buildings. As unmanned aircraft become smaller and quieter, they become easier to move and launch, and harder to detect in operation."[28]

26. Patrick Hruby, '*Citizen Unmanned Aircraft Warfare*': *Hobbyist Explores a Frightening Scenario*, THE WASHINGTON TIMES (December 17, 2012), *available at* http://www.washingtontimes.com/news/2012/dec/17/citizen-unmanned aircraft-warfare-hobbyist-explores-a-frighten/?page=all.

27. Kevin Johnson, *Man Accused of Plotting Drone Attacks on Pentagon, Capitol*, USA TODAY (9/29/2011, 1:16 AM), *available at* http://usatoday30.usatoday.com/news/washington/story/2011-09-28/DC-terrorist-plot-drone/50593792/1.

28. Peter W. Singer, director of Brookings' 21st Century Defense Initiative, in 2010, noting the constitutionality of privately owned and operated "self-defense drones" is, in fact, an "all too real question."

CONCLUSION

The extraordinary dangers unmanned aircraft are posing to individual security require more regulation and monitoring of all sources of unmanned aircraft use, be they public or private. Civilian unmanned aircraft use is a burgeoning area fueled by a remarkable convergence of many powerful technological advances. There are substantial commercial interests driving the integration and expansion of unmanned aircraft in the domestic airspace. Although unmanned aircraft offer real and far-reaching benefits, they also pose real and increasingly well-recognized safety concerns at the federal, state, and local levels. Therefore, a dialogue conducted with full awareness of this balance will be more likely to lead to positive policy outcomes. Accordingly, the FAA is likely to take a fair period of time to develop final regulations to ensure the safety and security of U.S. navigable airspace. In the meantime, state and local governments are likely to attempt to fill what they perceive as a regulatory void. Thus, it is likely that there will be continuing conflicts about the extent of the FAA's focused authority on federal aviation and the broader concerns state and local governments have under their historical police powers.

5

Unmanned Aircraft Risk, Product Liability, and Insurance

CHAPTER 13

Unmanned Aircraft Product Liability and Risk Management

Stephen S. Wu

Calvert Vaux Park in Brooklyn touches the water of Lower New York Bay. It lies between an inlet of the Bay and Belt Parkway, not too far from Coney Island Beach. A flat, grassy field in the park, by the baseball and soccer fields, plays host to hobbyists from the Seaview Rotary Wings club, who share a love of remote-controlled (RC) helicopters. On September 5, 2013, disaster struck this otherwise idyllic setting when 19-year-old Roman Pierozek Jr. of Woodhaven, Queens, lost control of his RC helicopter. Mr. Pierozek was no novice; he challenged himself to maneuver the RC helicopter with gravity-defying stunts and tricks.[1] On that day, however, Mr. Pierozek died when the helicopter struck him in the head.[2]

One hobby store worker commented about RC helicopters, "They crash all day long."[3] When asked about Mr. Pierozek's accident, he said, "It probably happened in a blink of an eye."[4] Fortunately, fatal accidents among hobbyists are infrequent.[5]

---

1. *See* J. David Goodman, *Remote-Controlled Model Helicopter Fatally Strikes Its Operator*, New York Times, Sept. 5, 2013, *available at* http://www.nytimes.com/2013/09/06/nyregion/remote-controlled-copter-fatally-strikes-pilot-at-park.html?_r=0.
2. *See id.*
3. *Id.*
4. *Id.*
5. *See id.*

On the horizon, however, are accidents between larger unmanned aircraft, possibly used for commercial purposes, and commercial airlines. Two close call incidents in 2014 raised the specter of such collisions—one near LaGuardia and the other near Los Angeles International Airport (LAX). The LaGuardia incident involved an unmanned aircraft with a 10- to 15-foot wingspan at 5,500 feet, and the LAX incident involved an unmanned aircraft the size of a trash can at 6,500 feet.[6] Moreover, we discuss elsewhere in this book how human error and the failure of certain key components of unmanned aircraft can cause accidents.[7]

The use of unmanned aircraft may significantly benefit agriculture. The innovative use of unmanned aircraft in the entertainment field is already starting. Unmanned aircraft may also assist in monitoring functions, such as security, checking on the environment, and infrastructure maintenance for facilities like oil and gas pipelines. Oil and gas exploration provides another compelling application.[8] Amazon founder Jeff Bezos told Charlie Rose of the CBS news show *60 Minutes* that the company has plans to use unmanned aircraft to deliver products to customers' homes.[9]

Despite the compelling commercial applications, and the likely growing popularity of unmanned aircraft for hobby, family, and personal uses, accidents involving unmanned aircraft will inevitably occur. Hopefully, the considerable benefits of unmanned aircraft technology will far outweigh the risks. Nonetheless, manufacturers will face the possibility of crippling product liability lawsuits. The threat of litigation may, in fact, deter some businesses from entering the market for unmanned aircraft. Further, foreign manufacturers may forego the U.S. market if they believe the risk of product liability litigation is too high. Finally, if an established manufacturer's loss experience is too great, it may exit the market. Consequently, the challenge for manufacturers is to determine how to commercialize compelling unmanned aircraft technology without going broke from additional costs to prevent accidents, defend litigation, and pay settlements or judgments.

This chapter identifies product liability risks to companies selling unmanned aircraft in the U.S. market, where those risks arise, and how manufacturers can adopt strategies to manage those risks. A focus on U.S. product liability law is important because the U.S. market is likely to be the largest one for now, and there is a widespread

---

6. *See* Craig Whitlock, *Close Encounters on Rise as Small Drones Gain in Popularity*, WASH. POST, Jun. 23, 2014, *available at* http://www.washingtonpost.com/sf/investigative/2014/06/23/close-encounters-with-small-drones-on-rise/.

7. *See* "Risk, Product Liability Trends, and Insurance in Commercial Unmanned Aircraft: A Data Centric Analysis" chapter 15 in this book.

8. *See, e.g.,* Matt Ball, *What Are the Top Ten Civilian Uses of Drones That Don't Impinge Privacy?*, SENSORS & SYSTEMS, Jul. 1, 2013, *available at* https://www.sensorsandsystems.com/dialog/perspectives/30861-what-are-the-top-ten-civilian-uses-of-drones-that-don't-impin.

9. *See* CBS Interactive, Inc., *Amazon Unveils Futuristic Plan: Delivery by Drone* (Dec. 1, 2013), *available at* http://www.cbsnews.com/news/amazon-unveils-futuristic-plan-delivery-by-drone/.

perception in the world that the legal climate in the United States makes it the most litigious country as compared to all other industrialized nations.

The first section of this chapter discusses the circumstances giving rise to U.S. product liability suits. It also mentions the reasons why juries in some cases award huge verdicts in favor of plaintiffs in product liability cases. The next section talks about the impacts of what can happen to an industry when companies fail to mitigate product liability risks. It uses recent automotive product liability as an example. After this discussion of impacts, the following section turns to the basic doctrines of product liability law. It covers possible causes of action a plaintiff can assert in product liability cases based on alleged unmanned aircraft defects and possible defenses a defendant can interpose. The next section moves to the topic of risk management. It discusses design practices and procedures unmanned aircraft manufacturers can adopt in order to reduce product liability. The final section examines other risk management strategies for unmanned aircraft manufacturers.

REASONS PRODUCT LIABILITY SUITS OCCUR

This chapter covers the phenomenon of "product liability." As usually understood, this term covers suits following some kind of accident based on strict product liability, as well as causes of action typically included in such suits, such as negligence, breach of express warranty, and breach of implied warranty. Nonetheless, this chapter also covers suits based on defects in unmanned aircraft that may not follow an accident. They may arise under consumer protection laws or breach of contract theories, and plaintiffs may base their suits on the diminution in the value of the product caused by a defect even when the defect did not cause an accident. Given the increasing popularity of economic loss litigation based on the diminution in the value of the product caused by an alleged defect, it is worth discussing in this chapter liability arising from defects generally. Thus, this chapter covers both economic loss litigation and product liability litigation arising from unmanned aircraft accidents. Both kinds of suits arise from alleged defects. Consequently, the risk mitigation strategies in this chapter will help to reduce defects and their legal consequences, regardless of whether those defects actually result in accident and regardless of the kind of litigation initiated by plaintiffs.

Having defined the scope of the "liability" covered in this chapter, we now turn to the phenomenon of "product liability" as a broad concept. Why do product liability suits occur? Frequently, an accident occurs, and the victims of the accident file a product liability suit. In addition, however, attorneys hearing about accidents or publicized instances of product problems carrying a great risk of accidents may file a complaint on behalf of other product purchasers who have not fallen victim to an accident but who have allegedly sustained economic losses because the products they purchased from manufacturers are worth less because of an alleged defect.

Using a car as an example, if a new car of Model X is perceived to have a fair market value of $20,000, and a consumer pays that much for one, but people later discover a defect in that model that lowers its fair market value to $15,000, the purchaser has sustained an economic loss of $5,000. For instance, Toyota faced product liability suits arising from accidents after the "sudden acceleration" phenomenon came to light. In addition, however, lawyers pursued separate suits consolidated as a class action in the U.S. District Court for the Central District of California. The class was comprised of consumers who purchased Toyota vehicles and sustained economic loss because of the diminished value of their vehicles.

As discussed below, litigation arising from product defects may result in huge compensation awards or settlements for plaintiffs. Perhaps the most famous huge-verdict product liability case occurred in the litigation involving Ford Motor Company's Pinto automobile. Here is how the appellate court described the basic facts of the most famous Pinto case:

> A 1972 Ford Pinto hatchback automobile unexpectedly stalled on a freeway, erupting into flames when it was rear ended by a car proceeding in the same direction. Mrs. Lilly Gray, the driver of the Pinto, suffered fatal burns and 13-year-old Richard Grimshaw, a passenger in the Pinto, suffered severe and permanently disfiguring burns on his face and entire body. Grimshaw and the heirs of Mrs. Gray (Grays) sued Ford Motor Company and others. Following a six-month jury trial, verdicts were returned in favor of plaintiffs against Ford Motor Company. Grimshaw was awarded $2,516,000 compensatory damages and $125 million punitive damages; the Grays were awarded $559,680 in compensatory damages.[10]

Although the court's statement of the case shows the seriousness of the accident, its dry version of the facts was different from others' accounts of the accident. For instance, *Mother Jones* magazine published a famous article about the accident. The writer, Mr. Dowie, describes the accident (using pseudonyms, evidently before the names of the victims became public) in much more colorful terms:

> [A] woman, whom for legal reasons we will call Sandra Gillespie, pulled onto a Minneapolis highway in her new Ford Pinto. Riding with her was a young boy,

---

10. Grimshaw v. Ford Motor Co., 119 Cal. App. 3d 757, 771–72 (1981).

whom we'll call Robbie Carlton. As she entered a merge lane, Sandra Gillespie's car stalled. Another car rear-ended hers at an impact speed of 28 miles per hour. The Pinto's gas tank ruptured. Vapors from it mixed quickly with the air in the passenger compartment. A spark ignited the mixture and the car exploded in a ball of fire. Sandra died in agony a few hours later in an emergency hospital. Her passenger, 13-year-old Robbie Carlton, is still alive; he has just come home from another futile operation aimed at grafting a new ear and nose from skin on the few unscarred portions of his badly burned body.[11]

Unmanned aircraft manufacturers should keep in mind that during any trial, a lawyer for an accident victim will likely tell a story about an accident victim in opening and closing statements much more like Mr. Dowie's description of the Pinto accident than the dry recitation of the facts in the Pinto appellate decision. Moreover, when future high-stakes lawsuits based on alleged unmanned aircraft defects come to trial in the United States, an unmanned aircraft manufacturer's fate will likely rest with a jury, which will decide whether to impose liability on the manufacturer, rather than a judge. Moreover, in any trial, the jury would likely see the victim of an unmanned aircraft accident seated next to his or her attorney. It is quite possible that the victim's accident would be disfiguring or even catastrophic. The image of these injuries would naturally have some effect on a jury, even though the judge would instruct the jury not to permit sympathy, bias, or prejudice to affect its verdict.

Another famous huge-verdict product liability case arose from the use of the pharmaceutical company Merck's painkiller Vioxx. A Texas lawyer obtained a $253.5 million verdict against Merck for Carol Ernst, the widow of Robert Ernst. Ernst died after he took Vioxx for eight months.[12]

Unmanned aircraft manufacturers should consider the realities of huge product liability verdicts when designing their products. In particular, executives of unmanned aircraft manufacturers should realize, first, that accidents will occur from their products, and second, that product liability litigation (as broadly defined above) is inevitable. The worst of those accidents may be dramatic and may involve horrific, catastrophic injuries to sympathetic accident victims. Moreover, executives should figure that there will be lawyers willing to take on product liability cases when injuries are catastrophic enough. In these kinds of cases, manufacturers face the risk of extremely large verdicts of the kind seen in the Pinto and Vioxx cases. These are simply the facts of life.

---

11. Mark Dowie, *Pinto Madness*, MOTHER JONES, Sept. 1, 1977, *reprinted at* http://www.motherjones.com/print/15405.

12. Alex Berenson, *Vioxx Verdict Raises Profile of Texas Lawyer*, NEW YORK TIMES, Aug. 22, 2005, *reprinted at* http://www.nytimes.com/2005/08/22/business/22lawyer.html?pagewanted=all.

Moreover, manufacturers' design teams will have an opportunity to consider safety when making engineering and business decisions about their unmanned aircraft designs. They will consider safety measures to take and how much they are willing to spend in effort and money to improve unmanned aircraft safety. When making these decisions, design team members may make clearer decisions and assess risk more effectively if they think about how they may need to defend their company's conduct at a trial in which the lawyers and jury will scrutinize and perhaps second-guess their decisions.

What motivates jurors to impose huge verdicts against manufacturers? The main motivation appears to be juror anger. "Angry jurors mean high damages."[13] More specifically, when juries become angry at the defendants' conduct, they use the only means at their disposal, the verdict and its size, to send a message to manufacturers and condemn their conduct. For instance, testimony in the Ford Pinto case showed that Ford was aware of problems with the Pinto's fuel system. In particular, during rear-end collisions, the Pinto's gas tank would split open. Ford also knew that a part costing only $11 could prevent the splitting problem.

Despite this knowledge, Ford decided not to spend the money to add the $11 part to the Pinto. Ford made this decision after conducting a cost-benefit analysis by comparing the additional cost incurred by adding the $11 part to the vehicle with the value of lives likely to be lost as a result of Pinto accidents arising from the fuel system vulnerability. Ford's analysis placed a value on each human life that it anticipated would be lost. In the end, Ford decided that the aggregate cost of adding the part to their Pintos was greater than the overall value of the human lives that the added part could have saved. Consequently, Ford made the decision not to change the Pinto's design by adding the part.

The jury found Ford's cost-benefit calculation and assignment of a dollar value on human life to be repugnant. The jury was aware that an $11 part could prevent the vulnerability of the fuel system. Eleven dollars is not much in comparison with a human life. Accordingly, the jury apparently concluded that Ford acted callously and placed its profits ahead of human life. Presumably, this callousness caused the jury to be angry, resulting in its $125 million punitive damage award.[14]

---

13. Robert D. Minick & Dorothy K. Kagehiro, *Understanding Juror Emotions: Anger Management in the Courtroom*, FOR THE DEFENSE, July 2004 (emphasis added), *reprinted at* http://www.krollontrack.com/publications/tg_forthedefense_robertminick-dorothyhagehiro070104.pdf, at 3.

14. The California Court of Appeal affirmed the jury's award of punitive damages. The court observed:
    Through the results of the crash tests Ford knew that the Pinto's fuel tank and rear structure would expose consumers to serious injury or death in a 20 to 30 mile-per-hour collision. There was evidence that Ford could have corrected the hazardous design defects at minimal cost but decided to defer correction of the shortcomings by engaging in a cost-benefit analysis balancing human lives and limbs against corporate profits. Ford's institutional mentality was shown to be one of callous indifference to public safety. There was substantial evidence that Ford's conduct constituted "conscious disregard" of the probability of injury to members of the consuming public.
    Grimshaw, 119 Cal. App. 3d at 813.

The Ernst-Vioxx case involved a similar situation. Internal Merck documents showed that the company knew that Vioxx created a risk of heart attacks to users before it began to market the painkiller. Seeing these documents apparently gave the jury the idea that the company placed profits above public safety and therefore made jurors angry. Based on the Merck executives' carelessness, the jury wanted to send a message that their conduct was unacceptable and that they should not hide information about the dangers of the drug.[15]

POTENTIAL IMPACTS OF ACCIDENTS

As discussed above, the Ford Pinto and Vioxx litigations resulted in huge verdicts. Nonetheless, the tide turned in these two particular cases when appellate courts reduced the verdict against Ford and overturned the verdict against Merck. More generally, however, product liability may cause significant financial losses to the industry and the loss of human life. In some cases, product liability has the potential for putting manufacturers out of business. For instance, lawsuits for damages caused by asbestos forced many asbestos-related companies out of business.[16]

Given that the market for unmanned aircraft is in its infancy, it is premature to predict the exact impact of product liability on the unmanned aircraft industry. We can, however, look to the automotive industry to see how product liability can lead to significant financial and human impacts in a more mature field.

One of the most prominent examples of recent product liability issues in the automotive industry has been the Toyota sudden acceleration phenomenon. People reported how their cars accelerated without warning and they were not able to brake the car.[17] Some reports contended that eighty-nine people may have died from accidents involving the sudden acceleration of Toyota vehicles.[18] The resulting lawsuits were transferred to the U.S. District Court for the Central District of California for coordinated or consolidated pretrial proceedings.[19]

15. Lisa Girion and Dana Calvo, *Merck Loses Vioxx Case*, L.A. TIMES, Aug. 20, 2005, *reprinted at* http://articles.latimes.com/2005/aug/20/business/fi-vioxx20.

16. *The Senate Fails on Asbestos*, CHICAGO TRIBUNE, Feb. 17, 2005, http://articles.chicagotribune.com /2006-02-17/news/0602170249_1_asbestos-litigation-asbestos-claims-trust-fund.

17. Ric Romero, *Sudden Acceleration Issue Spans Beyond Toyota*, 6ABC.COM (Jan. 4, 2010), http://6abc .com/archive/7200572/.

18. CBS News and Associated Press, *Toyota "Unintended Acceleration" Has Killed 89*, CBS NEWS (May 25, 2010), http://www.cbsnews.com/news/toyota-unintended-acceleration-has-killed-89/.

19. *In re* Toyota Motor Corp. Unintended Acceleration Marketing, Sales Practices, and Products Liability Litigation, No. 8:10-ML-2151 JVS (FMO) (C.D. Cal. filed Apr. 12, 2010) (cases consolidated by the Judicial Panel on Multidistrict Litigation in the U.S. District Court for the Central District of California).

An expert witness for the plaintiff in one of the cases looked into sudden acceleration in one of the cars and concluded that a software malfunction caused the accident.[20] He pointed out that Toyota's own engineers had trouble understanding the code, and they called their own code "spaghetti like."[21] Barr talked about his findings to a jury in a case pending in an Oklahoma state court. The jury ended up awarding the driver $1.5 million in compensatory damages, and it awarded $1.5 million to the family of a passenger who died in the crash.[22] The case, *Bookout v. Toyota Motor Corp.*,[23] settled before a punitive damages phase of the trial began.[24]

Although the cause of these accidents remained unclear, Toyota decided to start settling its sudden acceleration cases. Barr's testimony in the Oklahoma case may have convinced Toyota that it was time to settle.[25] Here are some of the amounts that Toyota has paid in settlements:

- $1.6 billion to resolve the multidistrict litigation financial loss claims[26]
- $1.2 billion to resolve threatened criminal charges Toyota faced[27]
- $25.5 million to resolve shareholder claims based on the company's failure to report safety issues[28]
- $65 million to pay fines arising out of federal vehicle safety law violations[29]

In addition to these settlement amounts, the total amount paid by Toyota to resolve the sudden acceleration claims may be more than $4 billion because in addition to these settlement amounts there are additional claims, hefty legal fees, and other internal expenses to investigate, recall, and remediate the issues with its cars.

Another more recent high-profile product liability issue affecting the automobile industry involved certain ignition switches in some General Motors (GM) cars. GM adopted new switches during the late 1990s in order to make them work more smoothly. "But as it turns out, new switches in models such as the Chevrolet Cobalt

---

20. Michael Barr, Rule 26(a)(2)(B) Report of Michael Barr April 12, 2013, in Estate of Ida St. John v. Toyota Motor Corporation, et al. 65 (Apr. 12, 2013) [hereinafter, "Barr Report"].

21. *Id.* at 39, 54.

22. Junko Yoshida, *Toyota Case: Single Bit Flip That Killed*, EE Times (Oct. 25, 2013), *reprinted at* http://www.eetimes.com/document.asp?doc_id=1319903&page_number=3.

23. No. CJ-2008-7969 (Okl. Dist. Ct. Okl. Cty. dismissed Nov. 20, 2013).

24. Jerry Hirsch, *After Losing Verdict, Toyota Settles in Sudden Acceleration Case*, L.A. Times (Oct. 25, 2013), *reprinted at* http://articles.latimes.com/2013/oct/25/autos/la-fi-hy-toyota-settles-sudden-acceleration-20131025.

25. "Legal analysts said that the verdict most likely spurred Toyota to pursue a broad settlement of its remaining cases." Jaclyn Trop, *Toyota Seeks a Settlement for Sudden Acceleration Cases*, N.Y. Times (Dec. 13, 2013), http://www.nytimes.com/2013/12/14/business/toyota-seeks-settlement-for-lawsuits.html?_r=0.

26. *Id.*

27. David Undercoffler, *Toyota and Justice Department Said to Reach $1.2 Billion Settlement in Criminal Case*, L.A. Times (Mar. 18, 2014), *reprinted at* http://www.latimes.com/business/autos/la-fi-hy-autos-toyota-justice-department-settlement-20140318-story.html.

28. *Id.*

29. *Id.*

and Saturn Ion can unexpectedly slip from 'run' to 'accessory,' causing engines to stall. That shuts off the power steering, making cars harder to control, and disables air bags in crashes."[30] The switch issue may have caused more than fifty accidents. "GM says the problem has caused at least 13 deaths, but some members of Congress put the death toll near 100."[31]

Before the accidents occurred, engineers at GM knew about the issue. Nonetheless, they opted against replacing the switches. Congressional hearings revealed an internal GM e-mail, which stated that using an improved switch design would increase the switch's price by 90 cents. Yet, such a switch would reduce warranty claims by approximately 10–15 cents.[32] "The part costs less than $10 wholesale. The fix takes less than an hour. A mechanic removes a few screws and connectors, takes off a plastic shroud, pops in the new switch, and the customer is back on the road."[33] "[T]o many people familiar with the automaker," the reason GM did not recall the cars sooner "is a corporate culture reluctant to pass along bad news. When GM was struggling to cut costs and buff its image, a recall of its popular small cars would have been a terrible setback."[34] "'It's pretty clear that somebody somewhere was being penny-wise and pound-foolish,' said Marina Whitman, a professor at the University of Michigan and a former economist at GM."[35]

GM paid a hefty price for not recalling the cars with the problematic switches. As a result of its conduct, a number of governmental entities started to investigate GM, including Congress, safety regulators, the U.S. attorney in New York, the SEC, Transport Canada, and forty-five state attorneys general. GM had to recall the cars anyway at a significant cost. Moreover, GM will likely pay $400 million to $600 million more after creating a compensation fund for families of crash victims.[36]

In addition to the compensation fund, GM said that it will spend $1.2 billion to repair the cars and trucks recalled during the second quarter, on top of the $1.3 billion it identified for repair costs in the first three months of the year. In

30. Tom Krisher, *GM's Ignition Switch: What Went Wrong*, COLUMBUS DISPATCH (Jul. 8, 2014), *reprinted at* http://www.dispatch.com/content/stories/business/2014/07/08/gms-ignition-switch-what-went-wrong.html.

31. *Id.*

32. E-mail from John Hendler to Lori Queen et al. (Sept. 28, 2005, 4:07 PM), *reprinted at* http://docs.house .gov/meetings/IF/IF02/20140618/102345/HHRG-113-IF02-20140618-SD036.pdf.

33. Michael Fletcher & Steven Mufson, *Why Did GM Take So Long to Respond to Deadly Defect? Corporate Culture May Hold Answer*, WASHINGTON POST (Mar. 30, 2014), *reprinted at* http://www.washingtonpost.com /business/economy/why-did-gm-take-so-long-to-respond-to-deadly-defect-corporate-culture-may-hold-answer /2014/03/30/5c366f6c-b691-11e3-b84e-897d3d12b816_story.html.

34. *Id.*

35. *Id.*

36. Chris Isidore, *GM to Pay Victims at Least $400 Million*, CNN MONEY (Jul. 24, 2014), http://money .cnn.com/2014/07/24/news/companies/gm-earnings-recall/.

addition, the company set aside an additional $874 million in the quarter for future recalls.[37]

When GM tallies its expenses arising from the problem switches, the price tag will be enormous: "All told, GM's recalls have cost the automaker nearly $4 billion this year."[38] Moreover, the costs will continue to accrue for the foreseeable future. Further, the cost for GM to resolve these issues will be in addition to the legal fees and other internal investigation and remediation expenses to look into and fix the problem.

Although cars and unmanned aircraft are different, the problems faced by Toyota and GM show the enormous human toll and financial impact from problems with the safety of products. Until suits begin to reveal problems with unmanned aircraft safety, the effect of product liability on the industry will remain unclear. Nonetheless, the Toyota and GM examples show the great potential for extremely costly responses to product safety problems. Severe problems may even lead to the bankruptcy of some manufacturers.

CLAIMS AND DEFENSES IN UNMANNED AIRCRAFT PRODUCT LIABILITY CASES

We have talked above about the risks to the unmanned aircraft industry posed by product liability, including the human toll and the considerable risk of financial loss. This section covers what plaintiffs must prove in order to prevail in a suit based on an allegedly defective product, as well as what defendants must provide in order to assert certain defenses. Plaintiffs filing a product liability suit to seek redress following an accident typically include claims in their complaints of three types: "strict product liability," "negligence," and "breach of warranty."[39] The governing law controlling the outcome of product liability cases in the United States is most frequently state law, rather than federal law. Moreover, product liability law varies from state to state.

Strict Liability Claims

Product liability plaintiffs face the lowest burden if they assert a strict product liability claim. Potential defendants in a strict liability suit include almost every business

---

37. *Id.*

38. *Id.*

39. "Deceit" or "misrepresentation" is another possible claim for plaintiffs. Liability for this claim arises from false statements made by the seller about a product. Such a claim, though, is the least asserted type of product liability claim. 1 FRUMER, LOUIS R., ET AL., PRODUCT LIABILITY § 2.05[1] (2014) [hereinafter Frumer]. A plaintiff may seek to prove that the defendant made misrepresentations, which may be intentional, negligent (careless), or innocent. *Id.*

in the chain of distribution starting with the extraction and sale of raw materials to component part manufacturers. Manufacturers of the finished product are often the principal defendant in product liability suits. Suits, however, may also include distributors and retailers of the product.[40] A seller defending a strict liability claim faces liability for selling defective products even if the defendant is not "at fault" in any way. It also does not matter if the plaintiff and defendant had a contractual relationship. Again, however, the states have different laws, and strict liability is not even a viable claim in some states. In general, however, most states follow the approach to strict liability described in Section 402A of the Second Restatement of Torts.[41] States may include this approach in statutory law or common law. According to Section 402A, a plaintiff must prove at trial the following essential elements:

- The defendant sold the product in question,
- The defendant is in the business of selling this kind of product,
- The product was defective and unreasonably dangerous at the time it left the defendant's hands,
- The product is expected to and does reach the user or consumer without substantial change in the condition in which it is sold, and
- The defect was the proximate cause of the plaintiff's injuries.[42]

A plaintiff asserting a defect in an unmanned aircraft will face the crucial burden of showing that the unmanned aircraft was "defective" in some way. "Defects" fall into three categories: defects in design, defects in the way the product was manufactured, and defects stemming from a defendant's failure to provide adequate warnings or instructions to a product's users. Manufacturers developing unmanned aircraft are going to be focused on design defect and failure to warn issues. Different states have different tests for determining when a design is defective. They are as follows:

- The "ordinary consumer test," which asks what an ordinary consumer would expect from a product; this test is typically used where the nature of the product makes a potential for injury clear to consumers.
- The "risk-utility test," in which a plaintiff claims that the risks from a design outweigh the design's benefits to the consumer or public.
- The "product manufacturer test," under which a court will consider whether a reasonably prudent manufacturer or seller, aware of the product's dangerous

---

40. 1 Frumer, *supra*, § 5.01.
41. RESTATEMENT (SECOND) OF TORTS § 402A(1) (1965). "More than three quarters of American jurisdictions incorporate all or part of this section in their own distinct brand of strict liability." 1 Frumer, *supra*, § 2.04.
42. *Id.* § 402A(1)(b).

condition, would not have put the product on the market if it had been aware of the product's condition.
- A combination test, which may shift the burden of proof to the manufacturer to show a lack of defect in certain situations.
- The ultimate issue test, which gives the jury the discretion to determine whether a design is defective.[43]

Design defect cases often require the assistance of expert testimony to explain the nature of a defendant's product and why the defendant's design is defective. Experts also frequently opine on whether an alternative design could have prevented the accident.

The second type of defect of interest to unmanned aircraft manufacturers is one in which a product is allegedly defective because the manufacturer failed to warn users of certain risks or characteristics of the product. A plaintiff could also say that the defendant did not provide adequate instructions about how to operate the product.

Negligence Claims
Negligence often appears in product liability complaints as an alternative claim, providing plaintiffs with an avenue for possible recovery in addition to strict liability. Negligence claims involve a plaintiff identifying the standard of conduct for a hypothetical "reasonable person." The plaintiff would contend that a defendant manufacturer's careless conduct fell below that standard and was therefore actionable. Negligence claims can be based on a product's design, the way in which the product was manufactured, or a manufacturer's failure to give adequate warnings or instructions. Negligence involves a higher burden for a plaintiff than strict liability, because the plaintiff must prove that the defendant was at fault in some way.

Under a negligence claim, the plaintiff must prove the following elements in order to prevail:

- The defendant owed a duty of care to provide a reasonably safe product in terms of design or manufacture, or to warn of dangerous defects; that is, the plaintiff must show a duty for the defendant to meet a standard of conduct to protect others against unreasonable risk.
- The defendant breached its duty of care by failing to conform to the standard of conduct required.
- The defendant's conduct proximately caused the plaintiff's injury.[44]

---

43. 1 JOHN VARGO, PRODUCTS LIABILITY PRACTICE GUIDE § 6.04 (2014) [hereinafter Vargo].
44. *Id.* § 6.03[1].

Breach of Warranty Claims

A plaintiff claiming a defect in a product can, in most states in the United States, assert a breach of warranty claim. Such a claim would arise if a product's seller made a "warranty," which is an affirmation or promise concerning a product. The warranty could cover a product's performance, features, or characteristics. For instance, a plaintiff could point out warranties relating to the safety of a product.

In a breach of warranty action, the plaintiff will contend that the product in question does not conform to the warranty because it does not perform as promised. Alternatively, the product may not have the promised features or characteristics. A plaintiff may use a warranty claim based on a design defect, a manufacturing defect, or a failure to provide proper instructions or warnings.

Like with strict liability, the plaintiff does not need to prove fault on the part of the seller. Rather, the issue in a breach of warranty claim focuses on whether the product is consistent with what the seller promised. A defendant, however, can assert certain defenses to a warranty claim, recovery on which depends on state law. For example, a defendant may be able to defend a warranty claim based on a "lack of privity" defense. The defendant can claim lack of privity if there is no contractual relationship between the plaintiff and the defendant.

Another common warranty defense is a claim that the plaintiff failed to provide the seller with notice of the breach. Finally, defendants will often use disclaimers in order to prevent the application of warranties.[45] Notwithstanding the historical use of privity as a defense, today the lack of privity does not, in most U.S. jurisdictions, prevent a product's purchasers or their family members from asserting product defect claims against companies in the chain of distribution under a warranty theory.[46]

A breach of warranty claim typically consists of the following elements that a plaintiff must prove:

- The defendant made a warranty,
- The product did not comply with the warranty at the time of the sale,
- The plaintiff's injury was proximately caused by the defective nature of the product, and
- As a result, the plaintiff suffered damage.[47]

Warranties typically fall within three categories. First, a seller makes an "express warranty" by explicitly making promises or affirmations about a product. These promises may appear in various kinds of documentation, including sales contracts, warranty

---

45. *Id.* § 6.02[4].
46. *Id.*
47. *Id.* § 6.02[1].

programs, advertisements, or sales collateral. A seller may make warranties in writing or orally.

Second, the law sometimes recognizes "implied warranties" in connection with the sale of consumer products. Implied warranties are not expressed by the seller but instead are recognized as a matter of law. For instance, the law may sometimes recognize an "implied warranty of merchantability." Under this implied warranty, the law deems that a seller is impliedly promising that a product is fit for its ordinary purposes. That is, the product should work as a consumer would normally expect. As an example, a seller would be liable for a breach of the implied warranty of merchantability if it sold a car whose engine fell out when the new owner was driving it off the lot. Product liability litigation about unmanned aircraft based on an implied warranty will most likely involve a claim for breach of the implied warranty of merchantability.

The other typical implied warranty is the "warranty of fitness for a particular purpose." Such a warranty arises if the seller knows the particular purpose the consumer has in mind for use of the product, and if the buyer is relying on the skill and judgment of the seller to select and furnish suitable products. In such cases, an implied warranty of fitness for a particular purpose arises as a matter of law, and the law will deem that the seller is promising that the product will be fit for the purpose intended by the consumer. As an example of fitness for a particular purpose, if a consumer wants to buy a saw blade for the purpose of cutting metal pipe, and the sales representative recommends a certain kind of blade, the law recognizes a promise that the blade can, in fact, work in a saw to cut metal pipes.

Claims Under Consumer Protection Laws

In addition to the common law or statutory tort claims, plaintiffs sometimes allege violations of state consumer protection statutes as the basis for a claim. For instance, a plaintiff may assert claims based on California's Unfair Competition Law (UCL),[48] False Advertising Law (FAL),[49] Consumer Legal Remedies Act (CLRA),[50] or their equivalent under the laws of another state. Different states have different laws, and some states do not allow personal injury claims under these consumer protection laws.[51] Plaintiffs, however, frequently use these laws to claim losses after purchasing a

---

48. CAL. BUS. & PROF. CODE § 17200 et seq.
49. *Id.* § 17500 et seq.
50. CAL. CIV. CODE § 1750 et seq.
51. JOHN ALEE, ET AL., PRODUCT LIABILITY § 18.02 (2014) [hereinafter Alee].

product based on the effect of a product defect in diminishing the value of the product. The typical essential elements the plaintiff must prove in such statutory claims are:

- A violation of the statute occurred
- that causes
- injury to a consumer.

In California, for example, the UCL prohibits unlawful, unfair, or fraudulent business acts or practices. The FAL prohibits untrue or misleading advertising practices. The CLRA contains a list of unfair business practices, such as misrepresenting the characteristics and qualities of a product, which the law prohibits.

Types of Defects

In any product liability case against an unmanned aircraft manufacturer, the key issue will be whether the unmanned aircraft had a "defect" of some kind that caused an accident or otherwise caused the plaintiff damages. It is premature to say what kinds of defects plaintiffs will likely claim in product liability cases. After all, the unmanned aircraft industry is still in its infancy.

This section, however, contains thoughts on possible types of defects that the courts may encounter in unmanned aircraft cases, based on the types of problems seen in product liability cases in the past, interviews with industry experts, and judgments about safety and other issues likely to arise in the future. Unmanned aircraft may face a wide variety of possible defects. Examples include the following:

- Mechanical or physical defects affecting different unmanned aircraft systems or affecting safety features of unmanned aircraft; for instance, claims may arise because a manufacturer used materials of insufficient strength or thickness.
- Electrical component or system defects; for example, defects may crop up because the manufacturer used incorrect or inadequate components, the components did not perform properly, or the components wore out prematurely.
- Defects in software,[52] including information security vulnerabilities.

---

52. By referring to "software," I also mean to encompass hardware or firmware code.

Perhaps more interesting are potential defects in autonomous unmanned aircraft. Unmanned aircraft may experience defects that human-controlled unmanned aircraft do not. Again, mechanical, electronic, or software defects may appear, such as:

- Mechanical or physical defects in unmanned aircraft control systems or in unmanned aircraft onboard sensors. For instance, a sensor needed to steer the unmanned aircraft might fall off if not properly attached to the unmanned aircraft, which might cause the unmanned aircraft to crash.
- The failure of electrical components in sensors or control systems for autonomous unmanned aircraft.
- Problems with the software used to operate autonomous unmanned aircraft sensors or control systems.

Software alone may involve a broad range of potential defects. For instance:

- Unmanned aircraft software may contain various kinds of information security vulnerabilities.
- The inputs to the software may come from inadequate sources of data, not enough data, inaccurate data, data of insufficient precision, or data input or processing of insufficient speed.
- The software used may not sufficiently recognize patterns such as obstacles or hazards to the unmanned aircraft's flight path.
- Unmanned aircraft designs may not adequately be able to execute safe ordinary maneuvers, such as takeoffs and landings.
- Unmanned aircraft may encounter other autonomous behavior issues, such as unpredictable changes in speed or direction.
- Unmanned aircraft may have problems in the algorithms used to avoid collisions.
- Unmanned aircraft software may not promote effective human-computer coordination. For instance, if an unmanned aircraft passes control from autonomous to manual mode, the unmanned aircraft must alert the pilot so that the pilot can take over control of the unmanned aircraft safely.

Moreover, commentators discuss design decisions that programmers must make when creating the logic for an autonomous vehicle in instances where the system believes the vehicle will inevitably and unavoidably collide. In these situations, the programmer may be able to make a choice to steer the vehicle to strike and perhaps harm different objects or persons. Professor Patrick Lin of California Polytechnic State University has published a number of articles discussing design dilemmas in the context of driverless cars. For instance, he writes about the dilemma a designer of a driverless

car would face in a scenario in which there is an unavoidable choice between causing a car to strike a motorcycle rider wearing a helmet and striking one without a
helmet. A programmer might decide that it is better, if a collision is unavoidable, to
strike one or the other. The programmer's implementation of that decision in designing the software may trigger product liability and a complaint from a person who is
hit because of the designer's decision.

Defenses in Product Liability Cases

Just as plaintiffs have a number of arguments they can assert to claim that a manufacturer should be liable for selling defective unmanned aircraft, unmanned aircraft
manufacturers have a number of defenses they can assert to avoid liability. Perhaps
the most common type of defense arises from the plaintiff's own negligent conduct
that might have contributed to an accident or other damages. For example, if the
family of Roman Pierozek sued the manufacturer of the RC helicopter he was flying
at the time of his death, the manufacturer might have a valid defense by saying that
Mr. Pierozek misused the helicopter by causing it to engage in extreme maneuvers
and his loss of control over the helicopter was the cause of the crash, not any defect
in the helicopter.

Depending on state law and the type of claim alleged by the plaintiff, a plaintiff's
own negligence may provide a partial or sometimes complete defense to a claim.
Moreover, a defendant could use the plaintiff's negligence to argue that it constituted a
superseding cause of the accident or other damages. Likewise, we may see unmanned
aircraft users modifying their unmanned aircraft, and sometimes modifications to a
product will cause an accident.

Another defense based on a plaintiff's own conduct is called "assumption of the
risk." If a plaintiff knew of a defect or safety issue and, despite this knowledge, the
plaintiff volunteered to use the product or entered a zone to encounter a known danger,
the defendant is not liable. One common example of assumption of the risk is a fan
entering a baseball stadium knowing that there is some risk a foul ball will hit the fan.

In any case, if the conduct of the plaintiff contributed in some way to an accident,
depending on state law, a jury may be instructed to reduce a plaintiff's recovery. For
instance, if a jury concludes that a product defect and a plaintiff's conduct contributed equally to an accident, some states' laws would require the jury to reduce any
award of damages by 50 percent. Even if a plaintiff's conduct did not contribute to
the occurrence of an accident, a plaintiff may have a duty to mitigate damages after
an accident, and a plaintiff's failure to mitigate damages may reduce the plaintiff's
recovery.

Defenses based on a plaintiff's own conduct, however, may not apply if an
unmanned aircraft was operating in autonomous mode. If the plaintiff was not flying

the unmanned aircraft and in control of it, the plaintiff cannot be liable for navigating it carelessly. Moreover, given the widespread use of unmanned aircraft today, a court is unlikely to conclude that the use of an unmanned aircraft by itself amounts to assumption of the risk, per se, the way piloting an experimental spacecraft might. If a user modifies or abuses an unmanned aircraft, its sensors, or its control systems for fun, however, that conduct might constitute assumption of the risk, allowing a defendant to assert this conduct as a defense.

Manufacturers may be most interested to know whether "state of the art" is a defense in a case. Manufacturers commonly defend their conduct when something goes wrong by saying that they used state-of-the-art technology to create their products or deliver their services, implying that it is unreasonable to expect that they could have done more. They say that they could not have produced a safer product at the time they designed it. The technology simply was not available then. And they should not be held to a standard of safety that was technologically infeasible at the time. The state of the art defense does exist in some states, although other states do not recognize it.[53] Other defenses to an unmanned aircraft product liability suit might include the following:

- A defense based on the "economic loss doctrine," which precludes tort claims when the plaintiff claims financial losses—rather than bodily injury or property damage (other than damage to the product itself).
- A defense based on the sophistication of the user or intermediary between the seller and the user, such as where the product is designed for professional rather than consumer use, or a professional chooses the product and delivers it, for instance where a physician prescribes a medicine for a patient to take.
- The government contractor defense, which permits a manufacturer to avoid liability in certain cases when the manufacturer built the product based on government specifications.

Finally, manufacturers or other sellers of unmanned aircraft built for purposes of fighting terrorism might have a defense based on the Support Anti-Terrorism by Fostering Effective Technologies Act of 2002 (the "SAFETY Act").[54] Manufacturers can apply to the Department of Homeland Security (DHS) for two levels of protection under the SAFETY Act, "designation" and "certification." If DHS gives an unmanned aircraft a designation as a qualified antiterrorism technology, then DHS will require certain levels of liability insurance but will cap damages recoverable against the

---

53. 1 Frumer, *supra*, § 8.04.
54. Support Anti-Terrorism by Fostering Effective Technologies Act of 2002 in the Homeland Security Act of 2002, Pub. L. No. 107–296, §§ 861–865, 116 Stat. 2135, 2238–42 (2002) (codified at 6 U.S.C. §§ 441–444).

seller at the amount of that insurance.[55] To qualify for designation, an applicant must make a showing, among other things, that the seller faces a large or extraordinarily unquantifiable liability risk and a substantial likelihood that the technology will not be deployed without the act's protections.[56]

Certification involves all of the benefits of designation, with certain additional benefits. Certification under the act requires an additional showing that the technology performs as intended, conforms to the seller's specifications, and is safe for use as intended.[57] If a technology is certified, the seller obtains the benefit of a rebuttable presumption that the government contractor defense applies; the defense can be rebutted only by a showing of fraud or willful misconduct in the application process.[58]

Additional SAFETY Act protections include the following:

- Creating exclusive federal jurisdiction over claims against sellers with a designation or certification.[59]
- Eliminating awards of punitive damages.[60]
- Limits on a plaintiff's ability to recover non-economic damages to cases of physical harm and only in an amount proportional to the percentage of responsibility of such defendant[61] (as opposed to the total amount of such damages requiring the seller to seek contribution from other defendants for their percentage of responsibility).
- Reducing a plaintiff's recovery by collateral sources of compensation.[62]

Not every unmanned aircraft can qualify under the act. "Qualified anti-terrorism technology" eligible for the act's protection "means any product, equipment, service (including support services), device, or technology (including information technology) designed, developed, modified, or procured for the specific purpose of preventing, detecting, identifying, or deterring acts of terrorism or limiting the harm such acts might otherwise cause, that is designated as such by the Secretary."[63] Not every unmanned aircraft will be intended for antiterrorism uses. Nonetheless, it is quite possible that a number of unmanned aircraft will qualify and can take advantage of the act's protections. Thus, unmanned aircraft manufacturers should consider whether their products can qualify under the act.

---

55. 6 U.S.C. § 443(c).
56. *Id.* § 441(b).
57. *Id.* § 442(c)(2).
58. *Id.* § 442(d)(1).
59. *Id.* § 442(a).
60. *Id.* § 442(b)(1).
61. *Id.* § 442(b)(2).
62. *Id.* § 442(c).
63. *Id.* § 444(1).

MANAGING THE RISK OF UNMANNED AIRCRAFT PRODUCT LIABILITY

The Risk Management Process

The second section in this chapter discusses accidents and safety problems as a cause for product liability litigation and juror anger as an explanation of huge verdicts against manufacturers. The third section discusses the potential public and financial losses manufacturers could incur for product liability. The fourth section covers claims and defenses in unmanned aircraft product liability cases. This section turns to the issue of risk management and how unmanned aircraft manufacturers can mitigate the risk of huge verdicts imposed by angry jurors.

After considering the fate of Ford in the Pinto case and Merck in the Vioxx case, manufacturers might think that when the inevitable suit is filed, they should hire really good lawyers who can present their case in a persuasive manner and prevent jury anger. In addition, they might point out that in the Pinto case and the Ernst-Vioxx case, an appellate court provided relief to the defendant, in the Ford case, reducing the punitive damages from $125 million to $3.5 million[64] and in the Vioxx case, overturning the jury's verdict.[65] Accordingly, they may think that they can save themselves on appeal by finding effective appellate counsel to overturn any large adverse verdicts.

Executives might also think that they can hire effective jury consultants to help pick a favorable jury less likely to become angry. They may also think about the use of mock trials and shadow juries to inform counsel about how juries are likely to react to the manufacturer's case. These mechanisms can help counsel find effective trial themes and uncover potential pitfalls. Executives may also think about using really effective trial experts to explain the company's safety practices to the jury. Finally, they may think that they will have good document retrieval practices to find the best evidence to present to the jury.

The above strategies are certainly helpful to the defense of high-stakes lawsuits. Nonetheless, all of these strategies are *reactive*. They are all put into place *after* a suit is filed, which is *after* an accident takes place, and all of which occur *after* the manufacturer designed and started selling the product involved in the accident.

Unmanned aircraft manufacturers, however, can manage their risks much more effectively with a *proactive* approach. By planning today, they can be prepared for the inevitable suits later. First, planning can enable them to make safer products that are less likely to cause litigation-triggering accidents in the first place. Second, by planning ahead, unmanned aircraft manufacturers can increase their chances of winning the

---

64. Grimshaw, 119 Cal. App. 3d at 823–24.
65. Merck & Co., Inc. v. Ernst, 296 S.W. 3d 81 (Tex. Ct. App. 2009), *cert. denied*, 132 S. Ct. 1980 (2012).

cases that accidents do trigger. A proactive approach to design safety with a comprehensive risk management program establishes upfront a manufacturer's commitment to safety. When the inevitable suit happens later, the manufacturer's counsel has a compelling account to share with the jury concerning why its products were safe and how the manufacturer cared about safety.

The next question pertains to what level of effort an unmanned aircraft manufacturer must undertake in such a proactive approach. One commentator has stated, "The most effective way for [counsel for] a corporate defendant to reduce anger toward his or her client is to show all the ways that the client went *beyond what was required by the law or industry practice*."[66] Meeting minimum standards is insufficient because of juror skepticism about the rigor of standards set or influenced by industry and because jurors expect corporate clients to know more about product safety than a "reasonable person"—the standard for judging the conduct of defendants under the law.[67] "A successful defense can also be supported by walking jurors through the relevant manufacturing or decision-making process, showing all of the testing, checking, and follow-up actions that were included.

"Jurors who have no familiarity with complex business processes are often impressed with all of the thought that went into the process and all of the precautions that were taken."[68] Even though accidents do occur, and in any trial setting if an accident did occur, a defendant's proactive approach would show the jury that the unmanned aircraft manufacturer tried hard to do the right thing.[69] Consequently, efforts to go above and beyond the minimum standards would diffuse juror anger and mitigate the unmanned aircraft manufacturer's risk.

Having discussed the importance of a proactive approach to safety, I now turn to one methodology for maximizing safety and minimizing risk: the risk management methodology. The remainder of this section describes what risk management is and how it can be applied to the unmanned aircraft industry. This section also refers to international standards that can be applied to the manufacturing of unmanned aircraft.

In general, risk management refers to practices and methods guiding an organization in its efforts to control risks that may thwart its ability to meet its business goals. An organization must have policies and procedures to provide a framework of guidance. They must also identify the organization's objectives and priorities. The executives of an organization must support the risk management effort and commit to executing the risk management strategy.[70]

---

66. Minick & Kagehiro, *supra*, at 2.
67. *See id.*
68. *Id.*
69. *See id.*
70. For a general discussion of risk management and the application of risk management principles in the information security context, *see* STEPHEN S. WU, A GUIDE TO HIPAA SECURITY AND THE LAW 29–36 (2007).

The first stage in the risk management process is a risk analysis. Risk analysis includes the following core processes:

1. Identifying the key processes, systems, and components that need to be protected and prioritizing their value.
2. Identifying the universe of possible threats to these key processes, systems, and components.
3. Identifying vulnerabilities in the form of an absence of a safeguard to prevent a threat or a weakness in a safeguard already implemented to prevent the threat or weakness.
4. Identifying and analyzing the risk arising from such vulnerabilities.[71]

A threat is a negative event that has the potential to damage an asset that is vulnerable to such a threat. Threats may be the result of intentional conduct or natural or physical phenomena. In the context of unmanned aircraft, there are a myriad of possible threats to address. Many of these threats are ones that would commonly come to mind, especially to engineers. One commentator listed the usual threats to human safety from robots generally as follows, which are particularly applicable to industrial robots:

> [T]he causes of accidents caused by robots can be grouped into three main categories: engineering errors, human mistakes and poor environmental conditions. Engineering errors include errors in the robot's mechanics (loose connections across parts, faulty electronics), errors made by the controller (programming bugs, faulty algorithm), etc. As a consequence, robots might, for example, fail to stop, or a robot arm might achieve high, uncontrolled speed, abrupt motion or acceleration. Accidents caused by these errors cannot be predicted even by the most attentive human operator. On the other hand, human accidents, which are more controllable, happen due to various factors, such as inattention, fatigue, inobservance of the guarding procedures, inadequate training programs or incorrect procedures for initial robot start-up. Adverse environmental factors refer to extreme temperature, poor sensing in difficult weather or lighting conditions, all of which can lead to incorrect response by the robot.[72]

A vulnerability is a weakness in a process, system, or component that allows a threat to cause damage. This weakness can stem from the lack of a control designed to prevent the threat, a weakness in such a control, or a characteristic of the process, system, or

---

71. *Cf. id.* at 30–32.
72. MILOS VASIC & AUDE BILLARD, SAFETY ISSUES IN HUMAN-ROBOT INTERACTIONS, at 1 (2013), *reprinted at* http://lasa.epfl.ch/publications/uploadedFiles/VasicBillardICRA2013.pdf.

component itself. Threats have the potential of exploiting these weaknesses to cause damage. Because vulnerabilities only exist in the context of a threat, a manufacturer must carefully consider which threats are relevant to them when assessing the vulnerability of processes, systems, or components to a particular threat. They should also prioritize which items require more protection. For example, unmanned aircraft components that serve only aesthetic purposes will be less important than structural protections, key electrical components, operating software, or safety features.

The risk identification step analyzes risk based on the likelihood that a threat will exploit a vulnerability and the impact that event would have on the vulnerable process, system, or component. The manufacturer can use existing questionnaires, interviews with experts, past history, and other means to determine the risks the manufacturer may encounter. The manufacturer should document potential risk elements as part of its risk management process.

Risk analysis may include both "qualitative" and "quantitative" processes. Each threat is analyzed in terms of its anticipated impact (severity) and its probability and/ or frequency (occurrence). Qualitative risk analysis classifies risks into categories of severity and occurrence, such as "high," "medium," and "low." Qualitative risk analysis is appropriate where the manufacturer does not have sufficient information to calculate the level of risk with mathematical precision.

By contrast, quantitative risk analysis would be possible where sufficient information exists to quantify risk. A good example is the use of actuarial data in the insurance industry to quantify certain risks of bodily injury and property damage for certain types of known hazards. With regard to unmanned aircraft, data may exist to identify the life span of a metal part subject to metal fatigue. A manufacturer may have the data to graph the likelihood of failure of the part over time.

Following a risk assessment, manufacturers can manage the risks they have identified. Risk management is a continuous, iterative process of:

(a) Reviewing the results of the manufacturer's risk analysis to assess the effectiveness of current or planned controls to provide assurances of safety in light of reasonably anticipated threats, and to identify any gaps in effectiveness that create risk.

(b) Analyzing changes to the manufacturer's circumstances over time, including such factors as (i) implementation of new technology and associated vulnerabilities; (ii) changes to the threat landscape, for example, because of changes in environmental factors or new threat technologies; (iii) changes to organizational structure and business goals; and (iv) changes in regulations.

(c) Measuring and prioritizing risks and corresponding mitigation measures and incorporating them into a Risk Management Plan.

(d) Implementing those mitigation measures defined in the Risk Management Plan.

The Risk Management Plan should address how a risk is to be managed to an acceptable level. Risks may be prioritized on the basis of degree of risk, magnitude of harm that a threat could cause, the cost to mitigate a vulnerability, business goals and critical needs, and expected effectiveness of mitigation measures.

Unmanned aircraft manufacturers may respond to risks in a number of ways. They may be able to implement controls to mitigate the risk of some threats. Other threats may be modest enough that the manufacturer may tolerate the risks of such threats. Other risks may be shifted via insurance or indemnity to others. Finally, in theory, a manufacturer may decide that the risk is too great to offer a certain set of products and decide to stop offering such products altogether. For purposes of commercializing unmanned aircraft technology, manufacturers will likely focus on the first three categories of risk management techniques.

For guidance, unmanned aircraft manufacturers have available to them standard risk management processes. One example is the international standard for risk management: ISO 31000 "Risk management —Principles and guidelines."[73] ISO also created related documents that cover various aspects of risk management, which would provide useful guidance for a manufacturer's risk management program.

A more specific international standard applicable to unmanned aircraft is the International Electrotechnical Commission's IEC 61508 Functional safety of electrical/electronic/programmable safety-related systems. The standard defines different safety integrity levels, which are categories that describe the risk associated with system applications. Safety Integrity Level (SIL) 1 applies to systems used where the consequences of an unwanted occurrence would be modest and the probability of an unwanted occurrence would be slight. SIL 4 applies to systems where unwanted occurrences would be likely and would cause a large number of deaths. SILs 2 and 3 fall between SIL 1 and SIL 4. This family of standards essentially describes a process for reducing risk to a tolerable level in the life cycle of an electronic product from initial design to decommissioning.

While adherence to the principles of international standards does not guarantee the avoidance of liability, adherence to standards bolsters the credibility of a risk management program. Moreover, the standards provide a framework by which manufacturers can build a set of controls for their risk management process. Consequently, a robust safety program built on international standards lays the foundation for a later defense of a manufacturer accused of building an unsafe unmanned aircraft.

In addition to threats arising from engineering errors, human mistakes, and poor environmental conditions, there are additional threats that may not commonly appear

---

73. International Organization for Standardization, ISO 31000:2009 Risk management – Principles and guidelines.

in the engineering literature but should be taken into account in the threat modeling done by unmanned aircraft manufacturers as part of their risk analysis and risk management process. These two threats are information security threats and threats to a manufacturer's supply chain.

Information Security Threats

When I think of information security threats to unmanned aircraft and systems to support unmanned aircraft, I remember the words of my collaborator, Marc Goodman, who briefed government officials on various security threats as part of his work for Interpol:

> [H]umans seem to have no limitations when it comes to finding ways to attack the computerized devices that others have invented. Attackers have successfully compromised computers, mobile phones, ATMs, telephone networks, and even networked power grids.[74]

The article Marc and I wrote was about neural devices, ranging from cochlear implants, to computerized prostheses, to "deep brain stimulators" implanted in the brain to assist in the treatment of Parkinson's disease, Alzheimer's disease, chronic pain, and other conditions. We continued:

> [W]e anticipate a wide variety of potential criminal threats to the human brain itself. . . . The media have publicized stories about hacking pacemakers and other medical devices. Attackers could use similar means to attack devices on board the human body, including wireless devices, controllers for prosthetic limbs, or deep brain stimulators.[75]

Another well-publicized security story involved a researcher hacking an insulin pump.

> A security researcher at Black Hat [Jerome Radcliffe] yesterday demonstrated how a hacker could remotely turn off a diabetic person's insulin pump without his knowledge. . . . According to Radcliffe, it is possible for a hacker to not only illicitly turn off the pump remotely, with the device only offering a small chirp as a response, but also to remotely manipulate any setting on the pump without it notifying the user at all.[76]

---

74. Stephen S. Wu & Marc Goodman, *Neural Devices Will Change Humankind—What Legal Issues Will Follow?*, The SciTech Lawyer, Winter 2012, at 12.
75. *Id.*
76. Ericka Chickowski, *Getting Root on the Human Body*, Dark Reading, Aug. 5, 2011, at 1, *reprinted*

I had the opportunity to meet Billy Rios of Cylance at a meeting of the Information Security Committee (ISC) of the American Bar Association Section of Science & Technology Law. Rios made a presentation at the February 2013 ISC meeting about research he had done to show how he and another Cylance researcher were able to compromise the security of a medical information management system manufactured by Philips. They were easily able to hack into a control system that could compromise X-ray machines and other medical devices attached to the Phillips system, which could in turn threaten patient safety.[77]

The stories about hacking medical devices should provide a cautionary tale for unmanned aircraft manufacturers. Attackers will have the means, motive, and opportunity to attack unmanned aircraft and systems supporting unmanned aircraft. In fact, an Iranian engineer alleged that Iranian electronic warfare specialists attacked and successfully captured a U.S. RQ-170 Sentinel unmanned aircraft by cutting off communications and reconfiguring its GPS coordinates to land it in Iran.[78] While the truth behind the event seems uncertain, if an Iranian attack did not bring down the unmanned aircraft, at a minimum, the downing resulted from a malfunction in its command-and-control system.[79] Information security issues not only include resisting attack but also include preserving reliability and preventing malfunctions that could lead to compromise.

Given the security threats seen with computers, networks, and other devices, coupled with stories about the downing of the RQ-170 unmanned aircraft, manufacturers should include information security threats among the threats they examine as part of their risk management process. Threats include the introduction of malicious code into unmanned aircraft, interception or malicious alteration of communications, and sending unauthorized control signals to unmanned aircraft. Workers with legitimate access to sophisticated unmanned aircraft include those maintaining or repairing unmanned aircraft; they could introduce malicious software into an unmanned aircraft during their work. Even those working for manufacturers themselves could introduce malware into unmanned aircraft.

---

at http://www.darkreading.com/vulnerabilities---threats/getting-root-on-the-human-body/d/d-id/1136133?.

77.   John Leyden, *Paging Dr. Evil: Phillips Medical Device Control Kit 'Easily Hacked'*, THE REGISTER, Jan. 18, 2013, *reprinted at* http://www.theregister.co.uk/2013/01/18/medical_device_control_kit_security/; Kelly Jackson Higgins, *Security Researchers Expose Bug in Medical System Used With X-Ray Machines, Other Devices*, DARK READING, Jan. 17, 2013, *reprinted at* http://www.darkreading.com/attacks-breaches/security-researchers-expose-bug-in-medical-system-used-with-x-ray-machines-other-devices/d/d-id/1138984?.

78.   Scott Peterson, *Exclusive: Iran Hijacked US Drone, Says Iranian Engineer*, CHRISTIAN SCIENCE MONITOR, Dec. 15, 2011, *reprinted at* http://www.csmonitor.com/World/Middle-East/2011/1215/Exclusive-Iran-hijacked-US-drone-says-Iranian-engineer-Video.

79.   *See* Dave Majumdar, *Iran's Captured RQ-170: How Bad Is the Damage?*, AIRFORCETIMES, Dec. 9, 2011, *reprinted at* http://archive.airforcetimes.com/article/20111209/NEWS/112090311/Iran-s-captured-RQ-170-How-bad-is-the-damage-.

If attackers are able to use malicious code to control unmanned aircraft, they could cause them to stop flying, steer in the wrong direction, or otherwise cause an accident. If infrastructure is used to control a fleet of unmanned aircraft or manage air traffic, attackers may seek to compromise the infrastructure to cause a cascading failure, resulting in a crash of all unmanned aircraft under control. The resulting accidents could be catastrophic.

Threats to the Supply Chain

Another threat that does not appear on the list of usual safety threats to unmanned aircraft manufacturers is the threat to manufacturers' supply chains. By "supply chain," I am referring to the network of suppliers that obtain or produce the raw materials for a finished product, the companies that manufacture components of the finished product, the manufacturer that assembles the components into a finished product, the distributors and wholesalers that deliver the finished product, and the dealers that sell the product to the consumer. For a manufacturer, the supply chain threat concerns suppliers of raw materials and components that the manufacturer purchases to assemble into the final product.

Consider the complicated supply chain involved in manufacturing a laptop computer. Figure 13.1[80] shows the countries where common laptop component suppliers are located.

In a way, the supply chain threat is an information security issue in that some of the threats may involve the introduction of malicious software into systems. Nonetheless, the threat goes beyond security. For instance, suppliers purchase counterfeit components and charge manufacturers the full price for genuine products in order to make extra profits. Suppliers providing counterfeit products are committing financial fraud, which harms manufacturers. At the same time, counterfeit products are frequently less reliable than genuine products, which may increase the risk of defects and component failures and thereby increase the threat to safety. Other threats concern availability and reliability of products and services. For instance, the March 2011 earthquake in Japan disrupted the supplies of certain kinds of memory chips, because such a large percentage of worldwide production of these chips came from areas in Japan affected by the earthquake.[81]

---

80. Figure 13.1 is reprinted from a GAO report: U.S. GOVERNMENT ACCOUNTABILITY OFFICE, IT SUPPLY CHAIN – NATIONAL SECURITY-RELATED AGENCIES NEED TO BETTER ADDRESS RISKS, at 5 (March 2012).
81. *See id.* at 14.

Figure 13.1

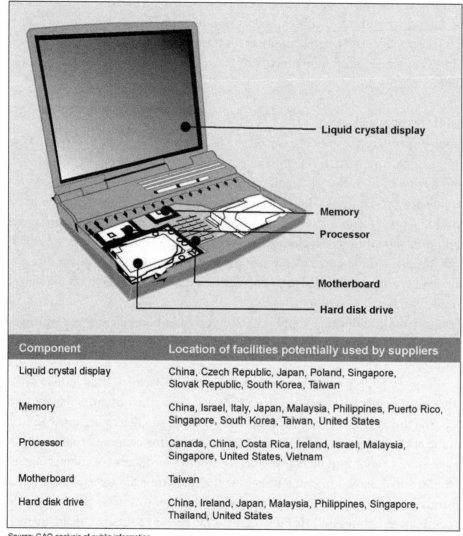

Component	Location of facilities potentially used by suppliers
Liquid crystal display	China, Czech Republic, Japan, Poland, Singapore, Slovak Republic, South Korea, Taiwan
Memory	China, Israel, Italy, Japan, Malaysia, Philippines, Puerto Rico, Singapore, South Korea, Taiwan, United States
Processor	Canada, China, Costa Rica, Ireland, Israel, Malaysia, Singapore, United States, Vietnam
Motherboard	Taiwan
Hard disk drive	China, Ireland, Japan, Malaysia, Philippines, Singapore, Thailand, United States

Source: GAO analysis of public information.

Laptop Component Sources (Reprinted from a GAO report: U.S. Government Accountability Office, IT Supply Chain—National Security-Related Agencies Need to Better Address Risks, at 5 [March 2012].)

In 2008, the Bush Administration began realizing that supply chain issues threaten the security of the procurement of products and services by the federal government and tasked federal agencies with coordinating supply chain risk management activities. Federal agencies including the Government Accountability Office (GAO), the Office of Management and Budget, and the National Institute of Standards and Technology began to study supply chain risks and coordinate efforts to mitigate the risks.[82] The GAO later reported performance audit findings to Congress concerning four national security-critical agencies, noted threats to supply chains, and made recommendations for additional steps to protect information technology (IT) procurement processes.[83] The GAO has identified certain key threats to IT supply chains:

- Installation of hardware and software containing malicious logic
- Installation of counterfeit hardware or software
- Failure or disruption in the production or distribution of critical products
- Reliance on a malicious or unqualified service provider for the performance of technical services
- Installation of hardware or software that contains unintentional vulnerabilities[84]

What the GAO is reporting also applies to the private sector. The kinds of problems that affect government equipment can also apply to unmanned aircraft manufacturers. In addition, government procurement favors commercial off-the-shelf (COTS) products.[85] To the extent the GAO is uncovering problems with COTS products in government procurement, private companies also procuring COTS products will encounter the same problems. Consequently, unmanned aircraft manufacturers, which need to procure hardware components and software, should heed the GAO's findings. To reduce the supply chain risk, the GAO is coordinating among agencies to adopt risk mitigation measures such as:

- obtaining and promoting a greater awareness of the threats, vulnerabilities, and consequences associated with acquisition decisions;
- the development and employment of tools and resources to technically and operationally mitigate risk across the life cycle of products (from design through retirement);
- the development of new acquisition policies and practices that reflect the complex global marketplace; and
- partnership with industry to develop and adopt supply chain risk management standards and best practices.[86]

---

82. *See id.* at 6–7.
83. *See id.* at 1–2.
84. *Id.* at 12.
85. *Id.* at 5–6.
86. *Id.* at 6–7.

In addition to these recommendation, the GAO reports the following measures mentioned by NIST:

- Conducting a due diligence review of suppliers prior to entering into contractual agreements to acquire information system hardware, software, firmware, or services;
- Using trusted shipping and warehousing for information systems, information system components, and information technology products; and
- Employing independent analysis and penetration testing against delivered information systems, information system components, and information technology products.

The lesson for unmanned aircraft manufacturers is that they should undertake the same kind of supply chain risk analysis that is now underway in the federal government. Moreover, manufacturers should adopt some of the risk mitigation measures recommended by the government. Finally, in terms of threats to reliability and availability, manufacturers should pay attention to what Apple is doing to manage the supply chain for components for its products. According to some, Apple's supply chain management is the best among technology companies.[87]

Other Strategies to Minimize Risk

The strategies in the previous sections emphasize engineering and technical measures to reduce the risk involved with commercializing unmanned aircraft. Nonetheless, lawyers can counsel their unmanned aircraft manufacturer clients on a number of procedural and legal strategies to reduce liability risk. This section describes some of these procedural and legal strategies.

First and foremost, unmanned aircraft manufacturers should obtain insurance to cover product liability risk. An insurance program would permit the manufacturer to shift product liability risk to one or more insurance carriers. Under their policies, insurance carriers will defend and indemnify manufacturers when they face third-party product liability claims. Insurance policies will pay for the cost of settlement and judgments. For a more detailed discussion of insurance for unmanned aircraft manufacturers and its usefulness as a risk management tool, see chapters 14 and 15

---

87. Adam Satariano & Peter Burrows, *Apple's Supply-Chain Secret? Hoard Lasers*, Bloomberg Businessweek, Nov. 3, 2011, *reprinted at* http://www.businessweek.com/magazine/apples-supplychain-secret-hoard-lasers-11032011.html.

of this book. In addition to insurance, unmanned aircraft manufacturers may want to consider:

- Participation in standards efforts to promote safety and security within the industry and among component manufacturers
- Collaboration with other manufacturers in trade groups and (subject to antitrust concerns) purchasing consortia; with the purchasing power of larger numbers of manufacturers, the industry may have greater leverage with component manufacturers to promote safe design and manufacturing processes
- Participation in information sharing groups that can share best practices to improve product safety

From a legal perspective, if the main risk is large jury verdicts, manufacturers would be well-served to analyze jury behavior and plan for ways they can appeal to future juries. For instance, they may want to engage jury consultants that assist the defense of product liability cases to identify risk factors for the manufacturer and the types of conduct that trigger juror anger. In addition, manufacturers may want to identify and cultivate a group of defense experts they can use to educate jurors about various engineering, information technology, and safety considerations. Finally, counsel for manufacturers may want to join specialty bar committees and groups for defense counsel for purposes of sharing information, briefs, and other work products.

Finally, manufacturers can maximize their success in future product liability trials by focusing today on effective records and information management (RIM). RIM may not be on the short list of things manufacturers consider when entering the unmanned aircraft industry, but effective RIM may win cases, while poor RIM may lose cases. Documents[88] and records play a key role in product liability cases. While a manufacturer can produce their employees as witnesses at trial to talk about the manufacturer's safety efforts, witnesses' memories fade and juries may be skeptical about witnesses shading their testimony to protect their employers. Documents and records generated contemporaneously with the management of a safety program, however, can corroborate the testimony of witnesses, provide a historical record documenting a manufacturer's safety efforts, and send the message that the manufacturer cares about safety.

In an insightful article entitled "Proactive Document Management," Minneapolis product liability attorney Kenneth Ross wrote:

---

88. By "document," I am referring to both paper documents and documents in the form of electronically stored information.

During the design, manufacturing, and marketing phases, a manufacturer's goal is to make a product that reasonably balances the risk of injury from the use of the product against the product's functionality, utility, durability, price, and other attributes. If accidents do occur and product liability claims and litigation result, hopefully a manufacturer will have evidence that it did sufficiently undertake measures to make a product considered reasonably safe. Thus, a manufacturer should have created and retained documents that evidence its interest in safety and regulatory compliance and describe procedures for evaluating a product's reasonable safety.[89]

The upshot of Ross' article is that "a manufacturer needs documents that describe the steps taken by the manufacturer to present an effective defense and to prove that the manufacturer was careful and prudent."[90] With all of the attention devoted to electronic discovery preparedness, the legal press has emphasized the need to have RIM policies, most frequently called "document retention policies," in order to deflect claims that a company failed to preserve and spoliated relevant evidence after a suit was filed against it or after it reasonably anticipated litigation. Document retention policies contain a "retention schedule" listing the types of documents a company will retain, how long it will retain each category of document, and a reference to the requirements for specific retention periods. They also discuss when and how documents should be destroyed when a business or legal need for their retention no longer exists.

Ross emphasizes that traditional document retention policies focusing only on what documents are retained for how long is inadequate to prepare for a strong defense of future cases. Instead, manufacturers "concerned about the use of documents in future litigation should implement a comprehensive document management program as part of an overall product liability program."[91] He advocates documenting a complete history of the life of a product from its initial design through the end of its life.[92] The idea of an effective policy is not to hide "bad" information or documents casting doubt on a product's safety but instead to gather all information, whether good or bad, and then make a written record about how management read, considered, analyzed, and responded to "bad" information.[93] Ross also provides practical advice on how employees should be trained to record information by avoiding overstating the urgency of problems, avoiding the use of legal terms of art, and avoiding inflammatory language. Employers should also train their employees to consider how future

---

89. Kenneth Ross, *Proactive Document Management*, FOR THE DEFENSE, March 2011, at 17.
90. *Id.*
91. *Id.* at 19.
92. *Id.* at 78.
93. *See id.* at 20.

opponents may selectively quote portions of records out of context. A full explication of effective RIM policies is beyond the scope of this chapter, but manufacturers should begin now to develop a RIM program that lays the foundation for a strong defense of future cases.

CONCLUSIONS

When it comes to commercializing unmanned aircraft technologies, unmanned aircraft manufacturers are likely most concerned about building safe products to preserve human life. From a legal perspective, they are likely most concerned about avoiding product liability lawsuits that threaten their ability to sell their products, or even their very existence. Manufacturers, however, have an opportunity now to win future product liability cases for products they have not even designed yet by a process of planning and risk management.

Risk management begins with a risk analysis. The chief risks from an unmanned aircraft engineering safety perspective include engineering errors, human mistakes, and poor environmental conditions. Manufacturers should also analyze less traditional risks, such as information security risks and risks to manufacturers' supply chains. From a legal perspective, the main cause for very large adverse verdicts following a trial is juror anger. Juries become angry at manufacturers when they seem to not care about product safety and seem to place profits over public safety.

Understanding the risks permits manufacturers to manage them. With guidance from international standards such as the ISO 31000 family and IEC 61508, unmanned aircraft manufacturers can manage risks throughout the life cycle of a product, implementing controls at every phase of the life cycle to mitigate risk, where safeguards are reasonable and appropriate. If safeguards are not reasonable and appropriate, manufacturers may be able to shift risk by insurance or indemnities, or they may decide to tolerate certain modest risks. Finally, manufacturers can undertake strategies with the assistance of counsel to prepare for tomorrow's litigation, such as by establishing an effective records and information management program.

In sum, the time for unmanned aircraft manufacturers to defend themselves in litigation in future decades is now. Reactive measures after lawsuits are filed only go so far. By preparing for accidents and litigation today in a proactive fashion, they can place themselves in the best position to maximize product safety and minimize product liability.

14

Issues of Unmanned Aircraft Insurance and Insurance Underwriting

David K. Beyer and Gale A. Townsley

"For autonomous and unmanned technology to become a reality in our world, the risk transfer abilities of insurance and risk management skills of insurers will be key."
—Gillian Yeomans[1]

Adequate policies for unmanned aircraft insurance must provide coverage for three major areas of risk exposure: safety, privacy, and cybersecurity for data and storage. The main challenges for underwriters of these policies include the lack of historical data for an actuarial approach to underwriting, the need to extrapolate from aviation risk data and military unmanned aircraft experience, and the highly regulated nature of the industry. Purchasers of unmanned aircraft insurance will want to carefully analyze their unmanned aircraft insurance needs and work closely with a broker familiar with the unmanned aircraft insurance marketplace to find a suitable carrier. Oftentimes, buying insurance coverage for specialty risks such as these requires buyers to understand the trade-offs involved with the coverage available at a price they can afford.

---

1. Gillian Yeomans, *Autonomous Vehicles, Handing Over Control: Opportunities and Risks for Insurance*, LLOYDS EXPOSURE MANAGEMENT (2014). *See* https://www.lloyds.com/~/media/lloyds/reports/emerging%20risk%20reports/autonomous%20vehicles%20final.pdf.

LIMITING RISK OF LIABILITY AND DAMAGES EXPOSURE THROUGH THE PURCHASE OF INSURANCE

To help understand the need and complexity around unmanned aircraft-specific insurance coverage, we offer the following scenario: Imagine that a videographer operating an unmanned aircraft has bought a standard one million dollar liability policy to cover himself if the unmanned aircraft fails or crashes at a spectator event. The unmanned aircraft crashes and hits an Olympic skier causing a serious, career-ending injury. The skier sues the unmanned aircraft operator for the loss of future earnings from endorsements amounting to millions of dollars and obtains a judgment against the unmanned aircraft operator. Alternatively, the unmanned aircraft merely gets in the way of the skier, adversely affecting performance and resulting in a lost medal and loss of revenue from future endorsements. Although difficult cases to prove, the likelihood of the unmanned aircraft operator being sued is possible, and even if the suit is unsuccessful, the legal defense costs of the operator may or may not be covered under existing policy language.

Where to Start—Identifying Key Risks

Darryl Jenkins, an analyst for the Aviation Consulting Group, set the scene when he said, "Insurance is the 800 pound gorilla in the room no one is talking about." Jenkins asserts: "While FAA integration is a sufficient event . . . insurability is a necessary event before businesses can successfully use UAS [unmanned aerial systems] in the National Airspace System . . . because no business is going to want to be on the line for the liability concerns."[2] He concludes, "Insurability will determine which sectors of the UAS market will grow and which will die."[3]

We know that the commercial use of unmanned aircraft will be a highly regulated industry, of significant concern to insurance underwriters. The FAA has said, "as safety is our top priority, UAS integration must be accomplished without . . . decreasing safety . . . or placing other airspace users or persons and property on the ground at increased risk." The FAA has identified another insurable risk as well: "While the expanded use of UAS presents great opportunities, it also raises questions as to how to accomplish UAS integration in a manner that is consistent with *privacy and civil liberties considerations*." (Emphasis added.)[4]

---

2. Brianna Ehley, *What's Grounding the Commercial Drone Industry?*, THE FINANCIAL TIMES (May 21, 2013), http://www.thefiscaltimes.com/Articles/2013/05/21/Whats-Grounding-the-Commercial-Drone-Industry.

3. Helicopter Association International, *Insurability of UAVs: The "Gorilla in the Room,"* ROTOR NEWS (Aug. 21, 2013), http://www.rotor.org/Publications/RotorNews/tabid/843/articleType/ArticleView/articleId/3393/Insurability-of-UAVs-The-Gorilla-in-the-Room.aspx.

4. U.S. DEPARTMENT OF TRANSPORTATION, FEDERAL AVIATION AGENCY, "INTEGRATION OF CIVIL UNMANNED AIRCRAFT SYSTEMS (UAS) IN THE NATIONAL AIRSPACE SYSTEM (NAS) ROADMAP" FIRST EDITION – 2013,

With respect to safety, air traffic control for unmanned aircraft will be a major factor in the speed at which commercial unmanned aircraft can be deployed on any significant and routine basis. Reportedly,[5] NASA researchers are developing an unmanned aircraft traffic management program that would, in effect, be a separate air traffic control system for things that fly low to the ground—around 400 to 500 feet for most unmanned aircraft. As controller of the skies, the FAA would have to sign off on any unmanned aircraft management system. Insurers will require assurances from insureds that requirements and obligations imposed on operators by whatever system of regulations and management is put in place are met.

Operational aspects of unmanned aircraft, all on their own, present serious risks to consider when underwriting unmanned aircraft insurance. Unmanned aircraft can be operated through communication with a pilot sitting in a ground station, but many will have autonomous capabilities where the aircraft will operate on their own. They will operate through advanced software systems coupled with sensing hardware and GPS navigation packaged in a highly maneuverable airframe. A key feature will be an autonomous anticollision system to protect the unmanned aircraft from collisions. They must be designed to handle lost links, in which communications are cut off and the unmanned aircraft must make decisions alone. In addition, depending on the type of unmanned aircraft, they will likely be gathering, storing, and transmitting a variety of data. As unmanned aircraft pivot through the national airspace, all of these computer and electronic communication-driven systems are exposed to all manner of cyber risk as well.

From an insurance point of view, then, unmanned aircraft risks fall into three broad categories that define the important directions in which unmanned aircraft insurance products must evolve: aviation safety, privacy, and cybersecurity. Those needing to limit these risks will include owners, operators, designers, programmers, manufacturers, distributors, component vendors, and end users. Insurers will be in a position to facilitate the transfer of the risk of operating unmanned aircraft, encourage high safety standards, assist in laying the groundwork for adequate regulation, and participate in determining how much testing and verification is required for public availability of UAS.

---

http://www.faa.gov/about/initiatives/uas/media/UAS_Roadmap_2013.pdf.

5. Conor Dougherty, *Drone Developers Consider Obstacles That Cannot Be Flown Around*, NEW YORK TIMES, September 1, 2014, http://www.nytimes.com/2014/09/01/technology/as-unmanned aircraft-technology-advances-practical-obstacles-remain.html?_r=1.

UNMANNED AIRCRAFT INSURANCE OVERVIEW

The length of the application to buy insurance, the amount of the deductible, and the cost of the policy are usually good guidelines to determine the scope and breadth of the coverage afforded under a policy. Long applications that ask detailed underwriting questions typically offer better coverage because the insurance company is able to more accurately qualify the risk. If the application and underwriting process is short, coverage is likely to be restrictive with significant conditions and exclusions.

Large commercial businesses with unmanned aircraft operations will likely find more options for coverage and limits than small companies and individuals who are not likely or capable of paying higher premiums for unmanned aircraft insurance. When buying unmanned aircraft insurance, it will be important to take the time to read specimen insurance policies, which brokers provide clients prior to making the purchase. Brokers have a responsibility to discuss the various coverages and restrictions with their policyholders to help them make informed decisions.

As unmanned aircraft become more pervasive in the market, more insurance companies will consider offering broader-based insurance policies designed to include aviation safety, privacy, and cyber risk protection. Insurers such as AIG and Lloyd's of London have a competitive advantage given their appetite for emerging risks and underwriting expertise on staff.[6] As unmanned aircraft operation historical data develops in each of these lines of risk, early market entrant underwriters will be able to use that data to suggest best practices behavior, provide good advice to operators, manage their own exposure, and price risks more accurately.

New insurance companies entering the unmanned aircraft insurance market will see opportunity, but will rightly take a cautious approach to offering coverage. They will have a limited appetite and will offer coverage that will be both restrictive and limited in scope by including strategies to restrict the amount of coverage for certain types of loss events (using sublimits to cap liability in specific situations) or by including exclusions to deny coverage for certain types of events. They may also seek to develop detailed underwriting questions to assess the enterprise risk of unmanned aircraft and may require the operator to meet more stringent conditions or engage in specific business practices in order to keep coverage in force. As more insurance companies enter the unmanned aircraft insurance market to offer coverage, enterprises will need to evaluate different coverage forms from different insurers to find the best fit at the best price for their situation.

---

6. London Underwriters also have the capacity and expertise to work with companies to custom tailor an insurance policy that specifically meets the needs of the policyholder seeking coverage. Custom tailored policies (called "bespoke" policies) allow a company to propose their risk story to underwriters, and together they work through what the important coverages are and craft a policy to suit the needs of the enterprise.

MARKET OVERVIEW

A nascent but growing insurance market provides limited unmanned aircraft insurance coverage to consumers and businesses today. Aviation insurers have been the first to market with insurance policies for unmanned aircraft. These policies are predominantly focused on the legal liability conditions arising from the use of flying remote-controlled aircraft or unmanned aerial vehicles (UAVs).

But a new generation of unmanned aircraft is flying in new territory with sophisticated onboard systems capable of capturing, storing, and transmitting vast amounts of data and information. These devices are entering the market at a time when laws and cases are struggling to define operating protocols; this creates underwriting uncertainty. Insurers offering coverage to help manage unmanned aircraft risks face not only operational and failure risk but also regulatory uncertainty and exposures arising from emerging technologies that are subject to significant vulnerabilities.

Aviation and cyberinsurance underwriters are likely to compete for this new emerging market since underwriters will need to price both "aircraft type safety" as well as "technology oriented data security and privacy concerns." FAA regulations and guidelines, new constitutional and privacy law cases, state and local attempts to manage and regulate unmanned aircraft, and autonomy and operational component vulnerabilities form a cluster of forces which will affect how underwriters draft policies, underwrite premiums, and handle claims.

Operators of flying unmanned aircraft need to buy liability insurance for when an unmanned aircraft fails and causes a loss. Companies looking to buy liability protection find very few insurance companies willing to offer them broad flight risk coverage that includes today's data risk and cyber exposure. So far, insurers that offer coverage in 2015 provide full coverage for the unmanned aircraft while in flight, loss or damage to the aircraft and associated electronic equipment, replacement of incompatible software following a loss, costs to investigate repairs to damaged equipment, and public liability insurance—personal injury and property damage cover for businesses.

Underwriters look at the number of hours of operation, the experience of the operator, and permission or certification compliance. Underwriters may require the insured to take security measures to protect the unmanned aircraft when unattended. Exclusions are many, and several key risks are not otherwise explicitly covered.

Today's aviation insurers have a good foundation of insuring flight risk and offer important coverage to protect operators, but they fall short of insuring many types of other risks that operators should consider when making an insurance purchase.

While some insurers are offering coverage for unmanned aircraft, observers do not expect the market to really take off until regulations are finalized by the FAA. Aviation practice leaders at major brokerages such as Marsh and Aon are excited by the potential uses of unmanned aircraft and the market that they could create. Michael J. Kerwin, Vice President of Analytics at Avemeo Insurance, an aviation insurer, anticipates a "fantastic" market for unmanned aircraft insurance "once the FAA and local governments figure out how they can safely allow people to monetize such aircraft."[7]

COVERAGES AND UNDERWRITING PRACTICES

Insurance coverage is frequently described in terms of first-party and third-party coverage. The most familiar coverage is third-party: You are liable for damage to someone else (a third party). First-party coverage applies when you or your unmanned aircraft are damaged.

Commercial Unmanned Aircraft Liability Coverage Scope
Property Damage
Commercial owners or operators of unmanned aircraft liability policies should seek coverage for both first-party and third-party property damage. The policy should cover first-party claims for damage to the unmanned aircraft itself and third-party coverage for damage to the property of others, including both fixed property, such as buildings, homes, and land, and mobile property, such as automobiles, livestock, and other tangible objects.

Personal Injury and Third-Party Loss
The liability section of the policy should provide an owner or operator with liability coverage for personal injury to themselves and others, as well as third-party liability coverage for damages arising out of privacy intrusions, security breaches, and communication network failures.

Data Liability
If the unmanned aircraft has the potential to collect, store, or send data, an unmanned aircraft owner or operator should seek liability coverage for damages arising out of the capturing or transmission of personally identifiable information/personal health information (PII/PHI), nonpublic personal information (NPPI), business PII, and NPPI (intellectual property, trade secrets, confidential or sensitive data, and location data).

---

7. Judy Greenwald, *Insurers Await Influx of Drones Pending FAA Rules*, BUSINESS INSURANCE, May 2014.

Other First-Party Coverages

Depending on the commercial enterprise deploying the unmanned aircraft, owners or operators may want to consider seeking first-party coverage for business interruption, unmanned aircraft loss of use or replacement costs, reputational loss (future earnings), data breach investigations and notification costs, and crisis management costs such as public relations expense.

Exclusions

As in most liability policies, underwriters are likely to exclude from coverage violations of law, criminal or malicious acts, gross negligence, acts of nature or *force majeure*, and terrorism. Numerous other exclusions may be added to these policies and should be carefully reviewed to be sure they do not remove key coverage of importance to the purchaser.

UNIQUE COMMERCIAL UNMANNED AIRCRAFT DATA PRIVACY AND CYBER RISK ISSUES

Coverage

Unlike most commercial manned aerial vehicles, today's unmanned aircraft may be outfitted with an array of software, sensors, and cameras to capture large amounts of data. This creates risks related to the software running the systems and the data captured during unmanned aircraft operation. Also, most unmanned aircraft will communicate with a cloud for remote communication and computational processing of information, creating additional unique risks that must be evaluated.

The Data

In standard property and liability policies, tangible assets consisting of physical objects or real property are a key policy language cornerstone. In those policies, digital data, however, is considered to be an intangible asset and is typically excluded from coverage. The new generation of unmanned aircraft liability insurance needs to provide coverage for emerging risks related to digital data.

Unmanned aircraft insurers will need to have experience qualifying and managing these types of risk and will likely turn to cyber insurance experience to blend underwriting talent with aviation underwriting. Combining these two areas of discipline will improve an insurance company's chance of entering the market safely and confidently.

If the unmanned aircraft to be insured has the potential to collect, store, or send data, an unmanned aircraft owner or operator should seek liability coverage for claims arising out of the capture, storage, and transmission of personally identifiable information/personal health information (PII/PHI), nonpublic personal information (NPPI), business PII, and NPPI (intellectual property, copyright, trademark, trade secret, confidential or sensitive data, and location data). Such claims would include libel, slander, invasion of privacy, copyright or trademark infringement, and misappropriation of advertising ideas, resulting in a blend of privacy and media liability.

Software failure to perform as intended could cause an unmanned aircraft to crash, resulting in personal injury or physical damage. Software can also fail by becoming corrupt, losing connectivity, or crashing, sometimes wiping or rendering itself unusable. The software could mistakenly send legally protected data to an unintended recipient, resulting in breach notification liability. Software data in transit could be hacked by a criminal who steals the data, or the unmanned aircraft itself could be hacked and taken over remotely. Hackers could also gain access to video, camera, or other sensor feeds and use the information gained to commit other crimes. Owners and operators of unmanned aircraft will need coverage for these risks as well.

The Cloud

As society moves toward the concentration of information and processing into cloud-based systems, new and highly complex risk scenarios emerge. Aside from the always-on dependency of an unmanned aircraft's need for Internet connectivity and the fail-over protocols required to complete tasks and avoid risk, the cloud introduces a host of new risks to unmanned aircraft operation that could give rise to liability exposure.

Intelligent infrastructure and artificial intelligence (AI) software is a significant development that will be a game-changer for determining who's liable for unmanned aircraft-related losses. Most unmanned aircraft will have onboard software hard-coded to perform a variety of tasks and functions. Many unmanned aircraft, however, will supplement their communication with cloud-based information that will push out instructions or commands to perform specific, semispecific, or learn-as-you-go tasks. These commands will come from databases of instructional applications.

Most commands will be preprogrammed with a variety of software applications. In application-based modular software programming, core software code underlies a platform that other software applications can run on and offers a dynamic palate of information that enables devices (such as unmanned aircraft) to receive up-to-date programming to perform new and specific tasks.

These tasks can relate to (a) performance (to optimize flight, landing, payload pick up or drop off), or (b) service (to take pictures or video of designated objects, track a person or vehicle, identify an address for destination). The programming may also include AI-based instructions to allow the unmanned aircraft to learn new things as part of their priority instruction (relay flight performance as it is impacted by weather conditions, relay traffic patterns to avoid congestion that may impact a delivery schedule, relay situational performance feedback for analysis and fine-tuning).

An exemplary headline grabbed the attention of the public: "The Robo Brain Project Wants To Turn the Internet Into a Robotic Hivemind." According to the article, "The goal is to create a centralized, always-online brain for robots to tap into. The more Robo Brain learns from the Internet, the more direct lessons it can share with connected machines."[8] This kind of functionality could align perfectly with unmanned aircraft communication and expand the utility of unmanned aircraft to develop great commercial opportunities. Such an uber instruction concept raises significant risk and risk allocation questions which would directly impact underwriting and coverage decisions for insurers.

Preliminarily, for example, if unmanned aircraft are drawing instructions via the cloud from the Robo Brain, the means used to determine if the instructions gathered by Robo Brain are accurate, complete, correct, or even appropriate for any given unmanned aircraft to use for the particular purpose intended will be a critical component to evaluate the potential level of risk. In addition, a key issue will be to whom responsibility should be assigned if flawed instructions are deployed and result in damage to people, property, privacy, or even the unmanned aircraft itself.

Other risks and potential liability exposures will arise, for example, if one unmanned aircraft's source code is infected with malware and through the cloud ALL of the devices become infected, or if corrupted, poorly written, or inadequately vetted software code is created, uploaded into the cloud, and disseminated to a fleet of unmanned aircraft causing adverse outcomes in unmanned aircraft operations. The gathering of data by unmanned aircraft has already raised questions of liability exposure for violations of personal privacy, intellectual property, or trade secret laws. Operators, for example, could be liable for royalty fees or fines for the unauthorized dissemination of intellectual property, intentionally or unintentionally, collected during use of an unmanned aircraft. Depending on the unmanned aircraft's construction, operation, deployment, and use, thousands of variables could impact the risk evaluation calculus.

As mentioned above, AI programming allows unmanned aircraft to perform both limited tasks and functions on their own. AI also enables unmanned aircraft to pull information from databases, integrate those commands, and learn how to perform tasks and functions on the fly. The range of limited tasks is far reaching, from specific A to B functionality to "do A, not B, if C happens."

The growing interest in enabling AI to learn on their own and become more human, however, adds another level of risk complexity. Behavioral optimization

---

8. Erik Sofge, *Robo Brain Project Wants to Turn the Internet into a Robotic Hivemind*, Popular Science (Aug. 25, 2014), http://www.popsci.com/blog-network/zero-moment/robo-brain-project-wants-turn-internet-robotic-hivemind.

allows unmanned aircraft to analyze, determine, and mimic human traits from a wide and growing range of attributes such as personality, integrity, empathy, frustration, and ethics.

A discussion emerging in the field of robotic autonomous automobiles illuminates concerns and risks related to unmanned aircraft enabled with AI functionality.[9] An article from *Wired* explains: "The way this would work is one customer may set the car (which he paid for) to jealously value his life over all others; another user may prefer that the car values all lives the same and minimizes harm overall; yet another may want to minimize legal liability and costs for herself. Other settings are also possible. Philosophically, this opens up an interesting debate about the oft-clashing ideas of morality vs. liability. The issue of "selectable ethics AI" will undoubtedly be important to the debate about unmanned aircraft deployment and who will be held responsible when unmanned aircraft go wrong, or when an unmanned aircraft "gets mad" or perhaps "goes mad.""

Cloud Architecture

Simply put, cloud architecture *includes* an information database made up of tens of thousands of applications that are designed to integrate and communicate with one or many parties. Rudimentarily and conceptually, this would arguably shift liability from a person to a thing. If the software fails, is corrupted, hacked, or taken over, and the unmanned aircraft becomes compromised, is a person or entity liable for any damage or loss that may result from the software risk? Technically, one could argue, the unmanned aircraft would be acting on its own if it is able to retrieve and execute commands without direct human intervention. With so many points of potential failure in the communication chain-of-trust, there surely will be failures, and the results could be catastrophic and systemic. Insurers face an enormous challenge in the effort to devise viable risk transfer products and adequate pricing for exposures of this potential scale, especially in an environment where regulation, laws, and their interpretation lag behind innovation.

Key issues arise from the emerging cloud communication infrastructure, including how minimum standards will be set, who will set them, the legal implications of those standards, who vets the software which operates unmanned aircraft, how the software is vetted, and how standards will be monitored and enforced.

Cloud architecture includes two primary options for cloud-based communications: closed-based systems or open-based systems. Closed-application clouds are cloud-based environments whereby application developers and their app products

9. Patrick Lin, *Here's a Terrible Idea: Robot Cars with Adjustable Ethics Settings*, by WIRED (Aug. 18, 2014), http://www.wired.com/2014/08/heres-a-terrible-idea-robot-cars-with-adjustable-ethics-settings/.

are subject to a strict set of development protocols, standards, and procedures that are governed, vetted, and approved by company oversight. Companies that manage closed-cloud systems police the actions of application performance and specifications, and can remove or shut off applications that do not meet the company's guidelines. (Apple's App Store is an example of a closed-based system.)

Open-application clouds are typically operated by a parent company that allows app source code to be made available to users so they can modify or alter the code to do different things. Many users who favor open architecture app environments make significant improvements to underlying code that can fix bugs, improve performance, add features and functionality, and share these new developments with others in the community. (Google's App Store is an example of an open-cloud system.)

Typically, parent company operators of open-cloud systems are less stringent in policing application market environments for good and bad behavior. Although this trend is improving, and more open-source app clouds are setting higher standards of both performance and conduct, the open-cloud concept will always be more risky to users since the underlying code work will be less subject to oversight in a community encouraged to fiddle with code. Open-cloud markets tend to be most sought out by bargain hunters and entrepreneurial or tech-savvy do-it-yourself developers that prefer free software or the ability to modify applications to alter their performance for their own objectives.

Open- and closed-cloud systems each have strengths and weaknesses and variable levels of risk. At this point, it is unclear whether one is safer or better than the other. Both are equally at risk, however, to the inherent vulnerability of heavy reliance on software that can be subject to a wide swath of corruption or utility dysfunction that can lead to individual or cascading risks.

Underwriting

Data privacy and cybersecurity are complex areas of risk for underwriters to understand in order to predict and price premiums for the wide range of evolving possible problems.

Cyber insurance underwriting focuses on the data: the type and sensitivity of the data and intended use; the practices, procedures, and security measures put in place to protect it; owner and operator care, custody, and control of the data; the unmanned aircraft vendor, manufacturer, and component parts suppliers and their care and control of data; and third-party access to on- and off-boarding of data, who will be granted access, and protections against unauthorized access.

For everything from software design and performance to network configurations, providers and cost will be reviewed in the context of the operator's experience and use of unmanned aircraft. Other key factors underwriters will review are Terms of

Service (TOS) and End User License Agreements (EULA) that the operator enters into when using an unmanned aircraft. Many TOS/EULA contracts will likely be written in such a way as to push liability onto the unmanned aircraft operator and away from the supplier, manufacturer, service or software providers, and venue stakeholders. Additionally, data risk can include requests, demands, or compliance orders from law enforcement and other government agencies, which may impose another aspect of operator liability in need of evaluation by underwriters before issuing a policy. Additionally, as noted above, if the data is in the cloud, an extra level of underwriting complexity is added.

As a result of the fast-paced evolution of unmanned aircraft deployment, communication, and functionality, most insurance companies that use static underwriting disciplines will be behind the curve in providing up-to-date coverage for real-time risk transfer if they take the traditional approach to insurability. Short of taking an all-risks coverage approach, by the time an insurance company understands a risk environment, agrees to cover certain risks, files their coverage forms with departments of insurance for approval, imports the underwriting procedures and policy information into their IT system, and pushes the product out to brokers with a marketing campaign, the insurance coverage intent will already *not* cover many of the new risks that will have emerged during that interval.

THE FUTURE: A POSSIBLE ALTERNATIVE MODEL FOR UNMANNED AIRCRAFT COVERAGE

With the wide and growing body of data available for harvest, visualization, and utilization, insurers may well be incentivized to adopt dynamic pricing and risk algorithms to change their methodology and approach to cover the unique commercial unmanned aircraft data privacy and cyber risks by adopting Usage-Based Insurance (UBI) technology and strategy.

UBI allows insurance companies to monitor behavior and price risk on the go. Currently the most widely deployed form of UBI is in the auto insurance market. UBI auto insurance requires automobile drivers to install a monitoring device on their vehicle that captures sensory data from the car, which is reported back to the insurer. The insurer is able to view the data and charge a price for the relative risk based on how the driver operates a vehicle. If the driver brakes hard, brakes frequently, swerves erratically, and speeds regularly, the price for coverage will be higher than if the driver drives in a safer manner.

Millions of automobile drivers around the world have agreed to allow their insurance company to monitor their driving behavior. Clearly, this arrangement results in the insured giving up a significant amount of privacy, not just in how they drive, but where and when. Many skeptics of UBI are quick to point out that UBI enables insurance companies to gather data that could give them greater justification to deny a claim and to adjust coverage mid-policy and instigate price-creep for higher rated activity. These are just a few of many valid considerations that need to be factored into the discussion when contemplating the adoption of UBI in new industries.

Conceptually, however, the UBI approach to insuring unmanned aircraft could be the optimal strategy for insurance companies to offer meaningful coverage for measurable risk. UBI would allow insurers to develop a baseline understanding of the unmanned aircraft platform, monitor the risk environment in which the unmanned aircraft operates, and provide guidance to users on how risk would affect insurance premiums. UBI would also enable insurance companies, based on the analysis of this valuable data, to fine-tune their loss exposure and loss ratios so they can bring critical value to the market by shouldering appropriate levels of risk, making it possible for widespread users to buy insurance and increase the adoption of unmanned aircraft technology.

15

Risk, Product Liability Trends, and Insurance in Commercial Unmanned Aircraft

A Data Centric Analysis

David K. Beyer, Donna A. Dulo, Gale A. Townsley, and Stephen S. Wu

"There are risks and costs to action. But they are far less than the long range risks of comfortable inaction."

—John F. Kennedy

The commercialization of autonomous unmanned aerial systems will make autonomous aerial systems pervasive and ubiquitous across the national airspace within the next few years. Yet even today with a highly limited number of unmanned aircraft operating in restricted airspace, accidents are making national news, including ones with fatalities and property damage. How can unmanned aircraft operators and unmanned aircraft manufacturers protect themselves from risk and liability once commercial operations intensify across many industries?

Unmanned aircraft are essentially robotic aircraft. They can be operated with a pilot sitting in a ground station, but many will ultimately have autonomous capabilities where the aircraft will operate on its own. The FAA currently bans fully autonomous operations but is being pressured to lift this ban as commercial entities develop architectures for autonomous unmanned aircraft operations for business areas such as parcel delivery, medical system emergency delivery, agricultural development, and many more. These autonomous aircraft will operate through advanced software systems coupled with sensing hardware and GPS navigation packaged in a highly maneuverable airframe. A key feature will be an autonomous anticollision system that must not only protect the unmanned aircraft from collisions with other unmanned aircraft but also protect it from collisions with birds, other aircraft, buildings, and structures.

The risks of crashes and incidents caused by unmanned aircraft in the national airspace are currently unknown. Risk profiles have yet to be determined due to the lack of available information. Insurance carriers may be able to extrapolate loss experience from the aviation industry but will need to be adjusted for the issues of robotic autonomy in flight, autonomy in collision avoidance, and autonomy in critical issues such as lost links, in which communications are cut off and the unmanned aircraft must make decisions on its own. Issues such as pilot command, sensor operator, and flight management systems will also be prevalent in risk profiles, as unmanned aerial systems operations can range from fully human controlled to fully autonomous, with many different degrees of both occurring in flight operations complicating the risk factors and triggers.

This chapter will discuss commercial unmanned aircraft in the national airspace from both an autonomous robotics and a piloted systems point of view. An original set of data will be presented with analysis based on studies of unmanned military aircraft accidents. These data and subsequent analysis of the data will be applied to the current issues of national airspace integration to help determine liability triggers and trends to help answer insurance underwriting trends and product liability questions. In addition, the chapter will discuss theories of product liability that plaintiffs may assert against unmanned aircraft manufacturers. For instance, plaintiffs may allege causes of action such as strict product liability, negligence, breach of warranty, and the violation of laws against unfair and deceptive trade practices. The chapter will apply these theories to the context of piloted and autonomous unmanned systems. It will also cover methods for mitigating product liability risks.

Finally, the chapter will discuss the unique insurance issues that may arise as commercial owners, manufacturers, and operators of unmanned aircraft seek to limit their risks of liability and damage exposure through the purchase of insurance. The chapter will discuss the current emerging market of available insurance as well as the likely trend of insurance coverage including scope, limits, restrictions, and availability as more unmanned aircraft are deployed commercially and claim experience grows. Both domestic and Lloyd's of London–based markets will be discussed.

THE FUTURE PERVASIVENESS AND RISK CHALLENGES OF UNMANNED AERIAL SYSTEMS

The mandate of the Federal Aviation Administration to integrate unmanned aircraft into the national airspace makes abundantly clear that the era of unmanned aerial systems is upon us. While estimates vary widely, we must assume that the number of unmanned aircraft that will enter and operate in the national airspace will be in the tens of thousands very soon. This includes unmanned systems of all kinds, from large government-operated systems to small personally operated systems such as model aircraft.

Regardless of the size or configuration of the unmanned aircraft, every aircraft that enters the airspace poses a particular danger. A model aircraft, for example, has killed a person in this country,[1] while the use of what is technically classified as an unmanned aircraft has not. So while the legal wrangling over the classification of an unmanned aircraft and which classification the FAA has jurisdiction over lingers, the overarching issue still remains: What are the potential risks and liabilities of operating an unmanned aircraft and how will they affect insurance underwriting trends?

This question is difficult to answer because unmanned aircraft are not flying at the rate that they will be in the near future in the national airspace. Thus, it may take a decade or more to establish accurate liability trends to be able to effectively gauge the true risks and liabilities of unmanned aircraft in the national airspace.

Unfortunately, operators are waiting in the proverbial wings to lift their unmanned aircraft programs off the ground. Major corporations like Amazon and Facebook have not been shy concerning their intended use of unmanned aircraft when technologically and legally feasible. Private operators are already putting their craft into the sky, for fun and future profit, edging as close to the commercial limitations as possible. As a result, the industry does not have time to wait to evaluate long-term liability trends and triggers.

Herein lies the challenge: Is there any accurate data available to assist legal professionals, insurance underwriters, unmanned systems operators, and interested parties now? The approach of this chapter is to study the current power user of unmanned systems, the United States Air Force. This study, while not directly applicable to the

---

1. A 19-year-old man lost his life while flying a model aircraft in a Brooklyn park due to the aircraft striking his head causing a partial decapitation. *See* http://www.nytimes.com/2013/09/06/nyregion/remote-control led-copter-fatally-strikes-pilot-at-park.html?_r=0.

commercial and civilian use of unmanned systems, does provide important information about the issues and effects of operating unmanned aircraft over an extended period of time.

Additionally, the study highlights possible and probable issues that may arise in the commercial or civil operation of unmanned systems in the national airspace, since the mishaps in this study are all noncombat flights and directly relate to the operation of the aircraft themselves without issues of malicious external forces at play when aircraft are operated in the heat of battle. The study, therefore, provides an initial level of theoretical guidance and practical applicability to the current integration of unmanned systems into the national airspace.

A FORMAL UNMANNED SYSTEMS MISHAP STUDY

The formal investigation undertaken in this chapter is a study of all U.S. Air Force Class A unmanned aircraft mishaps over a ten-year period, from fiscal year 2004 through fiscal year 2013. The U.S. Air Force defines a mishap as an unplanned event or series of events resulting in death, injury, occupational illness, or damage to or loss of equipment or property, or damage to the environment. It defines a Class A mishap as a noncombat accident that results in a death, a permanent total disability, or damage of at least one million dollars.[2]

The mishap studies in our analysis were of unmanned systems of all types operated by the U.S. Air Force. The accident reports were publically available from the U.S. Air Force Judge Advocate General's Corps Legal Operations Agency Claims and Tort Litigation site.[3]

The mishap reports are distinguished in the study between manned and unmanned aircraft exclusively. All other instances of Class A mishaps such as satellite, missile, ground station, and non-aviation-related mishaps were excluded from the study. Unmanned tethered balloon mishaps were also excluded from the study, as they do not fall into the category of unmanned aircraft but rather of tethered balloons under FAA regulations in U.S. national airspace.

The mishap reports provided by the Air Force are extensive and provide the results of formal investigations into the causes of the mishaps. It must be noted, however, as with all formal mishap and accident reports under 10 U.S.C. § 2254(d), the opinion of the accident investigator as to the cause of, or the factors contributing to, the

---

2. AIR FORCE SAFETY AGENCY. AIR FORCE SYSTEM SAFETY HANDBOOK. HQ AFSC/SEPP Kirtland AFB, NM (July, 2000).

3. US AIR FORCE JUDGE ADVOCATE GENERAL'S CORPS LEGAL OPERATIONS AGENCY CLAIMS AND TORT LITIGATION (2014), http://usaf.aib.law.af.mil/.

accident set forth in the accident investigation report, if any, may not be considered as evidence in any civil or criminal proceeding arising from the accident, nor may such information be considered an admission of liability of the United States or by any person referred to in those conclusions or statements.

The mishap reports cover the background of the unit operating the aircraft, the sequence of events, the maintenance on the aircraft, the aircraft systems, the weather, the crew qualifications, the operations and supervision of the aircraft, the governing directives, and any other areas of concern. Within the report, the Abbreviated Accident Investigation Board identifies a cause of the mishap by "clear and convincing evidence." Additional contributing factors are presented by a "preponderance of evidence" if applicable. All investigations were conducted in accordance with Air Force Instruction 51-503.[4]

Results of the Air Force Study

The first task of the study was to determine the frequency of manned mishaps versus unmanned mishaps over the ten-year period. The results of this analysis are rather striking and match the commercial news reports highlighting the high incident rates of military unmanned aircraft. For example, the Bloomberg BGOV Barometer statistics indicate that Northrop's Global Hawk and General Atomic's Predator and Reaper have a combined 9.31 accidents for every 100,000 hours of flying time, which is the highest rate of any aircraft of any category and more than triple the Air Force fleet-wide average of 3.03 accidents for every 100,000 hours.[5]

Figure 15.1 demonstrates the results of the study, which clearly show the high accident rates of unmanned aircraft. The solid bars represent all accidents of all manned aircraft in the Air Force while the striped bars represent the unmanned accidents of all unmanned aircraft models. The earlier years indicate a lower rate of mishaps, but this can be explained by the fact that all military services (Army, Navy, Air Force, and Marines) logged more than 500,000 unmanned flying hours in 2008, representing a sixteen-fold increase over 2002[6] due mainly to the advances in technology and the policies of unmanned integration into military operations.

---

4. Air Force Instruction 51-503. *See* http://static.e-publishing.af.mil/production/1/af_ja/publication/afi51-503/afi51-503.pdf.

5. B. McGarry, *Drones Most Accident-Prone U.S. Air Force Craft*, BGOV Barometer (June 17, 2012), http://www.bloomberg.com/news/2012-06-18/unmanned aircraft-most-accident-prone-u -s-air-force-craft-bgov-barometer.html

6. C. Bowie & M. Isherwood, *The Unmanned Tipping Point*, Air Force Magazine (Sept. 2010), http://www.airforcemag.com/MagazineArchive/Pages/2010/September%202010/0910rpa.aspx.

Figure 15.1

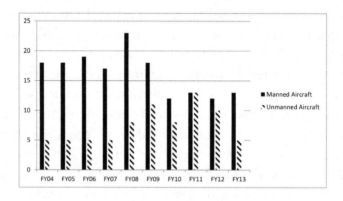

Air Force Class A Mishaps Ten-Year Comparison of Manned versus Unmanned Aircraft

Note in particular the fiscal year 2011 when the unmanned and manned mishap numbers were equal. This was the worst-performing year of unmanned aircraft in the study, although fiscal years 2009 through 2012 demonstrate a pronounced increase in unmanned mishaps while manned aircraft mishaps have decreased. To provide a further graphic illustrating the trend of unmanned mishaps, Figure 15.2 demonstrates the percentage of unmanned mishaps in relation to overall manned and unmanned mishaps.

Figure 15.2

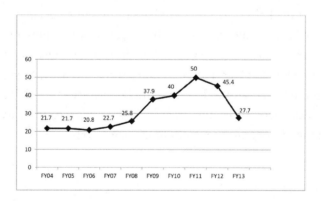

Unmanned Ten-Year Percentage of Class A Air Force Aviation Mishaps

As can be seen, the increased participation of unmanned aircraft in Air Force operations has resulted in a dramatic increase in the percentage of overall Class A mishaps. The fiscal year 2013 provided a respite, with an accident rate just slightly higher than the early integration years of unmanned aircraft. From fiscal year 2004 through fiscal year 2013, there were a total of seventy-five Class A Air Force mishaps, for which seventy-two accident reports or (in the earlier years) accident report summaries were provided by the Air Force Judge Advocate General.

The unmanned aircraft involved in the accidents during the ten-year study were the Global Hawk, the Predator, the Reaper, and the QF and QRF series Target Unmanned aircraft. The causes of the accidents are of critical importance to determine future risk and liability trends. As such, each accident report was carefully examined, including the cause of the accident as well as an analysis of the systems that failed as detailed in each report. Upon analysis, a specific set of categories was developed, and each primary cause was categorized into this set. These data are reflected in Figure 15.3. Aircraft categories were also noted as were the specific systems that were a cause of the mishap.

Figure 15.3

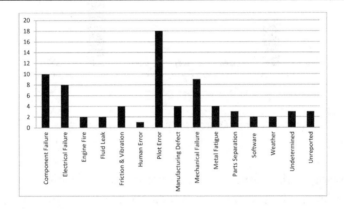

Air Force Class A Unmanned Aircraft Ten-Year Cause of Mishaps

Clearly, pilot error was a major cause of unmanned aircraft mishaps across the decade of the study. The human error category is slightly different in nature and reflects an incident in one of the ground stations where the pilot station throttle was improperly configured between unmanned aircraft models MQ-1 and MQ-9 resulting in an unrecognized command, hence the separate classification.

The aircraft hardware failures were led by individual component failures followed by mechanical failures of parts systems, followed thirdly by electrical failures which included short circuits as well as unexplained power anomalies. Weather was a minimal factor in the mishaps as was system software. In the midrange were metal fatigue and catastrophic damage as a result of friction and vibration. The difference between these two categories is that components in the friction and vibration category were from nonmetal sources or they were a component that was dislodged and jammed into a moving mechanical part resulting in the failure of the system. An example of this was a mishap caused by loss of control due to a partially dislodged computer chip in the right aileron.

Of all of the causes, in summary, pilot/human error accounted for 27.5 percent of the determined and reported mishaps, 3 percent were due to engine fire, 3 percent were due to software, 3 percent were due to weather, 6 percent were due to manufacturer defect in the hardware, while 57.5 percent were due to failure issues with the hardware of the aircraft. These data are represented graphically in Figure 15.4.

Figure 15.4

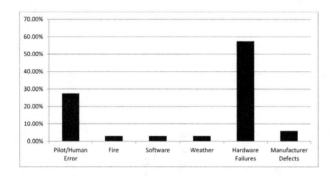

Air Force Class A Unmanned Aircraft Overall Mishap Cause Percentages

To further investigate the mishaps from a systems point of view, the causes were categorized according to the systems of which they were a part. Human and pilot errors, as well as weather and undetermined/unreported factors, were eliminated. Figure 15.5 demonstrates this system point of failure viewpoint.

The data clearly indicate that engine systems failure of various types is a major contributor to unmanned systems mishaps, followed closely by the electrical system, which included the alternator and the electrical circuitry in the aircraft. The variable pitch propeller in each system was also a central point of failure. The multispectral targeting system was the cause of one incident as was the tailboard system and the communications system. The throttle body, which was classified in this study as a separate system, had two incidents, as did the cooling system, which was also classified as a separate system from the engine, slightly dividing out the propulsion system.

Figure 15.5

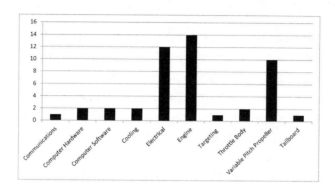

Air Force Class A Unmanned Aircraft Systems System-Point Mishap Causes

Of note is the low incidence of computer hardware and software causes of failure. The information systems of the mishap aircraft caused relatively few incidents, as both hardware and software had an equal faring in the mishap data. Due to the exponential complexity of software and the dynamics of the software–hardware continuum, this is an overall impressive result. The targeting systems and the communications systems also fared well, causing the least amount of mishaps in the study.

Study Conclusions

The Air Force study has several interesting points. First, weather was a cause in a very minor percentage of the accidents. This indicates the judiciousness of the operators in avoiding poor weather conditions, most likely through advanced meteorological systems provided by the Air Force. Second, computer and software problems were also low, which is a strong indicator of the positive viability of these systems given that they are computationally intensive and driven aircraft systems. Third, the high incidence of pilot and human error indicates training and human factors issues, which affect both the pilots and ground station operators. Finally, the high incidence of engine, propeller, and electrical systems failures indicates pervasive weaknesses in these systems overall that should be noted by future unmanned systems manufacturers and operators.

The study's results are by no means a comprehensive set of statistics for the determination of liability triggers and trends or comprehensive risk assessment. Rather, they serve as a starting point for the discussion. These statistics, combined with those of other services and thereafter combined with statistics generated from future nonmilitary incidents occurring in the national airspace, will give a clearer picture of the issues and risks associated with operating commercial and civilian unmanned aircraft.

PRODUCT LIABILITY IMPLICATIONS OF THE AIR FORCE STUDY

The study above discusses the investigation undertaken to study U.S. Air Force Class A unmanned aircraft mishaps from fiscal year 2004 through fiscal year 2013. The study shows high accident rates of unmanned aircraft and an increase in the accident rate over time, caused by the Air Force's increased use of unmanned vehicles. Figure 15.3 lists the possible causes identified by the Air Force, which the formal study groups into the categories of pilot/human error, fire, software, weather, hardware failures, and manufacturer defects. Figure 15.4 shows the magnitude of the causes attributed to these six categories of causes. Figure 15.5 focuses on the specific systems of hardware causing mishaps, such as electrical, engine, and propeller systems, in comparison with mishaps caused by computer hardware and computer software.

Based on the collected data highlighted above, the formal study points out the high incident of pilot error as a cause of mishaps. As shown in Figure 15.3, pilot error was the most common cause of mishaps. Nonetheless, when all hardware failures are considered collectively, hardware failures as a group are more common as a cause for mishaps than pilot error.

This section discusses the implications of the findings in the formal study from a product liability perspective. It describes the law of product liability and applies the product liability doctrines described to the causes of mishaps. What do the results from the formal study say about a hypothetical plaintiff's chances for succeeding in an action against an unmanned aircraft manufacturer assuming that civilian mishaps resemble the ones experienced by the Air Force? The final subsection of this section analyzes the conclusions we draw from the product liability analysis.

U.S. Product Liability Law as Related to the Study

In general, U.S. product liability law applicable to civilian commercial unmanned aircraft will be state law.[7] As such, the results of one legal case may not be the same as the results of a similar case in a different state. Commercial unmanned aircraft operators and manufacturers must therefore be mindful of each state's specific product liability laws. State law will dictate:

- The causes of action available to a plaintiff asserting a claim against a manufacturer arising out of an accident or other event.
- The essential elements the plaintiff must prove to establish a *prima facie* case of liability under these causes of action.

---

7. This subsection does not attempt to survey the product liability law of all fifty states and the District of Columbia. Instead, it identifies commonalities among groups of states; it notes majority and minority positions.

- The test the courts apply to determine if a certain product's design is defective.
- Whether the defendant ever has a burden to prove the absence of a defect in a product.
- The role of the plaintiff's conduct as a partial or complete defense to a product liability claim.
- Other defenses available to a defendant.[8]

These state laws may originate from statutes or the common law of torts. Tort law refers to law applicable to wrongs that give plaintiffs the right to seek remedies in a civil action. The common law has evolved over the last decades to create causes of action based on defects in products. Some states codified their common law in state statutory schemes to supersede state common law and implement the policies chosen by state legislatures.

Another persuasive source of legal doctrine is a series of books called *Restatements of the Law*. Judges, lawyers, and scholars in an organization called the American Law Institute write these books and attempt to collect, summarize, and identify trends in the law. Sometimes restatements persuade judges to recognize new doctrines in their individual jurisdictions. For this reason, restatements may change the direction of law. Nonetheless, the doctrines in restatements are not binding on courts when they determine the state of their jurisdictions' laws.

The Strict Liability Cause of Action

Strict liability or strict product liability is the cause of action easiest for a plaintiff to plead and prove against a manufacturer. Courts and legislatures have recognized a strict product liability cause of action in order to spread the risk of product defects and resulting accidents broadly through society and place the burden of managing the risk on manufacturers, rather than on users of the product. The theory is that manufacturers are best able to reduce risk and insure against hazards creating the risk. In the Air Force set of mishap reports, for example, the manufacturer is actively involved in determining the cause of the defect and is therefore quite familiar with the trend of mishaps relating to its particular unmanned aircraft product line. Through this intensive integration into the Air Force accident determination, the manufacturer is in a clear position to improve its product and reduce the specific risks of its products as discovered in the accident investigation process.

---

8. U.S. federal law may provide additional defenses. One example is the possible preemption of state law causes of action based on a conflict with federal law. Another example is the government contractor defense in which the federal government told the manufacturer to manufacture the product to precise specifications and the product conformed to those specifications despite the manufacturer's warning about the product. As a matter of federal law, the plaintiff cannot maintain a state law action based on a defect arising out of the danger identified by the manufacturer.

The inspiration for a strict liability cause of action is Section 402A of the Restatement (Second) of Torts. Many state supreme courts follow and incorporate Section 402A into state law when establishing common law principles of liability. In turn, states with product liability statutes also track the concepts in Section 402A to create a strict liability cause of action by legislation.

Section 402A says:

402A. SPECIAL LIABILITY OF SELLER OF PRODUCT FOR PHYSICAL HARM TO USER OR CONSUMER

(1) One who sells any product in a defective condition unreasonably dangerous to the user or consumer or to his property is subject to liability for physical harm thereby caused to the ultimate user or consumer, or to his property, if

(a) the seller is engaged in the business of selling such a product, and

(b) it is expected to and does reach the user or consumer without substantial change in the condition in which it is sold.

(2) The rule stated in Subsection (1) applies although

(a) the seller has exercised all possible care in the preparation and sale of his product, and

(b) the user or consumer has not bought the product from or entered into any contractual relation with the seller.[9]

A plaintiff asserting a strict liability claim against an unmanned aircraft manufacturer must plead and prove, under a typical state's law, that the defendant manufacturer sold a product that was "defective" at the time it left the defendant's hands, the product reached the plaintiff without substantial change, and the defect was the proximate cause of the plaintiff's injuries. A product may be defective for one or more of three reasons: (1) the product's design was defective, (2) the product had a defect in manufacture, or (3) the manufacturer failed to warn about a condition of the product.

A defective variable pitch propeller, for example, was the cause of several Air Force accidents. In some of the mishaps the propeller shaft had a design defect which affected the rotation of the shaft over time, while in others there was a manufacturing defect resulting in metal cracks and chips which wore out in operation due to accelerated metal fatigue.

A design defect occurs when the manufacturer fails to design the product to be safe. All copies of that product would be defective. A manufacturing defect occurs when one or a number of copies of the product are defective, even if the design was

---

9. RESTATEMENT (SECOND) OF TORTS § 402A (1965).

safe. For instance, if the stamping equipment caused a metal part to be too thin in one section, thinner than the design specifications, the defect arose from the manufacturing process, not the design. Finally, a product may be considered defective in the absence of essential warnings to inform users about certain potentially harmful or hazardous characteristics of the product.

In this subsection, which is based on the formal Air Force study, we are most interested in design defects and failures to warn. Methods to ensure safe manufacturing and uniform quality of completed parts and products are beyond the scope of this chapter.

Different states have different standards for establishing when a product's design is defective. The two main tests for the existence of a design defect are the consumer expectation test and the risk utility test. Under the consumer expectation test, a product is defective if it is "dangerous to an extent beyond that which would be contemplated by the ordinary consumer who purchases it, with the ordinary knowledge common to the community as to its characteristics."[10] For instance, if a consumer purchases a lawnmower and upon first use the blades shatter and fly out the side, that lawn mower is dangerous and does not work in a way that an ordinary consumer would expect.

The risk utility test is somewhat more complex. Under this analysis, a product design is defective if the product's risks outweigh its utility or benefits to users and the public. Frequently, a plaintiff points to an alternative design that makes the product as useful, but would not be unsafe. Another common issue focuses on the manufacturer's ability to reduce the risk of the design without impairing its usefulness or making it too expensive. Most states use the risk utility test for defining design defects. A much smaller number of states permit courts to use either test for defining design defects. A handful of states define a defect solely under the consumer expectation test.

Under some states' laws, once a plaintiff has made out a *prima facie* showing that a product is defective, the burden shifts to the defendant to prove that the product is not defective.[11] This burden-shifting process may play out at trial or in summary judgment proceedings. As a general matter, however, a plaintiff bears the burden of proof in a civil case to prove the essential element of the plaintiff's claim by a preponderance of the evidence, and expert testimony is nearly always required.

The Negligence Cause of Action

Under a negligence theory, a plaintiff would seek to show an unmanned aircraft manufacturer had a duty to exercise reasonable care in designing and/or manufacturing the unmanned aircraft, the manufacturer breached that duty, and thereby proximately caused the plaintiff's damages. A negligence claim is harder for a plaintiff to establish

---

10. *Id.* § 402A cmt. i.
11. *See, e.g.*, Barker v. Lull Eng'g Co., 573 P.2d 443 (Cal. 1978).

than a strict liability claim, because the plaintiff must prove that the manufacturer acted unreasonably. For instance, a plaintiff may contend that the manufacturer knew or should have known about a design defect, but failed to exercise reasonable care and sold the product anyway despite the defect.

Breach of Warranty Causes of Action

A warranty claim may be based on express statements from the manufacturer promising certain features or characteristics of the product that the plaintiff alleges are false. These express statements may come from advertising materials about the product or other communications by the manufacturer. The law may also imply a warranty that the product will not harm consumers who use the product for its ordinary purposes. This warranty is known as the "implied warranty of merchantability." Alternatively, if the seller knows that the product will be used for a particular purpose, and the buyer is relying on the seller's judgment concerning the fitness of the product, the law will imply a warranty that the product is fit for the contemplated purpose. This warranty is called the "implied warranty of fitness for a particular purpose." If the product does not conform to an implied warranty, a plaintiff could assert a breach of the implied warranty.

In order to prevail under a warranty theory, the plaintiff would have to show the existence of a warranty and a breach of that warranty. In some states, a plaintiff might need to be a purchaser of the product or a household member. Moreover, a plaintiff may need to prove that he or she provided timely notice of the defect to the seller.

Statutory Causes of Action

States have passed various kinds of legislation to protect consumers from unfair and deceptive trade practices of businesses and to give plaintiffs the right to bring suit for violations of statute. Examples include California's Unfair Competition Law (UCL),[12] False Advertising Law (FAL),[13] and Consumer Legal Remedies Act (CLRA).[14] The UCL strikes at any unlawful, unfair, or fraudulent business acts or practices. The FAL bars untrue or misleading advertising practices. The CLRA prohibits a list of unfair business practices, such as misrepresenting the characteristics and qualities of a product.

These statutory causes of action are interesting because a plaintiff can bring a claim even though an accident may not have occurred. A plaintiff could assert that a defect in the product diminished its value. For instance, if the plaintiff purchased a car for $20,000, but the car's defective state meant that the car was worth only $15,000, a plaintiff could assert that the seller sold the car for $5,000 more than it was actually

---

12. Cal. Bus. & Prof. Code § 17200 et seq.
13. *Id.* § 17500 et seq.
14. Cal. Civ. Code § 1750 et seq.

worth. Under the UCL, a plaintiff could seek restitution of the purchase price (the $20,000) or disgorgement of wrongful profits (the $5,000).

Defense Based on the Conduct of the Plaintiff

All states recognize a defense to a product liability claim based on the conduct of the plaintiff. In some states, a plaintiff's "contributory negligence" in using the product is a complete defense to a liability claim. Other states create a "comparative negligence" regime. Under a pure comparative negligence regime, a defense based on the plaintiff's negligent conduct does not defeat the plaintiff's claim entirely. Rather, the trier of fact (a jury or, in the case of a bench trial, a judge) determines what percentage of the plaintiff's damages were caused by the plaintiff's own conduct and diminish any award to the plaintiff by that percentage. For instance, if a jury found that there were two causes of the plaintiff's total damages of $100,000, a manufacturing defect and the plaintiff's negligent misuse of the product, and said 75 percent of the cause was the defect and 25 percent of the cause was the plaintiff's conduct, the jury would be instructed by the judge to render a verdict for the plaintiff, but award only $75,000 in damages. Some states have a modified comparative negligence regime. Their laws say that if a plaintiff's negligence is 51 percent or more of the cause of the damages, the plaintiff cannot recover at all. If it is less, then the plaintiff's negligence merely diminishes the plaintiff's recovery as described above.

APPLICATION OF U.S. PRODUCT LIABILITY LAW TO THE RESULTS OF THE AIR FORCE STUDY

Having discussed the different causes of action a plaintiff may assert and one major defense a manufacturer may raise based on the plaintiff's own conduct, we now turn to the product liability implications of the Air Force data.

The first result deserving attention is the attribution in Figure 15.3 to a small percentage of mishaps caused by manufacturing defects. We do not have enough information to know if the Air Force used the legal standards applicable to manufacturing defects described above. In fact, common sense suggests that investigators were probably not that precise in identifying manufacturing defects as a cause. Accordingly, the mishaps labeled as such may not have risen to a level sufficient to trigger manufacturing defect liability under the legal theories described above. Moreover, did the term "manufacturing defect" also cover the category of design defect? It is unclear whether these mishaps would have given a plaintiff a successful claim for either manufacturing or design defect.

It is also true that the absence of a designation of "defect" by the investigator does not mean the product would not, in fact, have triggered liability. The nonweather, non-pilot error causes listed by the investigators in Figure 15.4 focused on fire, software failures, hardware failures, or manufacturing defects. The fires, software failures, or hardware failures may have been caused by design or manufacturing defects. Again, there is not enough information about these mishaps to say that a manufacturer would have escaped liability in civil actions based on these mishaps.

In litigation, each side would have experts who would analyze all the information about a given mishap to not only identify the immediate cause, such as a hardware failure, but also determine why the hardware failure occurred. Was the hardware failure caused by a defect in the design, a defect in the manufacture, or some other cause? That other cause may have been ordinary wear and tear affecting a nondefective component. Each product has a life span and needs to be maintained. The failure to replace worn-out components may be the cause rather than a defect or the manufacturer's conduct. The information available for us to study is simply not detailed enough to answer these questions.

One final observation about the study's findings and product liability concerns pilot error. It is apparent that if these mishaps were the subject of civil actions, contributory/comparative negligence would be a key issue in these cases. The pilot's own error was the most common cause of mishaps. Nonetheless, a pilot error does not automatically mean the pilot was negligent. For instance, if the manufacturer failed to design the unmanned aircraft to prevent a reasonably foreseeable use of the unmanned aircraft or action by the pilot that might be erroneous, a trier of fact could find a defect notwithstanding the immediate cause of the pilot's error. There might be an alternative design that prevents the pilot error.

An analogy would be antilock brakes in cars. It is reasonably foreseeable that some people using older braking systems would cause their cars to skid on icy roads. The immediate cause of these accidents might be the driver's failure to pump the brakes properly. However, the alternative design in the form of antilock brakes can prevent skids caused by a driver's failure to pump the brakes properly.

In any case, even the incidence of pilot error does not show that a manufacturer would escape liability if these mishaps were ever the subject of a civil action. Again, the information available in the reports does not provide sufficient information to show whether the pilot that caused the accident acted negligently.

CONCLUSIONS CONCERNING APPLICATION OF U.S. PRODUCT LIABILITY LAW TO THE RESULTS OF THE AIR FORCE STUDY

Although the information in the mishap reports is not very precise, we can at least say that pilot error is a chief cause of the mishaps and raises the prospects of a large incidence of pilot error when unmanned aircraft are used for commercial applications. To manage these risks, commercial entities should train their pilots carefully to prevent accidents. They should also choose unmanned aircraft that are easy to use and have effective interfaces.

Manufacturers should implement risk management practices to reduce the incidence of mishaps caused by the particular components noted. There may be cost-effective engineering controls that could improve safety. Moreover, the results of this study can help them focus on particular components and systems that have proven to be the greatest source of risks. Figure 15.5 shows that the components and systems creating the greatest risk are the electrical components, the engine systems, and the variable pitch propeller. If manufacturers fail to address these system risks, they run the risk that plaintiffs will claim they knew of these potential risks and failed to exercise reasonable care to reduce them.[15]

INSURANCE UNDERWRITING IMPLICATIONS OF THE AIR FORCE STUDY

As noted in the summaries of both sections above, the Air Force study reveals two key findings: Hardware failures caused 57.9 percent of the mishaps studied, and human error or factors caused 27.5 percent. Although from a noncommercial context, these findings carry major significance from an underwriting point of view. The study can help underwriters focus their underwriting decisions based on the purchaser's response to questions relating to potential mishap causes demonstrated to be responsible for creating the greatest risk to the operation of unmanned aircraft.

With respect to both property and liability coverage, key underwriting questions should be directed to identifying and quantifying any specific hardware weaknesses of the unmanned aircraft sought to be insured. Underwriters should also be very concerned with the unmanned aircraft operator: their training, licensing or permitting, and years of experience with respect to aerial vehicles, both manned and unmanned, their experience with the components and systems that comprise and operate the

---

15. For a more thorough discussion of risk management methods in the manufacture of robots, *see* Stephen S. Wu, *Risk Management in Commercializing Robots* (Apr. 3, 2013), *reprinted at* http://conferences.law .stanford.edu/werobot/wp-content/uploads/sites/29/2013/04/Risk-Management-in-Commercializing-Robotics.pdf.

unmanned aircraft, as well as their understanding of privacy and data liability issues affected by the management, security, and protection of the unmanned aircraft and any data it gathers or uses for any purpose.

Property Damage

To determine whether to offer property damage coverage and at what premium, insurers will evaluate the type of unmanned aircraft, its design, including weight, range, capacity, payload, power train, and other onboard operational systems. They will also evaluate the costs of the unmanned aircraft, including repair, replacement, upgrades, and maintenance. The study suggests underwriters should pay particular attention to the quality of the electrical, engine, and propeller systems. Aviation insurers offering unmanned aircraft coverage are starting the underwriting process with applications typically used for manned aerial vehicles adapted for unmanned aircraft.[16] The more sophisticated the unmanned aircraft or its use, the more detailed information underwriters will seek in order to most accurately quantify the risk.

Liability

For liability risk underwriting, insurers will evaluate the type of unmanned aircraft, intended uses, and venues in which it will be operated or used. They will take into consideration whether the unmanned aircraft will be operated in urban or nonurban environments, from or over transportation arteries or densely populated areas, on or near waterways, in what airspace, and under what legal authority.

Underwriters will pay close attention to the legal requirements for use of the unmanned aircraft(s) to be insured and the insured's ability to comply with them, including unmanned aircraft licensing and permitting, authorized situational environments, and attendant duties of care. Whether the anticipated risks to be underwritten are negligence, strict liability, or ultrahazardous activities will affect premium, scope of coverage, and potential exclusions.

Unmanned Aircraft Manufacturer Liability Insurance Coverage

The good news is that there are reasonably substantial insurance policies available to unmanned aircraft manufacturers. The bad news is that these policies rarely cover any risk for data privacy or cyber liability. Limits are available, however, up to $100,000,000 and more with worldwide coverage territory. Nevertheless, the study suggests underwriters of this type of insurance should also pay particular attention to the quality of the electrical, engine, and propeller systems used by the manufacturer.

---

16. *See*, for example, Kiln Group Aviation Division UAS OPERATORS INSURANCE PROPOSAL FORM offered through the Unmanned Aerial Vehicle Systems Association at http://www.uavs.org/document.php ?id=168&ext=pdf.

CONCLUSION

Unmanned aircraft will become ubiquitous in the national airspace. At the same time, issues of risk and liability will move to the forefront as manufacturers and operators face significant challenges arising from aircraft operations. The risks and challenges will only increase as unmanned aircraft used in the skies become the norm rather than the exception.

Product liability issues will inevitably generate litigation, with causes of action such as strict product liability, negligence, breach of warranty, and the violation of the laws against unfair and deceptive trade practices facing all manufacturers of unmanned aircraft and their component parts. Insurance issues will also move to the forefront, as commercial owners, manufacturers, and operators of unmanned aircraft seek to limit their risks of liability and damage exposure through the purchase of insurance. Thus, through proper analysis, risk management, and observations of the liability and risk trends and triggers, stakeholders in the unmanned arena will be well equipped to handle the emerging unmanned systems market. The unmanned systems future is well on its way.

Table of Cases

Statutes and Laws

Index